A Sparrow's Flight

£1.50

A SPARROW'S FLIGHT

The Memoirs of
Lord Hailsham of St Marylebone

Fontana
An Imprint of HarperCollins*Publishers*

First published in Great Britain in 1990
by Collins

This edition first issued in 1991 by Fontana,
an imprint of HarperCollins Publishers,
77–85 Fulham Palace Road,
Hammersmith, London W6 8JB

9 8 7 6 5 4 3 2

Printed and bound by HarperCollins Book Manufacturing, Glasgow

*To all those whom I love
or who have loved me*

Contents

List of Illustrations

In the Engleberg, 1979
With the statue in All Souls, 1985
With the Duchess of Kent at Buckingham University, 1986
Our wedding, 1986
Final portrait (*Michael Ward*)

'"Such," he said, "O King, seems to me the present life on earth," as if . . . on a winter's night a sparrow should fly swiftly into the hall and, coming in one door, instantly fly out through another . . . Somewhat like this appears the life of man. But of what follows or what went before we are utterly ignorant.'

BEDE, *Ecclesiastical History*, II

'Are not two sparrows sold for a farthing? and one of them shall not fall on the ground without your Father . . . Fear ye not therefore, ye are of more value than many sparrows.'

MATTHEW, 10:29–31

Introduction

THIS BOOK requires some explanation, and possibly some apology. In 1970, when I was invited by Ted Heath to serve under him in his Cabinet as Lord Chancellor, I came back to my family and said: 'The next chapter will be "Eventide" or "Last Days".'

In March 1974, after the defeat at the polls of the Heath administration in the wake of the coal strike, my forecast appeared to have been reasonably correct. I was nearly seventy years of age. I did not expect another Conservative administration for another four or five years, and with the coming years in opposition on the front bench of the House of Lords there would be enough to occupy my time.

During my first term of office as Lord Chancellor, I had had several approaches from publishers on the subject of an autobiography, but with one exception I had set my face against them all.

Except for one short period in the war, I had kept no diary. Unless stimulated by conversation, my memory of past events is sketchy. I did not relish the long and tedious research into my own past which would have been necessary. There were almost infinite press cuttings, many photographs and, of course, in one House of Parliament or the other, nearly forty years of Hansard. So far as regards the details of political history, there were cartloads of papers, some now in the possession of a Cambridge college, some, to which I would have access, in the Cabinet Office or in the archives of the offices in which I have served. Some, of course, have already appeared in the Public Record Office under the thirty-year rule. But, above all, I have, as did Trollope, a certain contempt for autobiography as a class of literature. It tends to be either trivial, or self-justificatory and maliciously critical of others. In addition, as Trollope also pointed out, it can seldom be entirely candid. Even Cardinal Heenan's was entitled *Not the Whole Truth*. No one will willingly attribute to himself unworthy motives, even though privately he may be aware of them. Seldom, if ever, will the author disclose disgraceful actions not already known, and, if he does, he will tend to excuse them, with varying degrees of disingenuousness. Nevertheless there was one book I did sincerely wish to write. This was an account of my evolving beliefs in the fields of philosophy and religion. By 1974, it was to be an account of my gradual shift from a position of virtual agnosticism to one of acceptance of mainstream Christianity.

So, in 1974, I sat down and began writing *The Door Wherein I Went*, and it was published in the latter part of 1975. In writing it, I had intended it as positively my last word in public. Reading the book again, and especially the final chapter, I believe that anyone can see that such was the case. I thought I was bowing myself out, and that my public life was effectively at an end. I had no idea at all that in front of me there lay the greatest spiritual crisis of my existence, followed by my longest period in a single office. I was perfectly content. I had been married for thirty years, I had a marvellous wife and a family of five wonderful children, and was looking forward to a growing brood of grandchildren. By 1978 I had been a Privy Councillor for more than twenty years. In the war I had served in the profession of arms, and in peace had achieved a modest success at the Bar. I had held numerous offices of state in and out of the Cabinet, and for four years that of Lord Chancellor. I enjoyed a substantial pension, and my widow would enjoy one after my death. My wife was twelve years younger than I. I had numerous intellectual interests, and a wide circle of friends. I looked forward to a serene old age in modest comfort, supported by the companionship of my enchanting consort and a growing family. The seas were calm. The skies were clear of cloud, and I believed that, at long last, I was reaching port.

A little later, in a moment of time, in almost literally the twinkling of an eye, my whole life lay in ruins. At one moment my wife and I were riding joyfully on horseback together, talking together as happily as birds in spring. Not more, I believe, than ninety seconds later, I was kneeling before her unconscious body which lay in a pool of her own blood. She was unconscious but still alive. But she died either on her way to hospital or shortly after our arrival there, before I could even say goodbye or thank her for her thirty-four years' loyal, radiant and joyous companionship. As I write this, it was more than ten years ago, and eighteen since I came home with Ted Heath's offer of the Woolsack. Clearly there is now something more to be said, if only to tell you how I fared in that desperate time, a year or so in opposition, another book written and published, and, though I did not then guess it, another eight years on the Woolsack.

That therefore shall be accounted for in its place. But, whilst it had rather altered my ideas about not attempting any account of my life, it has not altered my opinion about the undesirability of embarking on the ordinary type of political autobiography. I simply wish to tell the story of my life, my youth, my family, my friends, my children, my adventures, my pleasures, my thoughts as I remember them now – apart from three terrible bereavements, eighty years happily spent in God's world, profoundly thankful as I remain for the gift of a long life of mingled joy and sorrow, and hopeful of a quiet and happy end, and peace at the last.

Obviously a narrative of this kind must be mainly structured on the chronological order in which things happened. But some strands have been continuous: my spiritual wanderings described up until 1975 in *The Door Wherein I Went*; my love of mountains, now, owing to my increasing infirmity, a matter only of memory; my family life; my fourteen-year-long farming and market-gardening career; my legal studies as student, advocate and judge; my domestic pets; my love of country pursuits; my brief experience as a poet. I look back without regret, but without any sense of self-congratulation. It has been a satisfying and varied life but it now draws towards its close, and I must take stock of it all, as I approach the last adventure. As an old Scottish MP said to me once as we sat together one evening in the Carlton Club: 'Life is like a journey from Waverley Station to King's Cross.' 'I', he added, 'have reached Finsbury Park.' So now have I. After that, as Rabelais said, 'Je vais chercher le grand peut-être,' without certainty but in complete and loving trust.

ONE

Nursery Days

ON WEDNESDAY, 9 October 1907, I was born, squalling, into the world. I was badly jaundiced, and slightly deformed. My right hand had six digits instead of the normal five. The sixth was firmly attached to my right thumb, but immediately and rather clumsily snipped off by doctors. The stump and scar are still faintly visible and capable of giving pain. There was still quite a lot of pain when I was young. Apart from this abnormality, both thumbs lacked a mobile top joint, or, rather, there was in each case a sort of top joint but it was fixed and incapable of movement. These defects were inherited from my mother's family, and I have transmitted them to some of my children. The peculiarity of this congenital deformity is that no two variations are exactly similar. My mother, who had strong views on certain subjects, saw to it that I was immediately circumcised. One would think that, even then, this was a fairly simple operation, but for some reason it was not completely or immediately successful. It had to be done again when I was nearly ready for my private school. I was not told that it was going to be done; no anaesthetic was administered; I was just laid across the doctor's knees and recircumcised (if there is such a word). I can still remember the pain, the blood, and my sense of total betrayal by the adult world. My younger brother, Neil, benefited by my misfortune. Deciding in future to trust only specialists in the matter, my mother engaged the services of a rabbi (if that is the right designation) to do the job on him, and this functionary, whatever his description, was entirely successful.

The place of my birth, and for the first eighteen months of my life my home, was 5 Cleveland Square, little more than a stone's throw from Paddington Station. I understand that many, or most, people do not remember events which took place before the age of five. This is not so in my case. I can distinctly remember the exterior of number 5, and was able to recognize it years later, and I can still see myself viewing the familiar exterior of the old Paddington Station from the interior of my pram. I can also remember a number of incidents which I can place confidently before Neil's birth in February 1910 when I was about two and a quarter years old. When I was about eighteen months old my family had moved from Cleveland Square to 46 Queen's Gate Gardens, where we remained until after my father had been elected unopposed for the old constituency of St Marylebone at the general election of 1922, which followed the downfall of the Lloyd George coalition government. It says something about the difference in social circumstances over my life that, though my father, mother, Neil and I, and my half-sister Isobel Marjoribanks and my half-brother Edward Marjoribanks, with our staff, occupied the entire house, when I visited it again more than fifty years later it accommodated about seven separate family units of approximately the same social class as we had been. My father was only a relatively young junior barrister, called at Lincoln's Inn after the South African war and dependent almost entirely on his professional earnings. There were at least eight indoor servants after Neil was born: butler, cook (Mrs Barker), kitchen maid, nanny (Mary Blencowe), nursery maid (Minnie Prevault), two housemaids (Mary Bird and her niece, Amy Bird) and a lady's maid ('Potty' – short for Poitiers, a French spinster). In addition, there was a governess (Miss Baster) who gave Isobel and Edward lessons in the 'schoolroom', a sort of excrescence at the back of the house.

My first nurse, Field, was sadly sacked by my mother when Neil was on the way, I think (and thought) unjustly because she had been seen to strike me in my pram. I was strongly bonded to her and missed her dreadfully for about a week whilst I was put in the charge of Mary and Amy Bird. The new nanny, Mary Blencowe, arrived shortly with presents to soften me up, and a further propaganda campaign was initiated to prepare me for the arrival of 'little brother' (as he turned out to be). Like most propaganda campaigns, this failed, because it was basically dishonest. They told me what a splendid little playmate he would be, but when the little pink object, utterly helpless, arrived, lying noisily but otherwise inert in a partially curtained cradle, obviously quite useless as a playmate, I was greatly disappointed. After about three months, I thought I would try an experiment. Deftly detaching the two fircone-shaped weights from the new cuckoo clock, brought by my parents the previous summer from Switzerland, I sought to interest him in these rather unpromising objects. The powers that be formed the impression that, out of jealousy, I was trying to murder the little creature – the first but not the last time in which I have been the object of unjust suspicion and my motives misunderstood. The one permanent lesson I learned from this episode is that even the smallest children (I was only two) have an acute sense of justice and bitterly resent a false accusation.

The world into which I was born was that of Edwardian England before the outbreak of the First World War. That war was by far the greatest social and political watershed of my lifetime. I believe that we were a happy family in that sunlit world. The servants, who were the great majority, were paid practically nothing, but were secure in their employments – all except the butlers, who tended to come and go – and all the servants lived like fighting cocks. Every Sunday two huge sirloins entered the house and were roasted on the kitchen range (on the bone, of course) with top cut and undercut complete, slightly underdone, and enveloped in delicious yellow fat which accompanied each portion. One sirloin was for the staff in the basement. The other for the dining-room and nursery, three floors up from the ground, and lifted by a curious contraption of ropes and pulleys. It was followed by one of Mrs Barker's famous plum puddings, dark brown in colour, less rich than a Christmas pudding, but served with cream and demerara sugar, and followed (in the dining-room only) with black coffee. Not for us the heresies of healthy eating favoured by Edwina Currie or the hypochondriacal fears of cholesterol. Vitamins, though not yet discovered, were seen to by apples (one of which a day was alleged to keep the doctor away) and green vegetables.

The servants, though ill paid and fearful of old age, were, I believe, cheerful and happy. Mrs Barker, who had worked previously for my grandmother, stayed with us to her last illness. My mother died in 1925 in the arms of Mary Bird, the head housemaid. She and Amy her niece were still working for my brother Edward at the time of his death in 1932. Nanny remained with us till long after we had ceased to need her services. Minnie, of French Royalist descent, left to emigrate to Australia only when I was ready for private school. No doubt there were social and political horrors outside, and we were well aware of fears and rumours of European war ahead. But, inside 46 Queen's Gate Gardens, peace and harmony were the order of the day.

My father belonged to a well-established professional middle-class family. His father, Quintin Hogg, died in his bath in January 1903, the victim of carbon monoxide gas emitted by an old-fashioned geyser for heating the water, after founding the Regent Street and other polytechnics. My grandmother, who survived until 1917, was a scion of the family which imported Graham's port which, under different management, is still on the market. My mother, from Nashville, Tennessee, was, at the time she married my father, the widow of Archie Marjoribanks (a younger son of the first Lord Tweedmouth) whom she married in Nashville at a time when he was equerry to the Governor-General of Canada. The Governor-General's wife, Ishbel, was first cousin to my grandfather.

My grandfathers had both died before I was born. I never knew my American grandfather, Judge Trimble Brown, and 'Granny over the Sea', whom I never met, contented herself with sending me, each Christmas, a gold five-dollar piece, which my parents, not foreseeing the future, immediately removed from me 'to be safe' and placed irredeemably in a banking account where they were each credited at the then par rate of four dollars and eighty-six cents to the pound. I recovered the proceeds only when I was twenty-one and 'Granny over the Sea' long dead. The only grandparent I knew personally was my father's mother, a devout Scots Presbyterian of the Church of Scotland who knew the Bible, both Old and New Testament, better than anyone I have ever known before or since. She was undoubtedly a saint, and my memory of her is as green and fragrant now as when she died, painfully of cancer, in 1917. She knew she was dying, though I did not, when Neil and I were introduced to her bedroom to be blessed. She did this in a long, humble, percipient, sincere and saintly prayer, interrupted for a moment when the nurse came in to give this wonderful woman a pain-killing injection.

There was a pleasant rhythm in the life of the nursery before 1914. It was punctuated with the usual holidays – Christmas with its stockings and presents, a short Easter holiday in lodgings by the sea, usually Weston-super-Mare, at the hospitable house of Mrs Spreadbury (a friend of Nanny's) at Cove View, 13 Manila Crescent. It was followed by a longer summer holiday when my father took my mother abroad without passport (save once when he visited Tsarist Russia) or traveller's cheques – which he did not need, since he had gold in his pockets, sovereigns and half-sovereigns which could be changed across the counter in any shop in Belgium, France or Switzerland at about twenty-five local francs to the pound. When we left Queen's Gate Gardens, a wagonette would arrive, drawn by two horses and with iron-tyred rattling wheels, summoned from the railway company to take our luggage on its roof rack and our little party of four, five or six (according as to whether Isobel or Edward were with us) on its interior benches. Until 1914 we never owned a motor-car or carriage. Our next-door neighbours (who were members of the Wills family) had at least one, a Minerva, and our doctor, Doctor Morgan, owned a horse-drawn brougham. For transport we either walked, at first pushed in a pram and a mail-cart by Nanny or Minnie, or, as a great treat, went by Metropolitan and District Line from Gloucester Road to Edgware Road to visit Granny's flat at 41 Cumberland Mansions, where she lived with her Swiss maid.

I vividly remember the outbreak of the First World War, not so much because I was in the least aware of the immense historical watershed that it portended, but since it approximately coincided with August Bank Holiday. We missed three trains running from Charing Cross to Westgate-on-Sea where once, in preference to Weston-super-Mare, we were booked into a boarding-house. When, after these three false starts from Charing Cross, we were ultimately embarked in an incredibly slow train from the South Eastern and

Chatham ('Slow Easy and Comfortable' was its nickname) end of Victoria Station and trundled through the Kent countryside at what appeared to be the speed of a hansom cab, interspersed by innumerable stops, I remember, almost as if it were yesterday, Isobel saying: 'Let's tell the driver that the Germans are after him.' Before we left Westgate that year for the first of several summers at Quainton Rectory, which my father had taken while the rector was on vacation so that the family could be reunited in the country, we could clearly hear the booming of the guns across the Channel.

After we got to Quainton towards the end of August 1914 an incident occurred which shed an extraordinary light both upon the great gulf which separates the beginning of that war from the other wars of the twentieth century and upon the extraordinary intrepidity and resourcefulness which always characterized my father, then a junior barrister of about forty-five. His younger brother, my uncle Ian, was a regular soldier. He had gone to France with the British Expeditionary Force in command of his regiment, the 4th Hussars, part of the Light Cavalry Brigade. He was a soldier of some distinction, having been the recipient of one of the very few prewar DSOs for service in Nigeria. On the night of 30–1 August the regiment was forming part of the cavalry screen covering the British retreat from Mons, and by 1 September (the very day when von Kluck made his fatal strategic error of turning towards Paris) he had reached the small town (little more than a village) of Haramont on the outskirts of the forest of Compiègne and a few miles further back from his previous night's stop at Villers Cotterets. News came through to Quainton, almost at once, that Ian was missing. 'I am going to find him,' said my father. In spite of being just under seven years of age, I realized that this was a foolhardy thing to do, began to cry, and was severely upbraided for cowardice by my mother, a lady of impeccably martial Southern spirit. My father bought a ticket to Paris, so far as I know as usual without passport, where he found the battle of the Marne in progress. Clad only in his civilian suit (blue with a light red stripe) and a small pork-pie hat, he boarded a French troop-train, bribed the appropriate sergeant, hid under the seat, and emerged only after the train had stopped and the soldiers got out and began engaging in a running fight with the Germans. My father got out from under the seat, climbed out of the train after the soldiers, made his way across the fields, and ultimately found the village, or town, of Haramont. In the presence of the mayor he was brought to a room where he identified the dead body of his brother. Ian had been wounded at the edge of the forest, captured by Uhlans and left behind there. He had died three or four days later. My father then returned to Quainton, where he told us of his various adventures which were later recorded by my grandmother. He did not bring back my uncle's half-hunter gold watch, embossed with the family crest. It had been taken from his body by the German officer when the Germans had retreated from Haramont. 'What a swine,' said my mother, 'to steal from the dead.' But she was wrong. The German officer knew enough about heraldry to know that, if he sent the watch to the College of Heralds in London, the watch would be returned to the family, and it duly came back to us, via neutral Holland and the College. When my father died, I inherited it, and it remained in my possession until it was stolen in one of my many burglaries.

Much of this story I was able to verify many years later, when, with my wife Mary and my younger son James, I was on my way back from a visit to my brother Neil, who owns a hotel on the outskirts of Lucerne in Switzerland. I came to Haramont late one Sunday afternoon in August when the whole town was asleep after their prolonged Sunday lunch. It must have been about 1960, since it was before the birth in 1962 of my daughter Kate. Only a wasp or two, buzzing around aimlessly, seemed alive in that deserted and somnolent place. Presently a very old man crept out of one of the houses and enquired my business. 'I have come to find the grave of my uncle,' I replied, feeling rather like an entry in an exercise-book in elementary French. I knew already that he was buried in the village cemetery since, not long before that, I had refused to allow his body to be moved to a military cemetery. To my astonishment, the man replied: 'Ah, you must be Monsieur Hogg.' 'Indeed, I am Monsieur Hogg,' said I, and my friend introduced himself as the secretary to the mayor. He led me to the mayor's parlour where the archives of the village were kept, in a sort of schoolroom bookcase, and pulled out a volume from the shelves. 'Ah, ce n'est pas ça,' he said, and over his shoulder I caught sight of an entry in the village archives in the beautiful sixteenth-century handwriting of the reign of François Premier. Eventually he found the right volume, and there was the story: how the Germans had brought Ian in, a prisoner and mortally wounded, how he had died three days later, how the Germans had left him there on their retreat, and how his body had been identified less than a week later by his brother. Afterwards, they took me to his grave, beautifully tended in the village cemetery with a headstone in English erected by my father and my grandmother. I photographed little James by the grave, and somewhere the snapshot still exists. They also took me to the place where Ian was shot and told me how it had happened, which coincided to a great extent with what my grandmother had told me from my father's account, except that what I saw and heard was far more convincing and in a way more moving.

There is a fine tradition in the British army that on a withdrawal the officer commanding must be the last to leave. Just outside Haramont, there is a little bridge where a lane leading to the forest of Compiègne runs over a sunken road. Ian was standing on that bridge waiting for stragglers to catch up, and saw some shadowy figures emerge from the forest some two or three hundred yards away. He made the signal to them to hurry up, waving his arm anticlockwise above his head. But they were not stragglers. They were Uhlans, and at that range they had no difficulty, even with their cavalry carbines, in shooting him in the chest. They took him prisoner and brought him into the village, where he died. There were fresh flowers on his grave when I saw it, laid by the schoolchildren of the village. As I came through Haramont, it was near the anniversary of his death. The story reads more like a tale from the age of chivalry than from our own time. But I tell it from my own recollection as it happened to me. Everyone comes well out of it: my uncle, my father, my mother and the German officer who had returned the watch. Things are not now as they were then.

TWO

Preparatory School

THE TIME was approaching when I must go to boarding school. Up to that point my education had been somewhat chequered. For a time in, I suppose, about 1912, I was sent to a little pre-prep school in Rosary Gardens, a brief walk from my home, across the Cromwell Road, but a terrifying one in winter in the horrific pea-soup fogs of those days, when the Cromwell Road, at the time served by horse-buses with open upper decks, had to be lit by flares. I must have been at this school only a short time. I was withdrawn, I believe, owing to the frequency of infection, and the fact that Neil had become old enough to be taught the alphabet (which I learned solely by hearing him repeat it). At all events the real foundation of my education was laid by private lessons from a governess in the day nursery in Queen's Gate Gardens. She taught Neil and myself so well that, by the time she left to marry a clergyman, I knew all five declensions of Latin grammar and all the four conjugations of verbs as well. The one thing she could not do was to pronounce French. This was later taught me by my mother, who, for an American, had a good ear.

I went to my private school at Sunningdale in the summer term of 1916. It is difficult to describe the trauma of moving from the protected surroundings of nursery and home, with nanny and nurse-maid to look after me, into the cold and unsympathetic atmosphere of school, with early school at 7.30 in the morning and compulsory games, in the summer term cricket, which I had not the smallest idea how to play, six days a week, chapel once a day every day, and life in a dormitory of thirteen or fourteen other boys, where the smallest eccentricity or weakness was treated with derision.

25

The hardest thing was the clothes. Until within a week of being transported into this alien environment I was in some sort of nursery costume prescribed by my mother. I had never tied a tie, and, though attempts were made to teach me how to do so in the three or four days available, they were wholly unsuccessful. The other garments were equally strange: knickerbockers with stockings and lace-up boots with eyes, again presenting difficulties to secure with bows, a Norfolk jacket with stiff collar, which, from the wash, soon presented a serrated edge to the neck, on weekdays, and on Sundays an Eton jacket (in later years known as a 'bum-freezer') with the same horrible collar, and a black tie tied in the regulation sailor's knot.

I have to say that the sanitary arrangements beggared description, all the more astonishingly because years later my brother Neil told me that, when confronted with them by a parent, the joint headmasters announced that they were unaware of their almost astonishing primitiveness.

There were two indoor loos on the two floors where the bedrooms and cubicles were situated, but these were for night use only. There were sixty-three boys in the school. For ordinary daytime use, we were expected to 'go across' (as the phrase was) to sixteen outdoor earth closets in a predetermined order written above sixteen little numbered metal tickets hanging on a hook. Each boy was assigned to a particular loo in inverse order to his seniority, in a written order which had to be followed regardless of need, and the tickets were handed from boy to boy as the appropriate loo in the correct order became vacant. I called them 'earth closets' a moment ago. But I did them too much honour. There was no earth in the hoppers above the seats designed to contain it. The war was on and in its most unfavourable stage, and the man employed to fill the hoppers had ceased to work for the school. The smell was indescribable, and why there was not a serious epidemic involving quite possibly a death in the school remains to me something of a mystery. The outer wooden frame of number 16 (used by the senior boys) was rotted away, and there resided an enormous toad of venerable appearance and age, attracted no doubt by the insect life which, naturally enough, was by no means absent. This toad was indeed venerated as an oracle. On days when the school was playing matches against similar institutions (St George's Windsor, Ladbrooke, Heatherdown or Earleywood) in the neighbourhood, if the toad could be coaxed out of the recess in which he normally lived, it was regarded as an infallible omen that our first eleven would be successful.

To say I was homesick, not only in my first, but in subsequent terms also, would be an understatement. There were no blinds in the windows of the Lower Dormitory to which I was assigned, and my bed was next but one to the window. I awoke in dismay extremely early and cried for some time until I could compose myself. One friendly voice invariably came to comfort me in my distress. It was May, and the dawn chorus was in full song. A friendly chaffinch uttered his repetitive song immediately outside the window. 'Don't don't don't don't don't you cry-eye,' the little bird sang. I have had a love for chaffinches ever since.

About my second year in the school there returned from the war – 'the Front' as we called it – a teacher of genius. His name was Ling, and I revere his memory. One arm had been shot away, and he had lost one eye. As I subsequently discovered, it was his good eye that had gone. In 1912 his brilliant teaching had won my brother Edward a scholarship to Eton, as it had for countless other Sunningdalians. When I was ready to join a scholarship class in 1918 or 1919, he got me the first scholarship in circumstances I shall describe. There were two other boys in my scholarship class: Griffin ('Gryps') and Lowry. They both got scholarships elsewhere.

I tell this story because, thank God, many years later I was able to repay this wonderful man for the incomparable debt I owed and still owe him. He had given me an understanding of the Greek and Latin classics, which has never quite deserted me. What he then gave me was the foundation which saw me through Eton, where I won the Newcastle Scholarship, and Oxford where I got a first in Honour Moderations and a first in 'Greats'. I owe it all to him.

Many years later, I came back to the school one sports day, suffering, as I always did at that time, miserably from hay fever. I was drawn aside by the then headmaster and it was explained to me that

27

Ling had gone completely blind and was having to leave. He was totally without means. This extraordinarily gifted teacher had never, so they told me, earned more than five hundred pounds in any one year of his professional life. Schools of that type were at the time owned by the current headmaster like a small business, and were passed on from hand to hand like a small sweet and tobacco store. There was no complete list of old boys, and Ling was not the beneficiary of any contributory pension scheme. What were they to do? Ling had a wife and either one or two children, I think grown up. I was not in a position to do very much myself, but what I could I did. There was in the school an almost complete collection of old school magazines, *Sunningdale School Notes*, and these invariably contained congratulations to the boys who had succeeded in getting scholarships from the school from about 1907 onwards. I was able to trace most, or at least many, of the survivors of these and, being an MP and employing a secretary, was able to send a circular letter to those I could trace telling them of the plight of our old friend and teacher. Between us we raised quite a tidy sum, and one of the most generous contributors was my brother Neil who had also obtained an Eton scholarship a few years after me. There were exceptions. One was from a man who had succeeded rather well in life and, like me, got a scholarship at Eton. He was a bully when I knew him at school, and he had not improved or changed with the years. He wrote back refusing all help, on principle, because, as he said, the school should have made provision for Ling. So, I quite concede, they should. But, for all this man cared, his brilliant teacher would have been on public assistance.

I cannot quite part from Ling without a short tribute to his moral character. If ever there was a patriot and a man of integrity, it was he. With his defective vision he was under no obligation to fight, but he volunteered from the start. He was not slow to teach his pupils the ideals of service to the State and to society owed by an educated man, as they appeared from the classical texts he was expounding. But for his example, these stirring sentiments might have fallen on deaf ears. Years later, I learned to my sorrow that he had no religious beliefs. This, too, has been a lesson to me. If heroism counts for anything, he is sure of his place in heaven. If it were otherwise, there would be neither justice nor mercy in God's universe.

On reconsidering all this, I must say that to do justice to the school, which still exists, I believe that all I have criticized seems to have been remedied. When my elder son came to the appropriate age, I visited it again and rang the front door to interview the appropriate authorities. The years fell away from me as I did so, and I was consumed with terror at what I was proposing to do. But, when I was conducted to the Lower Dormitory where my own bed had been during my first term, there, nestling on the pillow, was a teddy bear. In 1916 it would have been as much as my life was worth to admit to owning one, let alone to display it in public. Sometimes things do change for the better.

THREE

Public School

LONG BEFORE I WAS SENT to my private school in May 1916 I knew that I was destined for Eton. It happened in this way. We were seated on the lawn one August at Quainton Rectory. I was telling my father that I was having read to me at bedtime what must have been a told-to-the-children version of *Tom Brown's Schooldays*. I said what a wonderful place Rugby must be, and when my father confirmed that Rugby was still in being I expressed the hope I might one day go there. 'On the contrary,' said my father, 'you are going to the best school in the world.' In answer to my obvious question he identified this remarkable establishment as Eton. Though he did not tell me so at the time, he had already put me down for the house run by C. H. K. Marten (who later privately instructed the two princesses, Elizabeth and Margaret). My father's excellent but only reason for this decision was that by a sort of apostolic succession Henry Marten had inherited the house sports colours possessed in the 1890s by my father's own housemaster, whose name was Radcliffe. I am sure that I should have been extremely happy at Marten's. He was an excellent housemaster, the author of an excellent school textbook on British, and particularly English, history and employed a house-matron (in Eton parlance a 'dame') who was in her own field as good as he. His only fault was his devotion to a savage and dangerous pet raven called Boney which pecked my ankles ferociously when he asked me to breakfast on my first Sunday at the school. I am glad to say that in the end Boney received his deserts. He was poisoned by members of Marten's house. Quite innocently, however, and unaware of these plans, I frustrated my father's intentions to send me to Marten's.

By 1918 I was already aware that I was considered to be scholarship material, and at the Eton scholarship examination in the summer half (Etonese for term) of 1920 I was duly entered to sit. Since my private school was within easy reach of Windsor I was to sleep there and travel to Eton each morning by car. A magnificent vehicle supplied by the local garage was duly hired for the purpose. But on the day when the examination was due to begin the car broke down in the middle of Windsor Great Park, and resolutely refused to resume the journey. Being of a naturally nervous disposition, my morale completely collapsed, but not so badly as that of Mr Crabtree the headmaster. I can see him now wildly seeking to flag down each car in a whole column of traffic, his arms flailing, his red moustache quivering, the picture of agonized dismay. At first his efforts were vain, but after the best part of an hour a Good Samaritan was found and I eventually arrived at School Hall completely demoralized and something like forty-five minutes late for my first paper. By some miracle, however, I survived this preliminary misfortune, and when the time for the viva-voce examination arrived the assembled authorities asked me one, and only one, question. If I were to be awarded a scholarship, would I wish to take it up as a King's Scholar, boarding in college with all the other scholars, or would I prefer to enter as Oppidan, a commoner, in an Oppidan house? The question seemed to me to be superfluous. 'Of course, sir,' I replied politely, 'I should prefer to go into college.' I have never regretted this decision. Thanks to Ling, but to my astonishment, I came in top of the examination.

So my father's intention was thus frustrated by my innocence. I have never regretted this for a very simple reason. I regarded the scholarship as something which I had won by my own merits in a fair and open competition. I wished to be a Colleger and not an Oppidan. At that age I wished already, so far as possible, to stand on my own feet and, so far as possible, not to be beholden to others, not even to my parents. College, I believed, presented me with a better chance of a better education than that which would have been mine had I opted for an Oppidan house. Moreover, I would be among my intellectual equals. In England, brains are never popular. We are the only country in the world, apart perhaps from the United States, in which brains, and many other forms of distinction, are suspect as a sign of moral obliquity, and 'cleverness' is spoken of in accents of contempt. I had had to put up with enough snide remarks at my private school. In college I would be part of a community dedicated to hard work, scholarship and achievement.

I afterwards discovered that my expressed preference to go to college was ascribed to my father instead of to me and was made the occasion of criticism of him by some radical members of my far-flung family. By sending me to college it was claimed he had robbed some poorer boy of a valuable place. If I am not mistaken, the critics were a wealthy banking family, who afterwards also sent both their gifted sons into college at Eton with scholarships the same as mine. This is not the only time in my life that I have observed that circumstances have a way of altering cases. So far as I was concerned, a competition is a competition. I had won it, fairly, and was making a substantial contribution to the cost of my own education.

Ever since, I have always sympathized with the gifted boy, and despised those who condemn a community of the gifted as elitist. The pursuit of excellence is an essential part of a healthy society, whether it be in the Army, in music, or in the arts, and the number of 'elitist' societies which have added to the glory of Britain is too numerous to enumerate. The Royal Society, the Royal Academy, the Household Brigade, the Rifle Brigade, the Marines, All Souls College, Oxford, come to mind all too readily. But there are so many others.

They do not deprive anyone else of anything. Their members respect one another while entering into a competition of excellence. These bodies immensely encourage higher standards in lesser institutions in the same field for whom, in a real way, they act as pacemakers. I well remember an occasion when Harold Macmillan, as Chancellor of Oxford, was presiding at the annual banquet in Christ Church Hall after the Encaenia, the ceremony of the giving of honorary degrees. He was then very old and frail, and everyone was wondering whether he would make a significant speech. He rose, somewhat unsteadily, to his feet at the end of dinner and broke into a panegyric on the value of loyalties within a free national society, and their compatibility with one another even while they are competing in the same field. 'Of course', he said, 'there are the great loyalties, God, country and so on. But then there are the lesser loyalties, college, regiment, and of course', he added to his Christ Church audience with characteristic effect, 'I am a Balliol man myself.' The lesser loyalties are as important in their way as loyalty to the whole. Indeed, they are what sets the seal on the greater loyalties. Long live elitism and the benefits elitism brings.

FOUR

Eton

HUMAN INSTITUTIONS are of two kinds, the traditional and the contrived. Most partake of some elements of each, with one or the other predominating. The papacy and the British monarchy are obvious examples of the traditional; the American constitution, the Fifth Republic in France, the German Federal Republic and the Soviet Union are examples of the latter. The difference resides in the fact that, whilst everyone knows that no human institution lasts for ever, and that every long-standing institution develops its own customary ethos, contrived institutions look for intellectual justification in terms of the ideologies at the time of their creation, whilst the traditional are judged by the extent to which they are considered useful in practice for society now. The one question is 'How well does it work?' and, in judging how well it works, one can do worse than first consider how much it is loved by those who share its membership and dwell under its authority.

There is no doubt, of course, that the late Dr Arnold left the unmistakable impress of his personality on Rugby, and this influenced the development of all British boarding-school education at the secondary stage. During the course of their history the older public schools have usually developed on traditional lines, and they have, as it were, evolved different corporate personalities, which in turn impinge on the traditions of the others. Winchester has its own particularly esoteric 'notions', a tradition of almost medieval austerity, and unfailing urbanity and good manners. Harrow has its rich library of school songs. Rugby, Winchester, Harrow and Westminster all have their different games of football (Rugby's, of course, enjoying world-wide fame). Eton has two (the Field Game and the Wall Game), adapted to the peculiarities of the terrain on College Fields, and it once had a third ('Lower College'). At Eton, Fives Courts still bear the marks of the chapel buttress and staircase where the game was first played. Most schools have their private slang. This all contributes to the sense of corporate loyalty of which Harold Macmillan was speaking at Christ Church, and is particularly characteristic of these islands, particularly of England.

Eton was originally founded as an ecclesiastical establishment by Henry VI, and for long the governing body, the Provost and Fellows, formed a haven of rest for privileged Anglican parsons. But the foundation always included a school, composed at first of seventy 'poor scholars'. In those days 'the poor' did not imply a means test. All scholars were presumed poor, just as in Homer dawn was always 'rosy-fingered'. Side by side with the scholars, there grew up a number of boarding-houses run by independent, and not necessarily educationally qualified, men (tutors) and women (dames) of which one still survived in my father's day, run by the formidable Miss Evans. The boarders at these houses were able, on payment, to take advantage of the teaching facilities of the college. They were called Oppidans (or, literally, 'townsfolk') and gradually the 'tutors' and the non-teaching 'dames' became incorporated in the staff of the school. The original foundation remains at a closed seventy (and alone constitutes 'college'). Its members are entitled to the suffix KS (King's Scholar) after their name. But for many years the school has accommodated more than a thousand Oppidans, distributed among traditional houses scattered about the town, with traditional names like 'Baldwin's Bec' or 'Timbralls' and most of fairly ancient design and construction. The expression 'dame' (referred to in the third person as 'M'Dame' and in second person as 'Ma'am') is reserved currently for the house matron. A boy may have two tutors: a house tutor and, where the house tutor specializes in a subject outside the boy's course, a second tutor, in my day referred to as a 'moral' tutor, who supervises the boy's progress in the school. Both afford a friend to go to if the boy gets into trouble with the establishment. College is run by a resident 'Master in College' who is not technically a housemaster, assisted by a professional matron.

The advantage of these separate houses, running to about thirty-five or forty boys and scattered hundreds of yards apart, is manifest. It makes for increased order and better but relaxed discipline. In many ways Eton is more like a boy's university than a school. Tolerance prevails, and eccentricity is neither persecuted nor punished. There is no universally accepted school song. Three at least are in common use, and college has a separate fifteenth-century Latin hymn, sung to a swinging marching tune composed by a nineteenth-century Colleger, which we used to sing, when in a chauvinist mood, on field days in column of route. In this hymn King Henry VI is invoked as saint, and the actual meaning of the Latin words must relate back to a period shortly after his demise. There is also a very fine fifteenth-century Latin grace sung in college on Sundays or other high days and holidays in front of the Provost (resident chairman of the governing body), who, on those occasions, lunches in college hall.

I have always derided those who claim that their schooldays were the happiest in their lives. I make no such claim for myself. But when I remember my early days at Eton I get the impression, with one severe interruption, of years of pleasure, uninterrupted intellectual growth, and real happiness. Recently, it has been the fashion for intellectuals and others to deride their public schools. This does not coincide with my memories at all. With deep affection, I remember the beauty of the surroundings, the steady grind of scholarship, agreeable (but in my case hardly at all romantic) friendships, pleasant afternoons on the river, sculling my own boat to Queen's Eyot for beer and sandwiches through Boveney Lock, bathing at Romney, 'Athens', Ward's Mead and Cuckoo Weir, giving the Oppidans a good grinding at the wall game on St Andrew's Day, visiting home at 'Long Leave', skirmishing round Windsor Park on field days, at camp at Mytchett and on Salisbury Plain, tea in my own room in Lower Tower with three or four companions, breakfast and, later, dinner with the Provost (Monty James) or Headmaster (Cyril Alington), reading with H. E. Luxmoore at the Shakespeare Society at Baldwin's End. These were happy days, good times, and, although

I missed a very great deal of what was optionally on offer, I believe I enjoyed a very good education in terms of what was fashionable at the time.

I do not believe that there can be a good school which does not impart to its ablest boys at least a love of learning, demanding a high standard of scholastic discipline. By these tests, I still think Eton was a very good school indeed. Technically, it was a grammar school catering for, say, about the top 40 per cent in terms of ability. At its dismal bottom there were, no doubt, philistines and slackers in fairly considerable numbers. There was the occasional sexual scandal, though it is fair to say that never, in my six years there, did I ever come into direct contact with one of these. Throughout my time there was a succession of resident college thieves; I understand that there was usually at least one in most Oppidan houses. There was one case of blackmail when a boy was expelled. Though they must have happened, I never remember noticing a single case of drunkenness. In the main, I made few intimate friends. I suppose I was intellectually arrogant, a pot-hunter academically (though I won few school prizes apart from the Newcastle and Wilder Divinity Prizes), and a little difficult to know. I have no doubt, however, that the foundation of most of what I may have achieved since was either derived from my family, given me at Sunningdale by Ling, or acquired at Eton.

To modern eyes, the curriculum I followed would be rightly considered narrow and archaic. Compulsory subjects were taught: British history, in which I was well taught, the Bible ('divinity'), mathematics (elementary, and in my case also advanced), physics and chemistry (rather badly taught) and theoretical biology (very well expounded by M. D. Hill), and French. German and Russian were on offer (there was even a Newcastle Russian Prize), but I did not take them. These all with Latin and Greek, I pursued to School Certificate Level (Intermediate, I think between 'O' and 'A' levels and perhaps similar to GCSE) in which I passed with nine 'distinctions'. Thereafter I specialized in the two ancient tongues, which formed the basis of my education till I left Oxford. I was one of the last in the public eye, with the notable exception of Enoch Powell, to follow the traditional culture of the educated man which had dominated the curriculum since the Renaissance. Today, except for a few islands of specialists, it is almost as if it had never been.

Though I cannot complain of the reasons which led to their virtual extinction, I mourn the passing of the Classics. The modern world grew out of the ancient culture of the Western Church in the unreformed Middle Ages, and out of the study of Greek and Latin literature as developed by the scholars of the Renaissance and after. It is impossible to appreciate English, French or German history or literature without some knowledge of their roots in the past, religious and secular. Cut flowers never produce seed or fruit, and without a vigorous practice of religion and knowledge of the cultural past there is danger than the modern world becomes the prey of eccentrics, hypochondriacs and quacks, or, worse still, criminal lunatics and demoniacs like Hitler, Stalin and Mussolini, and their followers and imitators today who had better remain unnamed. The study of Classics and the scriptures certainly provided some safeguard against these, and we have not yet found an alternative in contemporary culture.

Nevertheless, the case from the other side of the educational debate is overwhelming. No one can now claim to be 'numerate', in the jargon later invented by C. P. Snow, unless he has pursued mathematics, at least to the level of the differential calculus, and acquired a sound knowledge, at least in theory if not necessarily in practice, of the fundamental conceptions of physics, chemistry, biology and Darwinism. It is wholly impossible to overload the young with a curriculum providing even a basic 'numeracy' and 'literacy'. It is wholly undesirable to attempt to concentrate on one of the two alleged cultures, the 'artistic' and the 'scientific', in any general system of education, or to avoid a sound general foundation in both in all the early stages. This would be to uncivilize the sciences and mathematics, and to deprive those primarily orientated towards the humanities of any understanding of the most characteristic feature of contemporary culture. There is no alternative to a sound general foundation prior to the age of specialization and, even after it, a continued interest in human activities of all sorts has to be specially catered for. Otherwise what I have always considered to be the wholly fantastic legend of the two cultures would become established fact. Apart from anything else, and whatever branch of academic study is afterwards included or abandoned from about the age of sixteen at one level and about twenty at the maximum at another, the demands of vocational training in practical skills are clamant and become an economic necessity. My own belief is that by far the most important general study in the humanities and the arts is the study of history, modern, ancient or medieval, and that this should always be orientated towards the history of ideas and language as well as the history of events, both of which should be related to the questions of the present day.

However, before I was led into this digression, I was saying that, for better or worse, I was well educated at Eton, and that, unfashionable as it inevitably must seem today, I became a classical specialist and remained so until after I had taken a first degree. The price I paid was that I did not begin my professional training in law until years after most of my contemporaries at the Bar. In mitigation, I can only say that I am quite certain that I was a better lawyer by the time I was forty-five than I would have been if my first degree had been in law, and that, when ultimately I came to be appointed to high office, I was far more suited to it, even as Lord Chancellor, than I would have been without my classical studies and general training in the history of ideas and of the Christian Church.

FIVE

The Death of My Mother

IN MY LAST YEAR AT ETON came my first great experience of bereavement. I happened to be in bed in the college sickrooms ('staying out rooms' in college parlance), ill of some kind of fever, at the same time as my brother Neil, by sheer coincidence, was also 'staying out' in the next room with one of the attacks of asthma which ultimately removed him from the school altogether. Suddenly, one Sunday morning I think it was, in May 1925, my brother Edward came into the room unannounced. He had come from London. I was pleased to see him. 'I am afraid', he said, 'I have come to bring bad news. Mother died this morning.' It came as a thunderclap. Had I been less innocent, I should have expected it. Two years before, when we were staying with cousins near Aberdeen, my mother had been taken ill with what I now know, and should even then have guessed, was a stroke. But all our elders conspired to make Neil and me underestimate its seriousness. Very likely they were wise, but the result was disastrous. To all appearances my mother recovered at first, as my father had done in 1917 when he suffered a serious bout of typhoid fever. Temperamentally she was considerably altered. Where on the whole she had been light-hearted and sparkling, she became irritable, short-tempered and hypercritical, and, wholly innocent about such things, I did not make allowances. Our relations, hitherto sunny and affectionate, became strained. Now she was dead. I had no power to make amends. Later, the Headmaster came in to comfort me, good Christian that he was, with the consolations of religion. Unpardonably, I was rude. I had obviously been aware of what I regarded as difficulties in the way of religious faith, and I suddenly realized that I had none to comfort me. It was not in the least that I lost my faith as the result of learning that my mother was no longer alive. It was the other way round. I learned that my mother was dead, was offered comfort, and suddenly realized that I had no belief in any religious doctrine at all to protect me against my grief. All that was beautiful and outgoing and loving about my mother had disappeared, all her pride in me and her other children had wholly vanished from the universe and was altogether absent. I do not think I ever became, in the strict sense, an atheist. I was simply a non-believer. There may not be much difference in practice. Emotionally, life was suddenly chaos. I never succeeded in asserting that there was no such entity as Good, or even God. It is fair to say that, though where there is no belief there can be no practice, in an abstract way I continued to believe in moral values, and to argue in favour of moral conduct. Much later, at Oxford, I can remember arguing in a purely academic way in favour of Kant's 'categorical imperative' and in favour of obeying its voice when it was unequivocably expressed and understood. It is here, I suppose, that my classical training in the works of the pagan philosophers came, to some extent, to my aid. But I think it is not too much to say that, for years after my mother's death, the Christian religion meant nothing to me.

The thing that saved me during the horrible week that followed her death was the manifest duty of doing something for my father. He was Attorney-General, a member of the House of Commons. My mother's death had knocked him sideways. I have never seen a man so stricken. He was even worse hit than I was later when I lost my wife Mary. He told me that during the week before her death the cloud which had descended on her personally for the last two years had suddenly moved away. They had just visited the Empire Exhibition at Wembley, and, he said, 'It was just like when we were first married.' For four years at least, and almost until he married again, he could be heard at night from his bedchamber, literally shouting with agony. He seemed to have no natural resistance to the tides of grief which were sweeping him away. In the mean time letters came pouring in, from political friend and foe, from the legal profession, from the judiciary, from relatives and acquaintances and strangers and, of course, the Polytechnic. The secretary answered those from well-wishing strangers. A very few he answered himself. The rest I answered for him in my own hand. One, I remember, came from Saklatvala, the communist MP for Chester-le-Street. It was a warm-hearted, charming letter. With a sob, my father was touched. 'And I always thought', he said, 'he was such a rotter.' This hideous week came to an end with the funeral, at All Souls, Langham Place, where we sang, inappropriately perhaps, though my mother had had a hard life, 'Fight the Good Fight'. After that, a long Via Dolorosa at a walking pace to Marylebone Cemetery at the far end of the old Finchley Road, where my grandfather and my grandmother also lay buried. It is a vast place, with literally hundreds of graves. As we walked from the little funerary chapel to the appointed place where a grave lay open beside a heap of excavated earth, 'Poor Myssie, she always hated crowds,' said my father. It was the first and only time I heard him call her by the pet name, originally given her by Negro servants when she was a child, in far-off Nashville, Tennessee. I never went near the cemetery for nearly forty years. But when I did I was able to find my way without difficulty. The grave, which was overgrown, is now well cared for by contractors. After the funeral, I was driven back to Eton, in the American car driven by the Master-in-College, Bill Marsden, who, with the Matron-in-College, was a tower of strength.

I think that, after that, I had almost a nervous breakdown. I continued my work at the school but would not take part in any school activities. I could not sleep. I was morose and neurotic. But time heals. Later, in 1926, I followed my brother Edward to Oxford. If I had not been so emotionally distraught, I think I could be described as a disagreeable boy, academically clever, but emotionally arrogant and extremely self-centred. It must be to some extent a mark of my emotional disturbance at the time that my last two years at Eton have left so small a mark upon my memory. Yet, academically, they were most successful. I was Captain of the School. I won the top classical scholarship to Christ Church, my two successful fellows being Denys Page and Donald Allan. Both had distinguished academic careers after leaving Oxford. Denys became Regius

Professor of Greek and Master of Jesus, Cambridge, and was only deprived of the Vice-Chancellorship by an intrigue. Donald was, I believe, a Fellow of Balliol and Professor of Greek at Edinburgh. They went on to win all the university prizes in Latin and Greek, in a competition with one another achieving standards no one else was able to approach.*

My school days were now at an end. Educational questions are always to be asked, but are never really capable of answer. I have already spoken of the peculiarities of a curriculum which characterized the learning I had acquired. These would never have occurred within the system provided by the State. I am sure, however, that I acquired more from what I have received from independent schools than I could ever have done had I gone to the nearest local-authority school and dined off the *table d'hôte* dinner there provided. Nor have I any shame at all in having sent each of my children to independent schools of my own, or their mother's, choosing of one brand or another. Between us we cost the State nothing, and for Britain we created five admirable citizens. By paying our rates and taxes, we also paid our full contribution towards educating the children of others, and thus provided the nation with citizens who received an education, the best at the time that a nationally funded and locally administered system could be expected to provide. During the period of my children's education, the provision of a single place in the national system would have cost the taxpayer hundreds or thousands of pounds a year, and, since the number of middle-class children at any given moment provided with independent education often at the cost of great self-sacrifice runs into hundreds of thousands, by educating these children at their own expense out of their taxed income their parents are making voluntary contribution to the revenue to pay for what in any case would have to be done and, as I believe, less well. So we are collectively conferring on our society an

---

*The final accolade came in Wystan Auden's first published book of poems where they appear by name: 'Allan and Page, like rival railway companies'. Wystan Auden, too, was an undergraduate of that year, reading English.

annual asset worth many hundreds of millions of pounds in total if you count every child educated from nursery-school age to first-degree level. The proof of this particular pudding is also in the eating. As wealth has increased, the demand for independent education has constantly increased with it. What we provide for our children is both popular, valuable to the child, and indirectly a contribution to the Exchequer and a public asset. So far from being sneered at as elitist, public statues should be erected in our honour.

One last memory of Eton. Long before my brother came there in 1912 the sixth-form lavatories in college were decorated with a strange epigram in heroic verse. It ran as follows:

> Fair Cloacina, goddess of this place,
> The accustomed seat of every child of grace,
> On thy fair throne let our libations flow
> Not rudely swift nor obstinately slow.

I have never discovered who was the witty and talented author. In the course of redecoration, the verse was frequently obliterated, but always reappeared. It existed in Edward's day. It existed in my day. As I have ascertained, it survived the Second World War. Alas, I understand it is no more. In my time a Greek version was added by my friend Anthony Martineau.

Whoever composed the epigram was evidently a scholar. During my time at Eton I had always assumed that Cloacina was an invented name. She was not. She really existed and was really worshipped. My authority? As I discovered only recently, it is St Augustine's *Civitas Dei* where Cloacina, goddess of sewers, is duly recorded and derided as part of the saint's condemnation of the Roman pagan religion.

SIX

Mediterranean Cruise

SANDWICHED BETWEEN my leaving Eton and my going up to Oxford in the autumn of 1926 were three successive events which had a bigger influence on my subsequent life than might at first have been supposed. These were my Mediterranean cruise, my part in the General Strike, and my journey to Aberdeen and back driving my mother's old 'T' model Ford in company with my brother Neil.

My father had promised me a trip round the Mediterranean as a reward for winning the Newcastle Scholarship. My real object was to visit Athens, but after toying with the idea of a Swan Hellenic Travellers trip to Greece I opted instead for a wider cruise on board an old RMSP vessel, *Arcadian*. This was to take me from Southampton right round the Mediterranean – Tangier, Naples, Malta, Phaleron Bay, Constantinople, Tunis, Algiers and Gibraltar. Being of a frugal disposition, my father had booked a cabin of the cheapest rank, two-berthed, somewhere in the bowels of the ship. When it was found, I discovered that the other berth was occupied by an old retired gentleman of very advanced age and in apparently frail health. I do not remember his name. But I also found that there had been a third berth erected, and shortly after my arrival, to my utter astonishment, in walked my half-brother, Edward Marjoribanks, carrying his gear. My relationship with Edward had always been affectionate and close. But this was the beginning of an even closer friendship which only ended with his tragic death six years later in 1932, the second of the worst bereavements in my life.

It is difficult to exaggerate Edward's charm and Edward's talent. He was eight years older than I, and planned to be everything that I, too, hoped to become in life. He was a scholar at Eton, a scholar at Christ Church, a double first in Mods and Greats, had been President of the Union of Oxford (where my father spoke at his invitation when he was Attorney-General), and designed to go into politics and practise at the Bar. He was a great friend and admirer of the famous jury advocate Sir Edward Marshall Hall, subsequently wrote his life, thereby founding a new genre in biography, and to my mind the very best example of a class of literature which otherwise I have never greatly admired, the legal biography which consists very largely of a list of famous cases in which the subject has been involved. In addition to this, unlike myself, he was a fine oarsman, which I also greatly admired, a member of the Leander Club, having rowed for Christ Church in a year when it finished head of the river and won the Ladies' Plate. None of this, however, gives an adequate idea of the real charm of his character. He wore his considerable achievements with an easy grace. He had inherited all my mother's electric, effervescent American charm. His vivacious conversation exceeded anything I had known, or was ever to know, in wit, knowledge and incisiveness. In addition to all this, and again quite unlike myself, he had made a great name for himself in the smartest London society. He was a frequent guest at Ettie Desborough's home at Taplow and at the dinners given by Emerald Cunard, to whom, when I learned that she was dying, I sent a special gift of flowers to remind her of her friendship with Edward, which I have reason to believe brightened her last hours.

Of course I was delighted to know that Edward was going to be my companion in my cabin, and that I was to enjoy the enchanting company which I knew he was able to offer on a voyage of which already I expected so much. But I was naturally curious to learn why he had not told me of his plan to join the ship, and how he came to occupy the same cabin as myself.

The reason, which I soon found out, was simple, and one which, though I did not realize it, was fraught with doom. Edward was courting Pamela Beckett, the youngest daughter of a Yorkshire banker, Rupert Beckett, and who was going in the boat, in far more luxurious accommodation, with her friend Patricia Herbert and her father. I did not know it at the time, but the courtship had been stormy, first up and then down, and then up again. She had first accepted him and then refused him, and then accepted and refused him again. Both of these delightful and attractive young people came to unhappy ends, but now Edward and Pamela, like some delicate Cartier jewel full of beauty and appeal, were full of hope. Edward and I were both welcome guests at Beckett's table and of course, while it lasted, it was an extremely happy party. It had a tragic end. Edward suddenly left the ship in high dudgeon halfway through the cruise whilst we were visiting Athens. The romance was over, and its end was, I believe, one of the decisive factors which ended Edward's young life, so full of promise, in the spring of 1932. By that time he was MP for Eastbourne, had written his successful biography and virtually completed the first volume of Carson's life. He had everything before him. Had he not died when, and how, he did, he could not have failed to achieve membership of the Cabinet, probably some time after 1939 (he was a friend of Winston and Brendan Bracken), and to have made a significant contribution to our national life. Alas, for what might have been. I have never ceased to mourn Edward, and to regret his passing, for which, as I will come to relate, I must to some extent accuse myself.

We came back to Southampton halfway through the General Strike, and I was kindly motored back to London in the Beckett Rolls. My father was then Attorney-General and in the thick of it, and I determined to be in the thick of it as well. This was not so easy. All the best jobs were already taken, and for about twenty-four hours I was at a loose end. The best jobs consisted in driving trains on the Underground and the main line, operating lifts, selling tickets and in every way showing that, whatever the merits of the coal strike which had triggered the whole business off, the country was not going to be held to ransom at the whim of the trade unions.

I was extremely frustrated at finding nothing to do. But fate suddenly came to my aid. For some reason best known to themselves, since their action was taken in defiance of the TUC, the refuse-collectors of St Marylebone, my father's constituency, who operated a fleet of decrepit Renault lorries from somewhere near Paddington

Green, stopped work, and the son of a friend of my father's and I were engaged to put them on the road again. Except in theory, I knew nothing at that time of the inside working of motor vehicles, but my colleague was an expert in mechanical engineering. We were twenty-four hours a day in the plant for about a week, only resting to eat and to sleep, putting those wretched machines, which I can only suppose had been sabotaged in various minor respects, more or less into working condition. We lived in great discomfort and had very poor food, but one by one, by using the manual lever in front, one engine after another would begin to fire. We were then joined by a group of Cambridge undergraduates to crew the lorries (it was before the driving test) and to take them on to the streets. We two remained behind, still struggling with the rest of the fleet. Unfortunately the grateful Marylebonians, discovering to their immense relief that help to remove their insanitary and deteriorating refuse was at length at hand, could not resist offering the crews hospitality as a reward for their coming. The result was inevitable, since the hospitality was repeated at every home. Lorry after lorry returned with an undergraduate crew in a state varying between mild insobriety and complete leglessness. Some of the drivers were sent home. But soon after this my father rang the depot to tell me that the strike was at an end, largely as the result of the efforts of J. H. Thomas, the railway leader. Years later, in 1963, this incident was brought up against me at the Marylebone by-election where I was described as an enemy of the working class. I derived some advantage from my experience since, under the tuition of my older colleague, I had acquired a little practical understanding of the working of the internal combustion engine.

Meanwhile I had acquired a driving licence. Of all the various motor vehicles I have owned or driven (they have ranged from motorcycles on Salisbury Plain to Bren-gun carriers in the desert) by far the most remarkable was my first, which I acquired in the months between my mother's death and my going up to Oxford. It was a 'T' model Ford open touring model constructed at some time before 1913, a circumstance which enabled me to get a reduced rate on my horsepower tax, in a 24-horsepower model then a fairly serious item.

My father and mother did not run to a car until 1914, when my mother bought her first Tin Lizzie, a beautiful contraption with a brass bonnet, and took my father on a motoring tour in East Anglia. In 1915 she changed this model for what afterwards became my own first car. Apart from the disappearance of the brass bonnet, there was little difference between the two. Both were open touring four-seaters with no protection against the weather except a hood, attached to the windscreen by straps, and side-curtains, connected with one another and with the hood by straps and buttons. The side and rear lamps, which frequently went out, were illuminated by oil and wicks. The headlights were electric but, since there were no batteries, ran directly off the engine, emitting a brilliant beam when the engine revved up, but going down to a dull glow when it was idling. There were two forward gears, bottom and top, operated from what, in a modern car, would be the clutch pedal. You depressed this pedal if you wished to engage bottom, and released it when you wished to get into top. Neutral was halfway, but you could not stay there unless the handbrake was on. Reverse was obtained by depressing the centre pedal. There was no gearbox, the gears being epicyclic. There was no accelerator pedal, revolutions being increased or reduced by the use of a manually operated level on the steering column. The petrol-tank was immediately under the driver's seat and fed the engine by gravity. You ascertained the depth of petrol in the tank by using a calibrated dipstick. There was no spare wheel. In cases of puncture, which were not infrequent, temporary relief was obtained by what was called a Stepney Wheel, a gadget with tyre tread affixed which clamped on to the outer rim of the wheel with the punctured tyre. This was not very convenient, as, in the nature of things, the diameter of the Stepney was wider that that of the ordinary wheels and caused the vehicle to run, as it were, on an uneven keel. Moreover, it did not always stay on firmly even when attached. Starting was by starting-lever, and when the engine fired at all it sometimes fired backwards, threatening the owner, unless he knew the knack of avoiding the kick, with a broken wrist. Cruising speed was 28 miles per hour, although the engine could be induced, with an angry snarl, to move the car at a maximum of thirty-five. My mother ran the vehicle throughout the First World War and, so far as I can remember, nearly until her stroke in 1923. Thereafter it remained on wooden blocks at home in Sussex until I was seventeen when, after my mother's death, it was rewired and delivered to me. It remained in my possession until 1928, when I sold it to a local sawmill near Hailsham for £2 10s (£2.50). It did yeoman service there, sawing wood for its owner from its offside back wheel, jacked up and attached by a belt to a circular saw. As a museum piece it would today be worth a small fortune.

Such was the vehicle in which I first visited Oxford in 1926, driving my elder brother, Edward, and carrying all my worldly possessions to Christ Church. I was not permitted to retain the car at Oxford, since during the first year freshmen were not permitted to own a car. After their first year, they were required to display an attractive little green light. But by the time I had the right to one of these I was the proud owner of a twelve/forty Alvis, which I christened Artemis after the Greek name for Diana the huntress, a miniature statue of whom I put on the bonnet as a mascot.

In the mean time, in the summer of 1926, Neil and I made the journey to Haddo House, near Aberdeen, in the Tin Lizzie. Haddo House was the home of Neil's godfather, the Earl of Haddo, to which we had been invited as guests. We broke the outward journey at Peterborough, Lincoln, Newcastle and, I think, Edinburgh, which we reached by Carter Bar. The coal strike, which had been the cause of the abortive General Strike, was still firm, and it was sad to pass through one coalfield after another, with all the wheels at the heads of the shafts standing idle. It was my first experience of industrial strife, and its outcome led me to believe that, whatever their merits, stoppages carried out on a national scale to bring a whole industry to a standstill were almost certain to be counterproductive for the workforce, as well as exacting a terrible toll of unemployment not confined to the industry itself. I thought, and still do, that, useful as it may have been in the days of Mr Gradgrind and the tommy shop, a strike on a national scale is certain to inflict disproportionate damage on the public and on workers in other industries, and, if prolonged, is nearly always certain to damage the prospects of the workers in the industry itself.

We crossed the Forth by the old Burntisland Ferry. The return journey we completed in two days, stopping for the night only in Newcastle. On the way down to the Forth we suffered what might have been a serious accident. I was descending the hill in neutral, which I managed to maintain by keeping the gear-pedal halfway up with my foot, and thus attained the unprecedented speed of 50 miles per hour. This was too much for Tin Lizzie. There was a hideous lurch, and Neil and I were astonished, and not a little alarmed, to see the back near wheel running in front of the car, which followed it with a series of sickening leaps and bounds. Happily both it and we came to rest in comparative safety. How exactly we found a garage open (it was Sunday) and prepared to repair us, and how, thereafter, we got to Newcastle that night, I do not exactly remember. But I have a clear memory of the moon over Carter Bar, and of cheering myself up with somewhat raucous singing.

My holiday ended with a conventional visit to Oxford by train, and I was installed, after being introduced to Dean White, in Staircase 8:3 in Peckwater Quad opposite the rooms of Roger Chetwode, the son of the field-marshal of that name. My fellow classical scholars were the Allan and Page already mentioned. Another contemporary was Patrick Gordon Walker, for a brief and rather inglorious period Foreign Secretary under Harold Wilson. But I was not a particularly social or gregarious figure. My closest friends at the House were Richard Best, the son of a Lord Justice of Appeal in Northern Ireland, Billy Loudon, Bill McElwee (later a history master at Stowe) and Hilary Magnus. All are now dead. My greatest interests were in my work (Honour Mods and Greats), which I took extremely seriously, in the Union, where I learned to speak and debate, and ultimately became President, and in various clubs and societies, like the Canning, and the Christ Church Essay Club, which met after dinner to drink mulled claret and to discuss serious questions in an amiable and frivolous spirit. I tried rowing, but gave it up after one Torpids and one Eights, and the Oxford Artillery, where I attended one camp on Salisbury Plain and rode enjoyably, in early mornings on Port Meadow and over the jumps in the riding school, but which I had to give up owing to pressure of work. With my father already Attorney-General, I believe I was an exceedingly earnest and ambitious politician, and, when my degree was over, eager to be called and practise at the Bar.

SEVEN

Christ Church

MANY PEOPLE have written about the Oxford of the late twenties, and I have seldom recognized the picture that they painted. Of course I knew most of the people. Maurice Bowra had examined me for the Newcastle; Professor Lindemann, as the result of his friendship with my brother Edward, entertained me in his rooms when I entered from Eton for the scholarship and also in Christ Church hall, where I first enjoyed the delights of champagne in a pint mug and I first met Richard Pares. Betjeman and John Sparrow were my fellow-guests my first term at a luncheon-party in Tom Quad. Barrington Ward (who first set my sights on a Prize Fellowship at All Souls) was my tutor for Honour Mods during my first two years, and Gilbert Ryle, Robin Dundas, Michael Foster and Bobby Longden, whom I knew from Eton days, successively taught me for Greats in Greek and Roman history and in philosophy, ancient and modern. Gilbert Ryle was so friendly to my efforts that I verily believe that I would not have got my first class had not Michael Foster torn me apart and taught me just in time how little I knew about Kant and Hegel. David Cecil came to lunch in my rooms, and Freddie Furneaux and Basil Ava and Randolph Churchill were close friends if not constant companions. Lindemann ('The Prof') used to have us in his rooms when he entertained F. E. Smith, Lord Birkenhead, and Winston to quite extraordinary evening colloquies. At that time I and, I believe, most of us, but certainly I, would have committed the greatest historical misjudgement if we had been asked to judge between the two. We would have thought Winston's career had reached his zenith by his being made Baldwin's Chancellor of the

Exchequer. Birkenhead still dazzled by his conversation, his arrogant gift of crushing repartee, and what we then quite wrongly believed his brilliant swashbuckling career at the Bar and in politics. In fact he had less than ten years to live and is now memorable mainly for his property reforms, a project which he had inherited from Haldane and which was ultimately carried through by Cave after a brilliant *tour de force* in draftsmanship by Sir Benjamin Cherry. No one foresaw either Churchill's years of self-imposed exile and isolation or his triumphant return to save his country in the Second World War. But the firework display touched off by the contact between those two brilliant and iridescent personalities in Lindemann's rooms was quite unforgettable. On Sundays there was the possibility of a four-mile walk to tea with John Buchan at Elsfield. On certain fortunate days Sligger Urquhart (to whom, again, I was introduced by Edward) would hold an agreeable open salon for undergraduate friends in his room in Balliol. Sligger (Francis) Urquhart, son of a former ambassador to Constantinople and founder of the Hammam Turkish Bath in Jermyn Street, was a history don and one of the most famous characters of the day. In addition he was one of the most agreeable men I have ever met: a Roman Catholic by religion and a saint.

From the start, I was interested in the Union. Again it was Edward, who had been President, who gave me ideas in that direction. Alan Lennox Boyd was President in my first term, and encouraged me to speak, and, unless I am mistaken, gave me my first real chance to speak 'on the paper', that is, amongst those advertised in advance to participate at the beginning of a given debate. I started with one great advantage. I had already learned to control and deliver my voice by speeches at Eton. These were declamations or recitations by members of the sixth form in the old 'Upper School' delivered in front of the Headmaster and an invited audience. When I first began to deliver speeches of my own composition, I learned my speech by heart before delivery (an apprenticeship far to be preferred to speaking from notes and, still more so, to reading from a prepared text). The real art of debating came slowly, and later, and was really only finally achieved as the result of practice at the Bar.

During my first term, I did one crazy thing which, by the merest chance, in the long run paid an immense dividend. At that time the Union was dominated by Liberals, and when the election for President came up before the end of term the Society was invited to make a choice between three Liberal candidates, Dingle Foot, Dick Acland and Aubrey Herbert, without either a Conservative or a Labour alternative. I do not know what possessed me to do it. I had held none of the three offices generally considered to be a *sine qua non* for the presidency. I was not yet even on either of the two committees; indeed, as a freshman, not merely in his first year, but in his first term, I had no standing in the Society whatsoever. I simply do not know how I had the gall to do what I did.

I stood myself as a fourth candidate in the Conservative interest, which gave me the right to take part in the Presidential Debate, the best-attended and most highly publicized debate of the term. In addition to the candidates, this debate was always attended by a national figure, and on this occasion the national figure was Lord Birkenhead himself, probably the best-known ex-President of the Union then alive.

When the day came, the debate was indeed one of the most memorable of my experience. On one side of the House were the three Liberals. On the other, sitting on the Committee Bench, were the former Lord Chancellor and myself. I do not remember the other speeches or my own, but I do remember those of Dingle (ultimately, and rightly, the successful candidate) and Birkenhead. Dingle recounted an anecdote, which I now know to have been a chestnut, and can be told either way, of any two brilliant undergraduates. In this case, Dingle told it of F. E. Smith (as he then had been) and John Simon talking together in their undergraduate days and agreeing that, as they were both of such outstanding ability, one or the other must certainly become Prime Minister one day, and therefore they could not afford to remain in the same political party. According to the version told by Dingle, they tossed for it as to who should remain a Liberal, and FE lost. Up to that moment, looking over his shoulder, I had seen FE, in his rather unformed schoolboy hand, making ordinary and rather conventional notes under headings such as

'Unemployment' and 'League of Nations'. But when Dingle told his anecdote these notes came to an end, and were jettisoned. When his turn came to speak in reply, FE, drawing himself up to his huge height, and delivering himself in his characteristic and fruity, but rather foppish, drawl, made use of the following passage, which displays him both at his brilliant best and, paradoxically, at the same time at his wholly deplorable worst. 'That anecdote', said he, 'bears all the characteristics of a Liberal pleasantry. In the first place it is a lie. In the second place it is not funny. In the third place it is calculated to give offence – not to myself, of course, because it is a matter of supreme indifference to me what my young friend may say or think. But think of the pain it will cause when I go back to Westminster, and recount it to my old friend and colleague Sir John Simon.'

When the voting took place, I found, to my huge surprise, that I was not bottom of the poll. Dingle, as he deserved, came first, Dick Acland second, I was third, and Aubrey Herbert was last. I have no doubt that this ludicrous foray in the field of calculated risk was one of the factors which set me on the road to become President three years later, in 1929, and so enabled me to set aside my last year to acquire my first-class degree in Greats. About forty years later my son Douglas was not so lucky. He, too, became President, but in his last year and at the expense of a first class in history, which I believe otherwise he would have obtained. He was following the conventional three-year course whilst my own, Honour Mods and Greats, took four years, which enabled me to have an additional year in order to make certain of my class. It was not the first, or the last, occasion when a calculated risk which I took paid a dividend. But I still regard my nerve in standing for President in my first year as a mark of folly rather than of foresight.

EIGHT

Sligger's Chalet

EDWARD'S EXAMPLE was what really taught me that the secret of success in Schools was work, and in particular hard, slogging work during the vacations. By itself talent is not enough for a first class. I still remember seeing Edward at our country home in Sussex reading in the garden all day and in his bedroom far into the night, filling notebook after notebook in his cramped handwriting with the notes which brought him his own double first in Honour Mods and Greats. Throughout my Oxford career I followed this example. Indirectly, however, this habit led me to one of the great loves of my life: walking, scrambling and climbing in the mountains and hills, particularly in the Alps, but also in the Lake District, Wales and Scotland.

In his youth, my father had been something of a mountaineer. Indeed, he had taken Edward on a walking tour in Switzerland, just about the time when he got his scholarship to Eton in 1912. Father used to tell me of a very exciting adventure in the Bernese Oberland when he was a very young man. He had set out to climb the Jungfrau with a guide, or perhaps two guides, and had got lost in a snowstorm on the way down and only found his position again after the guide's ice-axe cut through the snow on the roof of the hut itself, and the noise of the axe striking the wood of the roof of the hut instead of rock or ice both told them their exact position and afforded them shelter from the storm. But he had done more than this. Whilst my mother was still alive, between 1921 and 1924, he had brought Neil and me, with my mother, to the Polytechnic chalets near Lucerne and, using those as a base, had taken us on a brief walking tour

57

to Andermatt, Grindelwald and up the then recently opened Jungfrau railway to Jungfraujoch, where, with a guide, the three of us had climbed a small peak, then covered in snow, called the Mathildenspitze. By 1924 I had done some reasonably ambitious walking from Chamonix nearly all by myself, but once, with a guide, over the shoulder of the Moine to the Jardin de Talèfre and, by myself, up the side of the Brévent to Planpraz and to the junction of the two glaciers on the way to the Grands Mulets. By the time I was at Oxford, I was a fairly experienced walker and had conceived the ambition to make climbing and walking one of my main sporting activities.

My first real opportunity to make an independent effort to achieve these ambitions was when, in my first year, Sligger Urquhart asked me to join one of his reading-parties at his chalet in the French Alps on the shoulder of the Prarion mountain above St-Gervais-les-Bains, overlooking the valley of Sallanches, and facing the rugged summit of the Mont Percé. These reading-parties were among the most delightful experiences of my Oxford life. We travelled by train from Calais on a through coach to Le Fayet. We then changed to a rack-and-pinion railway known as the Tramway du Mont Blanc, which led to St-Gervais-les-Bains and a station known as Motivon. Then we walked by mule-path on to the chalet with our packs on our backs, leaving our luggage to be brought by mule-cart along the zig-zag path from the valley. We were expected to work on our academic studies both morning and afternoon. In the evening there were games on the rough lawn outside the chalet, and, more often alone but sometimes with companions, I would scramble up the 600 feet which separated us from the rough top of the Prarion, whence, on a clear day, you could see the whole range of the Chamonix Aiguilles, from the Chardonnet, via the Aiguille and Dôme du Goûter to the Aiguilles de Bionnassay and Trélatête in the west. Further away, just north of due east, you could see the Col de Bonhomme on the way to Italy, and below was the whole valley of Chamonix which Sligger often referred to as 'the Great Wen' from Les Bossons to Argentière.

The chalet itself was utterly delightful, smelling beautifully of pinewood. It had been built by Sligger's father from whom he had inherited it. Formally it was called the Chalet des Mélèzes from the larches which surrounded it, but in practice it was known locally as the Chalet des Anglais from the English who inhabited it in the summer. The view was spectacular, especially in the evening as the lights came out across the valley of Sallanches to the Mont Percé through the hole in which the evening sun would shine as it was about to set. I look on the days I spent there as among the happiest of my life, so much so that many years later I brought my beloved wife Mary to see it. We stayed then at Arbois opposite the Prarion, and a local farmer explained to me how he had been cheered at the worst time in the war when he had heard the 'bombardiers Britanniques' flying south across the valley and over Mont Blanc on their way to bomb Turin or Milan.

Sligger did not allow climbing from the chalet, for fear of accidents, but once or more during the fortnight of my stay we would take part in an organized chalet walk, to the Lac d'Anterne above Sixte, to the Cols de Bonhomme or des Fours or de la Seigne, or the little shrine of the Blessed Virgin at Notre Dame de la Gorge, and after our chalet stay was over we were encouraged to make use of the services of Louis Broisat, who looked after the chalet throughout the year and held a *brevet de guide* at St-Gervais. It was then that I made my first major climb, the Grand Charmoz, a rugged peak, within shouting distance of its famous sister, the Grépon, which rises vertically above the Mer de Glace and is reached by the Montenvers Railway and a night spent at the Plan de l'Aiguille hotel.

The Charmoz itself is not intrinsically a difficult peak. But, for a first climb of any magnitude, there is a good deal to be said for it. The way leads across the little glacier des Nantillons, where you have to run because there is an objective danger of falling séracs and ice fragments. The rest is a fairly easy rock-climb and scramble until the last pitch is reached. This consists of a lovely little granite chimney which can be climbed by the back-and-knee method, and the end of the pitch is a dramatic *coup de théâtre*. At the top of the chimney you swing yourself out over a vertical precipice. As you do so, down there and between your knees, you see the Mer de Glace two thousand feet below. This was my first big thrill in rock-climbing. The rock was warm and perfect. The sun was shining. The almost sensuous experience of climbing good rock has never left me, and this, my first time ever, did much to guide my permanent love of mountains, snow and ice (though I never learned to ski), rock and glacier, storm and sunshine. It never left me until, in 1974, my disability in my ankles, itself the result of two fractures acquired climbing in the Valais alps, put an end to my climbing, scrambling and even serious walking for ever. At the top of the Charmoz or perhaps eating my packed lunch just below the final pitch, we were entertained for nearly forty-five minutes by the sight and sound of two Englishmen climbing the famous Mummery crack on the neighbouring Grépon. This is a long fissure in the rock about sixty feet in length which can only be climbed by putting one's right fist and one's right knee in the crack and pulling oneself up. There is a small resting-place about halfway. The first Englishman succeeded relatively easily. But what we mainly listened to in the Alpine stillness was his encouragement of his far less experienced second.

After my experience on the Charmoz, there were, I believe, no years when I did not climb either in Britain or in the Alps at Easter, Whitsun and August, usually and if possible all three. My range was fairly catholic, scrambling or climbing in the Lake District, Wales, Fort William (Easter 1937), Savoy, the Valais, the Engadin, Austria, the Bernese Oberland (Bel Alp and Grindelwald), Norway (1939, when I had to scurry out as the Hitler–Stalin pact was announced and had to stay in the plane when our Fokker landed for a period at Hamburg). By the war, I had become a member of the Alpine Club (one of my great ambitions) and during my time in the Army my Alpine memories often comforted me in hours of loneliness, despondency and boredom. After the war my experiences became progressively less exciting owing to increasing physical incapacity, marriage and, later, a growing family. It all began with my visits to Switzerland with my father in 1921. And the decisive stage was reached after the reading-parties at Sligger's chalet, starting with small climbs and, more seriously, the Grand Charmoz in August 1928.

NINE

Campion Hall

I WAS BROUGHT UP to be a strict Protestant. When my first identifiable ancestor emigrated to Ulster, the family were Quakers, and I believe there are in Northern Ireland Hoggs who are Quakers still. But in about 1750 a direct ancestor married a Church of Ireland girl called Rose O'Neill, and for his pains was 'disowned' by the Society of Friends. Before the Treaty of 1921, we were all very conscious of our Protestant Irish connections and I was brought up a strict Protestant within the Church of England. Fundamentalism was not far away. My grandfather was thirteen when Darwin published his *Origin of Species*, and at first his whole world crumbled about him. With difficulty he recovered his faith, and his faith inspired his whole life of public service. But my great-aunts still believed in verbal inspiration. I well remember in about 1917 my Great-Aunt Annie expounding the theory that the entry of Allenby's forces into Palestine with his aircraft flying overhead had been directly foretold in some obscure passage of Ezekiel which spoke of an eagle (or eagles) flying over Jerusalem. My grandmother was a member of the Church of Scotland. Though he was a great and good man, I have never quite been able to make out what my father believed, though I am sure that he believed something. I never knew him take the Sacrament, even on his death-bed. He took the oath in the Scottish manner, with up-raised hand but not holding the book. My mother was certainly Christian, and claimed to be Presbyterian as she certainly had been when she left America with her first husband. But her church-going was entirely Anglican. About one thing, however, all my relatives agreed. The Church of Rome was

61

corrupt, superstitious, idolatrous, and much to be distrusted. Above all she was always eager to make converts, and extremely devious and ingenious in making them. I was heavily indoctrinated in these convictions. I was warned against mental reservations, the doctrine that the end justified the means, the 'worship' of images, auricular confession, relics, transubstantiation, the Pope, indulgences, the Latin mass and, perhaps above all, the Jesuits. Since, apart from one Roman Catholic in college at Eton who attended the ministrations of a certain Father Longinotti in Windsor and was much ridiculed because of the priest's Italian name, I had never knowingly met a Roman Catholic in my life and saw no reason to think that all my relatives were wrong, and until my mother died it never occurred to me that my own religious affiliations had serious shortcomings of their own. Anglicanism seemed to me all that was decent, common-sensical, progressive, well educated and undogmatic.

My education and my beliefs were held in separate compartments of my mind, when, as I have already told, my mother died and I found, not indeed that I had atheistical opinions, but that, in the place where religious belief should have existed, there was nothing but a void in my soul. By a curious incident I began to recover my religious convictions during my final schools in 1930, but during the time I was an undergraduate, I was still effectively in a religious vacuum.

I never knew quite how it happened that in, I believe, my first term I received an invitation to a meal at Campion Hall, then situated in St Giles Street somewhere near the Lamb and Flag pub. It came from Father D'Arcy of the Society of Jesus, and the real object of his interest was to introduce two of his undergraduate students to some ordinary inhabitants of the town. One of these subsequently became well known as Father Tom Corbishley. He became a life-long friend until he died in the St John and St Elizabeth Hospital in my constituency of St Marylebone. Apart from hospital staff, I must have been one of the last lay persons to have attended his bedside, and at his own invitation. Father D'Arcy himself phoned me from his death-bed to give me his blessing.

It has always seemed to me to be a matter of paradox that, though, when I returned by degrees to mainstream Christianity, I remained firmly Anglican in my allegiance and practice, by far the most intimate contacts I have made with my fellow-Christians have almost always been with Roman Catholics. My cousin Helen Asquith was exactly contemporary with me as an undergraduate. She was at Somerville and, like me, reading Honour Moderations and Greats. I was often asked to her home in Mells in Somerset. Her grandmother, Frances Horner, was a younger sister of my grandmother Alice Hogg, the widow of Quintin Hogg, my father's father. She had died in 1917 when I was ten. Helen's mother, Katharine Horner, had married Raymond Asquith, the son of the Prime Minister, who died heroically leading his company across the wire during the battle of the Somme. Katharine had been converted to Roman Catholicism by a Dominican priest, Father Vincent MacNabb, whom she revered almost as a saint, and whilst I was still an undergraduate her three children, Helen, Perdita, and Julian (now Lord Oxford and Asquith), successively joined her in the Roman Catholic faith. Normally, I believe, these intimate, and affectionate, friendships and contacts might have been expected to lead to my own conversion to their religion, as similar friendships have to many of my generation and before, to Newman, to Ronnie Knox, to Frank Pakenham and very many others, and I remain somewhat surprised that nothing of this sort ever occurred to me. It would have certainly caused great grief and, I fear, anger in my father and others of my family. But I am not conscious that this consideration ever crossed my mind. Harold Macmillan, as it now appears, was obviously a near miss but he died a regular communicant of the Church of England. So far as I know, I was never even a near miss. Nevertheless, if I am a Christian today, I believe I owe more to these Roman Catholic friends and relatives than I can ever repay. For the first time in my life since my mother died, I was brought into regular contact with a diverse and intelligent group of Christian people who actually believed and practised their religion in an organized, regular and wholly unsanctimonious way, always ready to discuss, but equally resolute to defend, their beliefs and practices. I have never really quite overcome my aversion to indulgences, pardons, regular confessions (though I have always confessed when I have done something truly awful, and in particular went when I determined to resume my real adhesion to the Christian faith). I do not believe in papal infallibility, the total inerrancy of Scripture, or even of Church Councils. I believe a lot of harm was done by the anathemas and recondite formulas about totally unverifiable propositions which formed such an extraordinary feature of church life in the two or three centuries after the conversion of Constantine. Though I love the Latin tongue, I regard the old Tridentine mass with the priest with his back to any congregation there might be, muttering incomprehensible syllables to himself, as a perversion of the primitive rite. I think it particularly fatuous to speculate in detail about what happens after death, beyond what we are bound to accept if we believe the Scriptures. I find infinite consolation in the Creeds, services and prayers that have come down to us from the past, especially when embodied in Cranmer's exquisite prose, in the Scriptures, whether in the English of the Authorized Version (the one translation incomparably more beautiful than the original text) or, in the New Testament, in Greek. I am sure, however, that my own contacts with Roman Catholics at a formative period of my life have had a decisive influence on my soul for good. In the restoration of my faith in the Christian religion I am sure that they operated as a sort of *preparatio evangelica* in the barren years of unbelief. I learned beyond doubt that their beliefs, which now very largely correspond with my own, were things which had to be taken seriously intellectually and were things not at all inconsistent, as I had been taught by my family to believe, either with Christian virtue or with the real essentials of the Christian religion, which they have preserved inviolate under constant discouragement and frequent persecution. I learned the beauty of their attitude to life and I thank God from the bottom of my heart for the inspiration and courage they have given me, especially at moments when my courage has begun to fail. They even tell me that in the end I may myself achieve salvation but, if so, only by my invincible ignorance.

TEN

Mods and Greats

No ACCOUNT of my Oxford life would be complete without an appraisal of my academic work. In my life it was more important than my activities at the Union, more important than my social contacts and more important than my leisure pursuits. It was the end and culminating-point of my general education. Whatever I may be today, my character, my cast of mind, I am what I am as the result of the rigorous discipline imposed on me by my academic training.

In Honour Mods there was one special subject which I selected which differed from that chosen by my contemporaries. This was formal logic, which involved a study of Aristotle's *Organon*, and had as its main English textbook *An Introduction to Logic* by H. W. E. Joseph, who also lectured on the subject. Joseph was not a profound philosopher, but he had a precise, rather pernickety, though extremely accurate mind. His book was notably an introduction to the formidable philosophical training exacted in Greats, but also opened a whole window for me in medieval thought and literature. The whole vocabulary of the syllogism, its premisses, its conclusions, its fallacies (*ignoratio elenchi, petitio principii*), its 'modes', its ingenious *memoriae technicae*, its technical terms ('property', 'substance', 'accidents', 'categories' and so on) are now things consigned to the lumber room and have no attraction to modern philosophers. They were, and are, known to me and, if not a guide to truth, they remain an excellent tool of thought. But they were the everyday fare of medieval theologians, and some ('substance', 'property', 'transubstantiation' and many others) are still necessary to a whole understanding of current controversy. One, 'property', occurs in the

65

prayer of humble access in the Book of Common Prayer, and is absurdly translated as 'nature' in the Alternative Service Book.

Two anecdotes of Joseph, who was a lovable and a good as well as a learned man, have always pleased me as illustrations of his character. When we read his *Introduction to Logic*, we invariably used the second edition. No one that I have ever met has so much as seen a copy of the first edition. This, it is universally believed, is because, on the day when it was published, an erratum-slip was pasted into the cover which read: 'For "carnal connection" read "causal connection" throughout.' This so embarrassed the poor little author that, although he was not well off, he purchased the whole of the first edition and had it pulped. The second edition fared better and has been an invaluable introduction to a not universally popular subject ever since.

The other anecdote comes from his tutorials with his pupils. At some stage in our studies for Greats, we were all asked to discuss the meaning and relationship of cause and effect. How can we predict that the same effect will always follow the identical cause? Pupils nearly always cited Newton's apple as an obvious explanation. 'It always does fall, whenever it is detached from the bough,' the pupils would argue, and claimed that it was logical to assume that next time it would do the same thing. 'Not a bit of it,' Joseph would reply. 'It ought only to cause you increasing surprise.' Indeed, the laws of chance should lead one to think otherwise. What Joseph was trying to instil into the pupils' minds was that a hypothesis of cause and effect was always present to the observer's mind before, and not as the result of, a predication following repeated occurrences.

I have been enormously helped throughout my life by the strict discipline of philosophical analysis. Although in theory the Greats course was limited to the study of ancient works (I read the *Republic* of Plato and Aristotle's *Nicomachean Ethics* at least sixteen times each), in fact our learning went right through from medieval logic to Descartes, to the English empiricists, to Locke, Bishop Berkeley and Hume, to Kant's *Critique of Pure Reason*, to Hegel, Karl Marx, and the objective idealists Bosanquet and Bradley. An old professor whose lectures I attended was still lecturing mellifluously on 'The Absolute' when I read Greats in 1929 and 1930. But we were on the eve of a new realism when I ceased. Wittgenstein was about to arise like a chariot of fire. Bertrand Russell had already written his *Principia Mathematica*. My tutor, Gilbert Ryle, was ready to write his *Ghost in the Machine*. The new realism and the new verbal and mathematical philosophers, Ayer and Austin, were already in the anterooms. When, many years later, I asked Isaiah Berlin what modern philosophy was about, he gave me the shrewd but unexpected reply: 'Philosophy is about the sort of questions which a clever child will ask when he gets the answer "Don't ask silly questions".'

Isaiah himself was perhaps one of the cleverest men I had ever met. When we elected him at All Souls as a Prize Fellow, it has always been alleged that the Fellows gathered round him to gain a little wisdom from one whose reputation was already legendary, and asked him what he believed. After a long pause he said: 'I believe there are ... propositions.' Six months later they asked him the same question again. 'What did I say when you asked me before?' he enquired. 'You said you believed that there are propositions.' The oracle was again silent for a while. Then he said: 'I don't think that now.' He vouchsafed no more. For me, by contrast, philosophy was the gateway back to the Christian religion. But that is another story.

I do not believe there is anything desiccated or unrelated to modern life about the other half of the course, which was ancient history. My periods were, for Greek history, from the beginning of Hellenic civilization to the defeat of the Athenian fleet at Aegospotami. In Roman history, I took the period from the death of Julius Caesar to the reign of Trajan. The set books ranged from Herodotus and Thucydides in Greek, to the *Annals* and *Histories* and *Agricola* of Tacitus and the biographies of the Caesars by Suetonius and the beginnings of Christianity. It was most exciting. To me the study of history is nothing except the precise and scholarly study of the past viewed simply as a relevant commentary on the present. I know of no commentary on the present day as good as Thucydides' history of the Peloponnesian War or his account of the class-battles fought out on the tiny stage of the Greek city states and their (by modern standards) lilliputian imperialisms and wars, nor any story of freedom fighters more moving than Herodotus' account of the heroic resistance of the earlier generation of Hellenes to the aggression of the Persian Empire. The Roman period was less instructive, but in some ways more intimate. The breakdown of the traditional Roman republic, the military dictatorships and proscriptions, the ultimate emergence of the Julio-Claudian dynasty, the Court gossip of Suetonius, the lapidary style and judgements of Tacitus, the abundance of inscription, the rise of the Flavian dynasty, the correspondence between Pliny and Trajan, and the wholly independent, but contemporary, documents of the New Testament are full of evocative parallels with the present day. For all the world I would not have been without these historical treasures, nor the works of literary genius which accompanied the events. There is much to be said for studying a period when the original materials are limited in scope and virtually all known.

ELEVEN

All Souls

ANYONE WHO has followed me so far will understand how closely my ambitions and actual achievements, whether consciously or unconsciously, had been modelled on those of my father, and of Edward, my brother, through private school to college at Eton, from Eton to Christ Church, Honour Moderations, Greats, and then via the presidency of the Union to the Bar, and now, if the omens were propitious, into politics and public life. Many others before me had followed identical or parallel courses. It was in fact one of the routes by which members of the professional middle class might enter public life and, if successful like Asquith, reach the highest positions in the State. My father was an exception, because, as the result of an injustice by his own father, he had been deprived of the advantage of a university degree. I was now, however, to take a step for which neither Edward nor my father offered any parallel. Early in my Oxford career my Mods tutor had urged me to set my sights on a Prize Fellowship at All Souls College. All Souls, one of the older Oxford colleges, was a medieval institution, but at the time unique at any English university. It was the foundation in 1437 of Archbishop Chichele, sometime Archbishop of Canterbury, one of the two prelates whose rather absurd colloquy begins Shakespeare's splendid *Henry V*. Whether or not his exposition of the case for the French Wars was, as I suspect, nonsense, there seems no doubt that, by the end of his life, some sense of guilt for his part in engineering the whole thing afflicted his conscience to the extent that he thought that it would be a good thing to found a college of priests whose main purpose in life, apart from the pursuit of learning, would be to pray

69

for the repose of all the souls of the faithful departed and particularly for the large contingent described so graphically by Shakespeare who had died in the French Wars. The college was not, by the standards of the time, particularly well endowed, but it contained amongst other things a barren tract of land known as the forest of Middlesex, which later included Willesden Junction. In later centuries this to some extent compensated the foundation for the loss of two of its principal treasures: a serviceable organ in the chapel, indispensable for singing at the requisite masses for the dead, and, even more importantly, a veritable tooth of John the Baptist, which pilgrims came to venerate from all over Europe. Both these treasures were taken away at the Protestant Reformation as aids to idolatry, but none the less the college itself survived, prospered and, after a period of comparative abuse in the eighteenth and early nineteenth centuries, was eventually reformed and virtually refounded under the famous Sir William Anson, the author of standard works on Constitutional and Contract Law, and in the House of Commons Member of Parliament for the University. Under his constitution which, in its essentials, though with numerous minor changes, survives to this day, the college became essentially an institute of advanced studies mainly revolving round the faculties of history and law, sponsoring various 'Chichele' and other chairs for professors, funding research fellows, senior and junior, and sponsoring various activities in the field of learning including seminars, invitations to foreign savants to act as visiting professors, and other activities ancillary to any good university, such as teaching, courses of lectures and learned publications. It has a splendid and immensely valuable collection of books and manuscripts, mainly in history, law (English, Roman and International) and literature, a beautiful library with facilities for students of all ages, and of course a medieval chapel. Unlike most other colleges of ancient foundation it never really included an undergraduate body. Until shortly before my time it boasted three individual undergraduates who were known as Bible Clerks, and played games as members of Trinity College. But by the time I got my fellowship even these had disappeared.

From my point of view, however, the most startling feature of the college was the institution of Prize Fellowships, which, each year on All Souls Day, were then awarded after examination, typically, one in history and one in law. These were eagerly competed for, and the awards were very highly prized as testimonials to academic achievement and capacity, and a final crown to first-degree graduates in the Final schools. Some Prize Fellows continued in an academic life. Others, like myself, pursued a professional or public career. With a number of changes I believe these Prize Fellowships have maintained their reputation and still serve a useful purpose. It was to the attainment of one of these that Barrington Ward had directed my attention when he was my Mods tutor.

From my point of view there was one serious snag. I suppose that, had I set my ambition on an academic career, teaching, lecturing, and researching into classical antiquity and history or in philosophy, ancient or modern, I would have had a reasonable chance of election either in the year following the schools or in the year after that, that is, in 1931. But I had no intention of pursuing an academic career at all. I meant to be a barrister and, if I could be elected, a politician. Under the law of the time, I was the heir to two peerages, the first a barony which my father had had to be granted in order to become Lord Chancellor in 1928, when he succeeded Viscount Cave, then fatally ill. A viscountcy was conferred on him in 1929, in, I believe, the dissolution honours of that year. I had been sorry when he accepted the Woolsack since, at the time, he was one of the two leading Conservative statesmen tipped to be the next prime minister after Baldwin. The other was Neville Chamberlain. Indeed, some time before Cave fell ill, Baldwin had sent for the two of them. I often wonder how matters would have differed had the cards between them fallen the other way. One thing I know is that, though the two were, and remained, closely allied on the question of disarmament, my father did, and Chamberlain did not, regard war as ultimately inevitable, ever since, just before Hitler came into power, Germany had walked out of the Disarmament Conference. Curiously enough, when it came to the crunch, Neville Chamberlain expressed the same doubts as I felt. He wrote: 'I regard his promotion as rather a calamity . . . and of course the tragedy is that he is barred from becoming PM when SB retires.' He added: 'I would gladly serve under him as I believe he would under me.'

However, this is a might-have-been of history. For me, the crunch had come in 1928 just after I had sat my examination for Honour Moderations. I was just about to go abroad on a tour of the South of France with my friend Richard Best. My father sent for me and informed me that Lord Chancellor Cave was about to resign and that Baldwin had advised him that it was his public duty to accept. At that time I did not know that he was about to marry his second wife, Mildred, and that she was strongly in favour of acceptance. I advised him to think long before making the irreversible move to the House of Lords. As matters then were, Baldwin's leadership of the party was constantly in question, and, although he was not yet in the House of Commons, my brother Edward was among the critics. I had the utmost respect for my father's judgement, and his almost uncanny capacity for discerning the crucial points in a complicated skein of facts. He was a first-class platform speaker. He had a wonderful reputation in the House of Commons and, most unusually, had been appointed to the Cabinet while serving as Attorney-General. I saw him as a potential prime minister, and at that date perceived but dimly the lure of the Woolsack to all professional members of the practising Bar. I left for France with the issue undecided, but on my way back, in Rouen, I learned that he had decided to accept. The exchange of correspondence between us has already been recorded by Professor Heuston in the first of his two volumes on twentieth-century Lord Chancellors. I sent my father a telegram on Thursday, 29 March, the day on which he received the Great Seal: 'Melancholy congratulations. Reform Lords.' This was followed by a similarly irreverent but affectionate letter.

Dear Father,
Some are born unto titles: some achieve them and some have them thrust upon them. Pity the poor third class! I fancy the spirit of Edmund Warre hovers satisfied behind the curved backs of the hack writers as they fill their fountain pens before writing once again the story of his true

prophecies. By the time this arrives in England Douglas Hogg will be Lord Chancellor. And what title is the most noble going to choose? Might I suggest Lord Hurstmonceux with a U as being slightly the most attractive? I fear Hellingly is not to be considered owing to its social and medical associations. Hailsham is possible. Magham Down, pronounced Maumdan, the same as Gilbert and Sullivan's. Polegate is doubtful. (Do you know Polegate? *Such* a nice little man!) Portland Place, though original, is slightly derivative. Warbleton is suburban: but what about Marylebone? I suppose it will be a barony: I shall not be Viscount Sterneaux? As you know, I would have seen you PM, but having achieved the honour which you have, you are most certainly to be congratulated even by the elder of your sons on having reached a position well in keeping with the family traditions. Chairman of the East India Company, founder of the Polytechnic, Lord Chancellor and Keeper of the King's Conscience . . . *et alors*. You set Neil and me a sufficiently high standard as it is: let me not hanker after anything higher for you, or we will have to heap Pelion on Ossa in order not to dishonour, let alone adorn your greatness. When I am at the age of 56, and earning £3,000 a year at the outside on running down cases, if I am lucky – by then this may be lucrative – I shall wave my finger at the House of Lords and tell little Douglas: 'If it hadn't been for old grandpa I shouldn't have been here.' But perhaps little Douglas will not be so little by then. Perhaps he will be old enough to answer (*sicut tuus est mos*) *erat hic non nomine tantum Nobilis.*

Had I known that in 1936 my father would suffer a crippling stroke which left him paralysed down his right side for the fourteen remaining years of his life, I would not have advised him as I did. I thought at the time that he would make a better prime minister than Neville Chamberlain and I knew that, since 1923 when Curzon was passed over, it was unlikely that there would ever again be a prime minister in the House of Lords. The Peerage Act 1963 was not then a blush on the cheek on the future second Viscount Stansgate. Indeed, the first Viscount had not then been made a peer. As the choice before my father then presented itself to me, it was between ending his career on the Woolsack and holding on in the Commons with the chance of leading his party. I advised him to make what as subsequently turned out would be the wrong choice. But my advice was sincere and, despite strong rumours to the contrary, I believe wholly disinterested.

I say 'I believe wholly disinterested' even though it was obvious to me even at that time that my father's decision would alter drastically the whole of my own subsequent life as well as his own. I was only twenty-one, and not merely the highest position of all, but most of the higher offices of state, including those of the two law officers, Solicitor- and Attorney-General, seemed likely to be closed to me for ever. By 1948 my father would have been seventy-six and my inheritance of his peerages could not be far away. I did not at that time foresee that my own career would be delayed for seven years by the war. But I correctly calculated that I was unlikely ever to be a Law Officer even if, as I hoped to do, I succeeded at the Bar. As a member of the House of Lords, I could not hope to become, for instance, either President of the Board of Trade, Home Secretary, Chancellor of the Exchequer or, indeed, any of the other offices for which I could contemplate myself as conceivably suitable. It never crossed my mind that I should one day myself become Lord Chancellor, of whose true functions, different as they then were, I was still very largely ignorant.

In 1930, when I sat my final examinations in Greats, the Conservative Party was in opposition. Ramsay MacDonald was in power, leading a minority party kept in office by Liberal votes. The National Government in 1931 (from which at first my father was excluded by Ramsay MacDonald by reason of his responsibility as Attorney for the Trade Disputes Act 1927) was unforeseen. But the one thing clear to me as the result of my father's decision two years before was that I must hurry on my call to the Bar, which would take at least two years, as quickly as possible. So far as All Souls, therefore, was concerned, I could not afford to compete in 1930, still less in 1931, for a Prize Fellowship based on ancient history, philosophy or a combination of the two. It must be law or nothing. I decided, concurrently with studying for the Bar examinations, to compete in the Prize Fellowship examination for 1931 offering law as my subject, a subject of which, apart from some Roman Law acquired in Greats, I had no knowledge whatever, except so much as had been imparted to me by my father in casual conversations from about the age of seven upwards. I began badly, with a second class in criminal law, after what I had regarded as a short period of intensive study between June and September 1930. That taught me a clear lesson. For all my examinations, including my finals, I took and paid for a correspondence course with Messrs Gibson & Weldon, a firm of solicitors who then, in addition to their solicitors' practice, ran an academic course of tuition leading to the Bar and solicitors' examinations. Quite in addition to this, I worked the longest-possible hours available to me in Lincoln's Inn Library and, when that was closed, in the nearby library of the London School of Economics, to which I obtained access by the good offices of the late C. E. W. Manning, who also arranged to give me one or two tutorials. I worked during term. I worked in the vacation. When my father took his holidays in Sussex I worked from lodgings in Guilford Street. I worked late into the night. When it came to the Fellowship Examination in November 1931, to my absolute astonishment, I was told at luncheon at Lincoln's Inn that I had been awarded a Prize Fellowship in law. I could hardly believe it. It was not that the competition was poor. So far as I can remember, one of the other candidates was Professor Herbert Hart. Another was Richard Wilberforce, who became a Prize Fellow the following year and had read Moderations and Greats with me. My association with the college has been among the happiest in my life. I was still a Fellow in 1938 when I stood in Oxford as a candidate in the by-election, though, since I had married by that time and was not following an academic career, I was not entitled to renewal after seven years. As a former Fellow, I remained associated with the college and a member of common room, until, very many years later, I was elected to an unremunerated Fellowship open to those who have distinguished themselves in academic or public life.

Needless to say, the Bar Finals examination which took place the following year might have caused me the maximum of embarrassment. If I did badly, it would have cast great discredit on the college for having elected me. Happily, thanks to Gibson and Weldon and the excellent law libraries at All Souls and Lincoln's Inn, I came top in the Bar Finals of 1932 and obtained the Certificate of Honour. I was now launched on a professional career with little or no hope of public life in front of me.

TWELVE

A Year of Disasters

DESPITE MY SUCCESSES at All Souls and the Bar Examinations and the great enjoyment I obtained in college, the latter part of 1931 and 1932 contained two, though very different, misfortunes, the memory of which has dogged me for the rest of my life, and still does not leave me unaffected.

I do not intend to be wholly candid about the history of my marriage to Natalie Sullivan. Poor girl, she is dead now, and I think that, however disastrously a marriage may end, the confidential relationship must remain totally intact, unmarred by indiscretion, still less by recrimination.

I met Natalie first on a visit to Salisbury when I spoke for the Conservative candidate there. She was the Conservative agent for the constituency, and was the daughter of an American mother and a fairly distinguished Canadian novelist, Alan Sullivan, who had come to live in this country in a picturesque house in Pluckley, Kent. She had two brothers and an elder sister, then married to a brilliant thoracic surgeon, Tim Nelson, who later died of septicaemia acquired during an operation on a patient. Her grandfather, a member of the Church of Canada, had been Bishop of Toronto but, at some time in 1926, Natalie had been received into the Roman Catholic Church, and at the time I first knew her was, I believe, a regular attendant at mass. She was about my age, six months older in fact, vivacious, ambitious and attractive. We were obviously mutually attracted, but after we became engaged it became obvious to me that, for reasons into which I will not enter, the marriage would not be a

77

success. Apart from anything else, I was not prepared to sign the documents which were then exacted of a Protestant intending to marry a Roman Catholic. I tried to extricate myself, but she held me to my word. We were married in the Church of England, and this rendered her an excommunicated person. So far as I know she never sought to reconcile herself to the church of her conversion. Our marriage lasted ten years, until the end of 1942 when I returned an ill and broken man after an absence of two years in the Middle East, ending in a serious bout of infective hepatitis from which I have never entirely recovered. She then immediately left me for a young Frenchman with whom she was having an affair, and whom she subsequently married. In her favour it must be said that during my absence in the Army she had conscientiously managed my affairs at home. I can honestly say that I was faithful to her during my entire ten years of marriage to her, and that includes two years in the Middle East when I was virtually deprived of respectable female company, except for the odd social contact in Cairo and Beirut. No doubt there were faults on both sides, and I bear Natalie no ill will. She and her French husband are both now dead, and she lies buried in the Protestant cemetery in Paris. I wish she had been reconciled to some form of religion. Before she died she gave me useful and generous help in enabling me to marry my present wife, since, according to Roman Catholic canon law, our marriage in an Anglican church was so absolutely null and void that it did not even require an annulment to enable me to marry. Without the information she gave me about her reception into the Roman Catholic Church, my present marriage prior to her death would have been difficult. Poor Natalie. She had many virtues, and suffered many illnesses, some as the result of a serious motor accident. I can only say that the marriage was a mistake on both our parts, and, as the husband, I must bear my full share of the responsibility. At the time of my marriage to my present wife I attempted to restore amicable relations between us, as I have done successfully with her family, with whom I am on terms of friendship. This attempt, however well meant, met with a rebuff. For the present I can only say that I pray that poor Natalie rest in peace as I trust she does. Whatever she or I did wrong, may we both have forgiveness. She at least had to pay very highly for a relatively common weakness.

I describe this event now because of the relationship between my courtship of Natalie and my poor brother Edward's misfortunes. Edward had been ill for quite a little time. After the failure of his romance with Pamela some years before, he had had a number of friendships with some charming women. He had written one bestseller, the life of Edward Marshall Hall, with whom he had been on terms of close intimacy, and was well into the first volume of his projected life of Carson, published after his death, but never revised and so with a number of blemishes which, though superficial, led to unfavourable reviews. (Of a novel, more or less completed, I, as its new owner, would not permit publication, judging it immature and unworthy of his best work.) After a slow start he was beginning to make good headway at the Bar. In 1929 he had been elected MP for Eastbourne, a constituency which, at that time, included my own Sussex home, in succession to Rupert Gwynne who was related to us by marriage. He had quickly made his mark, but rather as an associate of Colonel Gretton and the stern unbending wing of the Conservative Party than as a supporter of the official leadership of which my father was a leading light.

So, one day in the spring of 1932, Edward rang me up to ask me to lunch with him at the Travellers' Club. He was in trouble. He had not slept for days. The Pamela drama was repeating itself. The chairman of his constituency party had a beautiful daughter. She was entrancingly pretty, Dresden china, blonde, blue eyes, quite unlike Pamela who was a brunette. Her name was Helen. I knew her slightly as I had dined with the family more than once. She had at first been bowled over by the suit of this mature and brilliant man of thirty-two who was already making such a name for himself at the Bar, in literature, and in national politics. She had agreed to marry him, and then, finding him altogether too much for her, had called it off. Of course she was right. One is always right to call off a marriage when one is sure it would not work out. I wish I had had as much sense. But it set off all the frustrations and disappointments of Edward's highly strung nature. He was evidently ill. I saw his doctor. What was he to advise? He advised me that Edward was not to be left alone. Would it be all right if I brought him home to Sussex and handed him over to the care of my father and step-mother? Of course it would. I persuaded Edward to come and drove him down. I warned both my father and, I believe, Mildred, my step-mother, what the doctor had said, and they agreed not to leave him unattended. I left him in their care, and they did their best. But once a man has the thought of killing himself planted in his mind it takes more than a loving heart and a careful eye to deter him from his purpose. I left for Pluckley to see Natalie, certain that all was well. A brief moment before I went a thought came into my mind, which now haunts my dreams. Why not lock the gun-cupboard and take away the key? In the gun-cupboard was my most prized possession, a secondhand double-barrelled twenty-bore non-ejecting shotgun, bought for me by my father after my mother died a few short years before, and made in Dublin by a fine Irish gunmaker. 'Don't be absurd,' said my evil genius. 'Everything is all right now. Don't be neurotic.' I went away without locking the gun-cupboard and I have never ceased to blame myself ever since. I can only comfort myself with the thought that, had he not found that way, he would probably have found another. But I wonder. Anyway, my father carefully observed what I had said. On the Sunday (I think it was) afternoon they went for a walk together in the woods surrounding our home. Edward excused himself when they were some way from the house on the ground that he wanted to fetch a handkerchief. My father believed him and waited. But he did not return. He took the twenty-bore from the unlocked cupboard and shot himself with it. It is not particularly easy to shoot oneself deliberately with a full-sized sporting gun, though people have often done so by accident when climbing over a gate or through a hedge. I will never forget the woe of the next few days. It haunts me still. I returned at once from Pluckley. The house was besieged by reporters eager for a story. They tried to stop my car in the road as I approached. They tried to bribe the servants. I do not blame them. Edward was news, and his death was drama. It added to the macabre that the inquest, held in public, was in our own dining-room. Owing to the circumstances it was suggested that we should put forward a theory of accident. My father discussed the matter with me. Agreeable as the option was since it could easily have been made to wash, neither of us would pervert what we both knew to be the truth. Fortunately there was one quite certain fact that enabled us to avoid what would otherwise have been a verdict of *felo de se*. There could be no doubt in my mind or in my father's that, when Edward did that dreadful thing, the balance of his mind was disturbed. Sleeplessness and the whole unhappy history of his love-life had unhinged him. Had he had strong religious convictions, I believed they might have saved him. But these cannot be manufactured to order. Nevertheless, I testify, Edward was a good man, enchanting company, honourable, clever, brave and true. The garage man at Hailsham where he had serviced his car spoke for the public when he said to me of his former MP: 'He died for his country as surely as if he had been killed in battle.' Edward had overworked, had tried himself too hard in a dozen ways, and, when the crisis came, under the pressure of insomnia and nervous strain his reason snapped. I loved my brother then, and I love him still. His death left a permanent mark on me and, apart from anything else, it has left me with a permanent horror of suicide. If Edward had known what intolerable woe the manner of his leaving would inflict on those of us he left behind, I believe that, even in his inhinged state, he would never have done what he did. I have never ceased to blame myself for my part in the tragedy. I do not think my presence would have made any difference. I was far more gullible than my father. I was naïve and immature, and the gun-cupboard would certainly not have been locked had I remained at home. The law now requires it, but it did not then, and to do so would have been unusual. Nevertheless, I do not acquit myself. I should have loved him more or, rather, I should have shown more demonstrably the love and sympathy I felt. And I should have locked the cupboard door and gone away with the key. I disregarded the warning of my imagination. Or was it just imagination?

Edward lies buried in Herstmonceux churchyard. His sister Isobel attended the funeral. It was her last contact with our family, and in her kind heart she comforted me in my distress. I hardly ever saw her again.

One further ghastly circumstance I did not know at the time. Despite the verdict, Bishop Bell of Chichester tried to prevent my brother being buried in consecrated ground, and my father never forgave him. Fortunately, the rector, Rosslyn Bruce, had more sense and compassion than his ecclesiastical superior, and insisted on the funeral proceeding in the church. I only learned this later, when Rosslyn Bruce told me not very long before his own death and when my father had been dead for some years. He also told me that Bishop Bell had repented of this sin against charity. 'It taught me,' he told Rosslyn, 'that it is almost always wise to trust the men on the spot.' But he never apologized to me or, so far as I know, to my father, either, for having condemned us unheard in our hour of need. So much for bishops who try to exert their authority without either charity or natural justice. Nevertheless, in many ways, Bell was an admirable man. Though he did not extend his compassion to Edward, who was a member of his flock, in the face of considerable criticism, he was both brave and wise in his generosity to the defeated Germans after the war and he was the last bishop to exert real influence in the House of Lords by virtue of really remarkable parliamentary skills. But my father never forgave him. Forgiveness requires apology from the wrongdoer and an act of reconciliation. Neither was forthcoming from the bishop.

I do not seek total excuse from the responsibility for either of the misfortunes which beset me as I have recounted in this chapter, and, in a sense, though Edward's death came first, they were not wholly disconnected with one another, since my conviction has always been that, had I not been preoccupied with my courtship of Natalie, I might (*might*, not *would*) have been able to prevent the awful fate which befell Edward.

THIRTEEN

Junior Fellow

APART FROM the two miserable disasters described in the last few pages, the twelve months after my award of an All Souls fellowship were extremely agreeable. The days were spent in intensive study of law. The life in college was enjoyable and enriching. I was, of course, together with my 'twin', Goronwy Rees, one of two Junior Fellows. But both the senior members of the college and the older members of my own generation were a friendly crowd who treated each other and even us, the meanest form of life, on a footing of complete equality. They included the Tudor historian Leslie Rowse, Douglas Jay (now a life peer), John Sparrow, afterwards Warden, Denis Rickett, H. V. Hodson (later editor of the *Sunday Times*), Roger Makins (now Lord Sherfield), John Foster, and many others who remained friends all our joint lives. Leslie Rowse in particular was extremely kind to me in my agony over Edward's death. Incidentally, his life may have been saved by another fellow, somewhat senior to me, himself without medical qualifications but a specialist in the study of ancient Greek medicine. Leslie was looking and feeling extremely ill, and Reginald Harris claimed to recognize in him the so-called 'hippocratic face' which the ancient Greek practitioner asserted was an infallible mark of imminent fatality. Reginald took Leslie at once to the hospital, where he was found to be suffering from a perforated duodenal ulcer. He was just in time. Thus a doctor of the fifth century BC was able in the early thirties of the twentieth century AD to effect by proxy his latest and probably his last cure from what might have been a fatal illness.

But it was from the companionship of really senior members of the college that I derived probably the greatest pleasure. As the Junior Fellow, I occupied the menial position of 'Screw' whose function it then was to decant all the port consumed after dinner in considerable quantity and, since it was then the custom of many of the senior fellows to linger a long time over their nuts and wine, I was able from my humble chair at the far end of the table, or in the smoking-room afterwards, to enjoy a quality of interesting conversation which I should certainly have missed without membership of this distinguished society. There was Spenser Wilkinson, the Professor of Military History, John Simon (one of the most distinguished figures in public life), Wilfred Greene, then (or later to become) Master of the Rolls, Sir William Holdsworth (known from the immense size of his moustache as 'the Great Seal'), the historian of English law, and many others, scholars, authors, lawyers, civil servants, and, of course, their guests of equal standing, all of whom remained on easy personal terms with me, vastly their junior throughout their natural lives. Spenser Wilkinson could sometimes be induced to tell an immense story of how, before the First World War, he had been arrested as a spy in Cracow. There were two versions of this famous tale, the shorter of which lasted forty-five minutes in the telling. Greater kudos, however, could be obtained from eliciting the longer account which lasted far into the night. My own memory of Spenser Wilkinson, however, was of a tale of how, as a very young man, he had been introduced to an old fellow who had met Napoleon. I asked the obvious question. Imitating the voice of a very old man, Spenser Wilkinson replied: 'He said: "It was easy to see that Napoleon was not a university man."' The only comparable remark ever made about a similar figure was when Nancy Astor, fresh from a visit to the Soviet Union, was asked by the press what she had made of her conversation with Stalin. 'A nice, well-conducted little man,' was her reply.

John Simon was never a popular figure either with the public or even in college. I think he was misjudged. My father never tired of recounting Simon's warmth and kindness to him on his returning to the Bar after a nearly fatal dose of typhoid contracted as the result of eating an infected oyster purchased as a treat by his mother. I personally found Simon a person of profound integrity and considerable kindness, especially to the young. One night many years later, after the war, we were alone in the common room at All Souls when he told me the following story about the time when he was a young and struggling barrister, extremely badly off with a wife (whose premature death nearly broke his heart) and young children.

One night, Simon told me, he found himself asked to dinner by one of the great judges of his time whom he had never previously met. I rather think it was Lord Justice Bowen, but I cannot now be sure. At length, after dinner, the great man asked the young Simon if he had wondered at the reason for the invitation from a total stranger, and Simon confessed that indeed he had. At this the judge explained that he had heard of Simon, his talents, his lack of influence and his financial difficulties, and he added that he had a proposition to make to him. 'Come upstairs,' he said. At the top of the house there was a vast room occupying the entire top floor filled with the most complete and valuable law library that a young lawyer's heart could imagine. The judge told him that he wished to make him a present of the whole collection. 'There they are,' said the old judge. 'Soldiers, all ready to do your bidding.' But, he added, there was a condition attached to the gift. 'When you are old and about to retire,' said the judge, 'you must pass them on to some young man placed as you are now placed.' And Simon agreed.

Years came and passed, Simon told me, and came the Second World War, and the library of Simon's Inn of Court was bombed by Hitler, whose planes were constantly aiming at Fleet Street and constantly missing it. The Inn library was heavily damaged. 'I thought,' said Simon, 'that if he were alive today the judge would have wished me to give the books to the Inn instead of to a single impecunious young man.' And that is what he did. I judged him to have acted rightly.

At the very end of his life, about a fortnight before he died, I visited Simon in order to lobby him against the then Conservative government's plan for commercial television to which at that time I was violently opposed and of which I knew Simon to be critical.

Simon explained that he was not prepared to accede to my persuasion. He then told me that he had just seen the film of Shakespeare's *Julius Caesar* which was at the time being shown and, for the first time I believe, in colour on a wide screen. When the old man was trying to tell me how beautiful he found it he literally broke down and sobbed, and the tears came rolling down his cheeks. This is a very different figure from the cold, distant, arrogant Simon of popular opinion. About a month later, I went and had tea in the Commons tea-room where peers who have been Commoners are allowed to eat. Attlee, then quite recently retired from having been Prime Minister, was sitting next me, and I told him this story as we were talking of Simon, who had died just a week or two before. 'Ah, yes,' said Attlee. 'Inside there was a little pink quivering Simon struggling to get out.' Apart from being a shrewd Prime Minister, the Truman of British politics, Attlee was no bad judge of character and possessed a neat turn of phrase.

One night at All Souls I received a very useful lesson in advocacy from Wilfred Greene when he was Master of the Rolls, and I an almost totally inexperienced pupil at the Bar. Wilfred Greene had been a great classical scholar, was a superb judge of law on appeal and, unlike some judges, an absolutely first-class legal scholar who wrote many judgements still quoted in the courts. But, being a Chancery barrister, no one at the time rated him at his true worth as an advocate. Moreover he hated examining and cross-examining witnesses, and in his last years at the Bar virtually confined himself to advocacy in the appellate courts. I was sitting next to him one night at dinner or dessert in college, when he suddenly asked me a question.

'Supposing,' he said, 'you were instructed in a case where you had two points to argue, both of them bad but one worse than the other, which would you argue first?'

As, I suppose, most young men would have said, I replied fairly confidently to the great man: 'I suppose I would argue the less bad of the two.'

'Quite wrong,' said Wilfred Greene. 'You must argue the worse, and put your very best work into it. Eventually they will drive you into a corner, and you will have to admit defeat. You will then say:

"My Lords, there is another point I am instructed to argue. But I am not quite sure how to put it." And you will then put the better of the two arguments, but not quite as well as it could or should be put.'

After a little while, Wilfred went on, one of the old gentlemen will interrupt you. 'He will say: "But surely Mr Greene, you might put it in this way." And he will put it exactly as you really ought to have put it in the first place. At that stage you will lay your papers on the desk before you. You will raise your eyes to the ceiling. And, in an awestruck voice, you will say: "Oh, my Lord, I do believe . . ." And then you will be at least halfway to winning your case.'

All of which goes to show that the art of advocacy is not confined to the Rumpoles of this world or the Central Criminal Court.

During my first years at All Souls I nearly got myself into serious trouble. In the small Fellows' Garden behind the smoking-room there was then, as there is still, a half-sized bronze statue of a Grecian youth, entirely naked. The statue had been bought by an eighteenth-century fellow, then on the Grand Tour. But, at the time of my election to the fellowship, unlike the present, the statue was made decorous in the appropriate place with the addition of a fig leaf. There was a tea-party of some sort in progress, and the Warden's wife, Mrs Pember, asked one of the acknowledged experts on Greek art, Stanley (not Sir Hugh) Casson I believe it was, whether it was a genuine product of antiquity or not. Casson was a man who had a passion to *épater les bourgeois*. So he marched straight up to the statue, felt under the fig leaf and said, 'Manifestly not,' or words to that effect. Watching, I had grave doubts as to his methodology, and late that night, using my evening shoe as a hammer and something like a chisel as a weapon, I struck a series of felon blows in the appropriate place. After what seemed to me an appalling series of difficulties the fig leaf fell off with a clatter on to the statue's pediment. To my horror, there was nothing beneath it except an amorphous mass of cement which had been holding it in place. I was terrified at what I had done and dashed back into the darkened smoking-room to gather my thoughts, asking myself what on earth I, the lowest of the low in the college, to wit Screw, should do next. Presently my courage, and my scepticism, returned. No one, I argued to myself, ever put cement on a bronze statue for nothing. If there had been nothing to conceal, the fig leaf would have been cast as an integral part of the statue. I had never felt quite so badly about anything before, and would not do so again until 1941. Courage returned in due time. Armed once more with my patent-leather shoe and my trusty chisel I again attacked my adversary and bit by bit hammered off the cement. Victory crowned my efforts. My confidence was justified and my reasoning proved correct. Concealed behind the cement, now a jumble of powdered fragments littering the pediment and the distorted fig leaf, was a perfect male organ. Unhappily, as I could see even from the dim light of the smoking-room, while the statue itself was a weatherbeaten bronze, the organ, protected from the elements for, presumably, more than one century, was a bright arsenical green. I retired to bed in a mixed mood of apprehension and triumph.

Next morning, the college did not take it well. The organ was more startling and even greener than in artificial light. Never had there been such an outrage since the mutilation of the Hermae in Athens on the eve of the Sicilian expedition. Since no one had actually witnessed the deed, I was never quite sure why I was the only suspect. But there can be no doubt that, from the first, everyone knew that I was the culprit. I was the Alcibiades in the case. No one directly accused me of the crime. But I could see little groups of fellows eyeing me with malevolent glances and evidently discussing me amongst themselves. Later I was told that the least penalty being discussed was that the fig leaf should be replaced at my own expense. Strangely, but happily, wiser counsels prevailed. The statue, with emerald *membrum virile*, was left to the merciful operation of the elements of wind and weather and time's healing touch. It is now the same colour and the same weatherbeaten appearance as the rest of this venerable work of art. As I view it, in my octogenarian respectability, in the Fellows' Garden on a warm sunny day, I reflect that, with Chichele, Hawksmoor and Codrington, I, too, have left my permanent mark upon the college.

FOURTEEN

Foxhunting Interlude

THE TIME WAS APPROACHING when I would have to receive my call to the Bar. I had already lost a year compared with most of my contemporaries as the result of having read that four-year course at Christ Church as compared with the ordinary three. Those who had read in the honour school of jurisprudence were usually as much as two years ahead of me, as they could have taken their Bar examinations either in conjunction with, or at least almost immediately after, their Finals in Schools. In those days there was no vocational course as there is now; and pupillage, universal, though not then, as now, compulsory, could be taken after and not as a condition of call. However, I had taken the precaution three years before of joining Lincoln's Inn, my father's Inn, and eating my dinners, travelling up from Oxford in my old Alvis twelve/forty. In addition, I asked my father to persuade a judge to take me round a circuit as judge's marshal. In those days the marshal had a few ceremonial duties, such as swearing in the Grand Jury without whose 'true bill' a trial on indictment was impossible. But the real function of the marshal was to keep the judge company and, if possible, in good humour, to act as his aide-de-camp and social secretary, and, if need be, to smooth out difficulties of his travelling household, consisting of cook, butler and clerk. In those days it was relatively unusual for wives to travel with judges, though they came down and visited their husbands from time to time. All the staff, including the marshal, were paid by the day: in the case of the marshal, two guineas. But in 1931, as the result of the financial crisis which attended the formation of the National Government, the two guineas had been, if I remember rightly, reduced to two pounds.

89

There was, however, one serious obstacle. Apparently, the best judges played golf, and expected their marshals to play with them, and to me golf was as closed a book as Chinese characters. 'Then,' said my father, 'you must choose a hunting judge.' This both attracted and daunted me. I had never hunted the fox. At the same time I was not an altogether inexperienced horseman. I had spent one year with the Oxford artillery, then horsed, and had had some serious instruction in the riding school and on Port Meadow and one week in camp on Salisbury Plain with Kenneth Diplock, riding wheeler with a leg iron and dragging an eighteen-pounder gun behind me. I had also spent a week or two on Exmoor with the Devon and Somerset stag hounds hunting both stags and hinds in their respective seasons. The trouble about this last was that on Exmoor there had been no jumping. Still, the riding was fairly tough, as the horses were all hirelings, the ground was rough, and the form was to gallop down hill as well as up and on the flat – a difficult and sometimes risky activity, as any who have done it can testify.

So I tested myself by going out once with the Oxford drag; found that, thanks to my training in the riding school, my jumping of fences was in order; and, with my father's good offices, engaged myself as marshal to the formidable Mr Justice Roche, a commercial judge with a somewhat conservative view of life, who had the reputation of not suffering fools gladly. In fact, he was an admirable tutor, discussing the cases in the calendar before and after the hearings, encouraging me to read all the papers, civil and criminal, and commenting frankly, favourably or otherwise on the performance of counsel. He was, in very truth, a hunting judge, hunting whenever a list of his collapsed. His home pack was the Heythrop which hunted in a dark green and blue livery, as distinct from the conventional pink. It was stone-wall country, so that my experience over the fences with the drag stood me in good stead. The other country we mainly hunted with was the Berkeley (in primrose yellow and again not pink). Again, there were no fences, but formidable water-courses below the level of the fields and known as 'rhines'. These required a special method of negotiation, and we had two or three of the most wonderful hunting days of my brief hunting career. I heard the judge discussing his marshal with one of the Masters of the Fox Hounds of the circuit, and, to my infinite pleasure, I heard him say: 'Of course he knows nothing whatever about it. But he goes very well.' In fact, more by good luck than by good judgement, I had no serious falls, though there was one grim day at Gloucester Assizes when both judge and his marshal sat beside each other on the bench, each with a black eye of startling proportions. My own was due to a branch in a ride coinciding with a sudden jerk in the neck of my mount. The coincidence caused a certain amount of comment in court.

My mounts were cheap. With the Heythrop, I was generally mounted on a horse called Bowler, owned by the judge's son, Tom Roche. With the Berkeley and, on days when Bowler was not available, I hired from the local livery stables. The High Sheriff of the day, whose name was Tubbs, and his charming wife both hunted with the Berkeley of which he was also the Master.

At the risk of irrelevance, I cannot avoid a slightly ridiculous appendix to my account of my short and not particularly glorious career as a foxhunter. Many years later I was the author of a book on Conservatism which ultimately went into two editions, each separated by more than ten years. Endeavouring to show that it was a feature of Conservatism that Conservatives, unlike the ideologists of the left, do not think that politics is (or are) the most important things in life, I committed myself to the sentences (punctuated rather differently in different printings and editions):

> Conservatives do not believe that the political struggle is the most important thing in life. In this they differ from Communists, Socialists, Nazis, Fascists, social creditors, and most members of the British Labour Party. The simplest of them prefer foxhunting, the wisest religion.

More than thirty years after these words were first written, a university teacher came, for one reason or another, to consult me in my chambers, and casually let slip the fact that he had regularly instructed his pupils that I had once committed myself to the view that foxhunting was the 'wisest religion'. How any educated man could have read the sentence in this way I have never understood, because both at the time I wrote the sentence I was notoriously a committed Christian, and also the very next chapter in the book was entitled 'The Religious Basis of Society'. Indeed, how anyone at any time could have supposed that a man who had obtained a double first, including one in Greats, could have described foxhunting as a religion at all, let alone a wise one, makes my mind boggle. 'You ought to be ashamed of yourself,' said I to my client. He hung his head, and promised never to do it again.

But worse follows. When I resigned as Lord Chancellor in 1987 I was interviewed by two distinguished publicists, one of whom was Anthony Howard, of the *Observer*, no less. Both referred to the sentence, Anthony Howard actually asking me: 'Do you still believe that foxhunting is the wisest religion?' I gave them both their comeuppance, and have never thought of either of them quite so well since. But, for the record, I now point out that two sentences later I had written the words: 'The man who puts politics first is not fit to be called a civilized being, let alone a Christian.'

However this may be, I enjoyed a season with the Heythrop and the Berkeley in the winter of 1931, and, for those who think that blood sports are inherently cruel, I have one or two thoughts that perhaps they should bear in mind. Blood sports are the only method that I know that controls the numbers of a species, especially predators themselves, without endangering their continued existence as a form of wildlife. I hold no particular brief for blood sports where the quarry enjoys no chance of escape. But unlike most other methods of control, and particularly trapping, poisoning and shooting, hunting with hounds not merely controls the species without endangering it, but ensures the quarry either escapes completely or destroys it quickly and without subjecting it to prolonged agony. My own view, for what it is worth, is that these questions are best left to the individual conscience.

I do not wish to give the impression that we did not take the work of the Assizes seriously. The contrary would be the case, and I learned a lot. But the fact is, none the less, that in those days and right up to the war Assizes were a very different affair from the work of the

Crown Court and the civil list on circuit today. There were times, not so infrequent, though not while I was marshal, when the judge would be given a 'pair of white gloves' which meant that there were no criminal cases for trial at all. Most of the small housebreaking and larceny cases tried on indictment would be tried in Quarter Sessions before the County Bench and a jury, often with a senior magistrate in the chair who was possibly without a legal qualification and certainly without remuneration. Nevertheless, the criminal work on Assize was trifling compared with what it has become, since I remember, when after the Conservative defeat in 1945 I resumed practice at the Bar, how shocked I was at the swollen state of the criminal calendar with seventy or more cases even at comparatively unfrequented Assize Courts, and while the Quarter Sessions were still taking the lighter work. Since then, indictable crime has increased roughly at the rate of 10 per cent a year at compound interest, and, without the Assistant Recorders, Recorders, Deputy High Court Judges, Circuit Judges, and a vastly increased High Court judiciary which I inaugurated in 1971 after the Beeching Commission, the whole ramshackle system would have ground to a miserable halt.

However, at the Winter Assizes of 1931, we went to the old Oxford Circuit (vastly different from the new Midland and Oxford, again inaugurated by myself). We went from Reading to Oxford, from Oxford to Gloucester, from Gloucester to Monmouth, from Monmouth successively to Worcester, Shrewsbury and Hereford, and from Hereford to Stafford, where, for once, there was a purpose-built Judges' Lodging and where we joined the Midland Circuit Judge (Mr Justice Viscount Finlay, son of the Lord Chancellor) and Tom Talbot (son of Mr Justice Talbot), Finlay's marshal, with, so far as I remember, only one murder on the circuit and a few unlawful carnal knowledges between relatively innocent young people, no rape, nor any very serious woundings. Apart from motor-accident and employers'-liability cases, there were only two civil cases that I remember: an interesting battle about an allegedly forged cheque in which the protagonists were the leader of the Oxford Circuit, Sir Reginald Coventry, QC, and Rayner Goddard, QC, later Lord Chief Justice, brought up 'special' by the Midland Bank from the Western

Circuit, and a slander case between two local notables at one of the other towns.

The single murder, which had been moved from Oxford to Gloucester, was of a woman cyclist by a young soldier returning from leave somewhere on what is now the A40, high up in the Cotswolds. The motive was theft, but the soldier had got from the victim less than one pound. For that, he paid with his life, for he was hanged. I mention it, not because the case itself presented any particular interest, but because of the effect it had on the judge who was a tough old character and firmly believed in the death penalty. Nevertheless, and I have noticed it on later occasions in connection with other judges during the period when the death penalty was effective, the hideous penalty had a profound influence on the judge's mood. During the entire trial and up to and including the macabre ritual at the end when the judge, with the absurd black cap flopping about his wig, had to pronounce the horrible words, 'and that you be taken from hence to a place of lawful execution, and there be hanged by the neck until you be dead, and that your body be buried within the prison in which you have been last confined', the judge was a different man, miserable, lonely, moody and morose. The idea that judges enjoyed passing sentence of death should never be entertained for a moment, and the last words, spoken by the sheriff's chaplain, 'And may the Lord have mercy on your soul' sent a shiver down the spine of the young marshal, who had never heard it before, or even read of it, and this time it was no play-acting. It was for real.

For my part I have always believed in the right of the State to take life, and I am sometimes asked both for the reason of my conviction, and for the explanation why, at least in recent years, I have always let it be known that, as matters stand at the moment, I would not support its immediate reintroduction, except possibly for cases of terrorism. My reason for supporting the death penalty in principle is that without it there is a premium on deliberate murder. Every system of criminal law depends in the end on the identification of the criminal, and if – as, for instance, in the case of rape – only one pair of eyes has seen the perpetrator it must, as matters stand, pay him to close them for ever. As I write this, only the other day I read of a rape in which the victim managed to escape, but her attacker had said: 'If I cut your throat I shall only be inside for fifteen years at the most, and I shall not get very much less if I let you live.' Over the years I had read of many murders where the main motive of the crime, it has seemed to me, was that the murder was committed in the course of another crime which, if the criminal was identified, would undoubtedly attract a sentence of seven years or more, and where, therefore, as matters stand now, the balance of advantage clearly lies in favour of killing the single potential witness of identification. I wish abolitionists would face facts more honestly than in fact they do.

Why, then, it may be asked, am I not unequivocally in favour of reintroduction? My answer is threefold. In the first place, simply as a matter of practical politics, one really has to come to terms with the fact that, unwhipped, no House of Commons since 1948 has ever voted in favour of capital punishment, and what would be absolutely intolerable morally and practically would be if Parliament reintroduced it one year, and then, after a general election, fought mainly on other grounds, a new House, differently composed, abolished it all over again. If ever it comes back, it must come back permanently or, at least, for a very substantial time.

My second and third reasons are reasons of principle. In my view it would be quite unacceptable to reintroduce the death penalty for murder without redefining murder itself and clarifying the law of homicide in such a way as to distinguish between murder and the more serious forms of manslaughter. There is, at present, a large grey area which in practice makes it difficult to discern to which category the crime belongs. A question of life or death should not depend on the niceties of a complicated piece of jurisprudence. An attempt was made to remedy this in a half-hearted way by the Homicide Act 1957. But only absurdity resulted, including the continuing and ludicrous compromise of 'diminished responsibility' which was introduced from the Scottish law simply to salve the consciences of those opposed to the death penalty in any form.

The problem is much more difficult than it seems. A brave attempt at solving it was made by Lords Diplock and Kilbrandon in an appeal to the House of Lords in which I presided, and they both opted for a redefinition of murder in terms of an actual intention to kill. I did not, and do not, think that this really solves the problem at all; but, if it did, I do not believe that it could be done by a crude piece of judicial legislation. It is a matter for Parliament. Incidentally, it would exclude from mercy some of the cases which most cry out for lenience such as 'mercy killing'. I doubt myself whether the problem will be solved in my lifetime, basically because murder is not the name of a crime but of a whole bundle of crimes differently motivated, and of very different degrees of guilt, and having in common little but the result, namely the death of the victim within the purely arbitrary period of a year and a day. Who can doubt, for instance, that if the train robbers' victim, the driver of the train, had died at once, instead of some years later as the result of his injuries, the robbers would have been indicted for murder, and might well have been convicted? Terrorism is a rather different issue. Waging war against the Queen within her realm is, by definition, treason for which the penalty is still death, and that is precisely what the IRA and other terrorist organizations claim to be doing. The fact that they are not in fact indicted for treason must therefore be for reasons of policy which may or may not be good.

The third reason why I would not advocate an immediate reintroduction of the death penalty for murder is the total inadequacy of the machinery for the exercise of the Royal Prerogative of mercy. Prior to the abolition of the death penalty the ultimate decision rested with one man, the Home Secretary of the day. He might, or might not, be a man temperamentally or by training suited to the exercise of this momentous task. Presumably he was always given advice by experienced civil servants. But, in the end, the decision was his and, in my view at least, it is not a responsibility which one man should be asked to carry alone. An argument which one cannot wholly disregard in this connection is the irrevocability of the penalty once the execution has taken place. The Evans–Christie affair is often cited in this context. But to my mind this is not the crucial case, and I have my own views about its merits. But the fact remains that there are very much stronger cases than this. There is an irreducible number of cases, not necessarily of murder, but all the more illustrative for that, mostly of mistaken identity, in which the innocence of the convicted person has been established, not merely as a matter of opinion, but conclusively. In my extreme youth Adolf Beck was three times convicted of a series of mean frauds of which he was undoubtedly innocent. Nevertheless, on each occasion he was convicted on evidence which any normal jury would have treated as absolutely overwhelming. There was more than one positive witness of identification, and in one case at least this was corroborated by the evidence of an acknowledged expert on handwriting (incidentally the father of one of the two witnesses called in the very cheque case on the Oxford Circuit to which I listened as judge's marshal). The *modus operandi* in all three cases was the same. The victims were all certain in their identification, completely honest and independent of one another. If the charge had been murder and the death penalty had been in operation, Adolf Beck would undoubtedly have been hanged. What I am really saying is that unless the possibility of mistaken identity were eliminated the danger of the death penalty being inflicted on an innocent man would, in a small minority of cases at least, be extreme, and that, even if this possibility were disregarded, until some adequate definitions have been arrived at, murder being such an indefinite crime with such differing degrees of moral obliquity, the question of the prerogative of mercy would have to be adequately solved. Shortly before I became Lord Chancellor, I was myself engaged on legal aid to defend in a case when a jury convicted against, and in spite of, an impeccable summing-up. The year was, I believe, 1968, and on the second trial the accused was acquitted. The crime was undoubtedly a particularly brutal murder, and the question was whether the prosecution had charged the right man. If they had not, and if the appeal had been heard before 1968, my client might well have been hanged.

FIFTEEN

Pupillage and Call

BEHOLD ME, THEN, my education finally complete at the age of twenty-five, in November 1932, and my Bar exams behind me, called to the Bar and duly installed as a pupil to Theobald Mathew, a celebrated Pupil Master with three other pupils including Sir Ivo Rigby (later Chief Justice of Hong Kong and, even after that, many years a Metropolitan Magistrate) and Peter Thorneycroft (too famous for other reference and a life-long friend) in a pupil room above the arch in Crown Office Row where much talk and some work took place. Theo's chambers were on the ground floor of 4 Paper Buildings where at that time Lord Robert Cecil's name was supreme as the titular, but eternally absent, head. (My own is, or until recently was, there in its place.) Theo was so senior that he had run through several, quite different, Common Law practices. At the time I was his pupil, his bread and butter largely came from newspapers who regularly consulted him in libel cases which were almost always settled out of court, but which, awaiting their inevitable end, afforded us ample experience in drafting defences, demanding or affording further and better particulars of statements of claim or defence, settling replies and answers to interrogatories, writing opinions on the merits and the likely amounts to be awarded in damages (which, needless to say, Theo invariably spiked) and attending the bear-garden in the Royal Courts of Justice where the Masters of the Queen's Bench heard '1.30 summonses' or the nearby Judge in Chambers heard appeals from the Masters or granted or withheld interlocutory injunctions and applications for committal. It was not a bad initiation. Apart from Theo, the chambers were not particularly fashionable, but the other members had a reasonable run of work. I myself joined the old South-Eastern Circuit, the East Sussex Quarter Sessions and, concurrently, the Old Bailey Mess. At that time, as I have said, one was permitted to practise from the start, and it was not long before, thanks to the good offices of the clerk, Sydney Aylett (afterwards the author of a successful book *Under the Wigs* in which we all duly appeared), got quite a number of briefs of my own, either from my own chambers or from neighbouring chambers clerked by Sydney's friends. My first brief of all was thrown at me at short notice before the formidable Lord Justice Scrutton (author of *Scrutton on Charter parties*), who treated me with utmost consideration despite my manifest lack of experience. It is an honourable practice of Bar and Bench to be kind to young men, and to see to it, as far as possible, that injustice to the client does not result from their incompetence.

Contrary, I believe, to the general perception, success at the Bar does not demand profound learning or exceptional gifts of intellect. Obviously there are types of case which require high academic gifts, and appellate judges really do need some grasp of legal principle and learning. But certainly in the lower ranks, and for the general run of cases, diligence, application, common sense, humanity, a grasp of the essential demands of honesty and moral principle, good judgement in weighing conflicting arguments, and above all good health, without which all else is of no avail, are the essential requirements. In the end, when I come to lecture to students at Cumberland Lodge or elsewhere, I never tire of insisting that success at the Bar depends in the end upon the respect in which one is held by one's fellow-practitioners, including, of course, and perhaps particularly, the Bench, and not upon one's success in any individual case or run of cases. If you once take an unfair advantage or level an unjustified insult at an opponent, if you deceive the court either as to the state of the law on any particular topic, or as to the effect of evidence once it has been given, they will never forget it, never fail to hold it against you, and in the case of opponents will try to get their own back sooner or later. This does not mean that one should not take every legitimate advantage of mistakes due to incompetence or worse. If your opponent pleads fraud when it would have been enough to rely on breach of warranty, or, in a defamation case, if he pleads justification when qualified privilege or fair comment would have served, it is not merely your privilege but your duty to your client to exploit the error to the full. But it is never right to take advantage of a pure piece of inadvertence or to make him look a fool, or humiliate him in front of his client. These things are quite unnecessary. The Bar is one of the most competitive professions in the world but, like many other activities in life, it is a field where generosity, courtesy, chivalry and, above all, unshakeable integrity pay material dividends.

I am, of course, wholeheartedly in favour of the improvements in legal education, vocational training, compulsory pupillage, and, incidentally, training for judges brought about – more, I believe, than is generally realized – by the late Lord Diplock. Nevertheless, there is no substitute for experience and in-service training. Even after he was Lord Chancellor, my father used to sit as an ordinary magistrate on the Hailsham bench and at Lewes Quarter Sessions and had the opportunity of judging the performance of my brother Edward when he appeared as a member of the profession. As may be gathered from what I have written about him already, Edward was a person of abundant natural talent who could not have failed to achieve eminence in whatever walk of life to which he was attracted. Nevertheless, after he had died so tragically, I remember my father telling me that, even after four years' call, Edward was quite hopeless as an advocate, but that after seven he had become a seasoned performer well able to hold his own in any court.

My own performance was the same. For the first four years I must, but for the indulgence of my opponents and the occupants of the Bench, have been something of a danger to the public, deeply mortified as I would have been to be told it at the time. But, by the time the war came, and I voluntarily left the Bar for the Army, I believe that I was a competent and seasoned advocate, a formidable opponent and an asset to any client who made use of my services. My earnings, miserable as they were by present-day standards, fully bore this out. They rose quickly to a thousand a year, staggered for a year or two between one and two thousand, and thereafter began to rise again at a satisfactory rate. Odd as it may seem to a generation fattened on, though constantly complaining of, legal aid, this had been approximately my father's experience thirty years before. It is worth recalling that, in the terms of the gold currency of those days, my father, though in 1914 one of the more fashionable juniors at the Common Law Bar, was earning only about £14,000 a year. As Lord Chancellor I once had the privilege, by a courtesy of a well-known firm of solicitors, of reading an opinion of four of the most eminent counsel – including, I believe, three silks – who had been asked to advise on the question whether a Roman Catholic could become Lord Chancellor. They included Lords Haldane and Davey and Mr Justice Bray. The whole bill, so far as I remember, came to sixty-five guineas, certainly less than one hundred. The annual earnings of a top silk in these days may not unrealistically be estimated at £500,000.

Devilling for Harry Leon and the others was not very profitable in 1932 and 1933. But poor person's work had to be done for nothing. I made it my business to undertake the work of a 'poor man's lawyer' in Deptford, once a fortnight, and to do poor person's divorce suits where I first made the acquaintance of Rayden's standard work with its Appendix of Forms, enumerating the appalling sexual and marital offences of Adam Alpha and Benjamin Beta. For County Court experience I got my name on the list of the Bentham Society (run by D. N. Pritt, then, as always, an extreme socialist), and the Roman Catholic equivalent, the Society of Our Lady of Good Counsel. Thus in scope, if in nothing else, I was distinctly Broad Church.

Curiously enough, I remember little of my early cases at the Bar, and, although my practice was mainly civil, most of my recollections are of a sort of bargain basement in crime. They indicate something of the varied experience which goes into the life of a young barrister.

One of my first large cases, actually remunerated, which I must have obtained by some form of influence, was a will case in the Probate Divorce and Admiralty Division. I was to appear, suitably led, for the trustees and executors of a deceased testator who, at his death, stood possessed of a considerable fortune. It was an old story, the well-known situation in which an elderly man, comparatively late in life, married a comparatively young woman and left his property to her at the expense of his nearest relatives who had long-standing and legitimate expectations to succeed to it. Although, of course, as executors and trustees, we stood by the will, the real contest lay between the family, who disputed the testamentary capacity of the deceased at the time at which the will was executed, and the young widow who stood to gain by the disposition of the estate in her favour. The case came on for trial, and the contest was by no means a foregone conclusion, but it was ultimately settled, not necessarily amicably, but at least wisely, on terms which I had originally suggested fairly early on in the proceedings; the lady was allotted a life interest, while the remainder went to the relatives. I was considerably the gainer by this, not so much by the fee, though this was considerable by the standards of the time, but because in the course of it I acquired a fairly good knowledge of the law and practice of the Law of Probate, which stood me in good stead more than once in my career and which, at least at that time, formed no part of my studies for the Bar Examinations. Either during the course of the preliminary skirmishes during this litigation, or during my unpaid practice in poor person's divorce, I have a clear recollection of the almost totally blind but exceedingly learned author of *Mortimer on Wills* being led round the courts to do his work by his young son John, who had presumably read his father the briefs he had to do in order to enable him to conduct the case as he did exceedingly ably, in court. He was to become in due course the subject of an exceedingly moving play by the young man called *A Voyage around My Father*, and, less convincingly, I can trace an occasional element of his father's quirkiness and gift for spontaneous quotation from Shakespeare in the totally impossible character of Rumpole by the same talented author. But my recollection is of an old man of learning and professional skill, bearing an appalling infirmity with incredible fortitude, and led gently about his business by a young son who so obviously loved him – by any standards an affecting, even an inspiring, sight.

When my father became Attorney-General, he once told me he had done only three criminal cases, and those only in his early days. But, in those days of my father's early experiences, outside the Chancery Division virtually every issue of fact was tried by a jury, whether breach of warranty, defamation, breach of promise of marriage, the negligence of a cab-driver, adultery or 'criminal conversation' in divorce, lunacy such as the verdict which overtook poor Mr Jorrocks in Handley Cross, the amount of damages in the absence of defence (tried by a sheriff's jury in Red Lion Square), not to speak of the coroner's jury which then had a much wider jurisdiction than today, and for instance even committed Lord de Clifford to the ordeal of trial by his peers on a charge of manslaughter (presided over, incidentally, by my father, then acting as Lord High Steward). A jury of matrons decided whether a woman on trial for murder had within her a child *en ventre sa mère* as legal jargon had it. A jury also had to decide whether an accused felon was fit to plead, and, unless I am mistaken, another jury was sworn to decide whether an accused person who failed to plead guilty or not guilty on arraignment was 'mute of malice' or simply 'mute by visitation of God'. It took two world wars to get rid of this mumbo-jumbo, and even now we see nothing strange in condemning twelve men and women to determine, after a trial lasting six months or more in which they have to sit day after interminable day, an issue of fraud depending on reading interminable documents, double-entry accounts, sometimes in two separate versions, one genuine and one carefully doctored to deceive either creditors or the Inland Revenue or both. So it did not much matter whether my father, on the eve of office as Attorney-General, had taken part in three criminal cases or three thousand. Every experienced common-law barrister was a seasoned jury advocate. He had pleaded in the High Court before common juries, special juries, special juries of the City of London, and in the County Court before juries of seven.

It was otherwise when I began. Most trials, as now in civil cases, were by judge alone, and I therefore made it my business to learn jury advocacy in the most obvious way, by frequenting the Old Bailey, the Newington and the Middlesex Sessions, and generally wherever I could get a brief in the criminal courts everywhere.

There was no legal aid in those days. But an accused person could apply to the court for poor prisoner's defence (which meant a fee of four guineas or thereabouts to the advocate). That was at the expense of the public purse. Alternatively, if he could produce out of his own pocket the princely sum of £1 3s 6d (one guinea for the barrister and half a crown for his clerk), he had the privilege of choosing any junior barrister not otherwise engaged and actually present in court.

I can remember two cases in which I was the fortunate recipient of such briefs (out of which category I have long since forgotten). The first of these was at the Old Bailey, when I was briefed to defend a miscreant who had inflicted really rather serious injuries on an unfortunate woman and was charged on an indictment which, had it been made good in its entirety, would have landed him in prison for a considerable number of years. I read the depositions (borrowed from my prosecuting opponent), and duly went down to the whitewashed undercroft of the court to await my client. I had expected to find him (as I had my back to him when selected) a veritable Bill Sikes of a man: tough, gnarled, muscular and extremely formidable. Presently there came a rattle of chains and keys and a tramp of warders' boots, and round the corner there appeared one of the smallest and feeblest-looking specimens of the male human being I had ever cast eyes on. He sat down beside me at the table, and I asked him to tell me his side of the story. To my surprise and embarrassment he burst into uncontrollable tears.

'It was the drink that made me do it,' he said between sobs. 'But you can't make much of that.'

'Well how much had you had?' I asked.

'Not much,' he replied. 'Nobbut thirteen or fourteen pint.'

Wondering at the apparent impossibility of such a feat in so comparatively small a man, I asked him to elaborate a little on what had actually happened. It seemed that the victim was a whore who had agreed to commit with him the deed of shame for half a crown – not, as I subsequently learned, at that time a particularly low fee for that kind of thing. His real story was that after a long bus-ride towards the land of Eldorado where the happy event was to take place the good lady had bilked him of her wares, and he had then set about her good and proper. I decided to negotiate with the prosecution to accept a plea of guilty to a lesser offence and to tell this pitiful tale with the maximum pathos I could command to a sympathetic judge. I succeeded beyond my wildest dreams and got him off with three months in gaol. But, on leaving the court, I received an unfriendly welcome. The victim had invited a select band of her closest friends to witness her triumph over her assailant. She, and they, were by no means pleased at the outcome of my endeavours and, hat-pins at the ready, they proceeded to show every sign of making a murderous assault upon my person. Thinking discretion the better part of valour, I turned and ran, wig precariously perched upon my head and gown flying, away from the concourse and in the direction of the stairs. They had nearly cornered me, when my guardian angel intervened. A lift miraculously appeared and disgorged its burden. I leaped in. The doors closed, and I well remember seeing, through the closing doors, my pursuers clawing in impotent rage as I was wafted aloft in the direction of the barristers' robing-room. A Horatian tag from the ninth poem of the first book of the Satires came into my mind. 'Sic me servavit Apollo.' My father had chosen this poem for one of his sixth-form speeches at Eton.

Lewes Quarter Sessions was the scene of another of these episodes. This time I am pretty sure it was a dock brief. My client was indicted with another defendant for stealing a small quantity of money from a kiosk on the Eastbourne front. His co-defendant had pleaded guilty, but he did not. When I saw him in the cells behind the court I was disconcerted to find that, so far from denying the offence, he simply said that he had been drinking at the relevant time. Now, this put me in a quandary. If I put him in the box, he would certainly be convicted, and since he had confessed to me, albeit *tête-à-tête*, I could not call him to give any alternative account of the matter. He could go back into court and say that he had lost confidence in me and engage another counsel. Alternatively he could retain my services but, however oddly he might think I was behaving, he was on no account to show the slightest surprise. I gave him the option. He opted to retain my services, and we went back as a united team. I had spotted the fact that the only evidence against him of any kind was that the money stolen consisted of a quite abnormal quantity of farthings and that when he was arrested in company with the other defendant elsewhere in Eastbourne a quite abnormal quantity of farthings had been found in his possession. My problem was that I could not call my client to give evidence contrary to anything he had told me in the cells, nor could I cross-examine the witnesses for the prosecution to cast doubt on the accuracy of what they said. The choice was to go all out for the failure by the prosecution to discharge the burden of proof connecting the defendant with the crime. I could do this in either or both of two ways, either by way of submission to the chairman, who was legally qualified, that there was no case to be left to the jury, or by a powerful speech to the jury to the same effect. I decided in favour of the latter course, and that for the very good reason that I was not going to call my client, a tactic which I had had put into my mind by someone wiser and more experienced than myself when discussing, some time before, the course to be pursued in just such a predicament as the present. The argument, which has always seemed to me to be irrefutable, is that, if you call no evidence and the jury convicts, your submission of no case is equally valid in the Court of Appeal. If on the other hand you make a submission even in the absence of the jury and there is just an arguable case to go to the jury, the jury will know that you have been submitting no case and that the decision has gone against you, and that you have not ventured to call your client to deny the prosecution evidence. In the existing case, there was nothing to lose, as my client would quite certainly have given himself away had he gone into the box. So I decided to play the idiot boy, a course which quite unnerved poor Mr Cautley, KC, who presided in the chair. As each prosecution witness came forward and testified, he invited me to cross-examine, and I invariably replied: 'No questions, sir.' At the end of the prosecution case Mr Cautley asked me whether I wished to make a submission. 'No, sir,' I replied, and poor Mr Cautley, evidently concluding that the accused was defended by an imbecile, lost his nerve, and said as I had hoped but hardly dared to believe he would, 'Then, I rule there is no case to answer,' and my client was duly acquitted without a stain on his character or mine.

After my pupillage I went upstairs to the chambers which my brother Edward had formerly occupied, led by Freddie Van den Berg, KC, a brilliant young commercial silk. I had two room-mates. One was Gordon Alchin, a well-grounded lawyer and a considerable scholar but no advocate, who became a County Court judge after his heart had been broken by the premature death of his beautiful wife Sylvia. The other was Hugh Boileau, a fine advocate but no scholar. He survived the war, but had a sad end, since he suffered from a brain tumour and, when it recurred, took his own life. In the interval he came back to the Bar for a brief period, and since he was too infirm for junior work I persuaded Lord Chancellor Jowitt to give him silk, the only time I ever intervened actively in such matters. He would certainly have succeeded as a leader, had he lived to do so.

Soon after I moved upstairs, I became involved in one of the most spectacular cases of the day as a very unimportant junior to James Cassels, KC, subsequently a High Court judge. One summer evening in 1934, when I returned home to Natalie at our house in Victoria Square, I brought back a large square brief tied up in white tape (paradoxically the Government never use red), the mark of a brief for the prosecution. The brief was labelled 'R: v: Notyre', and there fell out a bundle of photographs, the first one of which, catching my eye, was one of the most sickening I have ever seen. It was the deliquescent body of a woman lying in a trunk. Universally in the press the case had become famous as 'Brighton Trunk Murder Number 2', since the trunk had been discovered in a basement flat in Brighton, when its presence had made itself too unpleasant to be any longer concealed. It was July, in a hot summer, and the death had taken place some time in April. The victim was a prostitute operating a bargain-basement business at about half a crown a time. The accused was a man with whom she had been living. He was not known to the press as 'Notyre', the name by which he was indicted, but as 'Toni Mancini', one of the names he had used when he made himself scarce. My own case involved no point of law since, according to my recollection, the case for the defence was that the accused had not killed the victim at all, and that any suspicious actions on his part were to be explained by the belief he said he had entertained that suspicion was likely to fall upon himself. Cassels and myself were prosecuting, and the accused was represented by Norman Birkett,

KC (then acknowledged to be one of the most powerful jury advocates at the Bar), and two juniors from his clerk Bowker's Chambers: John Flowers, later QC, and another. Although, in the event, my own part in the case was minute, and confined, as the transcript shows, to examining in chief one or two uncontentious witnesses, I was in fact present at every preliminary view and consultation before the trial and every conference during it, including consultations with the expert witnesses and, in particular, Sir Bernard Spilsbury, at that time the best-known forensic expert practising in that field. The judge, Mr Justice Branson, was a commercial judge, eminently fair and experienced in crime mainly as the result of his travels on circuit. The case has been written up so often, that I shall not attempt to do so myself, except to say that the acquittal of the accused was generally acknowledged to be one of Norman Birkett's finest performances, and that the decisive factor was almost undoubtedly Birkett's final address to the jury. In my experience, this is a comparatively rare occurrence, whether in criminal or civil advocacy. The normal way in which the cards fall is that the opening by the prosecution, being the first important thing the jury ever hears, has a profound effect, and that, if the defence is to succeed, and the case is not to be won or lost on contemporary documents or other types of 'real' evidence, like fingerprints or bloodstains, the cross-examination of the main prosecution witness, which is the earliest moment the defence can make an important impact, is the time at which an acquittal can be achieved by means of advocacy. Of course the judge's summing-up is listened to attentively (the late Mr Justice Swift was a master of the art), but juries are quick to react strongly if they suspect partisanship, real or imagined, coming from the Bench, either from the viewpoint of the prosecution, or, perhaps less commonly, from the point of view of the defence, and to assert their own right to make up their mind for themselves. In the event, in the present case, James Cassels, usually a powerful advocate, was suffering too much from bronchitis to make a strong impact by his opening. Mr Justice Branson's summing-up was a rather colourless affair. But Norman Birkett was at his towering best, dominating the court with his final speech, which ended with a magnificent gesture with his long bony fingers and a final sentence of just two words: 'Stand firm.' The jury were out for a long time, and even at this long distance it would be a contempt of court for me to recount what Charlton, the Irish circuit butler, afterwards told me about their deliberations as the result of his subsequent potations in the bar of the White Hart and elsewhere. But they returned, as in those days was necessary, a unanimous verdict of Not Guilty. Majority verdicts, in the introduction of which many years later I played a modest part as opposition spokesman on Home Affairs, were then something hidden in the far-distant future.

It is, however, interesting to reflect that, though legal aid in criminal cases was also not to be introduced for nearly another thirty years, the accused man in Brighton Trunk Murder Number Two was able to count on the professional services of so eminent an advocate as Norman Birkett. Nowadays, long before the case had left the magistrates' court, he would have been assigned legal aid, with the assistance of two counsel, as well as of a firm of solicitors. But it is quite unlikely that he could have counted on anyone of anything like the eminence of Norman Birkett. No doubt Birkett must have accepted the case at something much less than Bowker would have exacted from a paying client. (In fact I was actually told what it was.) But he was not paid the miserably inadequate sum he would have had to accept from the poor prisoner's defence. Instead, if my information is not wholly incorrect, the defence in spectacular murder cases was actually financed by the press, one of whose members would have been rewarded, in the case of a conviction, by some exclusive stories emanating, in the last resort, from the accused person himself. If this is correct, they were deprived of any reward whatever worth the having if the defence secured an acquittal. No doubt, at the time, the practice was a rather unsatisfactory way of financing the defence in important criminal cases. (Legal aid is the newest of our social services, the product, after the war, of the labours of the Rushcliffe Committee.) But, at least in civil cases, it saved the victims of motor accidents from the clutches of the speculative solicitor and counsel, 'the ambulance chasers' as they were known, and in criminal cases ensured adequate professional help, which, although it does not normally run to the equivalent of Norman Birkett and his learned friends, at least does not compel the profession to take the wholly unrealistic rewards of the poor prisoner's defence or, worse still, the dock brief without the benefit of adequate preparation or of solicitors at all.

SIXTEEN

Political Endeavours

ALMOST EXACTLY AT THE SAME TIME as the Spanish Civil War broke out, my father, then Lord Chancellor for his second term of office, suffered from a serious stroke. By this time he was living with my step-mother at 17 Bryanston Square. He recovered, but for the remaining fourteen years of his life he was paralysed all the way down his right side, in a condition which filled those of us who knew and loved him with a mixture of admiration and sympathy. In many ways he was appallingly handicapped. His right hand was virtually useless, and he had to teach himself to write, painfully, slowly, and almost illegibly, with his left. He could no longer shave himself properly and, though his mind was as clear as a bell and he soon recovered his highly critical sense of humour, he was incapable of delivering a coherent speech, and even in private conversation, after about five minutes of serious talk, although he knew exactly what he wanted to say, he would falter pitifully for the right word. Even after he had recovered, his condition required constant nursing assistance. To one who had known him as a man of indomitable energy and activity, his condition was truly pitiable. But his courage and patience were heroic. He had, of course, to abandon the Woolsack. But he remained in office as Lord President of the Council until after the Oxford by-election, when *Punch* published a friendly little cartoon in which Father, his public innings closed, was depicted carrying his bat honourably into the pavilion, and meeting halfway his son, suitably labelled QH, who was marching out, bat in hand, to take his place at the wicket. During the entire war, Father was a regular attendant at the House of Lords. Though he declined the office of President, he regularly took the chair at the meeting of governors at the Polytechnic, right through the war.

Father's illness and incapacity greatly changed the course of my life. From the time when he accepted the Woolsack and a peerage I had been working on the assumption that the highest offices in public life would be closed to me. I had been ambitious for myself until 1928. From then onwards I had turned my main attention to the law. Father encouraged me in this, and firmly discouraged any inclination I might have had to become a candidate for the House of Commons, being convinced that, prior to any such candidacy, I should first mature at the Bar. In practice, this attitude of his amounted to an absolute veto. In those unregenerate days before the so-called Kilmuir reforms, it was virtually impossible to become a Conservative member of the House of Commons without contributing generously to, or occasionally even funding, one's local constituency association. In one East Anglian seat, to my certain knowledge, the wealthy Member actually contributed £3,000 a year. But par for the course was very much less. When, as I am about to relate, I was put on the list of approved Conservative candidates I was informed that I was unlikely to get away with anything much less than a guaranteed minimum subscription of £400 a year. Of course, such a sum was wildly beyond my means unless my father was prepared to underwrite it. In fact, however, it never came to a disagreement between me and him, as his advice, even if unpalatable, was clearly right. I retained my political interests. My first election speech was in the general election of 1924, when I spoke at an overflow meeting in the White Hart hotel in Windsor, on behalf of the Conservative candidate, a retired Eton master. I was aged seventeen and still a boy at the school. I have spoken in the Conservative interest at every general election since then, 1924, 1929, 1931, 1935, 1945, 1950, 1951, 1955, 1959, 1964, 1966, 1970, 1974, 1979, 1983 and 1987, sixteen general elections in all and a number of by-elections (including my own two) as well.

But for my father, I might well not have been a Conservative. But I loved him dearly, and he was a persuasive advocate as well as a generous and just parent. So long as my father was alive, I was determined never to do an Oliver Baldwin and, when I was approached from the opposite end of the spectrum to join Beaverbrook's Empire Crusaders or the anti-Baldwinites, led by the Colonel Gretton whose views had so attracted brother Edward, I equally firmly refused. There have always been those who regard such an attitude as weak, dishonest or even cravenly subservient. But I had my own standards of honour, and, even before I returned to the Christian faith, loyalty to my father was one of them. I suppose that, had my father been a man less wholly admirable than he was, things might have been very different. But he was not, and they were not. In any case we discussed political matters openly together, sometimes in agreement, sometimes otherwise. I can remember a heated and prolonged discussion when, with my step-mother, he entertained me to dinner at the Ivy restaurant at the time of Mussolini's cynical and shameful invasion of Abyssinia. We did not disagree about the hideousness of the whole transaction, accompanied as it already was by numerous breaches of international law including the use of poison gas. Neither of us thought much of the efficacy of 'sanctions', even the 'oil sanctions' and 'collective security' which were then the watchwords and shibboleths of the left. I was frankly for declaring war. My father deployed the practical arguments on the other side: the absence of adequate ammunition for the fleet at Alexandria, the danger, as he saw it then, of driving Mussolini into the arms of Hitler. My father always consistently exposed the Germans to me as the real enemy, even before the rise of Hitler, ever since they had left the Disarmament Conference. But, although I remained unconvinced of the correctness of his view, it never occurred to me to make my opinions public. Obviously, coming from the son of a cabinet minister they would have attracted a good deal of attention. But I have always thought that, whatever the merits, there is something peculiarly ignoble about a son cashing in on his father's reputation in order to attract attention to his disagreement with his father's views. No doubt there must be exceptions. But, as a general principle, silence is always an option, and I was not slow to remind my father of the reverse principle when much later he showed signs of wishing to advert critically to some of my public attitudes. Being a just man, my father saw the sense of this and acted accordingly.

Nevertheless my father's illness in 1936 generated a real watershed in my intentions towards public life, and when he was sufficiently recovered I thought it right to raise the subject with him. I pointed out to him that his acceptance of the Woolsack in 1928, together with the peerage which that involved, effectively debarred me from a career in the House of Commons such as I had previously contemplated for myself. I said to him that, if I was to be a really effective member of the House of Lords when the moment came, at least a short period of membership of the Commons prior to my succession to the peerage would at least be a significant asset. Rather to my surprise, my father readily agreed and accepted the financial implications of my decision. It must have been late in 1936 that this conversation took place. My father agreed to introduce me to the then Lord Stonehaven, the current Chairman of the party. A *tête-à-tête* conversation with Lord Stonehaven followed at, I believe, St Stephen's Club, then at the corner of Bridge Street and Westminster Bridge on the other side of the road to Big Ben. The next thing I knew, I was on the approved list of Conservative candidates and hawking myself round the constituencies in search of a seat whenever a vacancy was announced either actively at a forthcoming by-election or prospectively at the next general election, then confidently expected to take place in or before the summer or autumn of 1939.

It was easier said than done. Then as now, there was a general impression that the sons and daughters of prominent men are born with a silver spoon in their mouths, and by the working of the so-called 'old boy network' can get more or less what they like when they want it in the way of public advancement. My own experience has been that, both in politics and at the Bar, the opposite is the case. Of course, there are items on both sides of the balance-sheet. As I have said, with my credentials and qualifications, and a consistent record of loyalty to the party, there was no difficulty at all in getting myself on the approved list, and with my father's undertaking to support me financially there was no difficulty in the way of my mortgaging my whole parliamentary salary, then £400 a year, in support of the association, in addition to which, of course, there would be election expenses amounting to perhaps another £1,000 at each contested vacancy.

Nevertheless, it was one thing to get my candidature approved by Central Office, and my financial worries taken care of. It was a totally different thing to find a constituency which would select me. It was not for want of trying. Selection committees are shy of barristers. They think, with some reason, that instead of paying sufficient attention to the interests of their constituents the prospective candidates will be pursuing their own professional careers. They do not pause to consider that, *mutatis mutandis*, the same is true of anyone who is neither unemployed nor younger than retirement age, unless he is also a millionaire. But worse still befalls the son or daughter of a famous father. In whatever party, there is a natural bias in selection committees against what they see as influence or privilege, and this tends to make them fall over backwards in defence of the inexperienced, the young and the unknown. My son Douglas was to sustain the adverse consequences of this effect for a long time when he, too, was seeking a constituency which would have him. But there is another, and related, disadvantage in being the child of a well-known parent. The child, immature and relatively inexperienced, is compared to his parent at the height of his powers. 'He is not a patch on his father', is the general verdict, whether it be on the young advocate who, as every novice does, makes a *faux pas* in court, or whether it be on the aspirant to the House of Commons, when, desperately shy, nervous, and obviously eager to make a good impression, he faces his worldly, experienced and slightly cynical interrogators on the Constituency Committee selecting a prospective candidate. Apart from anything else, the child of a nationally known parent is less than likely to be thought to have the potential local appeal of a neighbour inhabitant from the constituency itself. At all events, after two years of effort there was only one constituency which even short-listed me for interview, and that was East Willesden. In the event, quite rightly in my opinion, I was passed over in favour of an experienced and successful business man who, in the time available to him before the débâcle of 1945, made for East Willesden an admirable representative in the House of Commons. By the summer of 1938, I had virtually given up hope of ever serving in the Commons before succeeding to my father's two peerages. I did not then know, nor could anyone, that my father would live another twelve years, and I suppose his known invalidity was another factor subterraneously militating against me every time when I came up for selection. At that moment the totally unexpected occurred.

SEVENTEEN

The Famous Oxford By-Election

ALTHOUGH I HAVE SAID that my marriage to Natalie was probably an error from the start, and although we were both bitterly disappointed at her inability to have children, a fact which she was noticeably less willing to accept than I, it would be hopelessly inaccurate to suggest that by 1938 our marriage was on the rocks. We had had our ups and downs, but we occupied the same bedroom and remained on reasonably affectionate terms. Indeed, I am inclined to think our marriage might have continued indefinitely had it not been for my absence abroad on military service between the end of 1940 and the end of 1942 which seems to have thrown her into the arms of her second husband. I had, and have, a strong religious objection to divorce. I was genuinely fond of her and, from my point of view, I wished the marriage to continue. I was almost incredibly innocent at the time and, though I do not now believe she was faithful to me, apart from one painful incident I did not at the time have suspicions of her fidelity.

There was one feature of our marriage, however, which even now would be considered unusual. It was our habit to take separate holidays, I for a few days at Easter to the Lakes, Scotland or Wales, and in the summer on August Bank Holiday weekend to climb in Wales, and she usually to Scandinavia or East Prussia. The reason for this was, I have to say, my addiction to mountain-climbing and hill-walking which I had carried on continuously since 1938. The faded pages of my photograph-album show annual visits to the chalet until 1931, which was the last year that Sligger was able to visit it, though even then he had to get there on the back of a mule. But, in addition to this, there was a climbing tour in 1929 with Michael Vyvyan and Harold Freese-Pennefather to Fionnay, Arolla and Zermatt which I had to break off at the Mountet hut owing to a high fever, and broke my ankle on the way down. There was a long walking and climbing tour with Neil in 1930, an Alpine tour in Chamonix after one of my chalet visits in which I seem to have climbed the Peigne and the terrific but roped precipices of the Dent du Géant. There was another Alpine tour in 1931, a visit to the Oetztal in Austria in 1933 (when Hitler had refused to let the Germans visit the country). I visited the Engadin in 1934 when, with a porter of eighteen, I traversed the Piz Palü. In 1935 I climbed at Zermatt, from Kandersteg in 1936, in the Oberland with M. N. Clark via Belalp in 1937. I went to Chamonix again in 1938, where we had to be rescued from the Aiguilles Dorées after a night of storm and thunder on the mountain. I did not leave Britain out of my climbs. There were Easter visits to the Lakes in 1933, 1935 and 1936 (with a professional guide) when on Scafell Pinnacle I saw the Brocken spectre for the first time. In 1937 I went to Fort William to climb the Combes of Ben Nevis and the Aanochs. In addition there were my annual Bank Holiday visits to Wales in August.

In 1938, since Natalie had not yet returned from her own European jaunt, I had accepted an invitation to one of the highest shooting-lodges in Scotland, Fealar, about two thousand feet above the sea on the remote borders between Perthshire and Aberdeenshire. It was surrounded by rocky mountainous country over 3,000 feet high (Carn Righ, Benn-y-Gloe and other hills). We would shoot grouse over dogs during the day (or ptarmigan at 3,000 feet), or sometimes hook brown trout out of the burn with an unsporting worm as bait, and in the evening after dinner would listen to the wireless amid general talk and rounds of drink. My host was the late Sir Alexander Spearman, later the MP for Scarborough.

One Sunday evening, late in August 1938, the nine o'clock news announced that on that very day the Deputy Speaker of the House of Commons, Bobby Bourne, coming out from church had suddenly felt tired, sat down on a rock and died. He was at the time MP for Oxford City (in those days there were two other members representing the University), and his death meant, of course, that there would be a by-election. I was reasonably well known in Oxford, being a Fellow of All Souls, and had actually spoken for Bobby Bourne at the Town Hall at the previous general election (and, I rather think, at least twice before that).

'Why don't you apply?' said Alec.

'What use would that be?' said I. 'I have hawked myself round the constituencies for two years, with no result at all. Here we are, two thousand feet above sea-level and fifteen miles from the road and the nearest post office.'

'Look,' said Alec, 'if you will write out a telegram tonight, I will send the car to Enochdhu [the post office] in the morning.'

So it was decided. On such, almost chance, events, the whole course of my life was changed. If I had not sent that telegram, it is reasonably certain that I would never have been elected to the House of Commons at all. I might well have been killed in the war, as my military career would have been wholly different. If I had survived, 1945 was hardly a propitious time for a Conservative to get a winnable seat. My father eventually died on 16 August 1950 after one further inconclusive general election, and I would then, despite my wishes, have been wafted aloft to the House of Lords, never having been an MP, never having held office, and without any experience at all of public life. As it was, the next thing I knew was that at thirty-one I was the Conservative candidate in what was perhaps the most spectacular and widely reported by-election of the century.

The campaign began like any ordinary boring by-election of that time. There were three candidates. Patrick Gordon Walker (as I said, later briefly Foreign Secretary), who had sat at the Scholars' table with me twelve years before at Christ Church, was the official Labour prospective candidate for the constituency. There was a Liberal, Ivor Davies, who continued to contest the constituency unsuccessfully in the Liberal interest for several elections afterwards. He was previously unknown to me. The constituency, which did not then include either Headington or Cowley, was a small one and due for redistribution at the next Boundary Commission. It all looked as if we were in for a fairly dull time, arguing about local issues like the Cutteslowe

Walls, or travelling round the weatherbeaten track of unemployment, housing, rearmament, Abyssinia and the League of Nations. It did not quite happen like that.

Before nomination day, it became clear that we were in for an international crisis of the first magnitude. The crisis was about the future of Czechoslovakia. It would not be quite suitable for me to recount the three momentous meetings at Berchtesgaden, Godesberg and Munich, the obsolete anti-aircraft guns deployed in St James's Park, and the shifting sands of hope and fear, doubt and despair which gripped the entire British people. The actual dispute was about the future of the Sudetenland, a German-speaking and German-orientated enclave within an otherwise Slavonic population consisting of various nations, themselves not by any means united by religion, language or race, but with a few exceptions none of them eager to be absorbed into the greater German Reich.

As this, one of the great dramas of the century, unfolded, week by week and almost day by day, it was all rather a lot for a complete novice in politics to master. But I had one great advantage which others did not possess. I was able to discuss and analyse events as they happened. I had discussed public affairs with my father all the time that he was in the forefront of politics. Thus I knew that Chamberlain was not the soggy sort of appeaser that he was already being painted. He genuinely wanted a lasting peace, based on negotiation. But for years he had been struggling from within the Cabinet for a proper reappraisal of our armed forces. He was no enemy of what the left never tired of calling 'collective security', but he rightly appreciated that without Soviet Russia, or an alliance with France, this was impossible. Without this he knew we could not rely on Belgium, Holland or Denmark, and that, when the chips were down, all these, unless directly invaded, would take refuge in neutrality. He would greatly have liked an agreement with the Soviets. But he very soon learned that this could only be obtained from Stalin on terms rather similar to those which Stalin later obtained from Hitler as regards the Baltic states, Lithuania, Latvia and Estonia. None the less, after Godesberg, Chamberlain was reluctantly prepared for war and believed it to be inevitable. Munich followed, and it is difficult to realize the sense of immense relief which swept over the country when war seemed to have been averted. As Chamberlain returned through the cheering crowds I believe he was infected with the prevailing rejoicing, and it was then that, from the window at Downing Street, he gave voice to the terrible error of repeating Disraeli's famous phrase after the negotiations at Berlin: 'I believe it is peace for our time . . . peace with honour.' It was, so I have been told, put in his mind by a press secretary as he went out to address the crowd. I have never doubted that when it was attempted the Munich agreement was justified. The nation was not prepared for war, either morally or militarily. It was possible to conceive that, once the ethnic Germans were accommodated within the Reich, Hitler would keep his side of the bargain. Otherwise Munich was a carefully designed trip-wire, representing the utmost limit to which the democracies were prepared to go, under pressure, to accommodate German ambitions. I thought at the time the Downing Street declaration was a hostage to fortune which should never have been given. There was within it just that element of hubris out of which the great Greek tragedians built the frightful misfortunes which afterwards overtook their heroes.

In the mean time I had my own election to consider. The feeling of public, almost universal, euphoria which followed the relaxation of tension was followed by a strong reaction against the Government, and the reaction was accompanied by a totally new, and to me unexpected, development in Oxford. The two opposition candidates both withdrew, Ivor Davies gracefully, Patrick Gordon Walker unwillingly and under compulsion from his party. He was the Dr Beneš of the scene, masterminded as I have since been told, and believe, by Frank Pakenham, who, originally a Conservative, was by this time a prominent member of the Oxford City Labour Party. It was a shrewd move. Both opposition candidates disappeared, and their place was taken by the universally respected, but less universally admired, figure of Sandy Lindsay, the reigning Master of Balliol, as a sort of Popular Front candidate – a man, it was thought, to suit all tastes, although not by any means a man for all seasons. However, at this stage, the opposition made a serious tactical error. They extracted from Lindsay a promise that, if elected, he would not stand at the next general election. Since this was then confidently expected to take place the following year, a more preposterous promise was surely never made. Did Lindsay give it voluntarily as a price for agreeing to stand for election to a body to which he never wanted to belong? Was it the price the Labour Party demanded as a condition for supporting the Popular Front? Was it, as I rather uncharitably was inclined to suspect at the time, a clever ruse by Frank Pakenham himself, hoping, once he had got rid of Gordon Walker, to have the reversion of the seat himself after the political balance had been shifted against the Conservatives after the inclusion of Cowley and Headington? Though somewhat Machiavellian in design, there would have been nothing improper about this if it were once conceded that the Popular Front candidate was only politically acceptable as a device to unite the opponents of Munich, and that the alliance was certain to break up before the general election. At any rate, the emergence of the Popular Front candidate was certainly successful in achieving the first objective, but the publication of the condition attached to it was certainly a tactical mistake of which I made full and legitimate use. The plan was to leave Oxford represented for twelve months effectively by a dummy Member who would retire at the end of that period once the immediate objectives of the Popular Front had been obtained.

Sandy Lindsay was a Christian Socialist, a good man and a reasonably good scholar, but not a man of particularly sound judgement. He was so keen on preventing extravagance on the part of undergraduates that it was always said that he proscribed the provision of Lobster Newburg, a dish of which the Balliol chef was a renowned expert, in order to show solidarity with the unemployed. How exactly abstention from Lobster Newburg, or any other delicacy, by any Balliol undergraduates lucky enough to be able to afford it would actually assist the unemployed I never quite understood.

These, however, were trivial matters compared with the tremendous issues on the Continent. The scene was set for what I still look back on as the most sensational by-election that I can remember. Most candidates come to think of their opponents as unscrupulous, and I fear that I was no exception. Every attempt was made to blacken me personally. The walls were daubed with the absurd slogan 'A vote for Hogg is a vote for Hitler', to which I replied contemptuously: 'Vote for Hogg and save your bacon.' There was an occasion when my own office attributed to me words which I had never spoken and which clearly accused Sandy Lindsay of saying what he did not believe to be true. I went round to see him at once and apologized on behalf of my organization, and explained that what had happened was the ill-judged zeal of my subordinates. He accepted my apology and we shook hands warmly. This was the only direct contact between us, and I believe it did us both credit.

It cannot be said that my opponents managed their case well. Success in litigation and largely in politics lies in identifying the winning points in advance, concentrating on them, and brushing all irrelevance aside. I had various Conservatives fighting against me. But, on the whole, like Hannibal's elephants, they did more harm to their own side than to me. They included, I believe, Harold Macmillan, Randolph Churchill and, I have always been told, though at the time I had never heard of him, a young undergraduate President of the Union called Edward Heath. These were they who, very largely with my agreement and support, argued that there must be no further concessions to dictators. With this I concurred, but with the proviso that, Munich having been agreed, our word was our bond. We should see whether the other side kept their side of the bargain and in the mean time use the time we had bought to repair our woefully inadequate defences. As it turned out, this reply was apter than I knew. It was during the nine months which we bought as the price of Munich that the eight-gun fighters which won the Battle of Britain in 1940 came into squadron service. In the autumn of 1938 we would have been fighting the ME109s and the Heinkel and other blitz bombers with Fury biplanes, armed with little better than First World War machine-guns. There would have been no Hurricanes and no Spitfires, and there would have been no radar to identify enemy bombers before they reached the coast.

The left wing of the Popular Front was contemptible to the point of being ridiculous. Apart from the parrot cry of 'collective security', the exact meaning of which they were unable to explain, since neither America nor the Soviet Union would co-operate and the smaller European neutrals were unwilling to fight, their contention was that Hitler and Mussolini (by then known as the Axis Powers) were merely 'bluffing' and if we 'stood up to them' (whatever that might mean) despite their military readiness and superiority they would then retreat without a fight. There is a curious belief amongst the English that bullies are cowards. In my experience this is not the case when they are faced with a manifestly weaker opponent. That is why they are bullies. That they only fight those whom they believe, rightly or wrongly, to be much weaker than themselves is manifestly true, and it is also manifestly true that they will make a treacherous and unprovoked attack on an unsuspecting victim. In this sense it is obvious that bullies are cowards. But that they are cowards in the sense that they will run away from a contest in which they have an obvious advantage and are likely to win hands down does not accord with my experience.

As I faced the by-election, I had absolutely no doubt that, after Godesberg, Chamberlain had an absolutely straightforward choice, between, if the French would co-operate, starting a Second World War with all its consequences, as he did over Poland a year later, and something like Munich, which, at the expense of yielding to the threat of force in clear breach of international law, but giving due weight to the principle of self-determination for ethnic minorities, would operate as an acid test, a trip-wire, a litmus paper which would determine the possibility of maintaining peace decisively, once and for all, and fighting a year later if the wire was tripped. I have absolutely no doubt, in the light of subsequent events, that Chamberlain made the right choice, even though he was carried away on the balcony at Downing Street in the euphoria of his own relief and that of the cheering crowds that he had brought back peace with honour. My conviction is strengthened rather than weakened by a factor which I did not mention because I had not calculated on it at the by-election. This was the weakness of France. Fighting in 1939, and persisting after the fall of France in 1940 alone until Hitler's assault on Russia and the Japanese attack on Pearl Harbor, we fought as a united nation, with the Hurricanes and Spitfires to defend the Channel from day attack, with radar screen in place across the Pevensey Marshes and along the south and east coasts, with our land forces brought to a certain degree of readiness and saved miraculously at Dunkirk. Fighting in 1938, which was the only other option, we should have entered the war a divided nation, armed with obsolete aircraft and without radar or even, I think, barrage balloons, for what they would have been worth, allied with a French Republic as divided and unready as ourselves, and, as we subsequently learned, an incomplete Maginot Line and a moral inability to stay the course.

In the end I won by the not insubstantial majority for that constituency of over 3,000. The other by-elections which followed were less fortunate for the Government. One can never tell how much in an election campaign was due to one's own effort and correct analysis of the situation or how much to spontaneous movements of opinion. But I have never doubted that I took the right line at the Oxford by-election, or that, at an absolutely critical moment in our nation's history, and totally unprepared and inexperienced as I was, my victory at Oxford played a not unimportant part in our nation's ultimate salvation. The other by-elections which followed may have been less fortunate for the Government. But they were less important than this, the first after Munich.

One word more I must add to the honour of poor Natalie. Throughout the campaign, in public and in private, she had been a glamorous, supportive and affectionate wife. She nursed me devotedly through a devastating attack of pleurisy contracted only four days before the campaign began and which threatened to put me *hors de combat*, and it certainly would have done but for her loving care and the skill of Dr Hobson who attended me at Arthur Goodhart's house on Boars Hill where I was staying. In view of what happened afterwards and what I have already said, I owe it to her memory to make the avowal. From first to last no candidate could ever have expected a better or more supportive wife.

To this account of the matter I must add two postscripts, one personal, one contained in immortal words uttered by Winston Churchill. For me, the trip-wire was decisively tripped by Hitler's invasion of Prague in March 1939, and, being a totally unimportant backbencher whose words by this time meant nothing in the international scene, I felt free to make my own personal declaration of war against Hitler the very same evening at the annual railwaymen's dinner, held, so far as I can recall, in Cornmarket Street in Oxford. 'I prophesy', said I, with a theatricality not altogether characteristic, 'that one day the dogs will lick the blood of Hitler in the streets of Berlin, as they licked the blood of Ahab in the valley of Jezreel.' I got into terrible trouble for saying this from Joc Lynam, the headmaster of the Dragon School, who had been a tower of strength in the by-election six months before. He came up to me after the dinner and said to me: 'I can never support you again for saying what you did about the head of a friendly state.'

'Say that to me again', said I, 'in six months' time.'

He did not.

The other postscript, which I cannot forbear to quote, because it is such a perfect example of his style, came from Winston Churchill. It was Sunday, 3 September, and I had just crossed St James's Park from 1 Victoria Square to the House of Commons which, for the only time in my lifetime, had been summoned to meet on Sunday. I had been listening to Chamberlain's broadcast to the nation on the declaration of war. As I crossed the park on that bright autumn day, dramatically enough, the air-raid sirens went. I had no means of knowing that it was only a single friendly plane crossing the coast. The House met in a tense atmosphere, and presently Winston Churchill rose to speak. His speech lasted only five minutes by the Hansard clock, and this is what he said, epitomizing better than any words of mine could do the message that I had been trying to get across at the by-election the previous autumn.

> In this solemn hour, it is a consolation to recall and to dwell upon our repeated efforts for peace. All have been ill starred. But all have been faithful and sincere. That is of the highest moral value, at the present time, because the wholehearted concurrence of scores of millions of men and women whose co-operation is indispensable and whose

comradeship and brotherhood are indispensable is the only foundation on which the trial and tribulation of modern war can be endured and surmounted. This moral conviction alone affords that ever-fresh resilience which renews the strength and energy of people in long, doubtful and dark days. Outside, the storms of war may blow and the lands may be lashed with the fury of its gales, but in our own hearts this Sunday morning there is peace. Our hands may be active, but our consciences are at rest.

About Munich, Winston held views opposite to mine. But these words of his a year later epitomize my own verdict on that by-election, and will, I believe, represent the verdict of history.

EIGHTEEN

The Tower Hamlets Rifles

LIKE MANY OTHERS BEFORE ME, I have often reflected on the weaknesses of parliamentary government, and of democracies in their differing forms, the Weimar Republic in Germany, the Third Republic in France, the hesitations and vacillations of our own constitutional governments under different prime ministers and owing allegiance to differing parties and various political ideologies. Democracy at work is not an invariably inspiring example in this or any other age, until, like Winston Churchill, engaged on the same quest, one comes to compare the blunders and villainies committed, with very few exceptions the world over, by other regimes ruled by other types of political authority.

Whatever one's verdict on Munich or on any prewar British or western democratic government, nothing can equal in folly or villainy the blunder of Stalin in concluding the Hitler–Stalin Pact which was the decisive trigger which set off the Second World War, unless it be his obtuseness in failing to heed the Anglo-American warnings of the impending German attack in 1941, or Hitler's own folly in repeating Napoleon's mistake in 1812, or Stalin's paranoiac assault on his own people in 1937 during the purges following Kirov's murder. Even relatively minor blunders like Mussolini's agreement with Hitler on the Brenner Pass in 1935 as the price of allowing him to wage aggressive war on Abyssinia, or the unprovoked assault by Galtieri on the impoverished and wholly peaceful islanders of the tiny Falklands, who asked for nothing but to be left alone to live their own innocent lives undisturbed, were things which, in all probability, no democratic leader could have committed and, had they committed them, were hardly likely to have escaped un-punished.

Basing himself on Homer's dramatic story in the *Iliad* of the appalling evils on the rank and file of the Achaean army as the result of the idiotic and manic quarrel between two of their commanders, Horace wrote, 'Delirant reges, plectuntur Achivi,' but he might well have reflected that, unless the people were foolish enough to applaud the antics and initial successes of military dictators first, and thereby showed madness themselves, military dictators would never have had the chance to inflict these sufferings on their respective peoples. One has yet to see the end of the sufferings of the Iranian, Iraqi and Libyan peoples after the fall of their present notorious dictatorships. As the result of the Japanese military maniacs, the Japanese people suffered Hiroshima and Nagasaki.

From March 1939, I awaited events with a desperate sense of an impending and inexorable doom. Since I had already determined that, in the event of war, I would have to join the Army, it may be a matter of surprise that I did not volunteer for the territorial forces before the outbreak of war. But the plain fact was that I had to earn a living at the Bar as well as carry on my duties in the House of Commons. I made one abortive attempt to join a searchlight unit. I might, like my almost exact contemporary, Reggie Manningham-Buller, have made arrangements in the event of war to offer my service to the Judge Advocate General's department, for which my legal qualification and experience would, I suppose, have amply qualified me. I cannot say that this would not have been both a prudent and, in a sense, for I was already nearly thirty-two, a comparatively honourable course for me to pursue. I can only say that I did not even consider it, although I can remember that Val Holmes, by far the most competent junior counsel I have ever known, actually advised me to stay away from the forces altogether. 'After all,' he said, no doubt remembering the casualty rates for young officers twenty-five years before, 'there will be need for people of your calibre after the war.'

In the event I did nothing. When the courts and Parliament rose in August I went with my few friends in the Association of British

Members of the Swiss Alpine Club to Milestone Cottage below Tryfan for our customary August meeting in Snowdonia, and then betook me to Norway to climb with a professional guide at Turtagro above the Sognefjord, and thereafter, with Harold Freese-Pennefather, an Etonian friend then in our embassy at Oslo, in the district of the Romsdalshorn. We stayed in the little wooden town of Åndalsnes on the Romsdalsfjord, and I well remember after a bathe in the fjord with Harold and a friend of his (a lady-in-waiting to the King of Norway) discussing the international situation one Sunday afternoon in the second half of August. I looked across the water to the little town and said: 'What a peaceful sight, and how pleasant to think that this at least is safe from the danger of air attack.' As matters turned out, Åndalsnes was burned to the ground before a single bomb had fallen on London. Almost immediately after our bathe, the news came through on the radio (was it the twenty-second?) of the Hitler–Stalin pact. Tickets were hastily booked the same night on the sleeper to Oslo, and I flew back home on the first flight I could manage in a four-engined Fokker. Putting down at Hamburg, I did not even get out of the plane for fear of being interned. In fact there was no war for over a fortnight. There were, however, some fairly painful debates in the House in which the young, brilliant, charming, but, alas, doomed Ronnie Cartland made a famous, but I thought and still think, ill-judged intervention. War was inevitable, but it came as slowly as the crisis in a Greek tragedy. There were those in the Conservative Party (Ronnie included) who had taken the opposite side to myself over Munich in whom the illusion of an impending sellout died hard and gained momentum from the delay in the Allies' getting their act together.

After war had broken out, my main preoccupation was to join the Army. I could, of course, have waited until I was called up, or placed myself in a reserved occupation. But this seemed to me an ignominious course, particularly after the stand I had taken on Munich. The trouble was I was too old to be wanted as a junior officer, useless as a private soldier, and too young honourably to avoid armed service. There were others of my generation in the same plight – Evelyn Waugh, Anthony Powell, Freddy Birkenhead and Fitzroy

McLean (who only escaped from a reserved occupation by standing for Parliament). I had positively no qualifications except an infantry Certificate 'A' obtained at Eton in 1925 (or thereabouts) when Oliver Leese was Adjutant of the Eton Corps. At that time troops still formed fours and, apart of course from the trusty old SMLE rifle, which served the PBI almost as long as Brown Bess and was abandoned only after 1945, were supplied as a light machine-gun only with the First World War Lewis gun, a somewhat unreliable weapon which fired .303 ammunition from a revolving drum.

I was, however, in luck. My lifelong friend from Christ Church days, Hilary Magnus, afterwards an Income Tax lawyer of some note and later still a National Health Commissioner, had joined the first battalion, Tower Hamlets Rifles, and was able to persuade the Colonel, Eric Shipton, who was short of officers, to agree to take me on if I could get myself commissioned as a second lieutenant on the General List, with brass buttons and a 'Crosse and Blackwell' badge on my cap. I duly obtained my commission, and in fullness of time was permitted to wear the silver cap-badge, the black buttons, and the black and green lanyard expected of a junior officer in the Rifle Brigade. As matters turned out, it was one of the luckiest things which happened to me in the course of my life.

I found myself among as agreeable a group of people as ever I have known. The Colonel, who had seen service in the First World War (then only twenty years away), was director in a family firm of publishers who specialized in the production of travel guides. Hilary Magnus and Kenneth Elphinstone were fellow-members of Lincoln's Inn. But, at the beginning, I was a little bit of an outsider. Only a few weeks before they had all been together in a territorial army camp. They had their common recollections and their own private jokes. But they all made me welcome, and I was soon among friends. Amongst the most beloved of these was David Jacobson, a brother officer in my company who had been Captain of the School in college at Eton ten years after me, and he was for ever telling me extraordinarily funny stories about my exact contemporaries in college who had taken up teaching as a profession and come back as masters in the school after I had left. His father was well known to me as the senior partner in Guedalla & Jacobson, a firm of solicitors who had briefed me often enough, and in particular in a vast arbitral dispute heard at Leeds in connection with the complex coal legislation in force at that time. Old Ernest Jacobson had been a faithful client of my father, which was presumably why he briefed me. Although a Jew himself, he had brought up David as a Christian, and a nobler, sweeter or better example of young Christian manhood I have never known. David was so beloved by the members of his platoon, sentimental but typically tough East Enders like most of the other ranks in the battalion, that when he was transferred away to another company, they all clubbed together to give him a present. When I came back from the Middle East at the very end of 1942, I had the odious task of persuading old Ernest that his beloved child, whom he hoped had been taken prisoner, had in fact been killed in a desperate fight with a superior German force in the spring of 1941. My active service in the desert was not with this, the first battalion in which I served, but I had kept up my contacts. During the war and since I have had to comfort many victims of bereavement – husbands, wives, mothers, fathers, girl-friends, brothers, sisters. All these experiences are desperately poignant, but I think I have never known anything quite so bleak as the desperate grief of a widowed parent for an only son. Happily David's sister lived on, and still lives. But nothing could quite compensate this vast old Maccabee of a father for the loss of David when at last I had to bring it home to him that David was in fact dead. The only comfort that I could offer was that, at least to an extent, I shared his sorrow.

Our first military task was to guard vulnerable points, as they were called, in the East End. It was generally supposed that Hitler would employ a 'fifth column' as the jargon then was, borrowed from a phrase of Franco's in the Spanish Civil War, and my assignment, with my platoon, was to man a series of sentry-posts guarding a bridge over a canal, a strategic railway passing under another railway bridge, and another couple of posts in the immediate neighbourhood of Stratford atte Bowe, of Chaucerian fame. I was quartered in the parsonage of the church and every day I would hold a guard-mounting parade on a minute scale, each guard, so far as I remember, being composed of no more than two sections or so. They had in fact some ball ammunition, passed on, as it was in short supply, from sentry to sentry, and my only duty, apart from the guard-mounting and the administration of my platoon, was to get up every night at an unspecified, but different, hour and visit the posts. The approach at one post was somewhat scary, as one had to pass along the track of an underground railway tunnel with trains shedding showers of sparks dashing by at considerable speed some inches away. The post by the canal was quiet and peaceful enough, and I once found my sentry asleep at his post with his rifle leaning up against the bridge. I should, of course, had I taken my duties seriously, have instantly had him arrested and court-martialled, as, I believe, technically we were on active service, but as I was completely unconvinced of the utility of my doing so, and there was no one around to watch what I was doing, I took the rifle, touched him with it to wake him up, and assured him that in the First World War he would undoubtedly have been shot for his crime. Another sentry at the same post from the platoon which relieved mine was rather less lucky. Feeling rather tired, he retired to sleep in a barge which someone had thoughtfully tied up beside the bank of the canal. Unfortunately, whilst he was thus engaged, someone untied the barge and towed it silently on its way. He woke up in broad daylight to the sound of birdsong some fifteen miles away in the open country.

Such was my first experience of military life. The only good part was that I was occasionally able to visit my home and the House of Commons. However, this period of useless inactivity did not last long. The time was not far away when we were moved to Lincolnshire, near Market Rasen. My own company was reassembled as a single unit at the ancestral home, at Hainton, of old Lord Heneage. We were supposedly training, but there was little to be done except play football and engage in PT. Towards the end of winter, I was given the task of organizing a course for budding motorcyclists to become the dispatch riders of the battalion, who, though as yet without military transport, had been assigned the tactical role of a motor battalion. My own platoon, without any Bren-gun carriers, was to be the carrier platoon, and though I was reasonably expert in the driving of cars I had to organize and teach the would-be dispatch riders of the whole battalion the art of riding motorbicycles. This was difficult because I had first to teach myself. So I went to London and bought, for a relatively modest sum, a secondhand BSA motorcycle of, I think, 350 cc. It was still deep winter, the roads were icy, but as my first serious step I decided to ride the whole way back towards Hainton. I had never really ridden a motorcycle before, and I encountered some black ice somewhere just south of Peterborough; I arrived back at Hainton in a lorry and had at least one broken rib. I speedily acquired a high temperature into the bargain and spent the next ten days in bed. It had been quite a narrow squeak, one of several I endured during the war. As I skittered along on the black ice with my bike on top of me, I saw the front of a huge lorry looming over my face, and I thought I was a goner. Happily my guardian angel intervened, not for the last time. The lorry's bonnet was almost directly above me when suddenly it, too, encountered the ice, and waltzed away behind me into the nearside ditch. When I recovered from my escapade I had still to organize the DR course, which, on the whole with success, I did.

I stayed with the battalion for a long time into the summer, during the course of which I had to take one of the most difficult decisions of my life. I took leave to participate in the famous Norway Debate in the House of Commons.

I have called this the Norway Debate, and that is what in fact it was. Technically it was to be a debate on the war situation held at the request of the Opposition. The war had begun in a most curious way. Just as, at the time of Munich, there was absolutely nothing that could be done from the military point of view to save Czechoslovakia, since, even if we had had the forces, only a madman would have had the temerity to assault the Siegfried Line, so, when we intervened on behalf of Poland, there was nothing militarily which we could do, after the German military machine had obliterated the Polish forces, to prevent Hitler and Stalin carving up the unfortunate Poles and, for that matter, the Baltic States, in accordance with the terms of their infamous pact. The Phoney War, as it came to be called, took place entirely at sea, and consisted only of episodes, the sinking of *Athenia*, the battle of the River Plate, culminating in the sinking of *Graf Spee*, and the capture of *Altmark*. This last was a technical breach of international law after the fatuous and pusillanimous failure of the Norwegian gunboats to discover the three hundred British prisoners hidden on board when they claimed to have boarded and searched the vessel twice and discovered neither prisoners nor arms. (*Altmark* was in fact armed with two or three guns.) But, quite suddenly, the scene changed, again as the result of an attempt on our part to gain the initiative by mining the entrance to the West Fjord. The land war began in Norway, which the Germans treacherously attacked, allegedly in response to our mining operation. They also seized Denmark, but now at least we were able to respond by military intervention. In each case our operations ended in failure, though, by the time of the Debate, Narvik was still being besieged by Allied troops. Those who view the present military situation from a left-wing point of view might do well to ponder the appalling fate which awaits small neutrals who try to sit on the fence in an impending clash between Great Powers. By 7 May it was clear that the Germans had emerged victorious from their first land encounter with Allied troops. I went down to London from Lincolnshire in a thoroughly bloody-minded mood, determined to play a part in the debate and to speak highly critically of the Government's conduct of the war. For nine months I had been in a military unit which had neither the equipment, the training, nor the transport to engage in field operations. There had been no field exercises. There had been no use of weapons except on a miniature rifle-range with .22 ammunition, from which it was apparent to me that hardly a man in my platoon was in a position to fire his rifle at a human target at more than a hundred yards. There had been no contact with the gunners, the tanks or the sappers, still less with the RAF. We had been issued with no Bren guns, and effectively with no small-arms ammunition. Personally I was issued with a .45 Colt and three dum-dum bullets, the use of which would have been contrary to the laws of war. There had been no training at battalion level, and, though I had attended a young officers' course at Hendon Police College (which ended uproariously with a bayonet assault-course against a series of enemy figures stuffed with straw), this, and my unsuccessful effort to ride my own BSA bike from London to Hainton, was the only improvement I had had in nine months on my 1925 infantry certificate 'A'. There seemed to me to be a total nervelessness in the conduct of the war. The Labour Party and the trade union movement, and the Liberals under Archie Sinclair, stood aloof from government and carried on guerrilla tactics against the Chamberlain administration. This, in spite of the addition of Winston as First Lord, was basically founded on the same structure as had obtained in 1938. Only, by a series of masterly broadcasts, Winston had seemed to catch the ear of the nation. I was uneasily aware that, almost certainly, war was going to break out in the west, as it did on 10 May, about forty-eight hours after the conclusion of the Norway Debate. I went down to London determined, if I could, to speak, and determined to demand the formation of a National Government under Winston Churchill as Prime Minister. As I should certainly have made a fool of myself, it is fortunate that my guardian angel again came to my rescue and prevented the Speaker from calling on me.

But this was not the end of my dilemma. By the second day of the debate two things were apparent. The first was that the Opposition was determined to call a vote, and that without doubt they would be supported by a number of dissident Tories, notably Leo Amery, a respected colleague at All Souls, a young rebel called Harold Macmillan with whose antics at that time I had little sympathy, and the formidable national hero Roger Keyes, who in the full panoply of an Admiral of the Fleet had angrily accused the First Lord of the Admiralty, Winston Churchill, of pusillanimity in calling off the proposed attack on Trondheim, cruelly and, it seemed, unjustly implying that his nerve failed because he was haunted by the ghost of Gallipoli and the Dardanelles. To crown it all, the debate was to be answered on behalf of the Government, as indeed it had to be since Norway was primarily a naval campaign, by the First Lord of the Admiralty himself, the very man whom I had come down from Lincolnshire to proclaim as the desired, and desirable, head of National Government to put an end to fecklessness and unite the nation in what I knew to be a life-and-death struggle. How was it possible for me do this when he was the principal and legitimate constitutional target for the censure of the Opposition, backed by Conservative dissidents for whose behaviour I must say firmly I had neither sympathy nor respect? It was a real dilemma, and at first sight seemed to me to be insoluble.

Respect for Parliament and parliamentary institutions, of which the House of Commons is the essential feature, has been one of the fundamental political convictions of my life. But on three occasions, each connected with foreign policy, I have to confess that I felt the opposite. Here was the House of Commons at its deplorable worst – personal, factious, unconstructive, noisy, disorderly, and, as I then thought, totally unresponsive to the needs or the real wishes of the nation. It was true that, during the course of the debate, various flies were being thrown over Winston Churchill by prominent members of the Opposition, notably by Lloyd George, whose tragically anticlimactic career was now drawing, as I thought rather dishonourably, towards its close. He taunted Winston with allowing himself to become an air-raid shelter for the rest of his colleagues, clearly implying that at that time LG was wanting the very thing which I also wished to achieve: a National Coalition with Winston as Prime Minister. But he seemed not to realize that, the way the Opposition were playing their cards, Winston Churchill was not so much the air-raid shelter as its principal occupant.

There are facets of Winston's character which are constantly forgotten. One of these is that, savage as he was in combat, and even in debate, a trait which he presumably derived from his Sioux rather than his English ancestors, Winston was always at heart an English gentleman of the old school, honourable, courageous and, above all things, loyal to his allies of the day (not a trait which he necessarily inherited either from his Sioux ancestors or from the first Duke of Marlborough).

So, when he got up to reply, Winston was in no mood to conciliate those who had attempted to lure him to take their bait. He made no concession whatever to the Government's critics, save one, and that in a tone which was not calculated to mollify them. In his peroration he attempted, in words which neither then nor now I could ever hope to emulate, to appeal to the very need for national unity which I had come down from Lincolnshire determined to voice. 'Let all the strong horses pull together at the collar,' he began, amid rising uproar. 'Let all party rancour be forgotten.' And then, no doubt as the result of an interruption, he caught sight of Emmanuel Shinwell, standing on the opposition side of the House, somewhere level with the Speaker's Chair. The Sioux in him got the better of the gentleman, and his tomahawk began to wave. He shouted an insult, which, at the far end of the chamber, I could not quite catch, about 'There is the Right Honourable gentleman skulking in a corner', and the rest of the peroration was drowned in the uproar which followed.

The Speaker rose and put the Question for the first time. Of all the six hundred present my voice certainly remained silent. How on earth was I to vote? Or was I to vote at all in a situation which I thoroughly detested, and from which I could see no happy outcome at all? When the Speaker rose the second time, and before the door could be locked, I suddenly decided to vote with my guts. Had I voted with my head, I would either have abstained or voted with the Government. But my guts told me to cast my vote in the 'No' lobby. The present administration had to be brought to an end and a National Government formed, preferably under Winston Churchill, the one leader who, it seemed to me, could lead Britain to victory. It was not a logical decision. But it turned out to be correct. I seem to remember that I brought Godfrey Nicolson into the opposition lobby with me.

The vote was announced, and it seemed to me that I had achieved the worst of all possible worlds. With thirty Conservatives, of whom I was one, voting against their own leaders, including Winston, the Government had still won, and by the not inconsiderable margin of eighty-one. It was mortally wounded but could still continue in office. Scenes followed of, to me, extreme humiliation. The whole House was in confusion. My Conservative fellows in the lobby got up, and pranced and jeered. One whom I particularly remember was Harold Macmillan. Chamberlain was certainly not wholly responsible for the Norway fiasco. My heart went out to him in his humiliation. I did not then know he was suffering a mortal illness which would kill him within six months. I went back to Natalie that night with something like despair in my heart. The next morning, on a very slow train to Lincolnshire, I was made to drink the dregs. Walter Liddall, the twenty-stone member for Lincoln City, was in the carriage with me. As the train trundled down the old Great Eastern line at about 15 miles per hour, he kept on returning to the vote the previous night. 'Ye know,' he said in his Lincoln dialect, 'ye'll regret this for the rest of your life.' I had just spirit enough to reply, as I had done to Joc Lynam at the railwaymen's dinner in Oxford just over a year before: 'Say that to me in six months' time.' Neither of them ever did. But my constituents agreed with Walter Liddall. In the few days which separated the vote from the formation of the Great Coalition, Natalie reported that I received more than 300 letters of protest, most of them couched in immoderate terms complaining that I had betrayed the leader whom I was pledged to support. She did not send them on. I was back in command of the carrier platoon of Mark Clayton's company in 1 THR.

NINETEEN

MIR and the Blitz

SO I RETURNED to my unit in Lincolnshire, having pleased no one, least of all myself, and believing that my conduct had helped to achieve the worst of all possible worlds. In this last belief, at least, I was quickly proved wrong. Chamberlain was persuaded by the result of the division that he could no longer continue as Prime Minister, and he speedily discovered that neither the Labour nor the Liberal parties would join a Government of National Unity, the necessity for which he now perceived, under his leadership. Winston has given a graphic account of Chamberlain's private meeting with himself and Halifax. No doubt, like many others, Chamberlain distrusted Churchill's judgement, and for this he had good cause. But how on earth anyone could have supposed for a moment that, in time of war, the country could be led from the House of Lords I simply do not understand, especially with the memory of the choice 'in peace-time' of Baldwin instead of Curzon so fresh in the public mind. By the early hours of 11 May, Winston Churchill had taken office as First Minister of the Crown just at the time serious fighting broke out in the west. I am quite sure that the open defection of so many of the 'friends' to whom Chamberlain had misguidedly appealed in vain during the debate was the immediate cause of his change of mind. He has been a man unjustly treated by history, and I am sad, but not ashamed, to think that with others I played a small but significant part in the necessary removal of his administration, the essential condition for the formation of what, to the end, Churchill referred to as 'the Great Coalition'.

In the mean time, as Belgium and Holland and then France

successively collapsed, affairs in the battalion gradually improved. Our Bren guns arrived, and I spent a happy afternoon teaching my platoon of East Enders how they must be assembled, and how they were meant to fire. Then, or just before, the Bren-gun carriers arrived. They afterwards proved not much use in battle, as they were not designed as fighting vehicles. They were powered by Ford v8 engines of the type used in their production cars with an old-fashioned gate change. In addition to the knack which I had to impart to at least a minority of my platoon of double-declutching down and even up, there was another skill to be learned (which I had already acquired during a brief period of training on Salisbury Plain) of tilting the machine when it moved across country on its caterpillar tracks, so that you decelerated at the precise moment when you reached the top of a bank up which you had been driving at full power. I cannot remember exactly when, or in what quantity, any ammunition arrived, but its arrival momentarily preceded, so far as I can remember, my short remaining weeks with the battalion. My great pride and joy was my new scout car, a fast and serviceable vehicle of which, when on full establishment, my carrier platoon would have had two. But I already had one. The glorious feature of this vehicle was that, like the amphisbaena of Greek mythology, you could drive it as fast backwards and with the same number of gears as you could forwards, and by slightly swivelling the seat round you could also steer it from this position. I found great pleasure in practising with my scout car on the public roads, astonishing the natives by approaching them at great speed, braking firmly and disappearing into the middle distance equally speedily and without turning round.

During the death agonies of the Third French Republic, our life at Hainton, though strenuous, was idyllic. We were assigned a stretch of Lincolnshire coast, some miles away, to defend against the expected invasion. We had to stand to arms an hour before sunrise and one hour before sunset. In June and July this gave us a short night. But we endured this with enthusiasm. During the early-morning stand-to, one member of my platoon, a professional hairdresser in civilian life, would turn an honest penny by cutting the company's hair at 6*d* (2½p) a time. There is one extraordinary event I have never been able to reconcile with published accounts of the period, including Winston Churchill's *Second World War*. Against invasion, and as a sign that we must deploy against the enemy, we were given two code-words. One was 'Julius Caesar'. The other was 'Cromwell'. 'Julius Caesar' meant a rehearsal. 'Cromwell' meant the real thing. During the course of that summer we were brought out twice by these code-warnings. One was on 'Julius Caesar'. The other was, quite certainly, 'Cromwell', given the darkness in the early hours of the morning. Aware, as we were, of an almost total lack of training and the inadequacy of our equipment, one cannot be mistaken about these recollections. Our hasty movements, first to our dispersal-point, and then to our sections of the coast which we were supposed to defend, our studiously calm farewells to one another – 'Good luck, old chap' – and so on are not things of which we can be mistaken. It all turned out to be a false alarm, and was wound down from on high, in stages. When I got back to Hainton I parked my Bren-carrier in Lord Heneage's drive, and received an imperial rocket for my pains from our aged host. I replied pompously, in accordance with my latest counter-order: 'It may interest you to know, sir,' said I, 'that the Germans have landed, but not here.' Later, I received an apology from his Lordship. 'I am sorry that I checked you this morning,' said he, having obviously been in touch with higher authority. I also remember David Jacobson's comment, much later, after the whole thing had turned out to be a false alarm: 'I was hellish windy,' said he. So had we all been. The only thing which puzzles me about these recollections is that the only reference to any false alarm about 'Cromwell' in the official account related to 7 September the same year, by which time I was quite certainly no longer with 1THR, but in the War Office, and as to which, unless my memory deceives me, I have quite separate memories. I can only explain the whole thing on the basis that there had been two 'Cromwells' (perhaps Thomas and Oliver) and not one, one perhaps more local than the other.

Another, and equally absurd, event I seem to remember as 'the battle of Ing's Farm'. The name may be wrong, but it was certainly another mare's nest. We had an officer in our battalion (still alive, I hope, so no names, no pack-drill) who was much concerned with the danger of the so-called 'fifth column', fed no doubt by rumours of parachutists descending, one knew not whence, and one knew not for what purpose. Mysterious lights were seen, emanating from isolated Lincolnshire farmhouses. Obviously it was supposed they had been signalling to an equally mysterious enemy. One night I was awoken, and my platoon ordered out with quite definite orders. We were to surround, and occupy, a certain farmhouse quite certainly in correspondence with the enemy. I duly went, verified and deployed. The back door was open, or at least unlocked. I entered. On the landing the farmer was on the phone, engaged with a correspondent, obviously, I thought, some sinister figure.

'They are surrounding the house,' he was saying, and other things clearly describing our movements.

'Would you mind telling me, sir,' said I in my most military manner, 'with whom you are speaking, and about what?'

'I was speaking about the sale of a red poll bull,' was his surprising reply.

And I said with studied sarcasm: 'I suppose there was a red poll cock in it, too.'

A female dressing-gowned figure who had been listening, unseen to me, let out a screech: 'No British officer would ever speak like that,' she said.

At that moment our conversation was interrupted by the unmistakable sound of a man coming cautiously round the corner of the farmhouse. I turned and saw a cocked pistol aimed in my direction. It was held by Jackie Dawe, a brother officer in another company in my battalion. The farmer had been in touch with the police for some time. He clearly thought that his farm was under observation, he believed by the Germans, and my own platoon he had mistaken for German parachutists. 'Good morning, Jackie,' said I. We all left, feeling slightly ridiculous. Such was the atmosphere of these times.

Shortly after this, there arrived a bombshell from the War Office. I was to leave the battalion and report to the War Office in the Intelligence Directorate. I never served with the Tower Hamlets

Rifles again, although, as will be seen, I attempted to do so. They went out to the Middle East at the end of the year and they were dreadfully mauled in Rommel's first advance across the desert. From what I heard later, and from what I read in Churchill's memoirs, my fears about the adequacy of field training had been justified. But in the front line of the German advance they were in truth victims of our perfectly correct political decision to defend Greece and Crete, which in the event proved indefensible, and of their consequent lack of armoured protection, which had been withdrawn to defend our Greek ally.

My recruitment to the War Office as a GSO III (General Staff Officer Class III) was to a branch of the Intelligence Directorate in a supposedly highly secret branch under a talented officer, Colonel Holland. It was called MI(R), the 'R' standing for Research (the brackets were normally removed). At its disposal it had scientific and technical experts, whose function was to devise new weapons – the 'sticky bomb' was one. There was a small private force in training at Loch Ailort in Scotland which, I believe, subsequently developed into the Commandos, and they were privy to a number of clandestine operations. Although nominally concerned with research, we were basically a clearing-house for bright ideas, some of which came to fruition later in the war. I never knew exactly what became of it as a unit, since I was not with them for very long, leaving at my own request in the hope of rejoining 1THR when I learned that they were on the way to the Middle East. But I gained considerably from the experience. I attended fairly regularly at meetings of the Joint Intelligence Committee when Gladwyn Jebb was its Secretary. I was initiated into various existing anti-personnel and anti-vehicle devices, including land mines, which I later found extremely useful. I was taught how to blow up a railway line, and actually did so on a practice stretch. But I never had the chance to show my skills in combat.

I got to know a good deal about the structure of government. But the real value in experience which I obtained during my brief sojourn there was the fact that it compelled me to live, virtually as a civilian, throughout the perils of the Blitz, sleeping in the kitchen of my own

The last photograph ever taken of my parents together, at the opening of the British Empire Exhibition in 1925. My father was Attorney General. My mother died a week later.

He was a brilliant advocate – less remote than Simon, less offensive than F. E. Smith, more persuasive if less subtle than Rufus Isaacs, and a far better lawyer than Marshall Hall. He was among the most successful Attorneys General of the century, twice Lord Chancellor, Secretary of State for War, Leader of the House of Lords and Lord President of the Council. In addition, Baldwin always made him act as Prime Minister when he went on his annual jaunt to Aix-les-Bains. He was also a quite marvellous parent.

With my brother Neil *(left)* and my half-brother and half-sister Edward and Isobel Marjoribanks, taken just before the beginning of the First World War.

The College photograph at Eton, 1923. On my right is Noel Blakiston.

President of the Oxford Union, 1929. My father, on my right, came as my guest to the Presidential Debate in that year.

The summer of 1928: Neil and I at Haddo, and Neil *(above)* in my Tin Lizzie; *(below)* a tennis party at Olantigh. To my right is Constance Loudon, the daughter of the house.

The Balliol chalet, at the insistence of Sligger Urquhart *(right)* was primarily for reading, not a base for mountaineering expeditions. On the left, above, I am leaving the chalet, with apparent delight, to embark upon one.

In the Lake District, near Sty Head Tarn, in 1928.

My mountaineering passion:
on Dow Crag, 1936 *(left)*;
on the Col des Fours, 1927 *(right)*;
with Neil *(centre)* and Sam Lloyd
(fourth from left) in the Engadin,
1934 *(below)*.

My brother Edward campaigning in Eastbourne 1929; and I, with Natalie,
campaigning in the Oxford by-election nine years later.

house with Natalie, on camp-beds. At 1 Victoria Square we were very near Victoria Station, presumably one of the targets of the Luftwaffe's attacks. I was able to attend meetings of the House of Commons much more frequently than before and, on instructions, I prepared a paper on our long-term strategy of defence after the fall of France which got all the way up to Dalton, then Minister of Economic Warfare, who was so impressed with it that he offered me forthwith a job in his ministry. I turned it down on the ground that at my age my only honourable duty was to risk my life with my other contemporaries in the armed forces. From time to time the experiences I had there continued to be topical. I seem to remember that during the Falklands campaign of 1982 the present Prime Minister sought to give me instruction about the functions of the Joint Intelligence Committee.

'Prime Minister,' said I, to her evident surprise, 'I served on that committee in 1940, when Gladwyn Jebb was Secretary.'

'By God,' said Peter Carrington, hearing Lord Gladwyn's name, and evidently realizing that I was speaking the truth, 'so you did.'

As recorded by Winston Churchill, I was dining with my father during the Blitz in the old Carlton Club in Pall Mall on the night it was bombed. Though I did not in fact leave London until the night of 29 December, in the middle of a noisy air raid, the dinner was designed as a kind of farewell-party in anticipation of what was expected to be my imminent departure for the Middle East. The dining-room was on the ground floor, and we were sitting together with our backs to the street between two windows. The sirens had gone as usual at about five-thirty and, so far as I remember, by seven-thirty, when we were consuming roast partridge and a bottle of claret, things became a good deal more exciting. There was plenty of clatter and some bright lights as a stick of fire-bombs, flaring with magnesium, burst in Pall Mall exactly opposite to where we were sitting. The dining-room of the Carlton was pretty full, and a number of distinguished people were there. Almost immediately, the curtain beside us assumed a horizontal position, with the blast of high explosive outside, and almost simultaneously, with the hideous noise of the crack of doom, another high-explosive bomb burst inside the building and brought the ceiling down on us. For a brief flash by the light of the fire-bombs, I caught a glimpse of the entire dining-room, members, waitresses and all, in the Muslim attitude of prayer, bottoms up in what the doctors call 'Arthur's position', and the temple was filled with smoke, of a most mephitic kind, plaster, wood, and all kinds of debris descending upon us in a continuous cloud. My father, at this time half-paralysed from his stroke, had hold of the right heel of my boot, and there was a brief misunderstanding between us, since he was convinced that my right leg had been detached by the explosion from the rest of my body. I eventually persuaded him that this was not the case, and that our best chance of survival was for him to release my heel, let me get up, and carry him as best I could to the front door of the club. With difficulty we got there and found David Margesson, then the Chief Whip, counting us out into the street, as if we were Members of Parliament going through the lobby. Considering that, including staff, there were about 250 of us in the club, this required a good deal of sang-froid on his part. We were all alive, but, more or less as I reached the entrance, bearing my crippled father on my shoulders, the entire front of the building fell into the street beside us. As I looked back and saw the sky where the roof had been, I thought: Just like Aeneas carrying Anchises from the ruins of burning Troy. I notice that in his memoirs Winston, whether independently or not, drew the same analogy. Beloved old father, he had come up specially from my step-mother's house in Middleton Cheney to say goodbye to me at that dinner, and this was what he got. But we did not have to pay the bill. When we got out into the street we were still not out of the wood. My father could not walk, and it was more than half a mile to my house in Victoria Square. We met up with old Gerald Hargreaves, the County Court judge, before whom I had quite frequently appeared. Fire-bombs were lighting up the scene, there was a constant crash of high explosive, and most of the West End appeared to be on fire. And then, believe it or not, a miracle occurred. Out of nowhere a London taxi appeared in the midst of all this chaos with his flag up, and he agreed to take us to my home. By now it was quite late, and my last memory of that night is of Natalie sitting both old gentlemen down at the kitchen table and scrubbing the dust and filth from their bald heads with a basin of soap and warm water. Next day, my father went back to Middleton Cheney and gave a somewhat garbled account to my step-mother, and I returned to my work at MIR. I came by the ruins of the Carlton on my way to lunch (a friend invited me to his club in St James's Street). The road was cordoned off, and one bystander was saying to another: 'You know, one hundred and twenty people were killed there last night.' I was able to say as I passed by: 'I was there, and there were no fatal casualties.' I could see that neither part of my statement was believed.

Two other memories of the Blitz stand out in my memory. One is of the early daylight raid, I think in September. There was an air raid going on, and it was raining cats and dogs with a low-level cloud of, I should say, about 300–500 feet. I was doing air sentry on the roof of the old War Office. All of us young officers had to do air sentry in turn, and the turn was mine. Against the downpour I was wearing my anti-gas cape, the only purpose for which I ever found this garment of any use at all. I was armed, not only with my personal-protection weapon (a .38 revolver) but also with a very remarkable rifle indeed. It was known as the P 14. It was provided with a peep sight in place of the V-sight normally found in the SMLE. It had, apparently, been issued on a limited scale in about 1914 as a replacement for the SMLE. It held a magazine of five rounds similar to the SMLE itself, and I had four rounds in the magazine and one up the spout. I was on the roof of the War Office facing Horse Guards when from across the Thames behind me, with a tremendous roar, a vast aircraft appeared flying about 250 feet above me. It was gone in half a second, and I could not in that time make out whether it was one of ours or one of theirs, or what make of aircraft it was. The next thing I knew, it had bombed Buckingham Palace. The King and Queen were both at home. Thus I was the only member of the armed forces at any time in the war who was even in a position to fire a shot in defence of the person of his sovereign or his consort, and I had failed to do so. My only comfort is that a P 14 rifle would have been about as much use against a four-engined bomber as a pea-shooter. Still, it would have been a pleasure to know that I had had a go.

My other memory – equally, I think, from September – is of a rather different kind. I was night duty officer for the Intelligence directorate. There was another duty officer (from the Ops directorate) on the floor above, and we were connected by teleprinter with one another, and with the third duty officer, a female secretary, somewhere in the bowels of the establishment. There was the usual air raid on. But this was no ordinary night. Both duty officers had, for some reason, been expressly briefed that, on this night, the actual invasion was to begin, and we were given special instructions as to the action to be taken by us in that event. Nevertheless I spent a perfectly quiet night on the camp-bed provided, much safer in that strongly built War Office than in my kitchen in Victoria Square. I woke up in the morning to find that the teleprinter had been at work during the night, and, fearing that I might have failed my country in its hour of supreme peril, I read the exchange which had taken place during the hours which I had devoted to slumber. It was a conversation between my opposite number in Ops and the secretary below stairs. It ran something like this.

> *GIII Ops:* Have you got red hair?
> *The Secretary:* As a matter of fact, I have.
> *GIII Ops:* Meet me at the back entrance at 0830 for breakfast.
> *The Secretary:* OK.

I have a kind of feeling that GIII Ops was not fully aware that he was connected also with the Intelligence directorate. All the same, once again, I had missed an opportunity.

It was wonderful how the taxis kept going during the raids. There was an occasion when a farewell-party was held in Claridges. Present were David Jacobson, Kenneth Elphinstone (both of 1THR and both on embarkation leave), Natalie and I. On the way home by taxi via Victoria we drove down Whitehall when a bomb fell on the opposite side of the road. The taxi-driver euphorically began to address us as if we were a quartet of American tourists. 'On the right of us is Downing Street. In front of us is the Cenotaph. Further up on the right is the Home Office.'

But it was time for me to go. In one of the worst raids of the year I found no difficulty in getting from Victoria to Euston where we chugged off to Liverpool, and, via local public transport, to the new and unoccupied housing estate at Huyton where lay the transit camp in which we were to stay pending the sailing of our convoy (ws2, I seem to remember) to take us to Egypt. It was bitterly cold. The food-supply was nonexistent. There was no water, hot or cold. But I had my first sight of the Northern Lights from my bedroom window. And there was still the Adelphi Hotel for eats.

TWENTY

The Voyage of HMT Britannic

AFTER GIVING A LECTURE on some legal topic at Oxford recently, while being entertained to dinner, I was asked by one of my hosts which of my interests, law or politics, had most influenced my life. 'You have forgotten the Army,' I replied. Despite the apparent paradox, there was truth in that reply. It may seem strange that one whose military career in the strict sense was almost wholly undistinguished and comparatively brief, who had practised so long (although spasmodically and therefore without reaching the heights) at his profession, and who had held so many responsible posts should have made this answer. Nevertheless, it remains absolutely true that my joining the Army in September 1939 was a watershed in my life. From the first moments when I was quartered in what had been the ladies' lavatory of a charitable institute in Shoreditch, to the moment at the very end of 1942 when I returned from the Middle East, somewhat shattered in health, immediately deserted by my wife, and soon to undergo another quite serious illness, I was living a life utterly different from that to which I was used, being thrown into the company of officers and other ranks either much younger in age or in rank much senior to myself. Besides all this there is an enormous amount of sheer boredom in war which is likely to be forgotten among the relatively short periods of excitement and exhaustion, and the unexpected and often ludicrous incidents which inevitably accompany the most irrational of human activities. I was thrown heavily on my own resources, given a great deal of time to think and, after I reached the Middle East, life in an environment which was completely strange to me.

After a wearisome and uncomfortable stay in the new housing estate at Huyton, we were taken to the docks on Merseyside. I was one of a draft of more than a hundred officers, and we formed part of the complement of one of what was then the most modern ships, a motor vessel, as it was then called, *Britannic*, which in peace formed part of the fleet which regularly plied between Britain and New York. In the nature of things, the ship was heavily overcrowded and, as I saw for myself, the troops between decks, of which there were a large number under their own officers, had to undergo very considerable discomfort during much of the voyage. We were not particularly comfortable ourselves. But the other ranks had to suffer real hardships, particularly in the tropics.

We boarded the *Britannic*, so far as I remember, in the second week in January and did not arrive off Port Suez until the second or third week in March.

When we left the dockside in the Mersey we thought we were on our way. But in fact this was not so. We spent two or three days anchored off the coast of Wales within the sight of Snowdon and two or three more in Belfast Lough, admiring what I suppose were the Mountains of Mourne. When we did finally get under way, to avoid enemy action we went north almost as far as Iceland, west almost as far as the coast of America, and only then, since the Mediterranean was closed to us, slanted south-east on our way round the Cape. I seem to remember that part of the convoy put in at Gibraltar, but our own first port of call was Sierra Leone, where I spent one of the most uncomfortable weeks of my life. Conditions between decks were, as I have said, much worse. It was intensely hot and humid. For fear of disease we were not allowed to go ashore, and, because the powers that be feared air attack from Dakar where the Vichy French still smarted under the memories of Oran, we were totally blacked out at night. The bars ran out of drink, but, worse still, we became short even of drinking-water which had to be replenished slowly by a small boat named *Platypus*, which was said, perhaps incorrectly, to derive its supplies by distilling water from the surrounding seas. When we did set sail again we heaved a great sigh of relief. We duly crossed the Equator. I caught my first sight of flying fish, and at length, reaching South Africa, the convoy again split, part to put in at Cape Town, and our own portion at Durban. To one who had just left the blackout and the Blitz the sight of Durban utterly at peace and fully lit up at night was quite unforgettable. Unforgettable, too, was the hospitality shown by the English-speaking inhabitants. When at length we left, we put out to sea to strains of a pipe band in Highland dress playing 'Will ye no come back again? Better loved ye canna be'. Many of us did not, but I have always retained a soft spot for our generous hosts who opened their houses and clubs and plied us with food and drink. One small episode, however, less pleasant, sticks in my mind. On my return one night to the ship, I had my first and only trip in a rickshaw. It was drawn by an enormous black man with huge feet, wearing on his head the horns of a bull. As I reclined in the rickshaw in my lieutenant's uniform, I found this experience strangely degrading, not indeed to the black man who was glad enough to have a fare, but to me who was allowing himself to be drawn along by a fellow human being whom I was using as a beast of burden.

The convoy was heavily protected. There was at least one battleship (*Ramillies*, I think), an anti-aircraft cruiser (*Dido*, I seem to remember, and, if so, destined to be sunk off Crete), and numerous destroyers which shepherded the convoy like sheep-dogs uttering unmelodious hoots.

Life on board was not uninteresting. I learned my first few words of Arabic from a former Palestine officer named Miller, and tried to teach myself Italian from a primer I had brought with me. I was made to censor the troops' letters home (another exercise I found strangely degrading, not to the authors of the intimate confidences they contained but to me who read them). One, I remember, was headed 'HMS *Altmark*', which, of course, I should have cut out; but, having seen the conditions in which the men were living, I let it go. I attended as a junior member of a court of inquiry on the conduct of a young officer who, having undertaken to lecture to the troops on board, delivered himself of one on the Nazi regime which was thought to have been too laudatory in its tone. I myself did not take this at all seriously, regarding it as just one of those things which happen on board, but my seniors applied more rigorous standards. I would have thought a warning was sufficient, but as a whole the court insisted on an adverse report.

Our own contribution to the ship's entertainment was to stage a mock trial, with real witnesses and parties, pleadings, cross-examination and summing-up complete. The jury was composed of the audience. Beside myself, there were on board two experienced members of the Bar, and we staged a bogus claim for libel based on an article in the ship's newspaper. After the war, both the other participants became High Court judges. One was Seymour Karminski, then bearded and in the Navy, and the other James Stirling, then, like myself, in the Army. Karminski played the part of the judge, Stirling was for the plaintiff, and I for the defendant. I do not remember the outcome of the case, but I do remember that it was an immense success, the troops vastly enjoying their roles as jurors.

The seemingly interminable voyage at length reached its appointed end. We followed the east coast of Africa to the north, crossed the Equator again, were deposited by lighter at Port Suez, and my fellow infantry officers and I went by train to a transit-camp at Gineifa, where I spent a frustrating fortnight hoping to be posted back to ITHR (by this time incorporated into the Rifle Brigade as its ninth battalion) which was the only reason why I had come all that way. It did not happen so, and to this circumstance I probably owe my life or else my freedom from a spell as a prisoner of war, when my unhappy territorial comrades were so cruelly mauled by Rommel. At Gineifa I amused myself by bathing in the Bitter Lakes and scrambling along the sand and rocks of two neighbouring hills, known as the Big Flea and the Little Flea. But one of the most fortunate turns in my fortunes was about to take place.

TWENTY-ONE

The Second Battalion, Rifle Brigade

AFTER I HAD BEEN at Gineifa about a fortnight, there came, recruiting for the Second Battalion of the Rifle Brigade, its commanding officer, in fact about to be promoted brigadier. He was Callum Renton. The Second Battalion was one of the most seasoned regular regiments in the British army. Before the war, it had been some seven years in India where it had won numerous prizes for its marksmanship, and on the outbreak of war had been transferred to the Middle East. Prior to Italy's entry into the war, it had undergone eighteen months' intensive training in the desert in close conjunction with other arms, artillery, signals, wireless, sappers and such few tanks as were available. It had subsequently taken part in Wavell's spectacular advance to Benghazi. This had begun with the capture of the two Italian camps at Juma which won one young officer a well-deserved MC for a remarkable piece of reconnaissance, and it ended somewhere near Benghazi with a circling movement at night in which the battalion, only about 600 strong, captured something like 20,000 Italian prisoners. Apart from those newly out from home who had been sent as replacements, the men were seasoned soldiers, well disciplined and extremely tough, and the officers not only professionally proficient but also expert in the somewhat esoteric art of desert navigation. At the time when Callum Renton came recruiting at Gineifa, the battalion was at rest with the tactical task of guarding the Suez Canal against direct attacks from the acoustic mine, the latest scientific device the Germans had deployed against our shipping.

In the natural course of events, Callum turned his attention first to the young officers with the black buttons of his own regiment, and I was thus fortunate enough to be given an interview. Callum had known and had been friends with my brother Edward, and it may have been this which, despite my almost complete inexperience (shared, however, by the other subalterns available), turned the scales in my favour. Nevertheless I do not think that I was selected by this factor of influence. Compared with the others, I was mature in years, and despite the fact that I am not athletic I had years of mountain-climbing experience behind me which made me resistant to fatigue and well capable of looking after myself in a physically hostile environment. In the nature of things, though without desert experience, I was relatively good with a map and a compass. Moreover, when Callum needled me about my comparative inexperience and lack of qualification, I was able to tell him that I had come out with the express purpose of joining a fighting unit as an infantry officer, and had some elementary training in a motor battalion whilst I was at Hainton. At all events, Callum let me in, and, though my career in the battalion was relatively short and wholly undistinguished, it was one of the most fortunate things which have ever happened to me in the course of my life. I was posted to 'S' Company, then commanded by Douglas Darling, already a war hero. We were stationed at Port Said. The officers' mess of 'S' Company was in the Casino Palace Hotel. The rest of the battalion was strung out along the canal in the direction of the Bitter Lakes. After our short sojourn there, I never saw Port Said again until, as First Lord of the Admiralty, I saw the statue of de Lesseps gliding past my porthole window on board one of Her Majesty's cruisers during the aftermath of the Suez affair.

After a short stay in Port Said, the battalion was moved to Mena, a tented camp near the pyramids and the Sphinx, and conveniently placed near the Mena House Hotel. It was only a tram-ride from the centre of Cairo where there were luxuries like the Turf Club, of which all officers were honorary members, and the bar of Shepherd's Hotel at which it was said that if you visited it continuously for six weeks you would meet almost everybody (of course of the male sex) you had ever known in your life.

Owing to Rommel's sudden and successful advance, encircling

Tobruk and passing the Egyptian frontier, our stay at Mena was shorter than intended, but it gave me the chance to meet my brother officers, some of whom became my friends for life. Apart from the Colonel, by this time Archibald Douglas, who had won the MC in the First World War, the second-in-command, Hugh Garmoyle, who had sat next to me at Eton up to Mr Mayhew, and the Quartermaster, Jimmy James, I was the oldest, in years, of them all. I was also the junior officer, not merely in 'S' Company but in the battalion. The fact that I was also a barrister of seven years' standing and a member of the House of Commons gave rise to a little banter and not a little ridicule. But there is nothing like the comradeship in a regiment, and mine was unusually generous and kind.

Apart from training, the amenities of the area gave me great interest in my leisure-time. As the battalion moved up the road from Cairo the three great pyramids hove into sight. The thought came to me that, in the time of Herodotus, that is to say, about 450 BC, these extraordinary constructions were already the oldest man-made objects in the known world. The largest, that is, the pyramid of Cheops, is about the size of Beachy Head. It consists entirely of vast blocks of stone and it is entirely denuded of its original capping of polished stone, which, as originally constructed, would have made solitary climbing impossible. As it was, though the blocks were high and the physical effort not inconsiderable, there was no technical difficulty in getting to the top, and the view from the summit was tremendous. The neighbouring pyramid of Khefren, the second largest, was not so easy. From the lower slopes the capping was missing but covered with debris. On the last thirty feet or so the capping was smooth and intact except for a thin crack, obviously amenable to an experienced climber but, to a mountaineer of my modest attainments, I think too dangerous to climb alone. A fall from the top, especially in descent, would be serious, perhaps even fatal, as one would go down a long way. I funked it. A brother officer, Tom Bird, more intrepid than I, achieved the ascent and descent entirely alone. But, having reconnoitred the position right up to the base of the cap, I decided against the attempt, and Tom's success did not persuade me to change my mind. The third and smallest of the three pyramids offered neither attractions nor challenge, and I made no attempt on it. There were other pyramids not far away, at Beni Yusef, and I visited these twice, once on a hired stallion (Arabs, who are Muslims, do not cut their horses) called, I think, Sayyid – or something like it – and the second time, armed with a torch, I crept inside through one of the holes left by the grave-robbers. I crept my way (I think it was in one of the Beni Yusef pyramids) in total darkness with my hands pressed against the wall and found myself at length in an empty chamber where I shone my torch. Opposite me there was a most dramatic sight, the coloured, kilted figure of an ancient Egyptian, almost life-size, and seemingly also full grown, staring me straight in the face only a few feet away. The walls were covered with little vignettes of ancient Egyptian life, the river with all its birds, fishermen and boats, the peasants tilling the fields, carts, and other figures of a more religious aspect. Nowhere in antiquity have I seen anything quite so moving except, perhaps, the gold mask discovered by Schliemann the German grocer in Mycenae. But here, being alone, unguided, and in the dark apart from the light of my torch, the dramatic effect was enhanced. I also visited a spot where lay, recumbent and supine, a gigantic figure of a pharaoh. There was no one to tell me exactly who or what this figure was.

These activities led me to an absurdity of which I am still sometimes reminded when I attend regimental reunions. As part of the training assigned to young officers under his command, Douglas Darling decreed that we should reconnoitre and then lead 'S' Company on a route march. As I was the junior officer of all, my turn came last, and I found that all the most desirable routes had already been used. I therefore decided to lead 'S' Company up to the top of the Great Pyramid and down again. It was tremendous fun. But I had underestimated the effect of height on those unused to mountains. The result was that the officers and men of 'S' Company were soon festooned at various points of ascent and descent like the animals on the Mappin terraces at London Zoo. I ought, of course, to have known better. Liability to vertigo has nothing whatever to do with physical or moral courage or athletic ability but, though we are all liable to it on occasion (I remember a humiliating experience on the relatively mild Milestone Buttress of Tryfan), experience of the hills makes one a little insensitive to the disabilities of others. Not, I think, more than half of my comrades reached the top, and these did not include the company commander. But we all got down safely, accompanied by a large group of Egyptian small boys, who shouted encouragement to us all.

Soon, however, an order came that we were to go to the desert. Rommel had broken through and swept past Tobruk, which was invested, killing or capturing on the way a number of my old friends in 1THR, and had just passed the Egyptian frontier at Halfaya pass and Sollum with a mixed force of Italians and Germans. The moment had come for which I had been waiting for nearly two years. I was actually to fight for my country.

TWENTY-TWO

The Desert, the Coastal Plain

My wholly unmeritorious, but I hope still honourable, career as a fighting soldier divides itself naturally into two parts: my occupation of a platoon position a few miles south of Buq Buq and east of Sollum, punctuated by a brief period in hospital and a convalescent leave; and a second and rather less interesting period on what I choose to call the high desert, east of the frontier wire, south of Halfaya pass, but above the Escarpment.

As we moved north from Mena I had no idea what to expect. Dick Basset was now commanding the company. So far as I can remember, all the other officers had desert experience. I alone had no idea what desert warfare would be like. I suppose I expected something like Lawrence of Arabia, without, of course, the Arabs, camels and sheikhs. A little west of Alexandria, the desert was all our own, or the enemy's. Parallel with the coast was a desert track or road, partly made up by the Italians in their advance the previous year, and more or less viable to columns of vehicles. The area was interspersed with 'Birs' or cisterns, as far as Mersa Matruh almost all dry, and belonging, I suppose, to a period when the climate was different. There was a number of ruins, possibly of Roman origin. The vegetation was much more plentiful than one might suppose, composed in part of aromatic and rather prickly shrubs. The general effect seen from the Escarpment was dappled green and white, with the sea just visible in the distance. There were even one or two fig trees bearing fruit in one of the wadis not far from Halfway House (a track up the Escarpment leading off south-west from the coastal track). The plain came to an end at Sollum (then in the hands of the Italians) where the

Escarpment joined the coast at Halfaya pass. Sollum itself had been a small town in peacetime, but, except for the enemy, was now totally deserted. For their own safety, the Bedouin of the desert had been removed from where we were.

Our first night brought us to a group of Roman remains not all that far to the west of Alexandria. From there on we had to move entirely on our own for hundreds of miles till we reached our final positions south of Buq Buq and far to the west of Mersa Matruh. It took us at least a whole day to reach our final positions. My own platoon position I took over from a fine young ensign of the Scots Guards. I was thoroughly exhausted after what seemed to me an endless drive. Our orders were couched in rather dramatic language. We were to hold the position 'to the last man and the last round'. Happily such an unpleasant event did not occur.

My first surprise took place at the actual hand-over. The Scots Guards ensign showed me his section-posts, and, for the first time in my military career, I beheld weapon-pits constructed exactly according to the manual of infantry training. There they were, sump, firing-step and revetments, exactly as prescribed. At this magnificent sight I rejoiced too soon. I had overlooked the fact that riflemen are a trifle shorter in stature than men of the Brigade of Guards. The first section I put into this triumph of military engineering disappeared wholly from view, and, taking my advice from Sergeant 'Doggie' Nash, my experienced platoon sergeant, I caused my men to evacuate the position we were to defend to the last man and the last round, and to dig slit trenches, as they were well accustomed to do, about two hundred yards further back, on the forward slope of a slight rise in the ground. There was only a matter of yards between my section-posts and my platoon headquarters.

Another disconcerting surprise awaited me which was to cause me some embarrassment later on. The coastal track lay a short distance to the right of my platoon position, and roughly opposite to it was barred to traffic by two lines of oil-drums enclosing about twenty or thirty yards of track between them. This was a minefield which the Scots Guards officer had laid. 'How many mines are there?' I asked prudently. 'I don't know,' was the reply. 'In addition to our own we found a heap of Gyppo mines lying beside the road.' I decided, for the time at least, to let sleeping mines lie. I was afterwards to discover that the true count was in the neighbourhood of two hundred.

My third surprise, and the most unpleasant of all at the time, was that, almost as soon as my exhausted little platoon had started to brew up, an order arrived that we were to move about fifteen miles further west, and pass through our forward picket line in order to act as an infantry screen while an intrepid band of sappers led by a charming but, for the desert, elderly engineer blew up a dump of some 500 tons (it was said) of RAF bombs which had been carelessly left behind in the retreat and which it was thought expedient not to leave to be garnered by the enemy. So we left our position and, after passing the pickets, duly found the flat piece of desert where the explosives were supposed to lie. Happily the sappers and their white-haired leader seemed to know all about it and set earnestly to work. I only had to deploy my platoon to provide infantry protection. It seemed to me that we were dangerously near the Escarpment where, I wrongly supposed, the hostile forces would be watching us. With my soldier servant I went a little forward to carry out a little reconnaissance, and was nearly shot on my return to one of my own section-posts, which had challenged me rather too quietly to be heard. In the early hours of the morning the sappers and their leader returned and announced that the fuses had been lit and that we had better get out with all deliberate speed. Of course my platoon headquarters truck got stuck in the only patch of soft sand in the neighbourhood. The wheels revolved, but sank only lower and lower in the sand. Happily we all got out and pushed with some sense of urgency, and we were well on our way before the bombs began to explode. They went on exploding throughout the rest of the night, providing a most magnificent display of fireworks and bangs until well after dawn the following day. I was told later by an officer friend situated about twenty-five miles away that he was woken up by the series of bangs and thought that a battle was in progress. Thus ended the evening and the morning of my first day in really active service.

Life on the coastal plain was not altogether unpleasant. We were, of course, chronically short of water, which at that time was issued at about two gallons per man per day – a much more generous allowance, I was told, than had been obtainable during the Wavell advance. Out of that, however, it should be remembered we had to wash and shave at least once every twenty-four hours, wash our clothes, cook (each section had to have its separate cooking arrangements), drink, and finally fill our vehicle radiators. As my platoon were more experienced than I, they soon taught me how to recycle the water so as to use it more than once. An empty petrol-tin had its bottom pierced with holes, then part-filled with sand and used water poured through it into a second and intact can, where the surplus could be used for the humbler purposes of life. The 11th Hussars, who with their armoured cars formed our brilliant cavalry screen when we were on the high desert and were therefore further away from the water-point, were said to adopt even more desperate measures to fill their thirsty radiators, which lent a strange aroma to their vehicles. On the coastal plain we were never driven to such extremities.

One extremely bothersome feature of life in the desert was the dust storm accompanied by a vile wind known as the khamsin (Arabic for 'fifty'), as hot as hell and which stung the face and excoriated the skin with the particles carried in it with almost blizzard-like strength. A particularly annoying feature was that, from the direction in which it regularly blew, we always had it in our faces while our enemies only had to endure it in the back. It was said never to blow for more than twelve hours at a stretch, after which would come an utterly blissful calm. This relief, however, might only last for half an hour when the nuisance would begin again. I have known this to continue for two or three days at a stretch. The density of the sand particles varied exceedingly. But there was one occasion when, in what ought to have been midday, I could not stand up straight. I had to crawl for the twenty-five yards or so which separated me from my leading section and told my sentries to stand down until it was reasonably possible for a man to withstand the blast. The sand was so penetrating that even the ordinary wristwatch would stop unless it was protected by a special sort of case or, like my own wristwatch, bought at Simon Arzt at Port Said, of the waterproof variety.

A regular, and extremely fatiguing, feature of our work was the night patrolling at platoon strength. I seem to remember that these patrols took place more than twice a week. In our vehicles we would motor across country for something like fifteen miles, hide them behind any cover we could find, and proceed on foot for most of the night right up to the outskirts of Sollum or even beyond. It seemed that the Italians evacuated their day positions during the night and retired to some safer spot, and in fact, in spite of a number of false alarms, I never met any danger. But, further south, one brother officer was killed on patrol whilst I was there, I believe when he encountered a booby-trap of some kind. Despite the excellent morale and discipline of our men, and the explicit instructions of the manual of infantry training to the contrary, I found in practice that it was impossible to maintain the momentum and cover the necessary tract of ground unless I led the platoon in arrow formation from the front. Again contrary to practice, I carried a tommy-gun with which we had been newly issued, determined that, if I encountered an enemy (which, on these occasions, fortunately never happened), I would get in the first shot.

The air-intake of all vehicles had to be covered with air-filters to prevent the cylinders wearing with the sand, and if one went for even a short drive on the finest day one returned with face and lips covered with a fine white dust. Not long ago, after I had become Lord Chancellor, I found the green forage-cap I had worn in the desert with the dust still upon it. I think the powers that be were to some extent under the impression that we all wore topis and tin hats. In actual fact, however, we wore the most extraordinary amalgam of garments, varying from individual to individual and amusingly portrayed by a clever caricaturist known as Jon who invented two desert habitués whom he designated 'the two types'. I soon found that if I was to avoid desert sores, which on the coastal plain were particularly troublesome, long trousers were preferable to shorts, that shirts must never have their sleeves rolled up but should be buttoned at the wrist, and that desert boots, purchased at the officers' shops at the main bases, were *de rigueur* as footwear in preference to the ankle-boots which the well-dressed officer was expected to wear in uniform. Badges of rank were carried on the shoulder-straps of our shirts.

Wildlife in the desert was more plentiful than one might suppose. During my relatively short stay, I encountered bustard (which I failed to kill with my rifle), gazelle (not very common, but a welcome change from the eternal bully and biscuits), plenty of pigeons (but never available for the pot), a fox, a hare caught by an officer by jumping on it from a truck, and a chameleon, which genuinely changed colour when placed on different surfaces, and one runaway camel left behind by the Bedouin. There were also four kinds of scorpion (big black and little black, big orange and little orange), one of which spent a comfortable night in my sleeping-bag and scuttled away in the morning without harming me when I unzipped the bag to get up. The lagoons by the shore held considerable quantities of grey mullet which could sometimes be obtained by a judicious use of Mills bombs.

The nights in the desert were marvellous, and not at all what one might expect. If one took off one's clothes at night – and I usually did when not on patrol, or in the absence of any cause for vigilance – one would be very wise to cover them up with a groundsheet. If one did not, one usually found that, contrary to all expectations, in the morning they would be absolutely wringing wet with dew. I was not in the desert during the winter, but I was told that in most years there would be two or three days of torrential rain and, in the following days, seeds would germinate and the desert would, for a brief space, become radiant with flowers. There are passages in the Old Testament which seem to refer to this phenomenon.

The moon and the stars were of a brightness I have only seen in clear weather at high altitudes in the Alps, and I learned more in a week about the rising and setting of the moon than I had ever been told at school or anywhere else.

Both by night and by day, travel in the desert was by compass and the mileometer on the car applied by dead reckoning to the map. The art consisted in knowing how much to add to the distance measured in a straight line to allow for the deviations of the steering as the result of avoiding stones or other obstacles and soft sand. Even on a dead-straight road the addition is not less than 10 per cent. In order to assist the calculation, the experienced expert had a map of the tract of country likely to be met. Except for the Escarpment and the coastline, there were few features in the desert by which to mark one's position. Nevertheless an experienced officer (which, alas, never included myself) could travel fifty miles across country by night and come out within five hundred yards of a designated spot. I could do fairly well by day, but I never acquired this extraordinary skill in the dark. But the skill in the art of the more experienced officers accounts for a good deal of our superiority in mobility and, above all, for the specialist achievements of the Long Range Desert Group. I remember once, when the company was moving in column across an apparently featureless tract, the Company Sergeant-Major reminded the Column Commander that, eighteen months before, a quantity of beer had been buried at precisely this spot. Search was made, and the beer was found almost immediately.

TWENTY-THREE

Alarms and Excursions

As may be gathered, most of my brief period on the coastal plain, though relatively exhausting and uncomfortable, was not particularly dangerous. There was always the danger of an attack from the air, of which the Germans had superiority at that time. There was, in particular, a sinister figure in the shape of a single Messerschmitt 110, known as 'Lonely Bill', who prowled about, descending on an unwary traveller whom he easily spotted owing to the plumes of dust thrown high in the air by the wheels of any truck. One of our padres was killed in this way when setting about his pastoral duties. There was also a circus of three Messerschmitt 110s (of which more later) who attacked static positions. One officer, whilst I was there, was killed in this miserable way when on the loo.

The first adventure that I had was largely of my own making. Orders came down that I was to lift the minefield on the road left behind my Scots Guards predecessor. The difficulty which this presented was that he did not know, and therefore could not tell me, how many mines lay under the surface of the track. They had been perfectly concealed. He also could not tell me anything about their mechanism or the way in which they could be disarmed. I was inclined to assume, without feeling certain, that, having been laid on the track, they were anti-vehicle and not anti-personnel. But this did not tell me anything about the uncovenanted heap of Egyptian mines which the Scots Guards ensign had added to his own store.

Of the theory of land mines I knew something from my MIR days. I knew they were armed with a detonator made of fulminate of mercury, which was extremely sensitive and could blow off an arm or a leg, and whose function was to detonate the main charge. How you removed the detonator, or what exactly to do with it when removed, I did not know. I moved my platoon to what I regarded as a safe distance, and, accompanied by my very experienced soldier servant (whom I greatly trusted), who had shown himself surprisingly knowledgeable about the little red grenades the Italians had left behind, I moved in to tackle my task. Using my servant's bayonet (known to riflemen as a 'sword') I scrabbled away at the surface of the minefield and presently came upon the sinister surface of what was obviously one of the mines laid by the Scots Guards. It was of a type unknown to me, and there appeared to be no way of getting into its unpleasant contents. I sent my soldier servant some distance behind and regarded my enemy with distrust. I cannot help remembering, to my shame, that a little bead of sweat, not entirely due to the desert heat, formed on my brow and trickled down my nose. Still, I had to do something. I dug around the object with the sword and found, near the bottom of the case, what was obviously a bayonet fitting. In order to get at the innards of the thing I figured that it would be necessary to push the case down, and then up. Since I was not sure that the mine was not anti-personnel or armed with an anti-personnel device to prevent interference, I waited a minute or two to collect my thoughts, and I believe said a short prayer before pushing the case down. Sure enough, I was OK, and I pulled the case up again. The inner contents of the mine duly appeared, and there, in the middle, was what was obviously a brass detonator with some sinister-looking bits and pieces of wire. After further reflection, I decided that the only way in which the detonator could be removed in order to disarm the mine was by unscrewing it, and this I did, not without apprehension. I next had to instruct my platoon as to the detection and disarmament of the rest of the mines and the importance of not exploding the detonators when they had been removed. They raised over 150 of these objects and sent them to safety. I later learned that there were still one or more lying undetected in the sand. Still, I had done my best, and no one was hurt.

The removal of the minefield was, I suppose, the prelude to an advance on Sollum which took place some short time later. I was given the task of moving quietly into position the night before in order to give protection to the column advancing along the coastal road. I was told, correctly, that a parallel column composed of the Coldstream Guards supported by Matilda tanks would be moving in a northward direction along the Escarpment on our left flank in a sort of pincer movement at the top of Halfaya pass. I knew nothing of the dispositions of the enemy, not even whether they were Italians or Germans. We were in column strength, that is, 'S' Company, plus signallers, a few 25-pounders, some Australian anti-tank gunners, and, as it turned out, a few journalists. Dick Basset was again still in command. It was evidently not a very big show. We were specially warned against incurring casualties if this could be avoided; but as, apart from one big event to which I shall come soon, it was the first and only battle that I have ever seen, I think it deserves a place among my recorded memories. It has never appeared, except as a sentence, in the history-books. I suppose it was part of a design to take the pressure off Tobruk. But that I shall never know.

My platoon advanced all night more or less to the spot designated, and we assumed our positions. I could not help reflecting as we travelled through the night at the absurdity of a thirty-four-year-old barrister, with an Eton Certificate 'A', leading a platoon of infantry at the head of a unit of the British army in its advance over unknown territory. Presently, just about first light, the main body appeared and took up their positions. As we had been up all night, my platoon and I were in reserve at column HQ. Nearer the coast, it was not long before I heard the Bren guns of the platoon on our right flank engage in bursts of fire against an unseen foe in the neighbourhood of Sollum, and, more or less at the same time, on the top of the Escarpment, but below the skyline, a Matilda tank appeared, followed by a few Guardsmen of the Coldstream. They were met by machine-gun fire from the unseen enemy; the tank reversed for about thirty yards and halted. Presently our 25-pounders started firing from behind me. On the rear wireless link I heard a signaller passing on a request for 'help from above', not a very subtle way of asking for air support. But these were the days before elaborate codes. Presently a group of three Blenheims flew in from the sea and started dropping their bombs. The first stick fell, so far as I could see, in what I judged to be the enemy position, which caused loud sounds of satisfaction from the platoon. The second fell into an empty area of desert between us and the enemy. This caused less satisfaction. The third stick fell more or less in the middle of our position, and then, or later, my platoon sergeant was burned on the neck by a bomb fragment. This provoked considerable adverse comment, and I heard the signaller request that the help from above should cease, and their reply: 'We can't. It is already on its way.' The help from above went on unabated for a considerable time. Somewhere about half-past four I thought it was tea-time, and decided to boil up a tin of one of Groppi's steak-and-kidney puddings which a friend on leave had procured for me in Cairo, and to which, since I had had nothing much of anything to eat all day, I was looking forward with some relish. My platoon in their several sections were doing much the same. Our rations consisted only of bully and biscuits variously prepared, but most sections had procured additional fare of one kind or another. I was looking forward to my feast of tinned beefsteak and kidney, but it was not to be. As my first spoonful was about to enter my mouth, news came that the white flags had gone up. The Italian unit opposed to us had surrendered, and since I had been in reserve all day my task was to garner in the prisoners and take them to the rear. So I left my steak and kidney uneaten and drove forward.

The one thing I knew about taking prisoners was that one must begin by separating the officers from the men. This, owing to their badges of rank, was not particularly difficult. One tried to cheek me but desisted when I waved a tommy-gun at him in a menacing manner. I then addressed the Italians in the few phrases of Italian I had picked up in *Britannic*. 'Morte a Mussolini porco,' said I with unnecessary offence. 'Dove sono i volnerati?' I asked, borrowing the last word from Latin. I was given to understand that there were no wounded Italians. This was surprising as I later learned that our Brens that day had fired 1,300 rounds of small-arms ammunition. 'Dove sono i Tedeschi?' I went on, thinking I might have to deal with more formidable opponents. Again I was given a nil return. So off we went, through our own positions, dropping the officers there with column headquarters. The other ranks, 117 in number, could not be accommodated by any form of transport we possessed. So, to the rear, at about 2 miles per hour, we had to trudge, the victorious riflemen on their four trucks, the Italians being made to walk. We had not got very far when night began to fall. I suppose I should have kept everyone on the move. But we were all whacked, and presently I decided we could stand no more and we all went to sleep in the desert together, the Italians under armed guard; but, as there were 117 of them and less than twenty-five of us, I think it was perhaps as well that I had got rid of their officers. My last recollection of that evening was that of the smell which rose from the Italian ranks. It was the familiar, and not unpleasant, aroma of Alpine guides, somewhat reassuring in those troubled times. The Italians, who had had no washing facilities, were wearing, for the desert, wholly unsuitable uniforms of serge.

This was not quite the end of the affair. About three in the morning we were awakened from our slumbers by a terrifying series of crashes and flashes. I later learned that Rommel, who had prudently left the Italians as a screen, had counterattacked our troops, then in possession of Sollum and Halfaya pass, with Stukas and superior numbers. Not much later, I found that the coastal track by which I had camped was full of vehicles. The British units were in full retreat. What was I to do? If I attempted to evacuate the Italians, they would have to travel on foot, and I and my poor platoon stood in danger of being captured in our own turn. I obviously could not stay where I was. I could only guess what was happening. I took the only course possible. I stood in the middle of the coastal track like a traffic policeman, flagged down every fleeing vehicle as it passed and placed, according to availability of space, one, two or three of my charges on board. Presently there were few enough to take them aboard my own vehicles, and off we went with the rest. We stopped in our old platoon position which we had left about forty-eight hours before and awaited further orders. Happily none of the Italians was missing. A hundred and seventeen other ranks and six officers duly arrived back at the rear. Evidently I had done the right thing, even without the sustenance which I had hoped to obtain from Groppi's steak-

and-kidney pudding. So ended my first and only pitched battle with the ground forces of the enemy. Except for the burn from our own bomb which afflicted my platoon sergeant we had obeyed our orders not to incur unnecessary casualties. But we were back to square one. The enemy had regained possession of Sollum, and my platoon were back in the slit trenches which we had been ordered to hold to the last man and the last round.

Except for two final incidents, my inglorious career as a fighting soldier had come nearly to an end. On one of these, I was ordered to proceed to Halfway House, a track leading up the Escarpment and then in our possession. I was ordered to blow up the pass and was provided with an efficient detachment of sappers to assist me in the task. From my platoon position, the distance was considerable and the journey entailed a night out in the open, which I spent at the foot of the pass.

The pass itself was a narrow track not made up, and I had been instructed to blow up the defile at the top which led on to it. Then mines were to be laid in case any vehicle might escape beyond the blown-up defile. As we went up we found a place a little way below the summit which I judged suitable for mines. Unusually, I was wearing ankle-boots with leather heels, and, striking the ground firmly with the hard heel of my boot, I said to the section commander in charge: 'That is the place to put your mines.' The ground yielded a dull metallic sound, and a little scrabbling revealed a round metallic object just below the surface. Someone on the Italian side had evidently had the same idea in their retreat the previous year. Beyond this we found a vast stock of Italian ammonal which more than doubled our supply of high explosive. I resolved to use this in addition to our own in order to make my demolition the more effective. The sappers were summoned, the charges laid. The troops were sent a good distance away. But, out of sheer curiosity, I took refuge behind a rock somewhat closer but at what I judged to be a reasonably safe distance. I had miscalculated. When the charges went off with a satisfying roar, huge pieces of rock rose majestically, and surprisingly slowly, into the air and fell, somewhat more rapidly, around the rock behind which I had taken cover. Fortunately, but shamefacedly, I emerged unscathed. On this same occasion I had stopped to eat, and a piece of paper floated gently towards me in the desert breeze. I picked it up and read. It was written in Italian. It was a most moving and pathetic letter written by an Italian father to his embattled son.

The last episode, which nearly brought my career to a final conclusion, happened in this way. There had been a khamsin coupled with a sandstorm, which meant that my Bren guns were unlikely to work. Two I had dismantled and laid on groundsheets to be cleaned and reassembled. The remaining Bren, though probably useless, I placed on an anti-aircraft mounting to reassure the troops. This was just after the unfortunate officer had met his untimely end when seated on the loo. Behind the Bren I placed an air sentry with instructions that he be replaced at half-hourly intervals. I then went to carry out an individual task which had been set me by my company commander. Our friends in the Australian anti-tank unit had challenged us to a rifle-shooting competition, unaware, it would seem, that our best and most experienced men had, before they came to the Middle East, won almost every rifle-shooting competition in India. My duty was to lay out a makeshift rifle-range with empty beer-cans as targets, on which the match was to be carried out. This took some time, and when I got back to the platoon I found the air sentry on duty was one of a pair of identical twins who were serving with us. His name was Smith. No warning had been given, and the platoon was about its lawful occasions. But there was an ominous buzzing in the air. 'What's that?' said I to the sentry, calling him by his name. 'Aeroplanes, sir.' I looked up into the sky and there, in the eye of the sun, chasing one another like flies round a lamp, there were three Messerschmitt 110s. I was just in time. I yelled a warning which sent the platoon under cover, literally flung the air sentry behind a disused Italian sanga and took the gun myself. They came down on me in line ahead, and, as it passed, each plane treated me to a burst of cannon-fire which went off on the ground all around me like so many fire-crackers. I pulled the trigger, and of course nothing happened but a dull 'phut'. I was, and felt, the most obvious thing in the desert, but as the planes flew away I uttered a quiet prayer of relief and automatically recocked the gun. Unfortunately they came in again, and this time they machined-gunned me. The strike of the bullets kicked up the dust all around. Again I pulled the trigger. Again the gun said 'phut'. Unfortunately they then came in a third time, and this time I pulled the trigger twice. The first time the gun again said 'phut', and they dropped a series of anti-personnel bombs all round me in a circle of about thirty yards' diameter. I pulled the trigger a fourth time, at the retreating planes, and this time the Bren responded with a most satisfactory burst. But, of course, it missed, or at least did no visible harm. They were the only shots I fired at a human target in the war. I looked down for some reason and saw to my surprise that my right desert-boot was full of blood which was bursting from my knee. I was vaguely aware that at some stage of the encounter I had been on the ground, but which of the passes and which of the aircraft had inflicted this trivial injury I had no idea. Faces appeared from the slit trenches and the sangas. 'Does it hurt, sir?' said one, a newcomer named Rifleman Farquharson, solicitously. Truthfully, I replied: 'It does not.' Nevertheless, after making sure that no one else was hurt, I thought it wise to proceed to the Regimental Aid Post, which was miles away at battalion headquarters. There my wound was dressed and bandaged by the wise Dr Picton, our MO. I craved leave to remain at HQ for the brief period I judged it was necessary for the small hurt to heal, and was told firmly that regulations did not permit. I had to go back to the Advanced Dressing Station (about 140 miles away as I found out). The men at the ADS gave me a nice cup of tea and a clean bandage and sent me on to the Casualty Clearing Station at Mersa Matruh about 250 miles from where I was hit. I arrived there about three in the morning in the middle of an air raid. A truck was burning on the road, but the CCS, which was underground, was untouched. I was somewhat tired, and lay down on a camp-bed which turned out to be just outside the latrine. The latrine was overflowing. Later, when it was light, I transferred to a small ward where another officer was in occupation of one of the two beds. He looked like a plum pudding. He had blown himself up on one of Minis Jeffries's sticky bombs which he had been in process of demonstrating to the troops. 'Good God,' he said. 'My bloody MP.' 'Good God,' said I, or words to that effect. 'Not a f——g constituent.' We became, from that moment, fast friends. I was in the Casualty Clearing Station about five days. The surgical arrangements were spotless and first class. They told me one interesting thing which gave me pause to think. The missile, whatever it was, had made a minor groove at the precise point in my knee where the femur joins the tibia and fibula. 'Another millimetre up,' said they, 'or another millimetre down, and it would have had your leg off.' If that had happened, situated where I was, just south of Buq Buq, I should undoubtedly have died, as happened a little more than a year later to 'Peter' Baker, my junior clerk, when the same thing happened to him when he was walking along the front at Messina. From that moment onwards I have regarded myself as living on borrowed time. It had been a very narrow squeak. I later came to think that I owed God my life.

The medical arrangements and the food were as bad as the surgical arrangements were good. The Casualty Clearing Station, established and designed in the First World War to be about a thousand yards behind the front line, was entirely male-run. I will not recount the disgusting details, but my short stay there was probably the means of saving a number of lives. When I got back to the battalion about two months later I recounted what I had seen in the officers' mess. The arrangements were so bad that I thought it funny. The Colonel was not amused. He told me to write down what I had seen in the form of a letter. Prudently, I asked for a direct order, and he gave it. The letter reached HQ in Cairo where it became known as the 'black hole letter'. HQ responded immediately and with a complete remedy. In future the CCS was to be run by women, and a complement of female nursing sisters was supplied and saw to everything without need of further remedy. The CCS was as far back as it was, because it had to serve the needs of Tobruk, then besieged and evacuating their casualties by sea, as well as the Desert Force. The improvement came just in time to benefit the casualties from the break-out there. This was probably the most useful thing I have ever done, and it was not done by my own volition.

I was evacuated myself from the CCS by train for Alex after about five days, accompanied by an air-force casualty from Tobruk suffering from hideous burns. As we sat at a wayside station there came by an old Arab woman selling hard-boiled eggs and bread. Funny thing, I thought, that is the first female of the species I have seen since I left Mena. It was the end of May, or rather, I think, the beginning of June. Owing to the trivial nature of my hurt I was discharged almost at once and awarded fourteen days' convalescent leave, which I elected to take in Jerusalem. We crossed the canal at Kantara in an old prewar sleeping-car of the Compagnie Internationale des Wagon Lits with its somewhat primitive arrangements bearing the legend: 'Sous le lavabo se trouve une vase.' Unfortunately it was also infested rather badly with bed-bugs. On the platform on Jerusalem station I was tiresomely taken ill with sandfly fever. This is not a serious disease but it lays you out temporarily, and I was conveyed to hospital on a stretcher. They placed me next to an officer who turned out to be suffering from diphtheria, and this kept me in hospital during quarantine rather longer than would otherwise have been the case, and after that I spent another few days at Amdurski's Central Hotel in Ben Yahuda Street. After that I went back for a time to my unit, which by that time was on its way to the high desert, somewhere near the frontier wire and not far from Sheferzen. By then I was second-in-command of the Company and in charge of the rear link of the wireless.

The routine of life in the high desert was somewhat different from that on the coastal plain. At about three in the afternoon a dispatch rider (in a truck; motorcycles were not used in the desert) would arrive at wherever our day positions were, with a map reference – a different one every day. This was where we were to spend the night. It allowed us just enough time to get to the chosen spot, and the whole column, less one patrol, would form a close leaguer, rather like the Roman army on the march. The guns would be in the four corners, such hard-nosed vehicles as there were on the four sides, with the soft-skinned vehicles within. A brief social life then began in the centre. We were allowed two weak whiskies, diluted with the warm salt water, then the only drinking-water on issue, and then went to bed. Just before dawn we dispersed to our day positions. After some time in this life I lost my signet ring in a dawn raid by our 25-pounders which did not catch our enemies unawares. The Battalion then retired to rest at Gerawla, and that was the end of my desert career. A decree went forth from Caesar Augustus that if by the age of twenty-five one was not in command of a company one had to go out of the desert as undesertworthy, and I had to leave the Battalion. Although, as will be seen, I remained in the Middle East for more than a year after that, it was the effective end of my regimental soldiering which had been the only real purpose for which I had joined the Army in 1939.

TWENTY-FOUR

Cairo, August–November 1941

I HAD IN FACT another spell in hospital at about this time with a poisoned arm which I got from a wrestling match while bathing at Gerawla. But, effectively, I was posted to Cairo, then the headquarters of the British troops in Egypt, a formation subordinate to HQ MEF. We were in an office based high up in what had been the Semiramis Hotel. I once again achieved the rank of captain and the rating of General Staff Officer class 3. I shared a nice flat near the Bulak Bridge with a brother officer, 'Oscar' Norman of the Durham Light Infantry. We were looked after by an Egyptian servant, Abdullah, and life was as comfortable, even luxurious, as that in the desert had been rugged. Nevertheless, I was not happy. I felt I was *embusqué*, in a cushy job when others were risking their lives. People like me were referred to by the desert troops as chair-borne or, less politely, from what we wore at dinner, 'Gaberdine swine'. I was not with them very long, but after office hours met a number of friends on leave from the desert or whom I had met in the ship or in England. One was Randolph Churchill, who, about the time I was there, had become the editor of a popular newspaper for the troops. 'This, Quintin,' he said with a flourish, 'is the best newspaper in the world. It is composed entirely of scissors and paste.' So, indeed, it was. It consisted of extracts from the whole world's press, not excluding (though this caused unjustified criticism) that of the Axis Powers.

My work was concerned with communications. What led the powers that be to believe that I was particularly qualified to supervise the timetable of the troop-trains passing through Zagazig and elsewhere, I do not know. I can recall one abortive visit to reconnoitre what subsequently became the battlefield of Alamein – a fact which, with some prescience, I seem to have recorded in the diary which, from now on and for the first and only time in my life, I began to keep. It exists from about this time until just after my return to England more than a year later.

However, once again in my distress, my regimental friends came to my rescue. Earlier in that year Jumbo Wilson had conquered the Vichy French and, as GOC Ninth Army (as it was grandiloquently called), had established his headquarters in the summer resort of Brumana, just above Beirut. The political situation there was extremely complex and potentially dangerous, and he felt the need of a liaison officer who could have dealings with the Mission Spears (which was more or less the equivalent of an embassy if we could have had one), and with General Catroux (the French Resident General), who had joined de Gaulle and was operating from both Beirut and Damascus. Catroux commanded the Forces Françaises Libres and the Troupes Spéciales du Levant. There were also a number of British political officers, detested by the French and referred to as 'ces petits Lawrences', which they certainly were not. There were also a Yugoslav brigade, and a Greek brigade, a number of Australian troops, and various intelligence networks. If I was not to fight – and seemingly for the time being that was impossible – it was suggested to me that I might do a useful job there, and I thought I might. I remained in Cairo till the end of October, meeting Anthony Greenwood and Walter Monckton, who were on political missions from England, and Oliver Baldwin. I was already acquainted with each of them, but cemented or struck up friendship with them all.

One of the curious features of Cairo at this time was the enormous attendance in the English Cathedral at evening service every Sunday. I always went, usually in the company of Callum Renton, my former battalion commander but now a General. You had to be there at least half an hour in advance to get a seat, and there was a very large standing congregation of all ranks. The Cathedral was big, and when it was constructed under the auspices of old Bishop Gwynne it was treated as a sort of *folie de grandeur*. Now the old bishop's vision was fully justified and filled a great spiritual need, both for those on leave from the theatres of war and for those in residence in the capital. We were all far from home, and on these occasions all ranks worshipped together with an immense sense of purpose. The Cathedral is now no more, having been bombed by fanatics after the war in an outburst of anti-British and anti-Christian feeling. I have not seen its successor, but Gwynne's great church had already justified its existence.

TWENTY-FIVE

Lebanon, Palestine and Syria

I MOVED ON to my new post via Kantara, Jerusalem and Lydda, where Charles Mott Radcliffe, my predecessor and brother rifleman, handed over to me on Lydda airfield. I kept copious notes of the various briefing conversations I had with the various persons with whom I should have to deal. All are in my diary, but the bits I thought sensitive are almost indecipherable and, since the creation of Israel was wholly in the future and not yet dreamed of by any with whom I dealt, I doubt whether they are even of much historical interest. Nevertheless poor Lebanon is still much, and sadly, in the news, and the essential elements are still there. I think it therefore worthwhile to give some account of the year I spent working, based in Beirut and at Jumbo's HQ in Brumana, visiting the Mission Spears almost every day and General Catroux's HQ in the Grand Serail, and working the whole area between Latakia (Professor Evans-Pritchard the anthropologist being my contact there) and Aleppo, where I was entertained by the extremely civilized and pro-British Ernest Altounyan, a Rugbeian by education and an Armenian by race.

The Levant, from the borders of the Syrian desert to the Turkish border, including what was then Palestine, was once part of the province of Syria in the Roman Empire. But it had never been a single unit and, with the possible exception of Judaea before the days of Pompey, never self-governing. The Romans had it, then the Caliphs of Baghdad, then the Turks. After the First World War, Palestine was subject to a British mandate and Syria and the Lebanon to a French mandate from the League of Nations. The Turks had governed despotically but extremely erratically through the religious and ethnic heads of the various minorities, and it was Turkish policy to keep these minorities divided. When a particular minority gave trouble it was Turkish practice to execute and then replace the ethnic or religious leader. The almost universal language is standard Arabic. In Syria, the dominant religion is Muslim, but divided since immediately after the death of Muhammad into the mutually hostile Shi'ite and Sunni loyalties. Latakia is dominated by the Alawites, a heretical Muslim sect, the only one which does not consider it a sin to drink wine, and until recently ruled by the Old Man of the Mountains (Sheikh el Gibal).

In Lebanon and Palestine there is also the separate, esoteric and extremely warlike sect of the Druses, dominated by their feudal chiefs, the Jumblatts, and in my time the Atrash, who dwell both in the Lebanese hills and in what is now Israel.* They are not, as is sometimes thought, Muslims. Their day is Thursday, not Muslim Friday, and not the Jewish Saturday, nor the Christian Sunday. They derive from their founder, Hakim, who lived in Cairo, in, I believe, the tenth or eleventh century. Their true doctrines are kept secret from the main body of their congregations, rather like the Manichees in the days of St Augustine; and, though several books have been written about them, disclosure is said to be punishable by death. They are credited with venerating a number of 'prophets', twelve in number, of whom one is Iflatun, better-known in the West as Plato. They are said to speak an Arabic particularly pure and to treat their women better than – according to Western ideas – is common among Muslims. The men wear a distinctive type of turban-like head-dress with a red cap in the middle. There was a Druse village on the mountain ridge opposite to that on which Brumana is situated through which I passed during one or more of my travels.

The majority religion in Lebanon was Christian, of which I counted at least thirteen indigenous varieties, of various types. This

---

* The word 'assassin' comes from Latakia. The Old Man of the Mountains gave his military supporters a sort of Dutch courage in the shape of hashish, and the word is *hashashin*. Cannabis was grown habitually in Lebanon, and I suppose still is, but, since it was illegal, was usually concealed in a crop of maize or tomatoes, which were cultivated on the outside of the plots of hashish.

large number is partly due to the fact that, apart from Protestant imports, there are always two varieties of each type, one in communion with Rome and one not. But, although in theory in communion with Rome and therefore, also in theory, with one other, the various Uniate (that is, Roman) churches have different liturgies in different languages and quite different rites. Thus there was a Latin Christian congregation in Beirut, centred on the Jesuit University. The largest Uniate sect is Maronite with a Syriac mass, but Gospel and Epistle in classical Arabic, and the Roman chasuble. The village of Zahle in the Bekaa valley is Melkite (with a liturgy based on Greek rite). There is an Orthodox congregation corresponding to every Uniate group. There also Armenian Catholics twinned as it were with Monophysite Armenians, various American Protestant sects with local congregations, including Quakers, one of whose services (also in Arabic) I attended in Brumana itself. I have forgotten all the subdivisions, though at the time I made it my business to know the lot. There were Assyrian Christians (either Monophysite or Nestorian), persecuted across the border by Syrian Muslims but whose cause was enthusiastically espoused by Callum Renton. There was still one village whose language was Aramaic, as in the time of our Lord, and one more who worshipped the Devil under the emblem of the peacock, their argument being that, since God could be counted on to be good and therefore could be trusted to get on with it, the Devil was apt to be troublesome and therefore needed to be placated. The Lebanese are extremely cultivated, agreeable and civilized people with a strong commercial sense, and both Syrian and Lebanese had considerable expatriate communities in the United States and elsewhere who contributed generously towards counteracting the adverse balance of payments of the communities in Lebanon itself. There were numerous currency crises, generated by the different official exchange rates of the Syrian, Lebanese, Palestinian and Egyptian pounds, and each was accentuated, encouraged by vigorous black markets and supported by the vast amounts of trans-border traffic and cross-border trade. There is, of course, no obvious ethnic difference between Muslim Arabs in Jordan, Syria, Lebanon and what was then Palestine, and no language-barrier between them, since dialectal variations are trivial and at any rate completely unimportant in educated conversation in cultured standard Arabic, which differs from the classical tongue of the Koran certainly not as much as Latin from Italian.

Above this hotchpotch of ethnic and religious material stood the two European League of Nations mandatory powers. Both were different, often in bad temper with one another, and both had their bitter internal feuds. When Jumbo had sent the Vichy French packing in the previous spring, following the German attempt to capture the territory through Iraq, he gave their commanders, General Dentz and his supporters, the option of returning to the France of the Vichy regime, or of staying where they were and joining the Free French under General Catroux. Those who chose the second option were known as the 'nouveaux ralliés' and their loyalty was often doubted by the existing Free French, and often, too, by the British. Both the British and the French were bound by the terms of documents known as the Sykes–Picquot Agreement, but this did not prevent them from quarrelling in practice, and the higher their rank the more likely they seemed to quarrel, often over trivial matters. Charles Mott Radcliffe had warned me that, while Jumbo and Spears were reasonably friendly when together, they profoundly mistrusted one another when apart, and, once a week, he warned me, 'Spears would get a rush of blood to the head' and draft 'terrible signals', which, he said, it would be my duty to stop. He told me that 'Jumbo is a soldier and a damn good soldier at that, but does not pretend to understand the political aspect of affairs'. He was, of course, correct about Jumbo's military skills, but in my view underestimated his political intelligence.

After I had been there some time, I formed a totally different conclusion. Jumbo's pretence at not understanding the political aspects of affairs was purely a pretence. He understood them very well, and thought that the constant bickering between allies, and between the allies and the Lebanese and the Syrians, was interfering with military security and might present a serious danger if, as then seemed quite possible (this was before Stalingrad), the Germans secured some strategic advantage on the Russian front and Hitler sought to break through Turkey in an attempt to conquer our Middle Eastern forces. Rightly, in my opinion, Jumbo believed that the French (of both factions) and Spears were foolishly preoccupied by securing advantages for their respective countries after the war in circumstances which at that time neither could predict, and were ignoring the immediate future instead of leaving the more distant scene to look after itself. This, from the first, was my own view. I saw my function as, first, to secure Jumbo's confidence as a loyal subordinate (no man can serve two masters) and, second, to secure co-operation in everything possible to keep the peace generally as far as possible between all concerned. I believe I achieved these objectives. During the nine months Jumbo and I were working together, and despite numerous and often ridiculous alarms and excursions, we kept this extraordinary mélange of differing personalities on a relatively even keel.

But, in the summer of the following year, Jumbo went to PAI Force ('Persia and Iraq') and was succeeded by General Holmes. Not very long after that, an explosion took place in which there was a Lebanese insurrection which the French attempted to put down by force but were prevented, equally by force, by the British, and this had long-lasting results. It is clear from his memoirs that de Gaulle's opposition to our entry into the Common Market had a great deal to do with what happened then. On that occasion de Gaulle (by that time back in a liberated Paris) records in connection with this relatively small matter: 'I sent for the British ambassador [by that time Duff Cooper]. I made him sit down. I said to him: "Vous avez outragé la France, et trahi l'Occident. Cela ne peut être oublié."' It was not forgotten, with consequences which have not yet quite disappeared, though, of course, they cannot by any means be attributed to that single cause. At that time, however, if Spears, Winston and the French could have foreseen the present situation in the Middle East and the Levant, I believe much ill feeling would have been avoided. Jumbo, to whom very unfair references are made in Spears's reminiscences, had at least the wit to appreciate that, given the unpredictability of the future, it was obviously necessary to co-operate in the immediate present.

As was absolutely necessary, I maintained good relations with Spears, and with Mary Borden, his first wife, who were extremely kind to me both before and after I fell ill (Spears entertained me for three weeks in his house after I had left hospital and before I returned to duty), and after the war we remained friends to the very end.

One curious, irrelevant, and wholly disagreeable duty fell upon me during my stay in Brumana. It happened to be the case that I was the only legally qualified officer of standing east of the Suez Canal who was not already employed either in the Provost Marshal's Department or as Judge Advocate. The result was that I was constantly being asked to act as prisoner's friend in courts martial, in defence of either young officers or other ranks. I tried to avoid this duty. I was quite unused to King's Regulations and had never qualified in the Manual of Military Law. There were no law-books available. It was almost impossible to do the necessary solicitor's work in interviewing and taking statements from witnesses, and the actual time and place of hearing interfered a good deal with my liaison duties. But Shan Hackett, since a life-long friend, and then a major in the operations directorate at General Army HQ persuaded me that it was every officer's duty to perform this service for a comrade in distress. Some of the cases were rather bizarre, even if I did not do them particularly well. I successfully obtained an acquittal from a charge of stealing government tyres in or near the Street called Strait in Damascus, and of the soldier servant of the present Lord Gowrie's father on a charge of disobeying an order from an ordinance colonel and of burying some of his equipment under the sand of his tent. Most of the cases, however, were exceedingly unpleasant and often concerned charges of attempted homosexual acts. If convicted, as all those whom I defended for this offence in fact were, a period of imprisonment and reduction to the ranks was the unavoidable result. In one case I doubted the guilt of my client, and his attempts to clear his name when he came out of prison followed me for a long time after I had left the Army until he was killed in Europe in the last months of the war. The only benefit I obtained from this disagreeable duty was that, from the quite admirable Armenian consultant in psychiatry whom I was able to call and consult as a witness, I obtained a good deal of knowledge of the scientific aspects of this disagreeable subject.

By the summer of 1942 I was promoted major. Field rank gave me considerable advantage in my liaison and intelligence duties. I had thought a good deal on political questions during my Lebanese tour. I had sent a telegram of confidence personally to Winston on the occasion of the absurd debate on the misguided motion of Wardlaw Milne on the Central Conduct of the War following the fall of Tobruk and I had had a brief but friendly correspondence with Brendan Bracken who was by then Minister of Information and whom I knew slightly, both on my own account and because he had been a friend of my brother Edward while he was MP for Eastbourne. Natalie was looking after my constituency correspondence. In October 1941 she had wired: 'Remember 12th November our wedding day. No regrets. Natalie.' Though I was a little concerned by her sparse and erratic correspondence, I put this down largely to the vagaries of the post, which, apart from telegrams and microfilms, took about three months to arrive. I had no notion that things were going seriously wrong at home, and wrote to her regularly, usually by the microfilm service.

I see from my diary that I had a letter from Dingle Foot urging me to come home, dated 23 March, which did not reach me till 29 July, a day on which Hugh Garmoyle died of wounds and got a posthumous bar to his DSO; Shan Hackett his first DSO, which made him, at the age of thirty-four, DSO, MC, MBE, DPhil (Oxon), the last for his thesis on Crusader castles when on Service in Palestine before the war. Callum Renton also got a bar to his DSO. It all made me feel very small in my safe position at Brumana.*

---

*An odd thing happened when I was Lord Chancellor forty-three years later. I received a letter from Julie Hajjar, then head girl of Brumana High School when Lebanon was in the throes of civil war. 'We all remember you at Brumana', she wrote, 'as Captain Quentin [sic] Hogg. Will you write a piece for our school magazine?' I did so smartly, and the piece duly appeared. I was much moved.

TWENTY-SIX

Travels with a Donkey

A DAY OR SO AFTER Hugh Garmoyle's death, I was told that I was
due for fourteen days' leave, and was offered a place in the Officers'
Holiday Camp at Sarafand in Palestine. The prospect did not attract
me. The next suggestion was that I might go to Cyprus. But there was
the problem of transport, the absence of guide-books, the not
negligible cost, and my inability at that time, despite my acquaintance with the ancient language, to speak a word of modern Greek.
Instead, I invented a plan of my own. I had been longing for a
mountain holiday, which I had not enjoyed since the Hitler–Stalin
pact. I would go for a walking tour in the Lebanese mountains. There
were those who said I would be murdered. I did not believe them,
though, of course, I went in uniform and, in the ordinary course,
carried my useless .38 revolver. Maps were hard to come by, inaccurate, rather small scale, and in French. They told me I would have to
sleep out, which in the event I did not have to do, but I took a
rucksack and some bedding. I knew that somewhere about opposite
Jebail (Byblos) on the coast was the ancient shrine of Venus (Aphro-
dite, Astarte) and her lover Adonis (Adonai, Tammuz) where a wild
boar was sent by the King of the Gods to murder the mortal Tammuz
for sleeping with a goddess, and from whom Venus procured an
annual respite from death in the early months of the year when the
spring in the mountain-side runs red with his blood. In ancient times
the shrine was a great place of pilgrimage from the coast by the young
men and maidens along a sacred track from Byblos. It was not clearly
marked on my maps, but in ancient times it was known as Aphaca,
and modern Lebanese, having dropped the letter Koph ('Q'), now

pronounced it Af'a. I decided to try to find the place, which I was told was obvious and well known as part of a tour. About as far away again as Aphaca is from Brumana, but approximately on the same compass bearing, was one of the two small remaining patches of the ancient Cedars of Lebanon, from which Hiram, King of Tyre, had built his ships and Solomon, King of Israel, his Temple. Above the ancient cedars was the Col des Cèdres, clearly marked and rising to 10,000 feet with streaks of snow even in August, and even in the hottest summer. It marked the watershed of the Lebanon range, and on the other side was the Bekaa valley, which I though I knew well from my frequent visits to Aleppo via Baalbek (where I used to eat my sandwiches, and study the ruins and inscriptions, mostly in Latin, of the three temples on my way through Homs and Hama), and so home to Brumana via Zahle and a pass with more Roman remains to visit. I calculated the outward journey was about 200 kilometres, and perhaps a few less on the flatter route back along the bottom of the Bekaa valley, and that I should be able to make the journey with a day or two to spare. I acquired the services of a Christian Arab and, by great fortune, the Quartermaster told me that he could lend me a donkey named George, who had been entrusted to his care by an English lady who had left the country. The Quartermaster did not tell me that the donkey was not shod or broken in, but had been kept as a pet, and, though at four years old fully mature, as he fully demonstrated later, had never done any work at all. I learned the first point when I was telephoned by an Arab a day or two before my departure who enquired (*a*) whether I wished him to have shoes and (*b*) whether I wished him to have shoes 'on his hands or his feet'. I replied that I did wish him to have shoes and that I wished him to have shoes on his hands and his feet. The only other intelligence I received was from a brother officer, who assured me that at Beskinta, on my planned route, there dwelt a seer who spoke perfect English and whom I would find the wisest and most remarkable man 'since Jesus Christ'.

On the appointed day, George duly appeared, duly shod both on his hands and his feet, and accompanied by my Arab companion. We set forth on foot. George was laden, fairly lightly, with my bedding, my rucksack and my Arab's few necessities. There followed one of the most charming holidays of my life. The first day's walk was easy, terminating at an expensive gin-palace at the mountain summer resort of Deir esh Choueir, where the proprietor were glad enough to receive me as a guest. The next day's stop was at Beskinta where the seer dwelt and had been alerted to my arrival. He was certainly well informed and spoke good English, though his other qualities were not quite as distinguished as advertised. I stayed as a guest at a private house. The following day I climbed the Sannin (about 6,000 feet and highly visible from the bay of Beirut) but without George and the Arab. Our way on the next day would lead us, via the Shrine of Venus, to Mayrouba which I should reach on a Sunday.

At this stage, I should explain the nature of the country through which I should pass. My way out lay along a series of mule-tracks and footpaths just below the crest of the ridge on the seaward, and broadly Christian, side of the Lebanon range. It is utterly delightful, well watered, with many mountain inhabitants, little monasteries situated on hill-tops, plenty of trees, mostly Mediterranean pines inhabited by cicada, but with at least one patch of recently planted Lebanon cedars. With one important qualification, it reminded me enormously of what I imagined Switzerland must have been like in the eighteenth century before the arrival of the English tourists and, of course, without glaciers or snowfields. But the qualification is important. The structure of the mountain is utterly different. The crest of the range is easily passable by the tracks, but the lower slopes of the wadis or side-valleys are uninhabitable. For instance, the valley separating Brumana from the Druse village on the landward side was steep, full of thorn bushes, and inhabited by what I suppose were jackals which made howling noises at night and sprang from the bushes at one's approach. The mule-tracks and paths were well frequented with trains of donkeys, mules and the occasional horse, heavily laden with merchandise, jingling with bells on their harness and accompanied with cheerful, and by no means silent, muleteers. When one approached one of these trains, there was a halt. How are you? What is your religion? What is your age? How old is your donkey? How much did he cost? How many children have you? The

Lebanese jackass is a huge animal about the size of a pony, and George was a minute animal, the size of a child's mount by the seaside, so that my disclosure that he was four years old provoked some incredulity until he showed his virility by some unmistakable advances towards the questioners' mounts.

Between Beskinta and the Shrine of Adonis the Sacred Way was blocked by a landslide which must have taken place a hundred years or so before my journey. I spent a painful hour picking my way across a mass of sharp and disagreeable boulders. But, this obstacle overcome, the shrine itself was peaceful and unmistakable. Out of the mountain, through the mouth of a cave, gushed a river. Not a stream, a river. Below the fall a pool, below the pool a little ancient bridge over which the path went. It was not a difficult thing to see here the entrance to the womb of the Earth Goddess. To the right of the cave there was a stream in the summer little better than a trickle. In the spring it must be – it still, I hope, must be – fuller, and in February or thereabouts it must run red with the colours of the soil or, if you prefer, the blood of Adonis or Tammuz. To the right of the stream, if you face the mountain-wall, there were the remains of a small temple. It gave you an uncanny feeling since, whilst most ruined temples stand open to the sky, this one had fallen in on itself. It was as if there lurked a Presence inside. Out of the ruins grew a large fig tree, and from the branches of the fig tree, believe it or not, in the year of Our Lord 1942, there hung long pieces of string, and at the end of each strand was tied a piece of what appeared to be rag. They were evidently votive offerings. In a grotto which formed out of the ruins I found an icon of the Blessed Virgin and her Child. I am told that, had I proceeded into the cave, I would have found graffiti or drawings of the pagan worshippers of Venus (or Astarte, or whoever). But with my equipment this would have involved a short pitch of climbing, with a short rock traverse to the left, which I judged Grade 3 and did not attempt. I took off my clothes and briefly bathed naked in the ice-cold pool. Reclothed, I ate my sandwiches and drank from the Adonis stream. From the hills appeared shepherds (in appearance not at all like Adonis) and we shared our meals. We spoke in a mixture of kitchen Arabic and French.

'What is this place?' I asked.

'It is a church of the Blessed Virgin Mary,' said they.

'And what,' said I pointing at the fig tree and its offerings, 'is this?'

They pointed at the Adonis spring and stream. They said: 'This water brings fertility to a barren woman. We bottle this water and we send it to London, to Paris, to New York. And when the baby comes the mother sends its first clothes to us, and we hang the piece on the tree.'

Time was passing, and with mutual salutations the Arab, George and I went on our way across the bridge towards Mayrouba. The opposite side of the valley was in sunshine, and as warm, as easy-going and as fertile as our way to Aphaca had been boulder-strewn and forbidding. Fruit trees laden with plums and other fruit lined our path, and little terraces with houses began to appear. At one of the first a woman leaned over the terrace, and to my surprise offered me a single apple. I took it, and she invited me up. From her eminence above my head she appeared to be of preternatural size and beauty, and her lips and cheeks of purple colour. I accepted her invitation and mounted the steps to greet her. Alas, no. It is not as you think. Almost immediately there appeared a Maronite priest, and all three of us indulged in friendly conversation for a while. He had a good command of English, but we parted on relatively cool terms since, learning that in civilian life I was by profession a lawyer, he made an unseemly pun on lawyers and liars, and I an even more offensive joke in Arabic about Khouris (priests) and houris. Thereafter to Mayrouba and a friendly little inn, and mass on the Sunday at the Maronite church.

The following day we moved on to our next stop, a monastery at a place called Tannourin, where we were most hospitably entertained by the monks, and so on to the cedars themselves where we put up at a cottage. On our way to Tannourin I saw for the first time a large crop of cannabis concealed in a covering crop of either tomatoes or maize. When I told the monks about this they were not in the least shocked, but said it was no worse than smoking tobacco. They did not mention wine, which they produced themselves, a dark brown, sweet and rather cloudy liquid which, since they said they used it for their mass, must have been made from grapes. Otherwise I might well have mistaken it for something like a rather sweet cider.

The patch of surviving cedars was even smaller in area than I had been led to believe. But the trees were even more magnificent than I had imagined, and deliciously aromatic, a fragrance almost unbelievable. As I lay with my eyes closed in the midst of this tiny group of venerable monsters, the sole survivors of the once world-famous forests, and heard the soughing of the wind in their huge branches, I realized that nowhere in the Middle East had I heard this marvellous forest sound, and was filled with romantic thoughts about Solomon and Hiram, Ophir and the Temple with its seven-branched candlestick still to be seen in effigy on Trajan's arch when it was brought back in triumph to Rome.

After passing over the Col des Cèdres we walked across the floor of the Bekaa valley. This was the greatest possible contrast to the main range, relatively flat and broken into side-valleys running parallel to the mountains. Baalbek was out of reach on the other side of the valley beneath the Anti-Lebanon range. I knew it well from my journeys to Aleppo and other places, with its three magnificent temples of Graeco-Roman date: the vast temple to Baal, or Zeus Helios, the lord of the valley; the second, to Dionysus, much smaller, but with its peristyle standing, in which paradoxically you can still see lines of Stars of David clearly embossed. I was told that this was put because it was built by Hebrew slaves. I did not believe this, as they would have regarded it as blasphemous to place the holy symbol on a pagan shrine; I prefer to think it was, throughout the province of Syria, a symbol of the divine. The third temple, dedicated allegedly to Venus (Astarte), one could not enter. I was told that the Bacchantes, from the temple of Dionysus, used to take male pilgrims to this temple of Venus, for the purpose of prostitution after plying them liberally with wine from the cellars under the temple of Bacchus, though I know of no evidence to support this exotic legend. The temple of Baal itself is far larger than the Temple site in Jerusalem. But nothing remains save a number of pediments, which presumably supported statues inscribed with inscriptions often in Latin. It was built with vast blocks of a size much larger than even those which can still be seen on the Wailing Wall of Herod's Temple. One of these can be seen still in the quarry on the Anti-Lebanon from which it was hewn and in which it was shaped. The labour which must have been involved in moving them into the valley and placing them in position in the Hadrianic temple at the foot of the valley must have been past description.

At the other side of the valley where I now was, were much smaller Roman remains at a place called Yammouneh, with multiple springs gushing perennially from the mountains and an abundance of edible fish, always a rarity in the Middle East. I spent a happy hour in the ruins and went on. It was after this that my sketchy plans began to go badly wrong. Either from a faulty reading of the rough maps I had brought or because I misjudged the distance, I completely lost the way. The country was bare, but the track lay down a side-valley. The inhabitants were few, and the children (probably Muslim) ran away howling at the sight of my uniform. Some of them must have been Christian (Muslims not drinking wine), as there were from time to time extensive vineyards of white grapes. The grapes were ripe, and I exercised my traveller's privilege of plucking and eating them to slake a raging thirst. I noted watch-towers, like those mentioned in the Bible, to enable guards to protect the crops from depredation. The road went on and on. I was desperately weary, as was my Arab companion. We were hopelessly astray, and long after dark were constrained to knock up the muktar of a Muslim village who entertained us royally at his own house. As dishes were prepared there were numerous twitterings and chirpings from behind the curtain of the harem, but we were not permitted to view the female occupants of this humble dwelling. Being inordinately thirsty, and since there was nothing else, I drank copiously of the water provided, and, though I noticed nothing at the time, I have no doubt that therein was my undoing. Unknown to myself or to my respectable and friendly host, I had infected myself with the virus of hepatitis B. We were shown off in the morning and pointed in the direction of Zahle, our true destination, the penultimate stop on our planned tour, a lovely little Christian resort of Catholic Greek (Melkite) persuasion where we spent another blissful night in a tourist hotel. I had one more set of ruins to visit (as I ultimately did) on my way back to Brumana. Unhappily, in a narrow path, flanked by stone walls, George struck work. Like Balaam in biblical history, I was displeased, and so was my Arab guide, who swore fluently at him with the words 'Yuqsuf umrak', which I understand to mean 'May He [Allah, for Allah is the God of both Christian and Arab] cut off your life'. Terrified by this imprecation, and with more physical inducement, George was persuaded to go a little further, but then decided to lie down in the middle of a camp of Free French African soldiers, and neither curses nor tail-twistings nor buckets of water would induce him to go another inch. The French Africans gathered in amusement. 'Take me to your leader,' I said in effect. Luckily the commanding officer had a telephone, and I was able to telephone Brumana, which generously sent me a truck and removed George in great luxury in the back, together with my Arab friend, and my bedding, but not my rucksack. I thanked my Arab friend suitably as arranged, and, carrying my sack, finished my projected journey on foot, arriving the next day. But for the virus, unsuspected, which was reproducing itself quietly in my inward parts, my fourteen days' leave had been a great and enjoyable success.

TWENTY-SEVEN

The End of the Affair

THOUGH, AS MY DIARY SHOWS, I had no inkling of the fact at the time, the end of my affair with the Middle East was virtually at hand. I do not believe that I had advanced the course of the war by a hair's breadth. I had been able to comfort the widowed mother of a close friend made in *Britannic* since I had found out by research (which nearly got me into serious trouble with the authorities) that the official report 'missing believed killed' was in fact false and that, as turned out to be the case, he was almost certainly alive and a prisoner of war. My co-operation with Jumbo had probably saved a great deal of trouble by checking, and to some extent smoothing out, the constant bickering between the British and the Free French; and, had it lasted, might have prevented more trouble still. Above all, it had been an unforgettable interlude in a political and legal life. I had made some lifelong friends. What was more important when my health broke down, as it now did, was that my military service and the rather narrow squeak I had had during my encounter with the Messerschmitts enabled me, without self-reproach, to resume my duties in the House of Commons. My diary shows that I had returned from my travels with a donkey on 16 August, and the last entry before I began them was on 29 July. It also shows that for a week or two I spent a very busy time with a good deal of socializing of a distinguished kind. It was during this period that I believe General Holmes took over Jumbo's command, and moved his HQ from Brumana to Alex. De Gaulle came on a visit, and I met him with the Spears more than once. Between them they made a proper mess of things of which I was not fully aware at the time, in spite of my presence at a number of high-level meetings, social and otherwise. But by this time the hepatitis virus had decided it was time to take over my life. On the morning of 10 September, when the soldier servant came to wake me, I was unable to get up, and he had me moved at once to the New Zealand military hospital which served the HQ. They diagnosed me there as suffering from malaria. Happily jaundice has symptoms which even the most stupid medical adviser cannot mistake, and I was able to correct the record fairly soon. If I had been asked how long I remained there, I would have said 'about three weeks', but my diary shows conclusively that I was not discharged until 27 October with another fourteen days' sick-leave to follow. But I had kept my diary from about 26 September. I had lost over two and half stone in about a fortnight, and my blood count was still over normal. Owing to physical peculiarities in my veins it can only be taken away in sufficient quantities at the cost of considerable pain and severe bruising. My left arm, which was the site of the necessary punctures, showed an extraordinary appearance of bruising and subcutaneous bleeding.

Jaundice is a horrible disease. In my case, the symptoms were that, though I absorbed quantities of liquid, I would not eat any solids at all. So they tried to tempt me with all the most enticing food they could imagine. It was nearly always chicken, and I always rejected it. They became extremely alarmed. At length a clever New Zealand nurse realized that the clue to my character was not appetite so much as insatiable curiosity. One day she came into the ward with a warm smile, and said that she had just had a parcel from home which contained a tinned sample of a green oyster soup, the colour of green peas, which she thought I might like to try. She gave me the name. It was called Tehoaroa soup. Knowing that oysters do not have the colour of green peas, my curiosity began to stir. 'What does it taste like?' I asked. 'Oysters,' said she, and I accepted the gift. From that day on I began to mend. The characteristic of jaundice is such that when you begin to eat you go on eating. The clever nurse had in fact effected a cure. I did not fully realize at the time that, so very far from home, and with as few delicacies as we all had in those days, she had sacrificed one of the rarest and most prized delicacies in New

Zealand for the sake of a totally unknown British officer whose permanent health she thought to be in danger. I thanked her, of course, but not warmly enough. The story has a happy sequel. I have twice only since tasted Tehoaroa soup, the first when I was a special guest at the Reuter centenary dinner in London, the second when I was visiting New Zealand itself as Lord Chancellor in connection with a conference. In between these two times, the rarity and excellence of the soup had been explained to me, and, lo and behold, the clever nurse, reading my name in the New Zealand papers in some context or other, wrote to me and asked if I recalled the incident. I was able to write back and tell her that not only did I recall it after twenty years, but I also wished to apologize for not having thanked her enough, since, in my estimation, she had saved my life.

After I had begun to improve, I was also able to apologize to the young Armenian woman who used to sweep under my bed every morning. One of the characteristics of jaundice is that you hate the whole human race, and every morning I had been excessively rude. I apologized profusely, and we became fast friends. She taught me her greetings in Armenian. One sounded like 'Inspissik' and one like 'Hunky Stick'. One means 'Good morning' and one 'How are you?' I cannot remember which, but many years later I tried them out with surprising effect at an Armenian dinner in London to which as Lord Chancellor I had been invited.

It was a long time before I was able to get out of hospital, but I escaped at the end of October to convalescent leave. It was the fifth time I had been in military hospital in two years. This time it was with two provisos. The first was that I must stay on the water-wagon for six months. I adhered to this prohibition religiously, and could not help noticing throughout my period of abstinence how tiddly all my friends seemed to be getting at the parties to which I was asked. Mysteriously, this impression seemed to wear off the moment I started drinking again. The more serious condition was that my medical grading, previously AI, was how permanently altered to A2 which, I was told, meant that I could no longer hope to serve in an active theatre of war. I determined to come home and resume my duties as Member of Parliament for Oxford. I applied to be sent home. My last days in hospital, amongst poems and records of my blood count, were filled with speculations about the postwar settlement, including a more or less accurate forecast of the Nuremberg trials in preference either to clemency or instant execution (which was Winston's original idea). In one passage in my diary, clearly written from hospital, I was speculating about the House of Commons prior to the publication of the Beveridge Report which came out a little later. But about this time I wrote:

> What I should like to see is an inter-party committee of young MPs who would produce not a non-controversial programme nor a programme which any of them regarded as adequate, but a minimum programme on which they could all agree, sufficient to satisfy all doubts that, whatever party held power after the war, certain measures of social justice would be regarded as secure, and I should like to see this committee begin its work with a declaration of the rights of modern man on the lines of the Declaration of Independence. I have always been against legislating human rights as such as being contrary to the British tradition of law giving, but their enunciation in an informal document as the objects to be attained by formal legislation can, I think, do nothing but good.

It is clear that these passages were written in hospital during my slow period of recovery and before I was discharged. But they show, I think, that my serious illness had not been intellectually wasted. I had been thinking constructively on real problems. My thoughts were clearly turning back towards home and political responsibilities, and I had correctly forecast the Nuremberg legal process, the Universal Declaration of Human Rights and, on the Home Front, disregarding the non-partisan membership envisaged, the formation of the Tory Reform Committee which was, on my return, to be the main focus of my activities in the Commons before I joined the Government as Under-Secretary for Air early in 1945.

As is clear from my diary, the desert battle of Alamein had begun before I left hospital and the decisive breakthrough had evidently taken place soon after I was out and about again. There was clearly a brief time when I was back at HQ, now at Alex, even before my convalescent leave had expired, since by 8 November I was writing that I was thinking that at last the tide, which led to victory in the end, had turned, since our pursuit had now reached Mersa Matruh. My diagnosis that, with Stalingrad, these two victories were the hinge of the war was not, however, universally shared.

A fortnight later I was clearly back in Cairo with nothing to do except make contact with all my own friends in the Second Battalion including my old company commander from Mena days, Douglas Darling, now even more heavily decorated. I also met with Shan Hackett, now in Middle East Headquarters. Both spoke to me of the desert battle. Both spoke a little critically of Monty, of whom I was already an admirer. I asked Douglas whether Monty would improve. He said: 'I doubt it.' Both Shan and Douglas approved of Lumsden, whom Monty had dismissed, and thought critically of Oliver Leese who was my adjutant in the Corps in Eton. I also met Harry Leon, for whom I formerly devilled at the Bar, now Adjutant of the Queen's Regiment (on leave), Robin Turton (MP for Thirsk and Malton, with whom I talked politics) and my cousin Elizabeth Gwynne (later famous for her cookery-books as Elizabeth David) to whom I confided some anxieties I was developing about my marriage to Natalie. I also met John Witt, an old Eton friend, and Godfrey Morley (later President of the Law Society during my first term as Lord Chancellor, and at this time a major in my own regiment).

This, and my relatively few remaining days in the Middle East, convinced me that, if I had worked with an eye more to the main chance during the previous two years, I might have achieved more for the war effort. I remain convinced that this would not have been an honourable course. My purpose in joining the Army in 1939 had been to fight in a cruel war for which, in good conscience, I had felt it my duty to vote in the House of Commons.

In Cairo I was told that I would have to travel to New York by ship. The next day I was told that the ship was full. I was next told that there was room in a Liberator which would fly over enemy territory but there were some – I was not told what – political objections. By 3

December I was given a bit of good news: there was room in a
Liberator if I limited my baggage to 40 pounds. This was not an easy
matter as I was told I was to bring as much as possible. I could wear an
overcoat and scarf, and must carry a tin hat and gas-mask. I discarded
all solid suitcases and packed all in rucksacks. I would wear my better
service dress, pack one battledress and all nightwear and underwear
where possible. Then I remembered presents, which I would be
expected to bring. A panic visit followed to do some shopping. I
bought lengths of silk for a friend's fiancée and for my step-sister and
others, an amethyst brooch for my wife, and a spare scarab brooch for
emergencies. I then went in to weigh in, 90 kilos including my body,
8 pounds overweight in all. I decided to risk it. It was already 3
December and then the plane was delayed. At the last moment I was
told that our little complement was to contain two distinguished
Nazi officers, a major and a lieutenant who had been shot down on a
reconnaissance mission over the desert somewhere to the south, with
their escort. I tried to pick them out in the conveyance going to take
us all to the airport. I identified them at once: a tough-looking
individual disguised as a civilian but unmistakably carrying a cruel
Nazi face. He was in fact a distinguished neutral soldier. I identified
the lieutenant – a despicable type, I thought. He turned out to be a
government servant. At the airfield we met two distinguished-
looking specimens of young manhood wearing tropical kit, looking a
bit cold from unsuitable tropical uniform, but seemingly in excellent
good humour, presumably because they were going home. They
smile and bow and shake hands with the British officers in army
uniform other than myself. Both are wearing Iron Crosses, and the
British officers were their escort. The rest of us are a somewhat
ill-assorted collection. One, a group captain in the Air Force, I had
last met as an official in the Conservative Central Office. He had
helped me in the Oxford by-election. It is a small world. We were fed
on eggs, bacon, sausage, tea, brown sugar, milk, bread, butter and fig
jam, and introduced to our pilot, a Norwegian. The operation was
then postponed for a further twenty-four hours. We could get no
accommodation at Mena House, Shepherd's, the Continental, the
Carlton, the Metropolitan or the National. We spent an unpleasant

night together in a single small room in a transit-camp at Abbassiya. I
gave the bed to one of the escorts, and slept with the Germans, the
group captain and the civilians on an army 'biscuit' and under a
blanket. My baggage had already gone by sea, and in consequence did
not turn up in Britain for some time. The flight was postponed again
the next day, 5 December, when we again received a new addition to
our little company, a live guinea-pig in a little box with holes,
addressed to the 'Director of Pathology'. Fortunately, it was immediately removed, and we never saw it again. We got off, I think,
the following day. With their escorts, the German prisoners had the
best places, in passenger-seats, to prevent sabotage. With misgivings
that someone might play a practical joke, the rest of us lay on mat-
tresses in the bomb-bay. We flew due west over the Mediterranean
and put down in Gibraltar at the end of a tiring journey. I stayed
in the convent, with the Governor, Casey, and General Lumsden
who was in high dudgeon following his dismissal by Monty. We were
entertained by the Governor until we could take off from the newly
constructed landing-ground (still Gibraltar airport and still allegedly
on neutral territory). When we did leave we were overloaded and the
take-off was somewhat dicey. It was the same runway from which
General Sikorski and Victor Cazalet took off on their fateful journey
a little later. To balance the aircraft I was made to kneel uncomfort-
ably in an attitude of prayer among the suitcases in the nose of the
plane under the German prisoners. We made British landfall at
about 1.30 p.m. on Saturday, 12 December 1942, and I remember
noting, from the living-quarters of the Liberator, with an emotion
with which, in time past returning from abroad, Englishmen greeted
the white cliffs of Dover, the wonderful criss-cross patchworks of
English fields and the afternoon sunlight on the winter water. But I
had no time for sentimentality. We ran into turbulence on our way
down and before we landed were shaken about like corks in a rough
sea. We landed at Lynham and returned in a blacked-out train to
Paddington quite late in the evening. I had a large cargo of letters
from friends in Cairo to their loved ones, which I got by Customs and
censors without difficulty, having been instructed to leave the flaps of
the envelopes ungummed to enable them to be read if need be. They

passed on the nod.* After two years abroad my Middle Eastern adventure and, effectively, my military career were both at an end. Though I did not know it, it was also the end of my marriage to Natalie.

---

*I still remember that one officer, now a distinguished member of the House of Lords, on being told of this requirement, withdrew his letter, on the grounds that I wanted to read it.

TWENTY-EIGHT

A Soldier's Homecoming

IN THE NATURE OF THINGS, I had had no opportunity of telling anyone the date of my return, though my family knew, I believe, of my illness and of the general nature of my intentions. I arrived in London late on the Saturday night in the blackout, dishevelled, tired after ten days' travel, twenty-three hours of which had been in the air, and still broken in health. Throughout all my travels, on the voyage out, in the desert, on night patrol, in Cairo, in Lebanon and in Syria, as a sort of talisman I had kept the key of my front door at 1 Victoria Square, and, after stumbling up the steps in the dark, I put the key in the lock, and with a lump in my throat opened my own front door. I had no thought but to give Natalie a pleasant surprise, and the tiny gifts I had bought her. A startled voice from upstairs called out: 'Who's there?' I called out who it was, and went up to greet her. She was not alone. Fortunately, the full significance of what I found was not immediately apparent to me. I was introduced to a young French officer who – tactfully, I thought – made his apologies and left. Natalie gave me to understand that she was going to leave me, and I begged her not to. But the next morning she did and took the first instalment of her belongings. She appeared shortly for a brief period a few days later. I begged her to stay and give it a chance. But she persisted. She had taken a flat in Crawford Street, and she removed the bed, most of the bedclothes, some of the furniture. She told me she had sent all my civilian clothes for storage in the country. I was alone in London and alone in the house at the end of 1942, without ration-card, identity-card, clothes-points, much underwear, transport or immediate friends. The words I wrote in my diary some days later were: 'The kind of welcome I got when I came in had better not be described here.' My life was in ruins. But somehow I had to pick myself up and dust my trousers. Happily my father was in London, slightly better than I expected, and so, to my delight, was Neil, fairly recently arrived from his post at the embassy at Baghdad and, in addition to his work at the Foreign Office, currently serving several nights a week in a rocket battery in Hyde Park. I visited the Speaker, had an appointment to see Winston, made arrangements to get a ration-card and points for clothes, found how to get my clothes transported home from store. Friends to whom I confided my plight were incredibly kind. Winston, to whom I did not tell of my troubles, told me that he thought I was justified in resuming my parliamentary duties and that no one 'should presume to say', after two years' foreign service and a wound, that I was 'trying to shirk'. These words put more heart into me than anything else. But there was also a crisis in my constituency between my chairman, Lady Townsend, and the temporary agent, which I was able to patch up.

I must, however, take one matter out of its strict chronological order. I realized that I must come to some terms with the future of my personal life. During the whole of my absence and before, I had been physically faithful to Natalie. From the confidences of my friends I gather that in this respect I was the exception rather than the rule. One, I remember, a staunch Roman Catholic, with a wife and two children, told me of his frequent visits to a brothel in Cairo at £2 a time, and said, rather bitterly, 'and I hate every moment of it'. I do not think that my own abstention from this doubtful pleasure was due to any particular virtue on my part. I am fastidious, both as to what I eat and how I eat it, and in some other matters, rather than chaste. There were in fact a few attractive and respectable women in the Lebanon and in Syria with whom I had innocent friendships, some of which have endured ever since. But they were otherwise engaged, and in any event I had no desire to break up my marriage with Natalie, whom, apart from one rather strange glance between two Free French officers newly arrived in Lebanon from London, I had no reason to reproach or suspect, and whose infrequent messages (some complaining that I had not answered letters I had never received) I put down to the vagaries of the post. In my physical inclinations I am firmly heterosexual and, apart from the fact that my friendships were both more numerous and warmer than in peacetime, had no inclination whatever to imitate some of my court-martial 'clients'. In other words, though normally sexed, in my refraining from adultery or other deviant types of sex I was, on the whole following my inclinations rather than a conscious path of virtue. Physically, therefore, I was what at that time was somewhat complacently called 'the innocent party'.

None of this solved my immediate problem. After she had finally gone it was clear that I could not leave things as they were. My cousin, Mavis Tate, MP, informed me of numerous misdemeanours of Natalie's whilst I was away. But I would willingly have forgiven these as regrettable consequences of our enforced separation had she not made it unequivocally plain that she was not willing to return on any terms; and desired me, as she put it 'to give her a divorce'. I wrote to her in a perfectly friendly way, explaining my position and telling her that I could not leave things as they were and could not terminate our marriage even by way of judicial separation without some evidence which could stand up in a court of law. She did in fact provide me with this evidence, and I consulted Ernest Jacobson, the father of my poor and sainted friend David. But, even so, I did not at first make up my mind.

I had been a committed Christian since before my marriage to Natalie and I was nearer to the Roman Catholic view of the indissolubility of marriage than to any other. Of course, in the eyes of the Roman Catholic Church I had never been married at all, as I was perfectly well aware, having refused, at the time of my marriage to Natalie in an Anglican church, to sign their conditions about children which I thought unjust, and in consequence having been left in no doubt on this point. But I had myself no doubt about the validity of my own marriage to Natalie and was at first disposed to regard my future as one of bleak and enforced celibacy interspersed with some, probably squalid and immoral, deviations from the straight and narrow path.

It was my father and my brother Neil who dissuaded me from

these opinions and convinced me that I should feel myself free to form a new, legal and stable alliance, a preliminary condition of which was, of course, a petition and decree for dissolution on the ground of Natalie's infidelity with the young French officer. Quite apart from my own future, I think it was fair to consider Natalie's position had I declined to take proceedings or taken proceedings only for a judicial separation. In the event she married her lover and so remained for the rest of their joint lives. I shall always be grateful to my father and to Neil for this advice, which I accepted, and which led not long afterwards to thirty-four years of almost unadulterated happiness with the niece of my constituency chairman, Mary Evelyn Martin, and the birth of my five loyal and admirable children and, to date seven grandchildren. I married Mary in April 1944. As a result of my experience, and of much experience in the courts and elsewhere of the facts of other people's marriages, I have changed my views concerning remarriage after divorce. I continue to think of marriage as sacramental in character, and, in a life lived responsibly, it ought to be for life, and to impose a life-long obligation of mutual fidelity. But the fact is that marriages do break down, sometimes from the fault of one only of the parties, sometimes of both, occasionally as the result of circumstances outside the control of either. In such cases I believe that to impose an obligation of life-long celibacy on either or both of the parties terminable only on what has become the irrelevant duration of the other's life is in the interest neither of public or private morality, nor, indeed, of religious observance. I say this humbly, realizing as I do how difficult this view is to reconcile with the explicit teaching of the gospels and of the largest denomination in the Christian Church. None the less I have to say on this subject: 'I can no other.' I ought to add one footnote. I do not agree with those churchmen who allege, without I believe the smallest evidence, that all marital breakdowns are due to faults on both sides. Of course, none of us being perfect, no one of us is perfection in any human relationship either within the family or outside it. But what I write is based on a more than averagely wide experience of other people's marital affairs, and not only upon my own. Moreover I have heard judges of experience in family law much wider than mine, including one President of the Family Division, give voice to the same opinion. Before 1969, the secular law concerning divorce was fundamentally based on fault, and the courts, and therefore the profession, had to delve more deeply into the conduct of the parties than is now desirable or permissible. While I accept that in all human relationships no one is ever without fault, I personally seldom found the smallest difficulty, whether professionally or advising friends, given the requisite information, in deciding which of the two parties, or whether both of them, was or were responsible for the actual breakdown of a marriage, and this I believe to be the considered view of most of those who have professional experience of the subject. When I think what my life would have been like in the past forty-five years without my marriage to Mary and without, eight years after Mary's death, marriage to my present wife, I tremble to think what would have become of me.

In the mean time I had two further humiliations to suffer about which I felt bitterly at the time. Soon after my return I was bidden to what in wartime passed for a levée to meet the King, and as I had no civilian clothes available to suit the occasion I made a special pilgrimage to the War Office to beg permission as a special favour to wear my service dress uniform which I had done nothing to disgrace and was insulted for my pains by the chair-borne boffin to whom I was sent. I appealed to an old colleague, a junior minister by this time, I think, in the House of Lords – to my recollection the very same one who in 1940 had publicly suggested that the Home Guard should, if necessary, be armed with pikes to meet the Nazi invasion. He slammed down the telephone when I told him the nature of my request.

This made me angry at the time and it still makes me angry to think of it. The other humiliation cut even deeper. Before the war I had been one of the first MPs to hold what is now called a surgery, and, on my return to England, as it was my intention to resume my parliamentary duties, it was my intention to hold one shortly after my return. The difficulty was that at that moment there was no constituency office from which I could operate in Oxford. I therefore put a notice in the paper to the effect that constituents with problems were free on such and such a date to visit me at All Souls, which was virtually empty at the time. I saw no harm in this as, in common with all decent MPs of all parties, I made myself available to constituents of any political persuasion, and, in point of fact, there were in wartime more constituents with problems than there had been ever before in time of peace. Also the party truce was, at the time, in full operation. I found myself confronted with the then Warden who had been put up by some anonymous friend to accuse me of using college premises for party political purposes. The Warden was a kindly man and it is fair to say had no notion of my other troubles. But I think he was a little disconcerted when, faced with this final humiliation, I burst into tears for the only time in my public life. Shortly after, without bedclothes, or civilian suits I could decently wear, forbidden to wear uniform, but recently recovered from hepatitis, and deserted by my wife, I went down with a quinsy. During my illness, one pleasant memory stands out. I was visited by Chips Channon, whom I scarcely knew, but who had been a friend of my brother Edward, and had heard that I was ill. The memory of this act of pure kindness warms my heart to this day, and when Chips died I wrote specially to his son, Paul, by that time my colleague, to tell him of the debt I owed his father. In the mean time I felt myself to be a broken man.

TWENTY-NINE

Dusting My Trousers

MY SERIOUS PUBLIC LIFE really begins from the moment when I recovered from my bed of sickness. I determined to rebuild my life round attention to the public service. The opportunities were close at hand. Even whilst I was in Cairo, the Beveridge Report had been published and had made a tremendous impact on officers and men alike. Up to that moment, there had been practically no public debate and certainly no public consensus about postwar domestic policy, and yet we were all determined that the postwar world would be reconstructed around a more positive and imaginative approach to social policy than the world of the 1930s. Looking at my diaries in the Middle East I find I was constantly reverting in one way or another to this theme. By the time I was waiting for my Liberator I had already learned that in the following March there was to be a two- or three-day debate on the report, and I determined then and there to play a part in it and to give voice to what seemed to me to be not only my own but almost the universally favourable opinion held about it in the armed forces. This is hardly surprising, as, from my diaries, I see that I had moved very much to the left of my previous opinions, although I had always regarded myself as on the left wing of my party. I can recall a conversation I had in French whilst I was in the Lebanon. A French officer had remarked that it would be difficult after the war to avoid socialism. 'Au contraire,' said I, 'il sera impossible.'

'Pourquoi?'

'Parce qu'il est déjà arrivé.'

In this I was not far wrong, though at that time by socialism I meant something more like publicly organized social services than the common ownership of the means of production distribution and exchange or 'the commanding heights of the economy'. As regards public ownership, at that time I was much attracted to Harold Macmillan's Middle Way philosophy, which, so far as I then understood it, meant that there were certain natural monopolies, for example, broadcasting, which would be, and were being, better run as public services, and that there were certain other industries, which were necessary but not particularly profitable and which could not raise the resources required for capital investment except by subvention from the Exchequer. But, in the main, for innovation, salesmanship and exports I was as firmly wedded to private enterprise as the most right wing of my fellow-conservatives. On social policy, however, as soon as the Beveridge Report was published, I believed that it would be in the interest of the Conservative Party to support the main thrust of the Beveridge approach with enthusiasm. I was also disturbed at the apparently costive attitude towards it adopted by the leadership, including Churchill himself. At that time my formula was 'Publicly organized social services, privately owned industry'. When I returned from England, however, I discovered that the party as a whole was not taking this view. The cry was 'Where is the money coming from?' I still believe that I was correct in regarding Beveridge at the time as a relatively conservative document, and that neither the party nor the country had anything to fear from a national health service to replace the old system of panel doctors, or the declared objective of Beveridge himself of 'full employment in a free society'. In fact Beveridge had actually budgeted for an unemployment rate of about 10 per cent on the then method of calculation, and benefits far less extensive in range or ample in amount than those payable at any time since 1950. I believed that, after the war, there would, at least for a period, be such a vast demand for consumer goods that even with rapid demobilization unemployment on the prewar scale would not be a serious problem. I had no idea of the vast developments in modern medicine which have taken place in the past forty-five years and have proved so expensive, and my attitude to industrial injuries was based on a belief that a separate insurance scheme could be organized which would give benefits much more adequate than those provided for under the Workmen's Compensation Acts on the prewar level. I did not contemplate the total abolition of the old Approved Societies, and I still believe that these could have been retained within the new National Health Service and could have been used as a more flexible and less muscle-bound basis for National Health than the vast bureaucratic apparatus devised by Aneurin Bevan.

I do not, of course, now believe that anything the Conservative leadership could have advocated in 1943 could have prevented a Conservative defeat in 1945. But I still think that a more imaginative and positive response to Beveridge would have reduced the scale of the landslide and assisted an earlier recovery. I thought then that a more positive policy after the war in a party led by Churchill and with the prestige of victory behind it could win a postwar election by a substantial margin.

When I got home, I found that my views were already shared by a group of youngish MPs mostly returned from the forces who were meeting regularly for a dinner at a little restaurant in Charing Cross Road. They included Peter Thorneycroft, Viscount Hinchingbrooke (as he was then), Hugh Linstead, Alfred Beit and Norman Bower. This small group was the nucleus of the Tory Reform Committee which thereafter played a considerable part in the public debate on postwar social policy and, with the aid of a Conservative Fund called the Progress Trust, later published a series of political pamphlets which I believe had a considerable and beneficial effect on Conservative thinking at the time. The group, which had originally invited me to dinner on an experimental basis, soon asked me to join them permanently and we became fast friends and allies. Soon after we joined we moved our place of dinner to the Connaught Hotel, in which Alfred Beit had an interest, and were able to improve the heavily controlled wartime food with a delicious pre-prandial cocktail called Bacardi Rum, then still in plentiful supply. Though our visits, mostly on foot in the darkened streets of the blackout, became slightly more exciting during the flying-bomb period, they continued, I believe, until 1945, certainly until the time early in 1945 when, to my surprise, I was asked to join the coalition government as joint Parliamentary Secretary to the Air Ministry.

My intervention in the Beveridge debate was not quite so easily accomplished as I had expected after an absence of two years abroad. I went to see Mr Speaker Fitzroy (a rather terrifying old gentleman of royal descent, though with a bar sinister to the royal arms on his escutcheon) fully expecting to be told that I was certain of a place on his list. I was disappointed. 'But I called you only the other day,' was his response. 'But, Mr Speaker,' said I miserably, 'I have been out of the country for two years.' In the end, however, all was well, as the old gentleman had evidently verified from his clerks the truth of what I had said.

I had prepared myself ahead as well as might be for the ordeal. As a matter of fact I was more conscious of anxiety in advance than I had been for my maiden speech after my by-election in 1938. Then I was speaking on the Criminal Justice Bill, a technical topic on which I was reasonably well at home, though, in actual delivery, it had been quite a different matter. Then a sort of haze of apprehension enveloped me when I heard my name called, and realized I was actually speaking for the first time in the House of Commons, and although the speech was reasonably well received, both in the House and in the press, my stage fright must have been such that I actually remember nothing about it.

Now, however, I was to make a controversial speech in an important debate on a subject on which, though I held strong opinions, many of the more technical aspects were relatively un-familiar to me. The first thing was to get a copy of the report, which I had previously only seen through press coverage, and master its contents, which seemed to me, on reading it carefully, as it still does, to be far less sensational than was thought at the time.

There was, however, another occasion just before the debate when I had an opportunity of airing and sharing my views. Alec Spearman, who had been the very instigator of my appearance at the Oxford by-election, gave a wartime dinner-party at a hotel to discuss the debate. Alec was interested in the economic side, on which I could not regard myself as an expert. But I found during the discussion that there were others besides myself who were disappointed at the noncommittal, even half-hearted, attitude of the coalition, and believed that its Conservative members had missed a considerable opportunity in declining to give it a more enthusiastic welcome.

Looking back on that speech after a lapse of nearly fifty years, and remembering that I was still young, inexperienced and prone to arrogance, I cannot say that I am ashamed of it. I spoke, as I felt, of the need for a sense of national unity during the difficult period of reconstruction, when, as I correctly foresaw, we should still be under the necessity to ration food and other essentials; when, in the nature of things, we should be short of housing accommodation if only during the period of the repair of war damage; and when we should at the same time be under the necessity to reconstitute our export trade, which, under the need to manufacture munitions, was almost at a standstill. If I had my time again, I would not have used the unfortunate phrase 'redistribution of wealth', though I was at pains to explain it in terms of actual proposals in the report. But I was right to emphasize the need, if the necessary spirit of common purpose was to be attained, for an emphasis on the measures of reform and social justice which alone would sustain that purpose. I referred to these considerations as 'moral' and said that in order to make people understand that the Government meant business it was necessary during the war to take the immediate steps recommended in the report. These included institution of a department of social security under a minister, which would enable us to begin the work as soon as external circumstances permitted. The speech was well received, especially from the Labour back benches, and it attracted a good deal of support from our side as well, apart from a few snide comments about my being a 'young man in a hurry'. I still think the speech was moderately expressed in parliamentary terms, relevant and well argued, and showed no sign of the illness or emotional strain to which I had been subjected and from which I had not recovered. I notice that at the end of my speech, in reply to an interruption from George Griffiths, a Labour MP of the flat-capped breed, I described myself as a left-wing Conservative. All my diaries in the Middle East show that this was a correct description of my attitude on social policy at the time, and I still think it was the right line to take. Our social services were inadequately comprehensive, and benefits were unduly low in comparison with the national wealth even as it existed then. Reading between the lines, it is quite clear that I desired the party truce to continue for some time after the war. Events have shown that this was unrealistic, but I still think it was wrong for Liberal and Labour ministers to pull out after VE-Day and before the victory against Japan was complete. I do not know how many of the senior members of any party in February 1943 had been let into the secret of the atom bomb. I was certainly quite unaware of it, and when it was mentioned casually to me as a junior minister in 1945, not as an immediate reality shortly to be delivered, but as something in the offing which might conceivably come, I immediately expressed the strongest possible opinion that, whatever its ultimate importance might be, it could certainly not be made to work in the existing conflict. How mistaken I was. A few months later, already in opposition, and following the end of the caretaker government, I well remember the horror with which I heard the news over the wireless in my step-mother's country house that it not merely worked, but had been delivered on a Japanese city, and realized that a new dimension in the terrors of modern warfare had actually arrived. Incidentally, even now it is worth recalling the circumstances in which it came to be used. It was used by a power which possessed it against one which neither possessed it nor the means of combating it. It was used by a power that was already winning a war by 'conventional' means against one which was certainly losing it. It was used as a means of shortening a war which was already virtually won, and not as the ultimate means of defence. It was used in a war in which, even if it were not used, an Allied victory was already inevitable. If people would only digest this lesson, which remains as valid today as in 1945, we might hear a little less of the case for unilateralism. This is not the place for a moral judgement on these matters. The ethics of international politics, and in particular the ethics of warfare, are more complicated than many people appear to suppose. But the mechanics of them and the operation of cause and effect are somewhat simpler.

The reason why gas was not used in the last war was that both sides were equipped with chemical weapons and the means to resist them. The reason why chemical weapons in the First World War were used by the Germans against the Allies, the reason why mustard gas was used by Mussolini against the Abyssinians, and is now supposedly used by the Iraqi dictator against Iran and against Iraq's own Kurdish minority was again that its use by an adversary possessed of a real, decisive and supposedly superior weapon against an unprotected or inadequately protected opponent is decisive in the attack. A wise chief of staff once observed to me that no nation ever began a war which it believed would be long and hotly contested. When I was First Lord of the Admiralty the then Third Sea Lord warned me: 'Do not make the mistake of thinking that there is nuclear war and conventional war. There is only war.' This belief was so strong in me about the events leading up to the Second World War that it explains my violent attack on the late Professor Joad in the 'Brains Trust' at about the time I am discussing which at the time exposed me to so much criticism. Pacifism and unilateral disarmament are as much causes of war of which the victims of attack may be guilty as are aggressive intentions on the part of those who plan and execute aggression. It is arguable that both the terrible conflicts of my life-time could have been avoided if Britain had prepared herself adequately to meet her European adversaries.

Apart from my speech on the Budget statement in 1943, it is clear that, at the time, I was regarding myself mainly as a spokesman for the forces overseas and as a constituency Member. Although it would have been profitable to do so, I did not think it honourable to go back to the Bar while so many of my contemporaries were unable to practise, and in actual fact, since I was in junior office in the latter months of the coalition and the whole of the short life of the caretaker government, I did not return to it until after the general election of 1945. My whole activity was directed to politics, and in politics my whole thought was towards postwar reconstruction. There was, however, one episode about this time of which I am heartily ashamed. Sir James Grigg was a professional civil servant promoted by Winston to the War Office, and in the course of one matter connected with forces' welfare I became exasperated with what seemed to me his insensitive and wholly unconstructive attitude, as the result of which I allowed myself to indulge in a vitriolic and extremely personal attack which excited a good deal of publicity at the time.

Apart from one episode, in which I believe we were wholly in the right, it was no part of the policy of the Tory Reform Committee to embarrass the Government. What had brought us together was our feeling that the attitude of our leaders in the corridors of power as exemplified by their pussy-footing over the Beveridge Report was unduly unconstructive and unimaginative. They should have used the Party Truce to provide a basis of all-party consensus which I believe would have been politically possible in the atmosphere of the time. Their failure to do so, and in particular the evident resolve of Winston to rely solely on his Olympian prestige as the Saviour and Rallier of the Nation from 1940 onwards and (less sensibly) the man who was right in the period leading up to the war, was, I believe, one of the principal causes of the premature break-up of the coalition and, together with his lamentable election broadcast in 1945, contributed significantly to the scale if not the actual fact of our defeat. In the event, it was the Conservative Party who carried the can for the error of their leaders. Again and again during the 1945 elections I was greeted with voters who exclaimed to me absurdly: 'We want Winston as Prime Minister, but a Labour government.' When I explained patiently that that was the one thing they could not have, they were wont to reply: 'But this is a free country, isn't it? I thought we could vote for who we want.' *Delirant reges, plectuntur Achivi*. Winston played his cards wrongly. It was the rank and file of the party who suffered.

This was nowhere better illustrated than in the one exception to the rule that we did not wish to embarrass the Government in time of war. This was in the debate at the Committee stage of R. A. Butler's Education Bill in 1944, the one measure of postwar reconstruction which the coalition government had felt able to agree upon in advance of the peace. In itself it was a liberal and socially enlightened measure. It put an end, at least for the time being, to the absurd and irrational warfare between the various and quarrelsome Christian denominations. It provided for universal education at the secondary stage and, in my opinion rightly, provided for a variety of different types of secondary school according to the inclinations and ability of the pupils available. In the event, it stood the test of time, in spite of the failure of the experiment of 'secondary technical' schools and the inability of successive governments to introduce nursery education. Until it was destroyed by the fanatical egalitarianism of the Labour Party and the sheer educational philistinism of Shirley Williams as Minister, the Butler Act was the foundation of an agreed educational policy for a generation, and Butler could legitimately claim the loyal support of the Tory Reform Committee through Parliament.

To this generalization there was one curious exception. As is the case with most party groups, at our weekly dinners the first business of the Tory Reform Committee was to discuss the parliamentary agenda for the following week. Amongst our members, though not a regular attendant at our dinners (she was a Christian Scientist, a teetotaller and, I think, newly married to a *News Chronicle* journalist), was Thelma Cazalet Keir. There was one issue to which she attached enormous importance, and that was, of all things, equal pay for women teachers for equal work. We agreed with her, and even now I feel it difficult to see how any sane man or woman with an eye to the future, let alone the politically sensitive R. A. Butler, could have disagreed with Thelma or with us. I can only suppose that, secretly, he did agree. But the Government stood firm. Thelma had put down a highly responsible amendment on the order paper, which had attracted some backbench Labour support, and whose purpose was to give effect to the central principle involved. At our weekly dinner we decided at Thelma's request to back her amendment, if necessary by voting against the Government, and I cannot now see that we were wrong to do so. It could not by any conceivable stretch of the imagination affect the conduct of the war. It could not come into effect until after the war. It seemed to all of us that this was an elementary piece of social justice. After the debate there was a division, and in the division members of the Tory Reform Committee voted with the Labour backbenchers. The Government were defeated by one vote, and I well remember my delighted surprise when I saw the tellers come in with Peter Thorneycroft, senior teller, standing on the right of the line.

I was not able to foresee the sequel. I had assumed that the Government would accept the far from humiliating defeat as the opinion of the House of Commons moderately expressed. The only sane argument on the other side was that, as women appeared to be willing to do the work for men at a lower price, the Government would be foolish not to take advantage of this willingness – an argument which, for all its logic, would not necessarily benefit the interests of men who wished to enter the teaching profession. But this was not what happened. Within something like twenty-four hours Churchill announced the intention of the Government to seek to reverse the vote by issuing a three-line whip and making it a vote of confidence. We had no alternative but to capitulate. We could not vote against the Government on an issue of confidence in time of war. The only argument for Winston's extraordinary behaviour which I have ever heard advanced, and was reputed to come from his own lips, was that if it became known to the outside world that the Government was not able to command a majority in the House of Commons, even on a matter so apparently irrelevant to the war effort or its international standing, the Government he led would lose all credibility abroad with foes and allies alike. It was a naked demand for elective dictatorship, since the House of Commons had been elected in 1935 on quite other issues and had, quite rightly in time of war, prolonged its life by its own action beyond the five years allowed under the constitution. It is worth saying that the only reproach I had to bear at the time was one of pusillanimity at not sticking to my guns. I still think that in time of war we had no alternative but to support the Government on a vote of confidence which it was bound to win in any case, and which it was to the public advantage that it should win overwhelmingly.

I cannot quite pass over in silence the extraordinary way in which R. A. Butler deals with this strange episode in his memoirs, *The Art of the Possible*. I must make it clear that I was always one of Rab's admirers. Of the three up and coming postulants to the succession –

Eden, Rab, and Harold Macmillan – I had always favoured Rab. All three were on the progressive wing of the party. But, to my eye, Eden was too temperamental and Harold too unpredictable in other ways. I admired Rab's almost oriental inscrutability, his subtle mind, and his intellectual approach to practical politics. However, I never numbered candour amongst his virtues. Even by his own standards, however, he excelled himself in his book. He wrote:

> Many sensational accounts have been given of this incident. It arose because of the clear resolve of the Tory Reform Group, led by Quintin Hogg to whom I had quite fruitlessly appealed for a modicum of quite uncharacteristic restraint, to vote with the Labour rebels against the Government. Owing to their jubilant and overweening attitude, I did not think it right to adopt an appeasing line particularly as they had for some time been creating difficulties for my other colleagues in the Government.

And he went on to complain of 'the irresponsibility of a small minority in my own party'.

The only word of truth in this extraordinary summary was that, during the debate, in which he had clearly lost the argument, Rab did in fact ask me not to press the matter to a vote. And, since by his own admission he had offered no reason in the debate to lead me to acquiesce, and I thought in principle he was wrong, I gave him no joy in this request; and, had I done so, I could not have delivered except by going back on my word. As to the suggestion that I would have shown 'uncharacteristic restraint' and that the Tory Reform Committee 'had been creating difficulties for my other colleagues in the Government', I can only say that, to the best of my recollection, on no other occasion did the Tory Reformers bring any other issue to the vote since we always supported the Government on any matter affecting the war (especially about the Second Front Now campaign of the Communist Party and Lord Beaverbrook) and, so far as postwar behaviour was concerned, our policy was to express our opinion without bringing matters to a vote except in this one instance where actual legislation was involved. So far as causing trouble was concerned, it is quite true that I was deeply worried by the attitude of senior members of the administration to postwar policy and had thought it desirable to say so. I wholly disagree with the proposition that the issue of equal pay for equal work could not and should not have been settled in an Education Bill if only as an example of the line which was to be expected in social policy after the war, and which in fact was so taken.

The real truth behind this extraordinary passage emerges in a slightly frivolous anecdote on the following page of R. A. Butler's book. The explanation lies in his failure to control Winston's quite extraordinary inability to take seriously the overwhelming demand for social justice which led to our landslide defeat in 1945. Rab went to see the Prime Minister at a quarter to ten that night:

> We found Churchill in a very resolute and jovial mood . . .
> It was not the issue that mattered so much as the oppor-
> tunity to rub the rebels' [sic] noses in their own mess [sic].
> He had long been waiting for this opportunity. The by-
> elections had been going against him [indeed they had, and
> very largely for the reasons I have been giving]. Now the
> Lord had delivered the enemy [sic] into his hands . . .
> Happily he had the big battalions.

Churchill had indeed the big battalions. But the by-elections, instead of enraging him, should have sounded a clear warning which, had he heeded it in time, might well have enabled him to head, if not an immediately postwar government, at least an opposition of respectable size. As it was, the national coalition vanished after VE-Day, and the 'big battalions' which the Lord delivered into his hands vanished into thin air when the general election came in the following year. As Anthony Howard says in his biography of Rab, the extraordinary behaviour of the Government was an important factor in the landslide of 1945, and for every critic of Churchill before this behaviour there were three or four after it. The truth is that, although until 1963 I thought Rab was capable of being Prime Minister, as events both at this time and subsequently showed, he had not the stuff within him of which prime ministers are made. Politics may well include the art of the possible, but weakness on matters of principle, coupled with an inability to admit that you are wrong, limits the area of what is possible in given circumstances. The episode was bad for Churchill, bad for Rab, bad for the Conservative Party and bad for Britain. The only certainty is that Thelma Cazalet Keir and the despised Tory Reform Committee were right and the Government were the only personalities not showing 'restraint'. This absence of restraint on Churchill's part was certainly not entirely 'uncharacteristic'.

I do not wish to give a false impression of my immense veneration for the genius of this man. I have criticized what I believe were some of his errors of judgement, his childish behaviour over the equal pay amendment in the Education Bill in 1944, his mismanagement of the 1945 election and the numerous errors of judgement which kept him estranged from the Government between 1931 and 1939. I cannot retract any of these criticisms. I would like also to put on record my immense reverence. I do not use the word 'genius' lightly. It is as different from mere talent as sanctity is from mere virtue and godliness. It is an altogether different dimension. Winston was the only genius whom I can claim to have known well. Like all geniuses his defects were the reflection of his qualities. As the French say: 'Il avait les défauts de ses qualités.' But, at the end of the day, he was a portent. Cardinal Newman is credited with saying that, as a believer, he was always looking to see something which could be aptly and truthfully described as the finger of God in history, but that, looking at history, there was nothing he could see which justified that description. It was, he is alleged to have said, as if he had looked into a mirror expecting to see the reflection of his own face, and saw nothing. I suppose that, if we were honest, most of us would have to confess to something of the same experience. But in my own life there has been at least one exception. It is the career of Winston Churchill.

I first heard the name of Winston Churchill in rather curious circumstances. I can place the date almost exactly. It was March 1914, and I was less than seven years of age. It can only have taken place at about the time of the Curragh incident, and the sending by Winston whilst First Lord of the Admiralty of the Fleet to Lamlash. At that time small boys partook of Sunday lunch in the nursery, particularly on the occasion of a Sunday lunch-party presided over by my father in the presence of cousins, uncles and aunts and other grandees associated with the family. At the coffee stage, small boys, scrubbed clean, brushed, combed, and in their best suits, were sent downstairs, put on view, and fed like little birds with the crystalline sugar at the bottom of the adults' coffee-cups. On the occasion in question a name passed to and fro across the luncheon-table. My childish treble piped up: 'Daddy, who is Winston Churchill?' My father, normally the most compassionate and gentle of men, became aware that silence had descended and the eyes and ears of the family were upon him. He assumed a terrifying and uncharacteristic attitude of portentous gravity. 'My son,' he said, 'you know I have always told you [he certainly had not] that it is wicked to wish that anyone were dead. But, if ever I could bring myself to wish that anyone were dead, I would wish it of Winston Churchill.' My uncle Ian was then commanding Winston's own regiment, the 4th Hussars, at the Curragh as part of the Light Cavalry Brigade. He was one of the officers in that brigade who had signed the declaration, and his name even occurs as a footnote in some of the history-books which describe the incident. Winston and Ian had been the best of friends at Sandhurst, and Ian's presence in the 4th Hussars whilst they were serving in India was the main reason, I was told, for Churchill's transfer to the 4th Hussars from the 60th Rifles in which, I believe, he had originally been commissioned. Winston and my father had a curious physical resemblance to one another, and later that year, when my father walked down the Mall on the way to sign his name in the Palace Book on the outbreak of war, the crowds, thinking he was walking from Admiralty House, cheered him with the words: 'Good old Winston.' It is fair to say that in the 1920s I reminded him more than once of the incident at the Sunday luncheon-party in Queen's Gate Gardens, and he always denied it. But I do not think that my memory has deceived me.

I first met Winston face to face at Fuller's Cake Shop in Windsor whilst I was at Eton. I was being visited by my brother Edward shortly, I suppose, after my mother's death. Winston was crouched like a great bird over the unusually small table, giving tea to his son Randolph, several years younger than I. 'Meet my son, Randolph,' he said after Edward had introduced me. He later became a familiar figure in my life in his late-night discussions with F. E. Smith in Professor Lindemann's rooms in Christ Church.

Winston's meteoric rise met its first reverse after Gallipoli. Classical scholars have often compared that disastrous military episode with the equally disastrous Sicilian expedition which was the decisive turning-point against Athens in her famous war against Sparta. In some ways the parallel is curiously exact; but wholly unfair was the comparison, then often drawn, between Winston, the soul of patriotism and loyalty, and the treacherous but brilliant Alcibiades. What is true is that, if Winston's original plan of a sudden and unheralded descent had been accepted, the Dardanelles might have been a triumphant victory as indeed Athens's original design favoured by her best general of an unheralded descent on Syracuse might have been had it been permitted by the cautious Nicias. In both cases excessive caution was the cause of disaster. A calculated risk is sometimes the secret of success in battle, as well as in politics.

Winston's fall after Gallipoli was, however, an enormous blessing in disguise. Honourably, he afterwards had a taste of what the trenches were like. Countless lives were saved in 1942 by Winston's steadfast refusal, in the face of Stalin's reiterated demands, backed by the entire Beaverbrook press and the lunatic left of the Labour Party, for a Second Front Now. I believe that, more than anything else, it was Winston's experience in the trenches which prevented new holocausts like Passchendaele and the Somme which would certainly have occurred had he yielded to these powerful pressures.

Winston's errors over India and the Abdication, which were among the earlier and later causes of his alienation from his party in the 1930s, were also blessings in disguise. Had he recovered office after 1931, as he would dearly have liked to do, he would have been tarred, however unjustly, with the aura of appeasement which has stuck to the members of the Baldwin and Chamberlain governments. As it was, in 1939 he emerged with stirring speeches and broadcasts during the Phoney War, and as the leader of the great coalition which brought us from the jaws of annihilation in 1940 to ultimate victory in 1945.

One of Winston's great virtues was his magnanimity. When I was about to leave for the Middle East towards the end of 1940, the MPs who were serving members in the forces gave him a luncheon somewhere in St Martin's Lane and, because I was going abroad, I was placed on his right. I expressed the view that when we had won the war we should never again be able to forgive the Germans for what they had done and were then actually doing. The Prime Minister flatly rebuked me. It was the first time I had heard him explicitly expound his philosophy of 'magnanimity in victory', to which he lived up in his great European speeches after 1945. In 1940 that was quite something.

My last memories of Winston are sad. Old age is a strange trickster. In 1958 as the 'honorary Academician' he was present at the Royal Academy summer banquet. At the time I was Chairman of the Conservative Party and Lord President of the Council, and things were going badly for the Government and for the party. I was under constant and heavy pressure from the faint-hearted to persuade Harold Macmillan to go to the country. So soon after the Thorneycroft resignation it would have been a disastrous decision to take. At the banquet I was placed between Winston on my right and the Soviet ambassador who, quite legitimately, would have been noting carefully every word on my left. To Winston, I thought it right to talk about the past, and, in particular, about Winston's friend, my uncle Ian Hogg. Winston was already failing. 'Ian', said Winston, 'was killed at Gallipoli.' Quite wrong. Ian had died of wounds in France in September 1914. 'But are you not Ian's son?' he asked. Then suddenly, he was in the present again, with his genius fully alight. He grasped my wrist. 'Of course,' he said, 'you must hold on,' meaning, of course, that I must not allow Harold to dissolve that year. 'I have every intention of doing so,' I replied.

Our last meeting was the saddest of all. Not long before he died, I came into the smoking-room of the House of Commons which, as a peer who had been in the Commons, I was entitled to visit. Winston was sitting there, quite alone. He gave me a whisky and we talked. He asked me to dinner in Hyde Park Gardens, and I accepted. I expected a party, but when I got there I found we were *tête-à-tête*. He remembered that we both had American mothers and he spoke movingly of how all his life he had worked and dreamed of Anglo-American friendship. As we sipped our champagne a little budgerigar, 'Toby', was let out of his cage and flew about the room, and lighted from time to time on Winston's head. We moved into another room for brandy.

Long silence.

'Do you believe in the afterlife?'

'Why, yes, Winston, I do.'

'H'm.'

Long silence.

'You remember, Winston, when you were at the bottom of that coal-mine on the run as an escaped prisoner of war?'

'Yes.'

'You said you prayed for help and it always came.'

'H'm.' It was evident that his soul was clad in dust and ashes.

'And remember, Winston, that all over the world millions of men and women who remember what you have done will always bless your name. And I am one.'

'H'm.'

Long silence.

We parted warmly. It was the last time I ever saw him alive. As I went back in the taxi to my home in Roehampton, I cried silently to myself at the dark moment of despair which had befallen this giant among men.

THIRTY

Mary and Oxford

ONE OF THE FIRST THINGS I DID when I returned from abroad was to resume contact with my constituents. My revolt against Chamberlain's government in the Norway debate, at the time highly unpopular, had been altogether forgotten, but I soon found that my absence abroad had been more lastingly resented. I was first told about this at a constituency dance when my partner rebuked me for not having represented my constituency in the Commons whilst I was in the Middle East. I defended myself stoutly against her attack. I could not have faced my own conscience, I said, if I had supported the war in September 1939 without offering myself at the age of little more than thirty to face the enemy with my own body. The big decisions in my life have been taken with my heart rather than with my head. I do not despise brains, but there are things which only one's private *daimonion* (as Socrates called his) can tell one to do or not to do on great occasions. The worst mistakes, and sins, in my life have been due to ignoring either the warnings of this inner mentor or the more serious warnings of my religion rather than to any failure of intelligence or want of decision.

Soon after my return, I managed to arrange a little meeting in North Oxford, nominally public, but in fact mainly attended by members of my association of whom the chairman was Lady Townsend, the wife of an eminent professor of physics, Sir John Townsend. When the meeting had just started there came into the room a charming young woman who walked right through the crowd up to the platform, greeted Lady Townsend warmly with a kiss and was introduced to me as her niece, Mary Martin. Mary's parents had been working for most of their lives in Ceylon planting tea, though, having retired, they had come back to England and were currently in London at a flat in Kensington. For practical purposes, since the age of seven onwards Mary had been virtually brought up by Lady Townsend, her husband and their two sons, John and Edward, in accordance with the social custom of the time which did not favour a life in the tropics for young children – and well might it not, for by the age of seven Mary had already contracted amoebic dysentery and was not particularly strong. I had in fact met her once before at the time of the by-election when she was graduating from a secretarial school, and was employed temporarily to keep a check and report upon my own and my opponent's meetings. But I had hardly spoken to her and probably would not have recognized her in a crowd when she came to the North Oxford meeting in the spring of 1943. It was really, as she afterwards told me, Lady Townsend who brought us together, since she told Mary of the state of my affairs and actually suggested that, should I seek her company, she might like to go out with me. We were married the following year in April 1944 and there followed thirty-four years of happy married life, and the birth of five loyal and devoted children. Until our first child was born, we lived at my old house at 1 Victoria Square. When the second child was on the way Mary chose a larger house with a garden where we brought up our family. For the holidays we moved to my home in Sussex which we occupied for fifteen years after my father died. She now lies buried in the churchyard at Herstmonceux in what was then in full view of the family home she had made so happy.

In 1944 we were happy and together. In wartime there could be no question of a conventional honeymoon, but we spent a week at Brentor on the edge of Dartmoor on the recommendation of a climbing friend who had done the same. Outside the hotel was a little hill, dedicated to St Michael. One night, in the sky above, I saw two aircraft engaged in combat, shooting tracer bullets in the starlight.

It is curious how persons whose families have a connection with Ireland seem to find themselves drawn to one another. My own family came from the North, having entered as Quakers in 1722, but my branch of it became members of the Church of Ireland about

1750 when my direct ancestor, one Edward Hogg, married Rose O'Neill, the daughter of a Church of Ireland parson. Mary's origins were far more distinguished. The Martins came over with Strongbow and settled in County Galway. There were three branches of the family at first: the Martins of Spidal, the Martins of Ballinahinch (now a formidable-looking hotel) and the senior branch, the Martins of Ross, to which my new father-in-law, Dick, belonged. Ross was and is a fortress-like house near the Lough Corrib, with a large lake of its own, which the family vacated during the Troubles of the 1920s. There had been several very distinguished members of this branch. The family coat of arms was a cross, allegedly a Crusader's cross owing to some real or legendary connection with Coeur de Lion. But there were more recently memorable figures, too: 'Nimble Dick' who kept his estate through a judicious change of political allegiance; 'Humanity Dick' (also known as 'Hairtrigger Dick' from his duelling proclivities) who sat in the United Kingdom House of Commons and was one of the founders of the RSPCA; and, perhaps best known of all, Violet Martin, with Edith Somerville (also a relative) one of the partners of the Somerville and Ross books about the Irish RM and others. My new mother-in-law, Amy Martin, was equally born of a Southern Irish Protestant family, the Lamberts (also related to Edith Somerville). In the Irish RM books, old Mrs Knox, who travelled about in a donkey-cart, is a recognizable portrait of my father-in-law's grandmother, and other characters in the book are, I believe, recognizable portraits. Old Edith Somerville was still alive when Mary and I were married, and we used to exchange visits. She was a formidable old lady. She had rather blotted her copy-book with her admiration for Mussolini, but I never take much notice of temporary political and religious eccentricities. More eccentrically still, she was deeply addicted to spiritualism and continued to write under the names of Somerville and Ross long after Violet Martin had died, as she was convinced that her books' content was in fact partly the work of her dead relative, co-author and friend.

Mary's mother, Amy Lambert, as she then was, had been a famous horsewoman in her day and rode to hounds with the Galway Blazers. Mary ('May') Townsend, her sister, who had been Mayor (not then Lord Mayor) of Oxford more than once, was a veritable queen of Conservative politics in the city. During her mayoralty my own Mary had been her aunt's mayoress, at the unusually young age of fifteen, and so was admirably suited to be an MP's wife. At the time we met in the spring of 1943 she was a mature young woman of approximately twenty-five, secretary to one of the senior officers of MI5. When the war started they had been quartered in or near Oxford, first at Keble and then at Blenheim Palace. When I was going out with her, however, they had moved to London. Mary and her family had all the best qualities of the Southern Irish Protestants: a steely loyalty to one another and to the Crown, an unshakeable personal integrity, a nice sense of fun, and great personal courage. They lack the fierce Calvinism and garrison mentality of the Protestants of the North. They are wholly without fanaticism. They take their own Protestant Christianity for granted without flaunting their faith in the face of different persuasions. They treat the English with amused affection, but are as different from them as the Scots and the Welsh. They bitterly resent Sinn Fein, who have exiled them from their old homes.

Newly married in 1945, I was somewhat short of cash. My parents-in-law were definitely poor, and my father was not particularly flush. Since I had no income from the Bar we had to make do on my parliamentary pay, my earnings from broadcasting and writing, and the interest on a small capital sum my father had given me some years before. It was then that I conceived the idea of writing my first political book which ultimately came out under the title *The Left Was Never Right*, a title partly suggested to me by John Boyd-Carpenter, a friend from Oxford days and later the joint grandfather of two of my grandchildren. The idea of the book was to counteract the profound effect of a series of pernicious works published by Gollancz under the names of various Roman statesmen, who subsequently disclosed themselves as Dick Crossman, Michael Foot and Peter Howard, the last of whom later admitted his fault to me and we became fast friends. These pamphlets comprised partisan attacks on the patriotism and integrity of Conservative MPs and particularly of the senior members of the party. I had no particular objection to these gentlemen not taking their part in the fighting services. Of the three, Michael Foot and Peter Howard were almost certainly physically unfit and would have been rejected for military service. But, in 1940, when everything was at stake, the younger Conservative MPs were fighting, and the need above all things was for national unity, I took the view that all these books were morally wicked, unpatriotic and factually incorrect. *The Left Was Never Right* was an attempt to set the record straight and to establish that our unpreparedness before the war was largely the consequence of the policies of the parties of the Left, their espousal of the cause of unilateral disarmament, their resistance to any money being spent on the armed services, and their belief that, without powerful British forces and the participation of the United States and Soviet Union, the League of Nations could be made to work against the dictators and others by a process which they called 'collective security', and which could only properly be described as total unpreparedness and unwillingness to fight. I was entitled to make this case with complete sincerity since I had argued it strongly in public and in private during the notorious Oxford Union debate on King and Country in which I had participated, and continuously thereafter.

Apart from one unfortunate mistake which led to a perfectly well-founded action for defamation by John Parker, to whom I had mistakenly attributed a speech in fact made by another, the book was a success. Unfortunately it was too little and too late to counteract the impression made by the earlier Gollancz publications. I had two or three other writs for libel from various politicians from whom I had taken, with comments, quotations which were correct. But in the event they came to nothing. In addition to *The Left Was Never Right*, I wrote two other books about this time, one was called *The Purpose of Parliament* for the Blandford Press and the other *Making Peace*, each about the problems of the time, still of interest to myself, but now only of doubtful value to others. I also wrote regularly for the *Spectator* and other periodicals, and an account for the *Geographical Magazine* based on the last part of my diary, which I then still possessed, of my wanderings in the Lebanon. I wish now that I had taken up their offer to write about my climbing days in the Alps and elsewhere, then fresh in my memory but more faded now. Perhaps it was because I did not realize then that my days of serious climbing were nearly, though not entirely, at an end.

In April 1945 my connection with the Tory Reform Committee came to a sudden and unexpected end. At the very end of March the then joint Parliamentary Under-Secretary of State for Air, Commander Rupert Brabner, DSO, DSC, a war hero, was killed in an air crash on a political mission to Canada and to my surprise I found myself offered the job. I cannot now remember whether the offer came from Archie Sinclair, then Secretary of State, or Winston himself. I regarded the offer to serve my country again in time of war as a duty rather than an honour. But of course I accepted and found myself for the first time in my life a minister, complete with a car, an official driver (nicknamed 'Trigger') and a private office, with a Principal Private Secretary and two subordinate secretaries. I found my experience on Jumbo's staff in the Lebanon extremely valuable as a guide, and was given further help by the formidable Arthur Street, the Parliamentary Under-Secretary, a character infinitely more frightening but far less tortuous than the agreeable Humphrey Appleby of 'Yes, Minister'. I was also given some ministerial training by the eloquent Archie Sinclair, the Liberal leader and Winston's military colleague in the First World War. Despite his eloquence, he spoke with a slight stutter. He was constantly and quite unjustly under personal attack from Austin Hopkinson, one of the few truly independent MPs of that Parliament, but further to the right in his political views than anything to be found in the Conservative ranks. Archie sometimes took me on his trips in his Grumman Goose to East Anglian airfields where Bomber Command operated, to attend meetings where the young pilots of Bomber Command were briefed for their nightly flights over Germany. People now have forgotten how very dangerous these missions were. Bomber Command lost, I believe, 50,000 of its aircrews. They were not concerned with the military effectiveness, the wisdom or the morality of the strategic bombing policy of their commander, 'Bomber' Harris, whom I never met. Personally, having spent the three worst months of the Blitz in my own home in Victoria Square, I could hardly doubt the legitimacy in terms of the international law of war of the policy of reprisal and retorsion. But I did come to doubt its military efficiency. The later attacks on selected targets on the railway networks, especially the rolling stock, proved, I believe, more effective, after our invasion of the Continent began. But, both before and after D-Day, Bomber Command succeeded in detaching vast quantities of German military manpower from the Russian front, which we were unable to reinforce, and later from opposing our own invasion of Western Europe. Nevertheless, seated among the aircrew about to risk their lives that very night, I felt rather small, a young man in civilian clothes, when, after the technical briefing had taken place, they had to listen to Archie Sinclair's excellent but high-flown oratory. It was rather like a sermon in church. 'Too much bloody eloquence,' I heard one young man say to his neighbour in the row behind me, and, knowing from recent experience what it was like to go on night patrol, which in my case had been far less dangerous, I was rather inclined to agree.

I am, I believe, the last person to have been a member of the great coalition of 1940–5 still to survive in 1990 and even in retirement to hold the bronze medal struck for its members by Winston after the coalition's conclusion, which I have had carefully preserved in Perspex. I remained in active office in the same post in the caretaker government, this time under Harold Macmillan as Secretary of State, and in fact I was the last person to speak from the dispatch-box in the memorable Parliament which had lasted from 1935 until the general election ten years later.

Though my period of office was thus curtailed by events, and I only made one speech of any length (on 18 April 1945), this brief period of office was not quite so uneventful as the bald narrative of these facts might make it appear. A glance at the Hansard for my few weeks of office shows that my main menu was run-of-the-mill stuff. However, almost as soon as I arrived, I found a quantity of letters from members of service families expressing anxiety about their sons, as was increasingly the case, being transported by air. This seems incredible in this age of air transport only forty years later. But the anxieties of the mothers and fathers of that day were genuine enough

The Member for Oxford, 1938.

(Centre left) At Heliopolis, 1942.

Probably in Cairo the same year.

Carter's Corner, October 1957, with my glorious herd of Jerseys.

With my growing family at Carter's Corner in 1955. *(Right)*, with Douglas; *(below)*, Mary with Frances, *(left)*, Kate, *(centre)* and Mary Claire *(right)*.

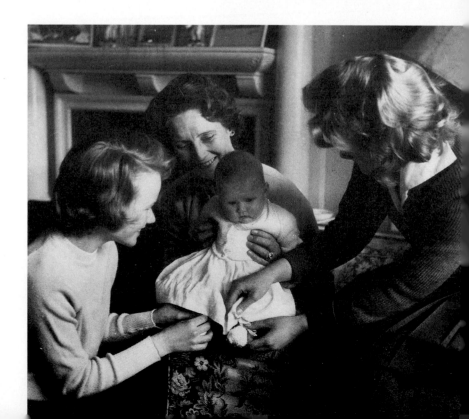

and increased both by my predecessor's death and that of other distinguished persons in air crashes. I therefore decided that every official journey I made – and most weeks there was more than one – should be by air, even, for instance, if they were as close as Oxford. At first I feared that this might be unduly expensive or unduly difficult, as indeed it would today. But in 1945 this was not the case. At the end of the war there were few places in the United Kingdom or at least in England which were much more than five miles from an airstrip or runway, and there were a vast number of pilots, some newly released from captivity as prisoners of war, only too anxious to get back into the air and make up their lost flying hours. I also determined to become a pilot myself as my predecessor had been. Unfortunately, my training was cut short by the general election and consequent loss of office. But I recently came across my pilot's log-book. I never completed my first solo flight, but I flew from Hendon in a Tiger Moth, under the tuition of a Group Captain Hannafin, newly released from Germany. I do not know whether I made an apt pupil, but Hannafin was a most agreeable companion, and it was the greatest possible fun. I have often seriously considered whether I would take it up again. But I have always decided against it. I can see no fun in it except as a means of getting from A to B, and the trouble and expense involved make it far from worthwhile.

I was fairly active both in Oxford and speaking for other Conservative candidates in the general election campaign, a somewhat odd one as so many of our younger constituents were in the forces and inaccessible to the ordinary process of electioneering. I certainly did not expect the magnitude of the landslide to Labour, and the only person I knew who did foresee not merely the result but the scale of it was Father D'Arcy of Campion Hall who asked me to a sherry-party to meet my friends there when the campaign was going on. Naturally enough, I was asked about my expectations of the result, and I replied, quite honestly, that I expected us to win by a narrow margin. 'Are you sure,' asked Martin D'Arcy, 'that it will not be a landslide the other way?' No one else had suggested to me that this would be so, and when, at the count, I had the usual conversation with my opponents about the national outcome both expressed the opinion that it would be a close-run thing. After the result was known, at the opening of the new Parliament, the new Labour Minister of Education, Ellen Wilkinson, processed with me in the wake of Black Rod to hear the King's Speech, and I asked her whether she, too, had been surprised by the result, and she told me frankly that she had. There seems to be a common agreement that the scale of the victory was due in part at least to the forces' vote. I believe that this was in part influenced by the manipulation of ABCA by the late Colonel Wigg (as he was then), one of the very few men in public life whom I would describe as evil. But, of course, one cannot explain portentous events of this kind by anything so trivial. It was odd, however, that Churchill's towering reputation at the time did not do something to stem the flood. I have already said that, everywhere I went, I was met with the cry: 'I want a Labour government with Churchill as Prime Minister.' Nevertheless, I believe that Churchill himself was one of the prime causes of the magnitude of the disaster. Despite his genius, which was amazing, his whole career shows him to have been one of the worst electioneers of the century. He had absolutely no idea of how other people felt or thought. He lost more seats at by-elections and general elections than almost anybody else in my experience. A glance at the number of seats he lost during his long career, Leicester, Dundee, Westminster, Oldham, et cetera et cetera, tells its own tale. In 1945 I happened to be in the Carlton Club among a group of interested listeners while Winston was delivering what I believe to have been his calamitous 'Gestapo' broadcast, no less calamitous in my view because it did in fact contain a germ of most important truth. All socialism contains within its body the cancerous seed of oppression which arises because it can only operate through a dictatorial party machine based on the principles of uniformity imposed from above by means of centralization. The listeners at the Carlton all appeared enthusiastic. 'That,' said one enthusiast, 'is the stuff to give the troops.' I was asked for my opinion, which, to their disappointment, was one of dissent. 'It may interest you to know,' said I, 'that in my opinion that broadcast will lose us between 250,000 and 500,000 votes.' My audience was not pleased. 'How marvellous,' was the comment, 'to be as certain of yourself as that.'

Nevertheless, I do not believe that that single utterance alone could have brought about that result and, in the ordinary course, the Conservative Party would have been due for defeat. The Gollancz productions, by 'Cassius', 'Cato' and other pseudonymous Roman Republican authors, had undermined the Conservative position. I had tried to counter this in *The Left Was Never Right* and, to some extent, I believe I succeeded. It was too little and too late.

But something more and something far more important was lacking which contributed to our defeat. Ever since the Beveridge Report, and in more fields than social policy alone, the Conservative Party had been almost entirely negative and unresponsive to the popular demand for some constructive vision of the future. Attlee and Morrison had not allowed this to pass unnoticed, nor had Bevin, who legitimately manipulated the big battalions from within the trade union movement without deviating one inch from his massive and instinctive Anglo-Saxon patriotism. Had our own leaders, and in particular Churchill himself, just heeded the warnings of the younger elements in the party represented by my colleagues in the Tory Reform Committee, instead of regarding us as 'the rebels' or 'the enemy' who deserved to have 'their noses rubbed in their own mess', I believe that we might just have edged ourselves to victory under the banner of Churchill's huge and fully justified personal popularity. For this failure, Rab Butler, Anthony Eden, Harold Macmillan, and perhaps also Oliver Stanley and Harry Crookshank, none of them on the right wing of the party, must share responsibility with the Prime Minister. The extent of our defeat certainly, and perhaps even the fact of our defeat, was due to the triumph of negativism in the higher echelons of the party. But the main responsibility must rest with Churchill himself, who believed that he could win through with his immense and deserved reputation as the Great Architect of victory who had snatched triumph from the very jaws of disaster.

The election itself, in Oxford, has left few impressions on my mind. The first is that for me, as it is for every candidate, every general election is a non-event. In a by-election, and especially for me in the by-election of 1938, one is the centre of interest, of attention of the media, in my case both at home and abroad. In the general election one may have one's little local difficulties – in my case a tiresome quarrel between my peppery little agent and the ladies who stuffed the envelopes – but in general, one's own contest, so important to oneself and one's own future, is completely lost in the maelstrom of events and the great swings and surges of popular sentiment. Occasionally, very occasionally, one's own reputation as a good, or bad, constituency Member may make the difference of, at most, 500 votes. But otherwise one is very much a pawn in a game. Since the advent of television this effect has, I believe, become even more pronounced. But even then, in the age of radio and the ponderous election broadcasts of the leaders, the individual candidate was just a pawn on the board.

I was faced, this time, with two opponents: the same Ivor Davies who was persuaded to stand down in 1938 in favour of Sandy Lindsay, and, as I had expected and as I believe he had calculated, Frank Pakenham.

I am in the unusual position of having contested both husband and wife in the same constituency in two successive elections. I was opposed by Frank in 1945, and by Elizabeth in 1950. Of my two opponents, Elizabeth, fighting the more difficult fight of the two, was by far the more formidable antagonist. Both, of course, are extremely intelligent and, thank God, I can also number both as my friends. But, quite apart from her striking good looks, Elizabeth's quiet and workmanlike handling of the campaign made her an adversary whom one would be unwise to take lightly. Frank crudely over-reached himself and, early on in the campaign, practised some sharp tactics which rebounded badly on his own head. In my adoption speech I had said what is usual on such occasions, and, in my case, what was more than usually sincere, namely that it had been a tremendous privilege to represent Oxford during the previous seven years and how much I looked forward to being again its MP during the transition to peaceful conditions.

It so happened that I was on the selection committee of the St

George's Division of Westminster in which, being near the House of Commons, I continued to reside. I cannot remember now whom we had selected as candidate, but my name was never among the possible choices, and if I had been offered it I would have refused. Someone had evidently got a garbled account of my membership of the selection committee, and in due course there appeared a letter in the *Oxford Mail* over the signature of a little-known, but quite real, Oxford trade unionist clearly accusing me of insincerity and saying that I had allowed my own name to be put forward for St George's. As there was not a word of truth in this, I immediately consulted a local firm of solicitors and threatened both the editor and the supposed author of the letter with a writ for libel if they did not immediately apologize and withdraw. I had hooked a bigger fish than I supposed. Next day the telephone in my office rang and I answered it. It was Frank.

'I wrote that letter,' he confessed.

'I would not have done the same to you,' said I, 'and, what is more, I shall put the facts before the electors in my speech this evening.'

And I did.

The only other clear incident I remember from the contest was that one day I was canvassing with my loudspeaker-car in North Oxford and a woman ran out of her house and started abusing Churchill on grounds which still seem to me somewhat bizarre. 'Show me his war wounds, show me his war wounds,' she cried. 'Madam,' said I, threatening to drop my trousers, 'if you are not careful, I shall show you mine.' My bluff worked, and the lady scuttled back into her house in a panic. If she had only known that all I had to show even at that early date was a red pencil-mark of scar between the fibula and the femur on my right knee, she would, I believe, have been rather less alarmed at the prospect. However, so far as I was concerned, the outcome was favourable, and after the result was announced from the Town Hall I walked out into the sunshine in St Aldgate's once more the Member for Oxford City, and altogether ignorant of the débâcle which was overtaking my party elsewhere.

So ended my first brief period in office. A new chapter in my life was to begin. A husband, and now the father of a son, I had to earn my living, and after an absence of nearly seven years I was determined to go back to the Bar.

THIRTY-ONE

Parenthood and Opposition

DOUGLAS WAS BORN to Mary and me on 5 February 1945, just before my appointment to the Air Ministry. It was a great moment in my life. Mary and I were both anxious to have children as soon as possible, and I was nearly thirty-seven when we were married. We consulted my doctor on the subject shortly after we came back from Brentor. 'Don't worry,' he said. 'You will soon be consulting me as to how to avoid them.' At all events, Douglas was on the way. It is a most rewarding period in the life of a marriage. The excitement of the coming event, the closer bonding of husband and wife, the solicitude of the husband for the wife's well-being, the selection of names for the coming arrival, all are marvellous experiences. Mary and I always chose alternative sets, one for a boy and one for a girl, usually one name from each side of the new arrival's family. We only had to make an alteration once. That was when our third child was on the way. If a girl, as she turned out to be, we were going to call her Frances after my great-aunt, Frances Horner, who had been most kind to me after my mother died, and Amelia after my mother-in-law, Amy Martin. But two days before the christening I woke up in the middle of the night and suddenly said: 'We can't call her Frances Amelia. She will be known all her life as "Sweet FA".' So we christened her Frances Evelyn after Mary's second Christian name, leaving Amelia to the third daughter Katharine Amelia who did not arrive in our midst till 1962, eighteen years after we were married. Whilst the child was expected, in order not to pre-judge the name or the sex we always referred to the coming infant as Algie, after the sad story of how Algie met a lion. The lion was bulgy, the bulge was Algie. I have since discovered that some other married couples have used the same device but nowadays parents can find out the sex of the child long before the actual birth. We called our son Douglas Martin, Douglas after my father and Martin after my father-in-law's surname. All our children were christened in St Stephen's Chapel, and the day we chose for Douglas's christening in advance was 9 May 1945, which turned out to be VE-Day. Being then a very young and newly appointed Junior Minister, we drove up to Westminster in my newly assigned official car. In Whitehall and at Buckingham Palace and in the streets the jubilant crowds were cheering their heads off. So we entered New Palace Yard to leave the car and carry the newly born infant through the Members' entrance towards my little office next to the barber's shop. As I alighted from the car to hand out Mary with the child in her arms, we were greeted by Beverley Baxter, also in the centre of Westminster to see the fun, and even from that distance the cheering sounded loudly all around from St Margaret's, from the Abbey, from the government buildings in Great George Street and all the way down Whitehall. 'Quintin, you showman,' said the beaming Beverley Baxter, and I loved the man ever afterwards. Later in the day, we joined the crowds in Whitehall where we met, of all people, Jean Crawford, who had been my first secretary in 1938 and fast friend ever since in good times and bad, and we all three thought it would be a good thing to go up to my official room in what was then the Air Ministry to rest weary limbs. The place was in darkness, and I switched on the light, only to find in my armchair the recumbent figure of my official driver in the arms of a young woman, and we beat a hasty retreat. When he apologized to me next day I was still too happy to care. 'Never mind,' said I. 'Christmas comes but once a year.'

Douglas was a precocious child, and by August was heard to make articulate sounds earlier than any other infant I have known, which both Mary and I interpreted as a deliberate, if unsuccessful, attempt to pronounce his own name. Oddly enough, my mother recorded the same thing about me at about the same age in a book she was keeping about my memorabilia. I was saying 'Cuckoo'; Douglas quite distinctly said 'Duggo'. All my children have marvellously enriched my life, and more than forty years after Douglas's birth I can honestly say they continue to do so.

After the general election the House reassembled in the new Parliament. Peter Thorneycroft, Reggie Manningham-Buller and I, as Junior Ministers in the caretaker government, took our places on the front Opposition bench with such of the grandees of the party as had survived the landslide. Neither Peter nor I stayed there long. Peter, I suppose, thought quite rightly that his outstanding talents would be displayed to better advantage, and over a wider range of subjects than would be allotted to him by Winston, who was, I think, still inclined to view the leading members of the Tory Reform Committee with the same distrust which he had shown in office. But, though the Committee was never, I think, formally disbanded, effectively it died with the election. It was thought by us all to be a little unsuited to what it was hoped would be a united opposition, rather than, as it had been before, a sort of ginger group, behind the Government in all essentials but urging it to take a more positive and constructive line on matters relating to social questions. It now fell, therefore, into desuetude.

My own reasons for leaving the front bench were a little different from what I suppose to have been Peter's. I simply had to earn my living, and, although I always supplemented my income with writing, the only real prospect for me lay in a return to the Bar. I had known, of course, from the date of my father's acceptance of the Woolsack in 1928, that my position as the heir to a hereditary peerage precluded my holding any of the more important offices of state occupied by members of Commons, including the two Law Officerships. So far as I then had any ambition, it was, I suppose, that by rebuilding my legal practice I might one day qualify for judicial preferment.

However, before I finally decided to leave the front bench, I made two speeches from the Opposition dispatch-box, of which, having reread them, I am not at all ashamed. On 24 August there was a debate on a motion by Herbert Morrison with wide terms of reference to consider the procedure of the House, and, on reading what had been said about procedure in various Labour Party pamphlets,

I became aware that what they intended to come out of the Committee, which of course had a built-in Labour majority, was nothing less than a guillotine on every measure in Second Reading, Committee, Report and Third Reading; and, further, to group amendments in such a way as to take away from the Chair the right to select them and to replace it with a provision that only one division should take place on each separate group. It is a particularly difficult art for a member of a defeated party to confront a triumphant government in the immediate aftermath of electoral victory and, even if it had not presented this inherent difficulty, it was obviously not possible to divide the House on a proposal so innocent as the setting-up of a Select Committee on a subject admittedly worthy of inquiry. Nevertheless, and in spite of a barrage of interruptions from the Labour benches, I believe I got the ear of the House, and I found myself not only quoting from the pamphlet proposals which seemed to me to present peculiar dangers, but also to have adumbrated many of the general observations on the dangers inherent in our constitution which many years later I described at length in my lecture on elective dictatorship. I also ended up by twitting the elated Labour majority (whose rules of discipline were, and are still, far tighter than those governing Conservative MPs) with being not so much representatives elected to debate the merits or otherwise of proposals laid before Parliament as delegates mandated to impose the will of their leaders irrespective of merits and often without any or any adequate debate. They were in danger, I said, of becoming 'lobby fodder', and the label stuck. I do not know whether the phrase was of my own coinage, but I rather think it was. I certainly know of no previous public use of the phrase, and I should like to think that I had added to the rich armoury of English political invective.

My second front-bench speech was on 12 February 1946 on the Second Reading of the Trade Union Bill which was introduced by Hartley Shawcross making his début as Attorney. The Bill repealed my father's Act of 1927, which had long been the focus of trade-union vindictiveness, putting nothing in its place. My father was in the gallery for the first part of the debate but did not stay to hear my speech, which was at the end. I began with a short paragraph in praise of my father, which was as follows:

> One good thing at least which this Bill can do is to give me an opportunity, not often accorded to sons, to say that I am proud of my father and very proud of his public work, part of which it is my purpose to defend this evening. But more even than my pride in his public work is the feeling of pride I have felt in the very high standard of public controversy which he adopted. There are some, but not many, in this House who can remember those debates. I at least have read them, and it has been a very moving experience for me to read how, reviled again and again, in language which was not always temperate, and pursued by arguments which were not always well informed and occasionally were a little disingenuous, he still continued to fight for principles in which he believed, and, I believe I am right in saying, secured a reputation, even among those to whom he was politically opposed, for his sincerity, patience and single-mindedness in debate.

I never said this directly to my father, and whether it was reported to him or he read it in print I do not know. But none of it was hyperbole, and in my own debating I have always tried to hold fast to the principles – sincerity, patience and single-mindedness – which I identified in him then.

My speech was intended as a full-blooded attack on the Bill as a thoroughly retrogressive measure. My father's Act had been based on four principles, each one of which had stood the test of time, having been in force virtually for twenty years. So far from being, as Hartley Shawcross had claimed, a vindictive attack on trade unionism, under the Act trade unions and the TUC had grown and flourished in numbers and reputation as never before in history, and in 1946 stood infinitely higher than now. The first principle of my father's Act, born of the experience of the General Strike, was to define in clear terms which strikes were legal and which illegal, whereas the matter, though strongly contested and argued, had never been authoritatively stated before. The effect of its repeal was to restore the law to the uncertain condition in which it had stood before Mr Justice Astbury's judgment. The complete efficacy of the definition in the 1927 Act was established by the fact that never once in the succeeding twenty years had it been necessary for either side in industry, nor for the Government, to test its provisions in the courts. My father's second principle was to outlaw intimidation in terms which would effectively have prevented the disgraceful mass picketing and flying pickets which we have now seen repeatedly on television, and which until again prohibited were actively encouraged or silently condoned by left-wing political and trade-union leaders. The third principle was based on the belief that subscription to the political fund of a union should be a voluntary political act only and not obtained by apathy, laziness or positive discouragement under the unjust system of 'contracting out'. Hartley Shawcross had endeavoured to defend this essentially corrupt, and corrupting, practice by saying that on average it demanded of a trade unionist less than a farthing a week. I said that this was only a version of the disreputable housemaid's baby argument brought up to date. The fourth principle, more obviously contentious, was the refusal to allow civil service unions to be affiliated to a basically politically orientated body like the TUC. I myself remain sure that the principle is inherently sound. Every government duly elected and appointed to office ought to be able to count on the unqualified and complete loyalty of its civil servants no less than of the armed forces, the police and the judiciary, all of whom are entitled to hold their private opinions but not to reflect them by concerted action whether or not favourable to their financial or other interests. If it be objected that this involves a curtailment of what in others would be regarded as a civil liberty, I would not disagree. But I would reply that public servants get, and should get, compensating advantages in return. They enjoy relative security of tenure, reliable pensions and, one would hope, reasonably secure, comfortable and hygienic working conditions. Obviously the last point is not applicable in quite the same way to public servants who run special risks like the fire services.

But one would hope that such partial exceptions could be made good by adequately generous compensation and pension arrangements.

At all events, my speech on this occasion was a success and received a generous tribute from George Isaacs, replying for the Government. I believe it was the last speech of any consequence I made from the front bench in the Commons before my succession to the peerage in 1950.

My return to the Bar after the general election of 1945 was by no means easy. Only two firms of solicitors of my former clientele actually remembered me from before the war, when, despite my relatively recent call, I had enjoyed an increasingly successful and prosperous junior practice. One was the provincial firm of Metcalfe, Copeman & Pettefar, run by George Pettefar with whom I had often crossed swords as advocate before Judge Farrant, the only County Court judge, I believe, who actually rode and finished in the Grand National, and in addition a fine judge of port and Stilton cheese. On the bench he was universally beloved, but had the unsatisfactory inclination to divide the plaintiff's claim by two and give judgement for that amount. My other friend from prewar days who sustained me during that difficult time was a Jewish solicitor, Herbert Baron, who ran a firm of his own from Queen Victoria Street in the City, and was at one time President (I believe) of the Jewish cultural society B'nai B'rith, which means in Hebrew, 'Sons of the Covenant'. My old chambers were open to me, however, though with a new clerk, and I soon picked up quite a lot of work, civil and criminal, on the South-Eastern Circuit and in London which kept me busy – indeed, in some ways too busy – and provided me with a modest, but not excessive, income to meet the needs of my growing family. I had to desert these chambers after they had been taken over by Eric Sachs, because the bulk of my circuit practice was in the northern part of it, that is, Norwich to Chelmsford, and it became increasingly difficult to combine the ceaseless travel involved with the demands of the Whips at Westminster. I went down a floor on the same staircase in Paper Buildings to Theo Mathew's old chambers, where I had been a pupil in 1932, and where the same clerk, Sydney Aylett, still reigned supreme. After his retirement Sydney wrote a book about us all called *Under the Wigs* in which I figured prominently.*

In the mean time my father's health was steadily declining. I remember sitting with him on the lawn in Sussex shortly before his death, when he knew that he had not much longer to live. 'I shall always regret', he said, 'that I never saw you in the front row' (meaning, of course, that I was still a junior barrister, and had never taken silk). 'But, Father,' I replied, 'I would have taken silk in 1941 [in fact John Simon afterwards told me he would have given it to me] but for the war, and I only went back to the Bar in 1945 when I had to start again from the bottom.' He had to be content with this. In fact three years later Gavin Simonds gave me silk on my first application, and I became a Bencher of my Inn in 1956. When my father and I had that conversation on the lawn of our Sussex home in the early summer of 1950 neither of us had an inkling that one day I should be Lord Chancellor for two terms of office, nearly twelve years in all, whereas he, a far more eminent lawyer than ever I was, had two terms in office each of only about two years or a little less.

During my last years as a junior at the Bar, my practice, although very general in character, had a very solid basis in personal injury cases, mainly road accidents and employers' liability. I was employed by most of the insurance companies for defendants and by some trade unions and others for plaintiffs. But, following my father's advice, there was almost no type of work I did not take. I had plenty of crime (mainly Attorney-General's briefs for the prosecution) and divorce. I had a nice line in Privy Council appeals (mainly from Canada). I appeared before numerous public local inquiries, and before professional disciplinary bodies like the General Medical Council, and one or two ecclesiastical cases about the union of benefices.

It had always been said that it was impossible to combine a junior practice at the Bar with membership of the House of Commons. This I did not find to be true, though, of course, it was a handicap, as

---

*When at length he retired full of years and honour, his former team gave him a dinner, and he left for Australia to join his family where he died in advanced old age many years later.

solicitors, reasonably but wrongly, thought one was not able to give undivided attention to one's work. One prominent industrialist, a very well known and wealthy person, once instructed his solicitors, a very eminent firm indeed, to withdraw instructions from me on party political grounds. He had no knowledge of me whatever, and I record it as an example of the meanest sort of political discrimination. On the whole, however, I managed pretty well. The House of Commons has an excellent law library, better than my own chambers, and nearly as good as those of the Inns of Court. In the nature of things, one is kept up late at night waiting for a division in debates on subjects one does not wish to attend. I used a dictating machine regularly, and could manage to get rid of anything up to sixteen sets of papers before I went to bed. Incidentally, the need to work kept me pretty sober.

My second and third children, both daughters, were born during my period of opposition. Mary, christened Mary Claire after an old friend who was Douglas' godmother, was born in January 1947, and Frances Evelyn in November 1949. When Mary Claire was on the way, my wife said that our house in Victoria Square was too small to house two children, and she chose a house in Roehampton where I still live. In the early days, food rationing was still in force under the Labour government, and I dug up part of the lawn to grow vegetables, and devoted another slice of the garden to keeping hens which we used to buy as pullets on the point of lay and allow to roam inside a fairly large pen. They were given a second season of egg-laying as a bonus, and then, alas, and to my tender-hearted wife's sorrow, we ate them. My gardening proclivities came to an end as far as vegetables and poultry were concerned after my father's death in August 1950, when I inherited the family home in the country. I had been twelve years in the House of Commons, of which three had been in the Army, two of these in the Middle East.

My return to the back benches did not in fact lead to a serious diminution in my activities in the Commons. It enabled me, however, to be far more selective in my choice of subject and to confine set speeches to subjects in which I had a genuine interest. The index of Hansard for each of the remaining years during which, for a full session, I was Member for Oxford, shows more than a hundred entries relating to my participation. Most of these, of course, were about matters current at the time, but now largely forgotten amongst the trivia of the past. But there are three or more occasions when I believe I spoke to some effect. In the debates in 1948 I intervened in what subsequently became the Parliament Act 1949. This was one of the more absurd and useless statutes passed by the Attlee government, and characteristic, I believe, of the muddled and unprincipled way in which Herbert Morrison managed the affairs of the Labour Party. What was under discussion was the future of the House of Lords, and what I said on that occasion has a distinct relevance to its future at the present time.

It is said of Lord Melbourne that when his colleagues raised a topic as a fit subject for reforming legislation his comments always included the question 'Why not let it alone?' This in fact would have been the real wisdom of the case in 1948–9, and Roy Hattersley would have been well advised to ask himself that simple question before he again introduced it into current politics in 1988.

The preamble to the Parliament Act 1911, which was the product of the unamiable folly of the 'diehards' in the Conservative Party after the débâcle in 1906, stated that the subject of Lords reform, and the substitution of an elective second chamber for the traditional House, as it then stood, composed of hereditary peers in their five degrees, the twenty-six archbishops and bishops of the Church of England, and the handful of Law Lords created in 1876 to perform the appellate judicial functions of the House, 'brooks no delay', and the elective principle was expressed to be the only respectable one to form the basis of the substituted body.

But, against a problem which 'brooked no delay' in 1911, the House of Lords has proved a strangely resilient body, and it probably enjoys a higher reputation today than at any other time in its long history.

It is, of course, obvious that no one could have invented the present body, and no one outside a lunatic asylum could possibly defend its present composition of powers on purely intellectual grounds. Like Topsy in *Uncle Tom's Cabin*, it has 'just growed' and, so far from reducing its anomalies, the changes which have taken place in my own time, that is, since the end of the last war, have only increased its reputation at the cost of multiplying the anomalies. The main change has been the introduction of lay life peerages on a grand scale. This has altogether altered the whole ethos of the body, and widely extended its usefulness, the quality of the membership, the number of attendances, and its actual influence on the course of legislation and, alas, also the length of its debates. The leave-of-absence principle which allows peers to strike themselves temporarily from the list of active members, brought about by the late Lord Swinton, has not greatly altered the course of events, but to some extent has mitigated the scandal of the absentee peer, also at the expense of increasing the anomalies, by enabling peers, if they wish, to disregard the unqualified words of command in the writ of summons. Lastly, the broadcasting and latterly the televising of debates have greatly increased the popularity and influence of the Houses of Parliament in general, by counteracting the animal noises and hooliganism of Prime Minister's Questions in the Commons, broadcast on Radio 4. On the whole the House of Lords provides a model of civilized, thoughtful and well-informed discussion on public affairs, and a real limitation of the party system, which, left to the Commons, might well convert Parliament, which under our constitution has no limitation on its legal powers, into a single-party, single-chamber elective dictatorship on the former Eastern European model.

The clue to the paradox lies in the fact that the one system which could never work at all would be an elected second chamber based on the same method of voting and the same principle of forming constituency boundaries as the House of Commons. Such a chamber would inevitably be either a mirror image of the Commons, in which case it would be useless, or of different composition and effectively of powers rivalling those of the Commons, which, if they retained command of their senses, the Commons would never tolerate. If by any chance they did countenance such a change, it would spell anarchy when, as would be inevitable, the two Houses, both elected, and therefore of equal political and democratic respectability, chose to differ. Long after the time of which I am now writing I pointed out that the one way out of the dilemma would be a federal or quasi-federal House based on regional constituencies (Northern Ireland, Scotland, Wales, and several provinces in England) probably elected but on a different method of voting and at regular intervals instead of, like the Commons, on a dissolution. But, this done, two further problems would remain unanswered; the question of powers, and the creation of subordinate provincial assemblies, based on the same regions and with defined legal limitations and demarcations of power. This the Westminster Parliament has so far never been willing to stomach after the defeat of Gladstone's attempt at Irish Home Rule in 1885. The ghost of another attempt, Stormont for Northern Ireland, created by the otherwise abortive Government of Ireland Act 1920, has now temporarily or permanently been laid to rest, and the parallel attempt of the Wilson and Callaghan governments to create separate bodies for Scotland and Wales without doing anything analogous for England has also proved unsuccessful. If anything were to be done on these lines, there would have to be more public opinion behind it than I can detect at present. In the mean time Lord Melbourne's question, 'Why not let it alone?', reigns once more supreme. Arguments against change can never be based purely on intellectual respectability.

The strength of the present House of Lords lies in its very anomalies. As Lord Whitelaw and I both pointed out in the Community Charge Debate, with its present powers and present composition the House of Lords cannot effectively set itself up as a Court of Appeal from the House of Commons. But it does retain sufficient authority, influence, powers and nuisance value, at least under a Conservative administration, to constitute one effective limitation on elective dictatorship. Contrary to the false legend sedulously promulgated from the Labour leadership, the House of Lords has no natural built-in Conservative majority. There have been more defeats of Conservative governments in the House of Lords than under any Labour administration. Under both parties with majorities in the House of Commons, the House of Lords has scrupulously observed the convention established since 1945 that it does not normally defeat on Second Reading a programme Bill proposed by the

Government if contained in their election manifesto (though what it would do to a House of Lords Abolition Bill, if produced, remains to be seen). In spite of a misguided attempt by a minority during the Community Charge Bill, the House of Lords has never challenged the primacy of the House of Commons consistently asserted since the seventeenth century in matters of finance and, unlike the elected second chamber of the Australian Commonwealth, has never since the fiasco of 1909 sought to establish a veto by denying supply altogether. What in fact happens is that when the Labour and Liberal parties whip (as I believe they almost invariably do on contentious matters) it only requires a small hostile vote from the cross-benches with or without a small dissident Conservative minority to put a Conservative government in the Lords in a losing position. The one, and only, argument against the Melbourne doctrine is, and has been since 1911, that a left-wing majority in the Commons might suddenly determine to impose unicameral government.

At the time of which I am writing, in 1948 and 1949, the Morrison Act served no useful purpose. The diminished legal powers of delay in primary legislation imposed by his Act have made no practical difference at all. Given the volume of primary legislation which it is now, as it was even then, necessary every session to place before Parliament, and the legal power, which the House of Lords retains, of vetoing every single instance of devolved legislation without deferment, it is evident that the real power of the House of Lords resides not in its legal powers but in the power of reason applied in debate, and the influence of convention which prevents both Government and Opposition from pressing things to extremes. Sooner or later Westminster may think it worthwhile to come to terms with federalism or at least with provincial government. In the mean time Lord Melbourne's dictum, which for seventy-five years has governed the practice of all parties, had better be followed.

The second affair of continued interest in which I was involved during these years was the curious business of the expulsion of Garry Allighan, the Member for Gravesend, for acts amounting to dishonesty and an affront to the House. Towards the end of 1947 there appeared in a journal called the *World Press News* an article over his signature which alleged acts of widespread corruption of Members of Parliament by the newspapers, which, he said, consisted in the payment of money to disclose confidential information, with subsidiary allegations of drunkenness. On the precedents cited in Erskine May these allegations seemed to me to be a gross breach of privilege and contempt of the House, and to this, at the usual time of 3.30 p.m., I drew the attention of the Speaker. The Speaker ruled that a prima-facie case had been made out. The matter was then referred to the Committee of Privileges in which, as Attorney-General, Hartley Shawcross bore a prominent part, and, after a considerable lapse of time, the Committee report was to the startling effect that apart from one other minor exception the only instance in support of the allegations which was established in evidence affected the conduct of the Member for Gravesend himself. The House began by accepting a motion by Herbert Morrison that he had been guilty of contempt. In the course of his speech Herbert Morrison had said:

> The Committee found him guilty of first a libel in the House, and secondly the acceptance of a bribe, and they stated that these offences were aggravated by his evidence in which he sought to cast suspicion on others and persistently to mislead the Committee.

The motion condemning Allighan and finding him guilty of contempt and of giving false evidence was passed without a division. A second motion was then proposed by the Government and opposed from the front Opposition bench by Jim Reid, at that time former Scottish Solicitor-General, and later, for over twenty-five years, a Law Lord and one of the best judges both of English and Scottish law that it has ever been my privilege to appear before as counsel or sit with as a brother judge in the Appellate Committee. This second motion stated that Mr Allighan had been 'guilty of dishonourable conduct which deserves to be severely punished'. It was hotly contested by our front bench, and according to my recollection the great bulk of the Conservative Party agreed with them. In this debate I strongly supported the Government, and on a division the motion was carried by 198 votes to 101. Against me, in my own party were

Winston, Clifton-Brown (later Speaker), Crookshank, Walter Elliot, Manningham-Buller, and of course Jim Reid and a number of Labour Members as well. The majority of the Labour Party and Clement Davies for the Liberals supported my view, and a few Conservatives, like John Boyd-Carpenter, Paddy Hannon and Thomas Moore, also voted with me for the winning Ayes.

But there was also a third motion which had to be considered. The question was what should be done with the unfortunate Allighan. Morrison proposed that he be suspended for six months without pay. This I thought was a dishonourable compromise, fair neither to his constituents, who would be effectively without a Member, nor to the House, nor even to Allighan himself, who would be a kind of pariah if he came back, and if he did not would be wise to resign at once, which in practice would be the same as expulsion. I therefore moved a backbench amendment to this effect, which in the event was carried by 187 votes to 75. This time the front bench (Winston, Clifton-Brown, Crookshank) and Jim Reid supported me. In effect I had carried the House with me against both front benches, against my own front bench on the first division, and against the Government on the second.

I have often wondered whether I was not too harsh. On the whole I believe I did right, and I am quite sure that, having passed the second motion, the House had no alternative but to pass my own amendment to the third in favour of expulsion. As Winston said, in the course of what, to me, was a compelling speech:

> [On the second motion] the arguments were exceedingly complex and difficult, and it was only after considerable heart-searching that I came to the conclusion that it was right to vote against the Government's motion. But now we have a new situation. All that is past. This is not a complicated or difficult situation. In my opinion it is an extremely simple one . . . How can you stigmatize a Member as dishonourable by the most formal and solemn vote, and then, after an interval, long or short, immediately resume calling him an Honourable Member?

I had set a precedent. As I said in my speech, my amendment for expulsion was 'an odious task'. It was odious. But I believe that the precedent I then set was a service to Parliament. The Morrison position was a dishonourable compromise. The first motion was a formality. The leaders of my own party were, I believe, guilty of pusillanimity and even of pedantry in voting against the second. But, the second having been passed by a decisive majority, as in my opinion it had to be, there was no honourable or practicable alternative to expulsion. Whilst, if the truth be known, I was extremely sorry for Garry Allighan, I only wish that, in this era of leakage of confidential information by those in receipt of it, more would benefit by his experience. The fact that he received payment for what he did clearly aggravated his offence, as did the fact that what he did constituted a contempt of the House and that his evidence to the Committee was held to be dishonest. But deliberately to disclose confidential information of any kind without a legitimate excuse does involve a breach of duty. Our system of government depends on mutual trust, between colleagues, between honourable opponents, between government and civil service, between government and the armed forces, between Parliament and the Crown.

After the Allighan affair, my intervention in debates by speeches on the grand scale diminished considerably, although, at least for a time, references to minor interventions were as frequent as ever. The reason was twofold. My junior practice at the Bar was increasing mightily, and it was obvious to me at least that my father's life was drawing rapidly towards its close. I fought the 1950 election when Attlee's immense majority dwindled to minute proportions. After the count, at which I was again returned for Oxford, I had to travel through the night to deal with a murder case in front, if I am not mistaken, of Mr Justice Croom Johnson, a small and somewhat pugnacious judge. Maidstone Court was then, although apparently he was unaware of it, on one of the main air routes for civil airlines between England and the Continent. Mr Justice Croom Johnson was under the distinct impression that the noises to which he was subjected were due to low flying from a neighbouring RAF station. As a result of this false impression, he sent for the station commander, who proved on arrival to be a group captain of proportions as relatively diminutive as those of the judge himself, with the distinct difference that on the left breast of his rather battered uniform – he had evidently not had time to change before obeying the judge's summons – there were seemingly at least four rows of extremely distinguished medal-ribbons. The two small men, the bemedalled veteran and the scarlet-gowned and bewigged judge, eyed one another combatively, the one from the judge's bench, the other from the witness-box. At that moment another civil aircraft flew over the court, no doubt on its way to Paris or some other European capital. 'If this goes on,' said the judge, 'I will ground your aircraft.' At the Sheriff's lunch afterwards, to which I was bidden, the High Sheriff enquired of me what on earth he should do if the judge attempted to carry out his threat. 'High Sheriff,' I replied, 'in that case you would have no option but to call out the *posse comitatus*.' Happily the matter was not further tested.

Shortly after that, my step-mother warned me that my father had had another stroke, and, with one exception, I took thereafter a somewhat perfunctory part in the affairs of the House. The exception was the debate on the Schuman plan, as it was then called, which took place towards the end of June 1950. Exceptionally, Winston asked me to make, from my place on the opposition back benches, the principal winding-up speech on the first day of debate, in support of an official opposition motion to be proposed by Anthony Eden imploring the Government not to miss the opportunity afforded by Schuman's invitation to take part in the discussion preliminary to the formation of what subsequently became the European Iron and Steel Community, the first of the three associations subsequently merged into the European Community.

I accepted with alacrity. Not only was I heart and soul behind the motion, but I also knew instinctively that it would be the last opportunity open to me to address the Commons before my father died and I succeeded to his peerage. The Government was hostile and proposed an alternative to our motion expressing willingness to join in the discussions, but refusing to subscribe to the essential conditions of doing so, namely the pooling of resources in the three commodities of coal, iron and steel and the establishment of a High Authority to implement the plan, which was of course to be supranational in character. In practice the Government's attitude was a polite refusal, and a disastrous piece of political blindness characteristic of the Labour Party's attitude towards the European idea. My principal opponent winding up for the Government on the first day was Dick Crossman, my exact contemporary at Oxford, brilliant in scholarship and with outstanding brains, but utterly devoid of principle or moral conviction. Rightly or wrongly I tried to give of my best to fulfil my brief, which was a whole-hearted support of Schuman's invitation, given me orally by Winston. I began by trying to expose the inconsistency and party prejudice underlining Crossman's arguments. His first objection had been that most of the existing European governments were, in effect, Christian Democrat, and therefore hostile to what he called socialism. To this I replied in effect that no discussion in 1950 could foretell how long existing governments would be in office, and that, in any event, one could not make conditions to independent nations embarking on discussions for co-operation about what sorts of government they could elect. His next objection was that the acceptance of the plan would inevitably lead to a European federation essentially undemocratic in character. This argument still has some relevance today, since then, as now, there were differences of opinion on this very topic, including, I must add, among very distinguished members of my own party. To this I replied that I was against a federation of Europe, but that this was not the necessary consequence of the proposed High Authority. In this, so far, I have been proved correct. But, because I knew these would be my last words spoken as a Commoner, I ended on a high note:

> For two thousand five hundred years the nations of Western Europe and their predecessors have struggled painfully, brick by brick, to build up a body of political doctrine, enshrining belief in the freedom of individuals and of nations, fortified by the rule of law, sustained and inspired in later centuries by the massive philosophy and

age-long tradition of historical Christianity, achieving, as I
believe, not only an unparalleled measure of human freedom, but also an unparalleled measure of human co-
operation. This is the western civilization of which we talk.
This is the Christian society. This is the thing which gives
us all a second country above and apart from that in which
we were born. This is the tradition which gave to our
constant internecine feuds the poignancy as well as the
bitterness of civil war.

It has not proved enough. The specific challenge of
history to our civilization has been its inability to solve the
problem of peace. We have never achieved liberty except at
the expense of a considerable degree of disorder. Nor have
we ever built up a system of order without sacrificing some
of the essential principles of liberty. Bloodshed has marked
the course of our career through time. We have all become
the children of Cain with his mark upon our brow, and if
this plan can, as I believe it can, offer a step forward towards
a specific response to this historical challenge, then I do not
think it will be in vain.

I went on to warn the House of the consequences of refusal, and,
although the consequences have not been as severe as those I then
apprehended, I believe they were severe enough. Had we entered the
Communities from the start, I believe what emerged would have
been much more to our liking than what ultimately appeared: a
bureaucratic Commission; a Parliament, seated in another capital,
oscillating between irresponsibility and impotence; a quarrelsome
Council of Ministers responsible each to his or her own Parliament;
an agricultural plan, flawed, not as Crossman had feared in the
direction of restrictions but in favour of wine lakes, butter mountains
and wheat surpluses; the de Gaulle veto; the Franco-German Axis,
directed, perhaps not intentionally, against Great Britain; and the
humiliating crawl back consummated in 1972 by an absurd refer-
endum and an Act of Parliament devoid, as Lord Diplock complained at the time, of any statement of principle.

As I spoke, I was of course aware that not all my party was with me. Harry Legge-Bourke, a narrow-minded but honourable patriot, was afraid that I had betrayed Commonwealth and Empire. Eden was, as I believe, lukewarm in his attitude, though he had proposed the motion. There were others who looked west to our becoming the fifty-first state of the Union. All, I believe, were misguided. The way forward was through Europe, and through Europe we ultimately chose to go, though at a price greater for us and, as I believe, for Europe, higher than either we or they needed to pay.

So, as I then thought, ended my career in the House of Commons. Mary was in the gallery, knowing the significance to me of the occasion, listening to what I had to say. My father died less than three months later, during the long vacation, and I became involved in a new, and personal, controversy.

THIRTY-TWO

Death of My Father

MY FATHER DIED on 16 August 1950.

The loss of a parent is always a landmark in one's life. Life is never the same again, especially when the parent is the survivor of the two. So long as one knows that they are in the land of the living, one is aware at the back of one's mind that somewhere, however far away, is one of the two physical authors of one's being, who welcomed the baby, housed him, fed him, saw to his christening, educated him, launched him into adult life. To say that one does not miss one's parents or either of them would not be true. Their loss leaves a gap which no one else can fill. Nevertheless I do not put the loss of my father forward as one of my great bereavements. Quite the contrary. For fourteen years, patiently and with dignity, he had borne an appalling affliction, all the harder to bear because in active life and robust health he had been so immensely industrious and successful, and all the time he had had to live tended by others and increasingly limited in almost every way, unable to shave himself or turn over in bed, writing illegibly with his left hand, and suffering increasingly from loss of those correct words he wished to utter. Throughout those years he had contrived to play a useful part, in the years of the war, actually including acting chairman of the Polytechnic. He was truly a noble man, giving me a splendid example of what a human being should be. But in the last years, and particularly in the last months of his life, though we never spoke of it to one another, I knew that he was waiting for the end, and desiring it to come. I was with him to within five minutes of his death, by his bedside. I had been summoned home to our Sussex home by Mildred, my step-mother, a fortnight before the end. One sunny August afternoon I had left him for five minutes to fetch a handkerchief or something from my bedroom, and by the time I had come back he had gone. I grieved, of course, and I grieve as I remember it. But all the same I was glad, and thanked God for having released him from the burden he had borne so well, and as I went out into the sunlight to be alone with my thoughts in the garden the hot August sun warmed me like a benediction. I never knew his true religious beliefs. I never knew him to take the sacrament, and in his last illness I knew that he expressly declined to do so. He was violently anti-papal in his expressed opinions. He knew his Bible well but he had no idea whatever of the spirituality or depth, be it true or false, of the Catholic religion whether as taught in Rome or in other mainstream Christian churches, and I think he simply did not wish to know. In my irreligious days, he showed himself profoundly shocked at some of my anti-religious outbursts – for instance, when I criticized the passage in the Acts of the Apostles dealing with the unfortunate affair of Ananias and Sapphira. When he took the oath to testify he told me he always insisted on taking it in the Scottish fashion, right hand up-raised but not holding the Bible. So far as I can remember, he never gave me any positive religious instruction, unless severe warnings against the Roman Catholic faith can be so called. I assume that, at Eton, he had been confirmed, but, if so, he never mentioned the fact to me. At one time in his life he had been an active Freemason, but when, in his last illness, I asked his advice on the subject he advised me against it, and I never became one. His most enigmatic utterance on the subject of religion I learned almost the other day. My step-sister, Domini, told me that, in the last months before he died, he said to her that he did not think it mattered what a man believed so long as he believed something. I do not think he can have meant quite that, but I do not know exactly what he did mean. I am sure he admired his mother's Scots Presbyterianism, and so do I, since she was manifestly a saint. But, so far as I knew, he never went to a Presbyterian church and he had his children brought up as Conventional Anglicans. What I do know is that he was a transparently honest, just, merciful, humane and profoundly patriotic man, and

lived a good as well as a distinguished life accordingly. Had his father
had the sense to send him to Balliol after he left Eton instead of
transporting him to British Guiana to grow sugar, he would have
been amongst those distinguished men from Wadham College –
Birkenhead and Simon, Roche and C. B. Fry – who made such a
contribution to sport, law and politics when they came to maturity.
His powers of persuasion and his gift for instructional exposition
were unsurpassed, and I would say unequalled. He did not really have
long enough as Lord Chancellor to make his true worth felt in that
office. His powers of factual analysis of a complicated case were the
best I have ever known anywhere. His lack of academic training
makes his judgements a trifle less exciting than some of the best by
those whom I have mentioned. I wish he were better remembered
now than he is. He deserves to be. But at least his son remembers him
and venerates his memory. His body lies buried in Herstmonceux
churchyard with Mildred my step-mother and beside Edward, my
brother and his step-son, and next door to Mary Evelyn, my wife and
his daughter-in-law, and I hope one day next door to my own mortal
remains, when my time comes to go there. I wish I were anything like
as good or as great a man as he, as certain of the reward that comes to
the true and faithful servant.

In the mean time I had to consider my own future. I still held
those views about my parliamentary ambitions which I had held five
years earlier. When my much loved and deeply admired father died, I
was still a member of the Commons, and I was asked by an enterpris-
ing reporter what I proposed to do now. I found myself answering,
with strange prescience, that 'in some twenty years from now, some
ass might make me Lord Chancellor'. At the time I thought that this
could only be because, for the love of law, and of the profession which
has never left me at any time in the course of my life, I might have
been thought worthy of a seat in the High Court Bench, and that
later some prime minister of the day might perhaps recollect that I
had once held Conservative opinions, and had had in the remote past
some parliamentary experience. Quite unexpectedly, and by a totally
different route, exactly almost to the month, twenty years from
my father's death, I was in fact to become Lord Chancellor,

though I devoutly hope that the prime minister to whom I owed this distinction and to whom I shall always be grateful, will never be thought to deserve the description I had forecast in 1950.

By the stop of a heartbeat I had ceased to be entitled to sit in the House of Commons. I had become the holder of two hereditary titles: the barony which my father had received in 1928 as a consequence of his tenure of the Woolsack, and the viscountcy which he received as the reward, in 1929, for his first successful period in that office. My constituents evinced no desire for a by-election. I had long determined what I would do. I wrote to the Prime Minister, Attlee, to do for me what Harold Macmillan afterwards accorded willingly to Anthony Wedgwood Benn when he became the second Viscount Stansgate. I did not expect to succeed in my request from that rather mean-minded, waspish man. But I believed that, sooner or later, reason would prevail, and I now think that my unsuccessful attempt may have been an indispensable preliminary to Anthony Wedgwood Benn's ultimate success.

What I did not expect was the fundamental dishonesty and misrepresentation of Attlee's reply. These frankly shocked me. My letter to the Prime Minister had made the nature of my request perfectly plain. I was asking for nothing for myself alone. Like Benn, I was requesting a change in the general law relating to the succession to a hereditary peerage, such as was accorded to Benn in the Peerage Act 1963. The only difference between my case and Benn's was that I chose to obey the law and become quickly a member of the Conscript Fathers, whilst he chose to defy it by trying to sit on in the Commons. Attlee elected to treat my request as a plea for privilege peculiar to myself. I did not believe at the time that this reply to me could have been written by an intellectually honest man, and I do not think so now. Perhaps there is something paradoxical in the fact that the unsuccessful plea was made by a Conservative to a Labour prime minister whose party was pledged to the abolition of the hereditary peerage on principle, while the successful plea was made by a left-wing Labour Member of Parliament to a Conservative prime minister who, though committed to the continuance of a hereditary

House of Lords, was at least prepared to admit the injustice to one who was admittedly unwilling to join its numbers.

Despite his disingenuousness to me on that occasion I rank Attlee relatively high in the hierarchy of postwar prime ministers. He was the Truman of British politics. Like Truman, no one would have given him credit for the qualities he showed from the moment he assumed his position at the head of affairs. To turn Tacitus' epigram on its head, Attlee was 'omnium consensu incapax imperii nisi imperasset'. I well remember one occasion early on in his government when Attlee had replied to a debate in which he scored a fair number of points against Winston who had been winding up for our side. When the division was called, it happened that I was immediately behind Winston as we trooped through the lobby. Winston turned back to me and said: 'Not a bad speech of Attlee's, just now.'

'No, sir,' I replied. (I always gave Winston an honorific 'sir'.) 'And do you know, I do not think he could have made it eighteen months ago.'

'H'm,' growled Winston. 'Feed grubs Royal Jelly and they become queens.'

Bob Boothby, who was standing to the right of Winston and in front of me, turned back and said to me: 'I bet you dine out on that story for years to come.' He was right. I did. But it still seems to me worth telling.

THIRTY-THREE

Carter's Corner

APART FROM MY TITLES, I had now become the owner of what at that time I regarded, and even now regard, as my home.

In 1917 my father had bought the freehold of a house standing above Pevensey Marsh about two and a half miles from the market-town of Hailsham and in the parish of Hellingly. Its name is, and as far back as human memory goes always was, Carter's Corner Place. As it stood then, it consisted of two parts, one dated over the front door as 1602, the last full year in the reign of Elizabeth I. The house, however, contained parts and materials much earlier than that date, and it is probable that there was a house there on the site at least since the fourteenth century. It overlooked Pevensey Marsh, and you could see across the sea as far as the *Royal Sovereign* lightship whose flashing lights were clearly visible on any night not obscured by mist. It was exactly opposite Norman's Bay, the exact spot, according to local legend, where William the Conqueror landed, though then, at high tide at least, the sea extended further inland than is now the case, right across what is now the marsh. His heavy cavalry, the real might of his army, he put ashore at Pevensey, where they captured the ruined Roman fort of Anderida. His infantry rowed across the shallows to the peninsula which now holds Hastings and Battle where Senlac (the lake of blood) gave the name of the encounter and where, in gratitude for his victory, William founded Battle Abbey, placing the high altar on the exact spot where Harold's body lay, not pierced through the eye by an arrow but foully murdered by William's brutal knights. They had ridden round from Pevensey, laying waste everything they could find, by what is now the lower road past

Herstmonceux. They found some friendly monks near the sea on that peninsula, and there awaited Harold, who for some reason gave them a pitched battle, instead of luring them on to face an uncomfortable winter in the Weald.

The house is pictured in a print in the British Museum dated 1745, a copy of which I still have. A fascinating story attaches to it by local legend. It is well known that in the reign of Henry VIII the Lord Dacre of the day whose home was at Herstmonceux was hanged for the murder of a bailiff of the Pelham family (the ancestor of the earls of Chichester, whose main seat was miles away at Stanmer more or less on the present site of Sussex University). The legend is that the bailiff lived at Carter's Corner and that the affray, a boundary dispute, which led to his death and was the cause of the trial was near by in a piece of forest now called Park Wood. The legend goes on to say that Dacre was in fact innocent, and was covering up for his party of guests who had ridden with him over from Herstmonceux to hunt deer in the disputed territory of Park Wood, and had been guilty of the actual murder. However that may be, when my mother was renovating the house in 1923, she pulled out the Victorian fireplace in the room we used as a parlour. Behind the fireplace she found a Georgian grate, and behind the Georgian grate was an open hearth, clear, through a great chimney, to the sky, and behind the open hearth was a Sussex Iron fireback impressed unmistakably with the coat of arms of the Pelham family, of straps and buckles.

The name of the house is something of a mystery. Local tradition associates it with a mythical first owner 'Carter' who was given a 'Corner' of land by a grateful employer. But I do not believe this. The name 'Corner' is a common enough place-name in that part of Sussex and is always associated with a road or junction, coupled with a specific geographical description. Thus there is a 'Woods Corner' and a 'Three Cups Corner' and other 'Corners' in the neighbourhood. Now, just below the house there is just such a junction marking the spot where the parishes of Hellingly, Warbleton, Herstmonceux and Hailsham theoretically meet, and I have often wondered whether the name, like that of Carfax in Oxford (*quattuor vias*) is associated with the French or Latin words for 'four'. Alternatively, the name may be associated with a sharp change of gradient in the road running by the house where it might be accepted that carters were used to lead their horses.

However, local legend has a habit of being right. I have already mentioned the coincidence of the Pelham arms on the fireback which obviously dates from a time earlier than the present house, and confirms the story of Pelham ownership of this site. But here is another coincidence. Local tradition has it that the Presbyterian owner of the house, after Charles II escaped from the battle of Worcester and was making his way to the south coast and his escape to France, sheltered and aided the royal fugitive, who rewarded him after the Restoration by giving him a royal licence to hold Presbyterian services on the property, probably in a granary now demolished. That such a licence existed there is no doubt, and my father once had the original, signed at the top with the royal sign manual.

The soil is hungry, sour and poor, almost all made up of Heathfield sand with a pocket of Midhurst clay. Apart from the rather modest farming operation carried on by my step-mother and consisting of a few pigs and hens and about fifteen Jersey cows with their calves and heifers and a bad-tempered little bull called Stylish Charlie, there was no serious cultivation going on. Every year one field grew cereals rotating with roots and a few potatoes. The cereals would be harvested in the old-fashioned way by reaper and binder, dried in the stook, and finally stacked prior to being threshed by a hired 'drum'. There was one old and another very old Fordson tractor, and there was a charming cart-horse called Nylon, who in better days had pulled a coal-cart and still retained the habit observed by horses pulling coal of heaving the cart into motion with a sudden jerk and then subsiding into a gentle amble, suitable for pulling the loaded sacks from house to house. There was a small walled garden and an outer garden devoted to vegetables and dominated by a huge mulberry tree. Most of the open land was covered in the summer with bracken and all the year round with scrub, mostly birch, amongst which a small tented camp had been used by the troops prior to the Normandy landings. There were two woods given over to the Sussex system of coppice and standards. The whole ground was populated by rabbits until these were exterminated at least temporarily in 1951 by myxomatosis. There was the occasional wild pheasant, and very occasionally wild mallard visited the one pond clean enough to allow them to nest.

I knew every inch of my father's property where, boy and man, I ferreted rabbits or waited for pigeons with my little spaniel bitch before she was killed on the road (by a motor-cyclist who never stopped) or with the gardener's terrier or, later, my own Welsh springer spaniel. From hard experience in Roehampton I knew how to grow vegetables. Of farming I knew practically nothing, except that the whole live and dead stock of the farm, but of course not the house, had been valued for probate so far as I now remember at £15,000. As I found it, the land was virtually unfarmable. But it was my home, and I loved it. Indeed, though I lost it, I love it still. The question was how I could keep it without going bankrupt. I was prepared to take a small loss on the market-garden. But the farm could not be left as it was. At first I employed a well-known firm of estate agents, but, when after two or three years, in addition to their management fee I found myself losing £1,000 or £2,000 every year, and was told by the agents that I would continue to do so, I said to them that I could achieve that result as well as they could for myself and farmed it personally together with my farm foreman, a remarkable character of Cheshire origin. In fact I farmed it altogether for nearly fourteen years. It either made a profit or broke even, and I ended up with a fairly large capital gain. I only gave it up because my wife Mary found that she could not bring up five children and run two houses. If she had let me stay on another five years, I would have been quite a rich man, for together with some adjoining fields I had bought for a song the land was by then selling at over £1,000 an acre.

By the time I had to leave at the end of 1963 I had brought the whole of the land into cultivation, except for the woodland (some of which I replanted) by a policy of uprooting hedgerows, clear felling, ploughing and reseeding the derelict land, and selling the timber. The policy of the Government of those days was to make two blades of grass grow where one had grown before. I actually brought into cultivation land most of which to my knowledge had not been cultivated for over fifty years. After some experience I abolished the pigs. But the foreman's wife continued to earn pin money from the free-range hens. I grew no more corn, and at the end almost the whole of the land was down to permanent grass, stimulated by fertilizers and manure. There I furnished myself with 120 milkers and their followers, and I had a contract with a Hastings dairy to sell farm-bottled Jersey milk. My father's bull, Stylish Charlie, was quickly put down, and I borrowed a fine bull from one of my neighbours and bought him later for a nominal sum. His heifers yielded an average of 10 per cent more than the Jersey herd average, and when they got a bit inbred I employed AI, or, as we called it on the farm, 'the bull in a bowler hat'.

In fact I could not have gone on indefinitely combining farming with public life. The farm foreman, Millington, would have been too old, and Mary died, tragically, in 1978. So I lost my home, but when I visit the neighbourhood, as I still do regularly to tend darling Mary's grave in Herstmonceux churchyard, I creep back to Carter's Corner like Mr Mole in *The Wind in the Willows*, and am always hospitably welcomed by one of the three households now occupying the house as three separate units of accommodation. Since, from the age of ten, I had been brought up in the country, I still think of myself as a country man, and am glad of my recollections of fourteen years of productive farming. Of course, nowadays with butter mountains and other surpluses I suppose I would be taking advantage of 'set aside'.

I sometimes think of these years as among the happiest of my life. I was out of office. Weekend by weekend we went down from Roehampton to Carter's Corner. I walked the farm and did some rough shooting on the Saturday, and on the Sunday read the two lessons in one of the two churches serving the parish – in the Authorized Version, of course, for none other possesses the magic of Coverdale's prose as only slightly altered by the editors of James I. My children were born or growing up during these golden years: Douglas born in 1945, Mary in 1947, Frances in 1948, James on Easter Sunday which, exceptionally, was Lady Day, in 1951, and lastly Kate, a year before we left Carter's Corner, in 1962.

I had of course made my début in the House of Lords shortly after taking my seat there, and thereafter attended fairly regularly, though I remained on the back benches.

My maiden speech in the Lords was, but perhaps did not deserve to be, something of a success. It did not deserve to be because it was both controversial and satirical of no less a personage than the then Chairman of the Governors of the BBC, Lord Simon of Wythenshawe, who on his own authority and without consulting his colleagues had stopped a television performance of a play which had already appeared on the stage and on the radio in consequence of an attack upon it in the *Daily Herald* complaining that it was a criticism of the Labour Party then in office and in power, the *Daily Herald* at that time being the official organ of the Labour Party and Lord Simon of Wythenshawe then a prominent Labour Party member. I had been advised that the rule that maiden speeches should not be controversial did not apply to those who had previously been in the Commons and succeeded to the peerage from there. I should not now advise a young peer who had succeeded to the peerage in circumstances such as mine to make a controversial maiden speech on such a subject, still less, which is what I did, to propose the substantive motion debating the question. But that was what I did, and I got away with it. I made my point, and it was a good one, even if it had better have been made by someone else.

I made two more speeches that session, one on marriage and divorce in which I clashed with the then Archbishop of York, and one on foreign affairs in which I castigated the pusillanimity, as it seemed to me, and hypocrisy on foreign affairs of the Government. But, for the main, I followed my plan of pursuing my professional career. In spite of the frequent breaks in this caused by military service in the war and my short period of junior office after it, this really took off after 1950 and, although I suffered the inevitable decline in income which followed my taking silk in 1953 (for the time being I lost my lucrative junior practice in personal injuries), my practice was beginning to build up quite nicely before the end of 1955.

In the mean time my plan was to play a conscientious but not conspicuous part in the business of the House of Lords whenever my professional engagements permitted. This was not as difficult as it would be now. Although membership was distinguished, attendance was usually sparse. Although they took place from time to time, divisions were relatively rare. Question time was usually perfunctory. Now, when the Liberal and Labour parties divide ferociously on nearly every contentious issue, where possible on a three-line whip, when average attendance runs into hundreds rather than tens or scores, and questions and debates are not infrequently televised, I would have found it much more difficult. The whole atmosphere of the House has changed. The vast influx of life peers, including a large number of former members of the Commons, has injected a note of purely party politics into debate, and makes the old ethos of leisured and civilized discussion more difficult to maintain. The greatly increased numbers and influence of the cross-bench element, coupled with increasing signs of independence on the Conservative back benches, makes the result of divisions more difficult to predict, particularly when a Conservative government is in office. I believe that television has greatly enhanced the prestige and influence of the House, which presents an intelligent and informed contrast to the monkey-house noises emanating from the sound radio recordings of Prime Minister's Question Time, especially since the disastrous invention there of the so-called 'open question'. The danger, which I pointed out some time ago, of our constitution, which depends so much on unwritten convention, mutual trust and political rather than legal checks and balances, degenerating into an elective dictatorship has led to a demand, both inside and outside the House, that the House of Lords should be used as a means of curbing more vigorously the authoritarianism inherent in a sovereign Parliament, especially under Labour governments, more controlled by than controlling the executive which is theoretically responsible to it. These factors make it much more difficult than it was in the 1950s for a backbencher, intent on earning his living at an exacting and competitive profession, from playing a useful part.

Looking back on this period in my own career, I thus think that I was extremely lucky to be as useful as I was. I may have been hampered slightly by my use of mockery and the biting phrase as a legitimate weapon in debate, but, considering the difficulties, I think I was fortunate. In November 1951 I made quite a contribution to the debate on the King's Speech, warmly endorsing the principle of the Welfare State, a phrase which was just beginning to come into use, but stressing the question of how it was to be funded in order to produce 'the best possible kind of welfare spent in the best possible way', and saying: 'Socialism may be an excellent way of sharing misery, but it is not a good way of creating abundance.' During the debates in the Commons on Aneurin Bevan's National Health Service, I had never been convinced that he had chosen to finance it wisely by wholly destroying the system of Approved Societies which offered some degree of variety in provision. I concluded in 1951 by claiming that the Welfare State was possible without socialism. I still think so.

When the next election came in 1951, I let Winston know, through Randolph, that I was not expecting office because I wished to concentrate on my career at the Bar. My sights were then concentrated on a possible seat on the High Court Bench, and perhaps beyond in the Court of Appeal. I certainly could not have afforded a return to political office and all the vicissitudes of general elections. I now had four children to educate and, without my practice at the Bar, it would have been quite impossible for me to do so within the independent system which, for both educational and religious reasons, was the only one I was prepared to tolerate for my offspring.

Between 1950 and 1956 I was a contented and happy family man, with a delightful wife and young children enjoying a happy life, with my legal practice flourishing if not spectacular, farming a small property, and had no ambitions beyond ultimate elevation to the judicial bench. The next chapter must describe how, from 1956 onwards, my life once more underwent an extraordinary, unexpected and, to me, unwished-for sea-change as the result of a return to political office.

THIRTY-FOUR

The House of Lords

ALTHOUGH IT HAS CHANGED VASTLY during the course of my lifetime, there is a sense in which the House of Lords has retained its identity through the centuries. It has never been representative in the sense in which, because from the beginning essentially elective, the Commons have been representative. On the contrary it has always been, and is now, a body of individual councillors of the Crown, summoned by writ to give their attendance and advice when, and if, a Parliament is convoked. Because it is not an elected body, and in spite of being called – to its great disadvantage – the Upper House, it has since the seventeenth century been condemned to perpetual subservience to the Commons in financial matters and, since the constitutional crises of the early twentieth century arising out of their attempted rejection of the Lloyd George Budget and the controversy over Irish Home Rule, it has never been in a position to challenge the Commons on whose confidence alone the government of the day has to rely. Thus it has never been in a position to constitute itself a sort of Court of Appeal to keep the Government and the Commons in order.

Nevertheless there is a sense in which, being a body of councillors either appointed or hereditary, it is representative in the sense that the individual members are truly representative of the experience, distinction, knowledge, sense of service and achievements of individual members of the community. Not being representative in the elective sense, and despite the unqualified language of the writ of summons, there is no enforceable obligation, moral or legal, to attend unless the individual peer has something to offer by way of vote or voice either generally or on a particular occasion.

The House of Lords to which I succeeded in 1950 had developed out of all recognition both in social quality and composition from that which had clashed with the Commons before 1914, and even from the body over which my father had presided in 1928 and 1935 or which he had led earlier in the 1930s. But it was even further removed from the House of Lords as it exists today.

Apart from judicial business, which before the war took place in the chamber itself between 10.30 a.m. and 4 p.m., the House met for its political debates about 4.15 p.m. and was usually up in time for dinner. I suppose the daily attendance was extremely sparse. The bombing in the war put an end to these convenient hours, and both Houses sat during daylight so as to be up before the sirens wailed and the raids began. After the House of Commons had been effectively destroyed by the raids of May 1941, the House of Lords vacated its own chamber and sat in improvised accommodation constructed out of the royal robing-room. It was there that I heard the dramatic defence of the American loan by the late Lord Keynes after a spectacular attack by Lord Beaverbrook. The smaller chamber, which today would be wholly inadequate to house the increased daily attendance, was admirably suited to hear Lord Keynes's quiet but beautifully modulated voice, which, without the microphones, would now be totally inaudible. Despite his occasional and often effective appearance in debate (he was no mean speaker either in Parliament or on the platform), Lord Beaverbrook was no great admirer of the House of Lords – the 'House of Make-believe', as he once described it to me. Once before the war I had exercised my right as the heir to a peerage to sit on the steps of the throne to hear the statement on the King's abdication. Apart from that, and my listening to the American-loan debate in the improvised chamber, whilst I was still a member of the Commons I had seldom attended, since I rather shared Lord Beaverbrook's views on the subject and, if asked, would certainly have said it would not last another quarter of a century.

After my unsuccessful correspondence with Attlee, I first attended the chamber on 12 September 1950 to hear Lords Jowitt (the Lord Chancellor), Salisbury, Samuel, Halifax, Maugham,

Mersey, Pethick-Lawrence (who was at Eton at the same time as my father), Simon, and the Bishop of Winchester pay generous and well-deserved tributes to my father as a lawyer and debater, as a former Lord Chancellor, as sometime Leader of the House, and above all as a man. It was, naturally, a moving occasion for me, and, apart from the fact that I remember being deeply moved, I have preserved no separate recollection of the speeches at all. But I cannot read them now without fond tears rising to my eyes. Maugham in particular described with deep insight the tragic paradox by which for fourteen years, with intellect unimpaired, the cruel stroke he had suffered prevented him from displaying his talent by public utterance.

Simon was equally moving about this. It is a great mistake to think of Simon as a cold, distant and unfeeling man. Simon has, on the whole, been judged unduly harshly by public opinion. His fine scholarly brain made him something of a loner. He refused the Woolsack in 1915, expecting, it was thought, to become Prime Minister. When, at length, he became Lord Chancellor, his judgements were of commanding and magisterial quality. He was no mean platform speaker, as all the pre-1914 political leaders had to be before the age of broadcasting. He was a generous friend. My father always had a warm spot for him and used to tell me how warmly Simon had welcomed him back to the Bar when he had been close to death from typhoid fever in 1917. He was intensely loyal to the institutions, his Inn, the Bar, All Souls, Oxford University, all of which claimed his affection. It is true that he lacked what is called the common touch. His tenure of the Home Office, the Foreign Office and the Exchequer all came at times when there were really no runs to be made, and his manner was gauche and, unless one knew him well, gave one the impression of aloofness. But in his own way he was a great man and, although I believe he retained no religious belief, he was virtuous and of the total integrity which marks all the leaders of the legal profession.

Meanwhile, during this period, I concentrated largely on constitutional and legal questions. In 1954 I was able to introduce at least two useful Private Member's measures of law reform which had come up from the Commons. (In those days, even more than now, shortage of government time made it necessary for the keener law-reformers to depend on Private Members.) Earlier, in 1952, contrary to John Simon's advice, I advocated the grant to the Court of Criminal Appeal (as it then still was) of the power in suitable cases to order a new trial, and supported Simon's minor attempt to improve the House of Lords as it then was by a limited infusion of life peers, and, in doing so, castigated both front benches for hypocritically shuffling off the issue in order to preserve the status quo. On that occasion I did not wholly endear myself to the late Lord Swinton by saying that he had defended his position with all the enthusiasm and vigour of an extinct volcano. In July of that year I participated in a somewhat ludicrous debate on the antics of the communist Dean of Canterbury, whom I think I designated a 'clown in gaiters' when he praised unequivocally the institutions of Soviet Russia, a favourite theme of his. The Archbishop of Canterbury also made a speech critical of the Dean, but somewhat ridiculously defended him by saying that he had never actually denied his belief in Christ or the existence of God. Seventy American clergymen had telegraphed the Archbishop demanding that the Dean be removed from his post. But I had to point out to them and to other speakers that deans of cathedrals were appointed, not by the Church, but by letters patent under the Great Seal which at common law are irrevocable, but that it was open to the authorities to discipline him without actually breaking the law of the constitution for his breach of the canons of 1603 by reason of his frequent absence abroad and breach by neglect of his canonical duties.

My main contribution to debates during those years was my bitter and wholehearted opposition to the policy of the Conservative government in introducing as its second network of programmes on television a new system, under an authority separate from the BBC, to be financed solely by advertisement and not by sponsored programmes. In this I found myself at one with Lord Reith, a number of senior Conservative peers, and other persons of Conservative cast of mind like the late Lord Waverley and John Simon. I was overwhelmingly defeated by the Conservative Party, and the embers of the controversy were eventually laid to rest. Once a decision of this kind is taken, like Bevan's choice of options for the health service, it cannot be reversed and is only seldom susceptible of fundamental change.

The general view at the time was that I had badly overstated my case, perhaps from excessive enthusiasm. I do not myself plead guilty to this. I was able to point out, on successive occasions, that the proposals had formed no part of the election manifesto, ran counter to the recommendations of successive Royal Commissions, were wholly anomalous in that they excluded sound broadcasting, and were based on pure dogma without a proper analysis of the real questions of principle involved. I tried, in vain, to insist on certain technical matters. It must be remembered that we were not at that stage concerned with the variety of channels which now exist, still less with the vast numbers now in contemplation by satellite. What we were concerned with was the creation of two alternative networks, one to be financed solely by licence fees through the existing BBC, and the other solely by advertising revenue, extracted by the programme companies under contractual licence but subject to a central controlling authority. I strove to point out that both systems were essentially monopolistic in character, that in neither case was there direct competition by purchase of goods or service at the point of use. I argued that children's programmes, religious and serious programmes, specialist programmes of all sorts would be liable to be squeezed out as not suitably attractive to the purchasers of advertised goods when true consumer choice would demand them. I argued that the real consumer choice would predicate two balanced programmes giving at the same moment programmes of widely differing character, and not two programmes at the same moment in time as like as two peas but competing for the attention of identical audiences, whilst minorities, who might collectively form an inarticulate majority of would-be viewers, might really want something different but rather special. My advantage in debate was that, even at that time, I had probably done more broadcasting, both on sound and on television, than most other active members of the House. If anything, I underestimated the prospective decline in values, the increase in sex and violence, trial by television, 'Death on the Rock', 'Tumbledown' and other horrors which have since been seriously and properly condemned. I greatly underestimated the value of the 'licence to print money' which subsequently occurred. I did not get everything right, and I got some things wrong. But I believe I saw more deeply into the question than my critics and I still regard what was done as an ill thought out piece of legislation introduced after inadequate preparation and probably for the wrong reasons. But I was greatly hampered by two factors, both of which were, in a sense, entirely irrelevant to the questions at issue. One was that my main support came from those who were either against television funded by revenue from advertisement as such, which I was not, or else against the American system of sponsored programmes which was not proposed by the Government and therefore strictly irrelevant to the debate. Still more I was hampered by the almost inspissated ignorance of the issues both of senior members of the Government and of the bulk of the members of our own side, who thought they were fighting for liberty and freedom of choice. On one side was the usual windy rhetoric from the left about the wickedness of profit, and the mythical but supposed subservience of Conservative leaders to those who make profits at whatever cost to aesthetic social or cultural values. On the other side there were grandiose and eloquent references to *Areopagitica*, and the puissant nation aroused from its slumbers – composed, it must be remembered, by that ruthless lackey of tyranny John Milton, the Latin Secretary to the Commonwealth. As a result I was soundly beaten and thought I had properly cooked my goose with the powers that be.

I was wrong about that, too. Late one night about this time, I was alone in the smoking-room of the Carlton Club, reading the periodicals, when who should come in but Harold Macmillan, then high up and of cabinet rank. Harold started talking to me about my future. I told him frankly that I considered my political career as effectively at an end. I had served under him briefly when he was Secretary of State for Air in the caretaker government. I was therefore on friendly terms and could afford to be frank. I told him I was only interested now in the law and my practice, that I saw no future for myself in politics, that I looked eventually for a judicial appointment, but that I needed to establish myself as a silk before anything like that could reasonably be expected to happen. We exchanged friendly drinks, and he went away, looking pensive. I believe myself that this conversation may have influenced future events. But this is surmise. What is certain is that from that date either in 1955 or in early 1956 a dramatic change came over the direction of my life. Indeed, I was almost fifty years of age and my real public life was just about to begin. Like the other great events which changed my fortunes for better or for worse, what happened was unplanned, unforeseen, and seemingly the result of chance.

THIRTY-FIVE

Suez

PATTERNS IN MY LIFE have a strange habit of repeating themselves.
I have already described how in 1938 my perfectly innocent attempt
to participate in public life by entering the House of Commons as a
preliminary to service in the House of Lords, started on the suggestion by Alec Spearman as the result of the six o'clock news, as a
three-cornered by-election of a humdrum kind, ended in the most
spectacular baptism of fire that could possibly have happened to
a fledgling candidate without previous experience of contesting a
parliamentary seat of any kind. My entry into office in 1956 repeated
this experience in an astonishingly similar way. I do not know how it
was that coincidence stretched its long arm in this totally unexpected
manner. Or is there such a thing as coincidence?

Not very long after my late-night conversation in the Carlton
Club I was summoned unexpectedly to an audience by Bobbety
Salisbury, then leading the House of Lords. He told me, much to my
astonishment, that he was authorized by the Prime Minister (then
Anthony Eden) to offer me the ancient but honourable post of
Paymaster-General. I enquired the salary. It was £2,000 per annum. I
was hardly flattered. I was nearly fifty and was busy trying to build up
my new practice as a silk and Head of Chambers, Diplock having left
us for the High Court Bench on his distinguished path upwards to
the House of Lords. I had two houses to keep up, and a young wife
and four children. I could no more hope to run my life on £2,000 a
year than I could fly to the moon. Oddly enough, in the good old days
of corruption, the office of Paymaster-General was, I am told, one of
the most lucrative under the Crown. To this day my own old-age

pension purports to be signed by or on behalf of the Paymaster-General. But, in those days, the funds placed at his disposal for the purpose were by convention paid to the forces or to whomsoever six months in arrear. In the mean time the fortunate Paymaster-General placed the funds on deposit at his bank or elsewhere and pocketed the interest. At the time, however, that Bobbety Salisbury made me the offer of Paymaster-General in 1955, I politely explained to him that it was financially impossible for me to accept the honour, and I went back to my chambers in the Temple, thinking that that, said John, was that. But, once again I was wrong.

I soon received another summons from Bobbety. This time it was to be First Lord of the Admiralty. This time I really was rather flattered. Of course, the office was not what it was when Winston had it in 1914 and 1939. It did not carry a seat in the Cabinet. At first I believed that since Walter Monckton, always a good friend of mine from the time my father had befriended him in his early days at the Bar, was Minister of Defence he would remain my superior. In fact, after October and during the Suez crisis, the office changed hands and it was Anthony Head whom I had known at Eton. I would also be working with John Hare, the staunchest of Tories, whom I only knew slightly, as my opposite number in the War Office. Nigel Birch, with whom also I had been at Eton, was in the Air Ministry; he proved to be nervy and prone to fits of threatening resignation.

I must admit it was a close thing. Not once or twice in the stresses and strains of the intervening years I have wondered whether I did wisely in accepting the office when I did instead of concentrating on the Bar. Had I known what was coming, I think I would have refused. Of course I consulted Mary before I took my decision. I was profoundly thankful for that twenty years later, since neither she nor I would have gone into it had we known that, indirectly, we were signing her premature death warrant. I distinctly believe that, had I said 'no' to the offer, as I very nearly did, Mary and I would now be living together in retirement as husband and wife after a life of relative calm and, I hope, distinction on the Common Law Bench.

In the end, however, acceptance was really inevitable. Even though no longer of cabinet rank, the First Lord of the Admiralty was still an office of immense distinction. When I left the Army in 1942 I had made a great resolution that, since I could no longer serve my country as a fighting soldier, my own life no longer really belonged to me. So many others had perished, and, through no virtue of mine, I had been preserved. I am glad to say that Mary wholly concurred, and during the four months in which we were at the Admiralty together I do not think I ever knew her happier. Nor has any other First Lord enjoyed a more supportive wife.

Of course, neither of us had an inkling of what was going to happen. At the time when the post was offered to me in the Leader's room in the House of Lords, I was told, and I believed, that my task during the next three years would be the finding of a new and honourable role for the senior service within an integrated combination of fighting forces, British and Allied, in the nuclear age. Stalin was already out of the way, and Bulganin and Khrushchev reigned in his stead. Like Walter Monckton himself, the existing First Lord, Jim Cilcennin, had been set on his way in his career by my father, but had now decided to retire. The change was originally to take place, so far as I remember, in the early summer. I was particularly anxious to keep my coming appointment secret, since when the secret came out, as it did, in the *Observer*, my practice at the Bar stood still over night. No one was likely to brief as leading counsel a First Lord of the Admiralty in waiting.

In waiting was indeed exactly what I was, since Jim's proposed resignation did not take place. This was the summer of the Bulganin and Khrushchev visit and the dismal and tragic end of Commander Crabbe in the midst of it. Though I never got to know the ins and outs of it, who ordered it, what it was hoped to get out of it, or why the political considerations of it were totally ignored, I always regarded this episode, now happily almost forgotten, as one of the most foolish, unedifying and dishonourable to this country in the whole of the postwar period. Bulganin and Khrushchev, rulers of the Soviet Union, were our guests, and we owed them, and on the surface showed them, every duty of hospitality. Diplomatically, in a sense, it was a breakthrough. It could have been seen – and, for aught I then knew, it was – a signal for an end to the Cold War. They came here in a rather elderly Soviet cruiser. No doubt the cruiser must have held on the bottom of its hull some military secrets which the Soviet naval authorities had rather we did not know. What they were I have not the slightest idea. But, even if we did not know them already, they were hardly likely to be matters of life-or-death importance, and, so far as I am aware, there was never any possibility of their being used in a hostile sense during the course of the visit. In these circumstances it seems scarcely credible that Commander Crabbe should be, if he was, commissioned to inspect the ship's bottom. I assume that his presence was detected, and he was killed by one means or another. But, for aught I knew, he may just as well have drowned or been snared automatically by some anti-personnel device. The result, however, was disconcerting in the extreme to myself. Jim Cilcennin's expected resignation did not take place, and I was left, absurdly, suspended in mid-air, without a practice, without my appointment, and without a word of explanation. Eventually, in despair, I wrote to the Prime Minister and was told that if Jim Cilcennin had resigned at the intended moment it would be thought that he had been dismissed because of what had happened as the result of the Crabbe episode. In the end, I was told that it had been arranged that he would go at the beginning of September and that I should take over then.

In the mean time I was reflecting on the role of a modern navy in the second half of the twentieth century. Not surprisingly in the absence of a tutor, I got it wrong, or, if I was right, the answer with which I came up is not the answer which has since been given by the military pundits. As a first step towards my understanding of the right answers I took the precaution of visiting the greatest Former Naval Person in the world in his home in Hyde Park Gardens. I went there at my own suggestion. I was cordially received and spent a long time in the great man's company. At that time, Winston was a little difficult to talk to. He had had more than one stroke. Words came out of him slowly, and there were gaps between sentences. There were those who said he was over the hill. I did not find him so on that occasion, though two years later he was capable of strange errors of fact. On the present occasion, I found him amusing and with judgement unimpaired. I began the conversation myself. I said that I

was about to be appointed First Lord of the Admiralty and had come
to ask his advice. 'I was already aware of this,' he said. 'I congratulate
you.' Long pause. 'You must get yourself a sloop' – the last word
pronounced with his usual lisp. He was referring to a replacement for
the old Admiralty yacht *Enchantress*. But I had not come to talk about
public relations so much as the fundamentals of modern warfare, and
I brought the conversation round to nuclear war. 'Indestructible
retaliation,' said Winston, almost shouting. 'Indestructible retaliation. That is the secret. Never forget that.' It was evident that he was
talking about an underwater launch-pad for a rocket, which was
exactly what Polaris and its successors ultimately became. This fitted
in exactly with my own thinking. I had long been of the opinion,
which I still hold, that nuclear war between the great powers (I speak
not of powers like Iran, India or Israel) would only take place if a
nuclear strike were launched, as were the bombs at Hiroshima and
Nagasaki, either against an adversary itself unprotected by a similar
capacity or, alternatively, by a power regarding itself as possessed of a
capability of smothering its adversary's retaliatory response. This, of
course, might happen if the aggressor was possessed of something
like President Reagan's 'Star Wars' weapon, which, I imagine, is why
the Soviets dislike it so much in American hands. At that time, my
thinking was (and it still is) that what was then most likely to happen
was not a nuclear war at all but a series of encounters with relatively
minor powers in various parts of the world, often at great distances
from the United Kingdom, which would require intervention at
relatively short notice by a force of conventionally armed troops,
transported by sea, with air cover provided from the sea, and
protected by anti-submarine and anti-aircraft capability from ships.
This was the role I had foreseen for the Navy in my inmost thoughts
and, although this does not correspond at all with what has been
done, I think that, if I had known how much money would be
squandered on Blue Streak, Skybolt, TSR2 and other fiascos, I would
have expressed my views even more strongly than I did. However,
other counsels prevailed. All the same, what I was then contemplating was not all that different from what has since happened at Suez, in
Egypt, Aden and Malaysia, and more recently in the Falklands. The

presence of such a force in the Mediterranean, backed by a task-force of commandos, might well have been useful more than once in the last quarter century. Of course, the argument on the other side lies in the land frontier with the Warsaw Pact, their vast superiority in numbers of men, and in tanks, artillery, land-based aircraft and other conventional weapons of war. This is not an argument which I feel myself any longer in a position to pursue, still less so after the unexpected events of 1989 and still in progress.

Events were taking on a most sinister appearance. Before my appointment was made public, Nasser had nationalized the Suez Canal and was proceeding, in defiance of his treaty obligations, to claim the right to hold staff talks with the other Arab states surrounding Israel and, soon after my appointment, to interdict to shipping the arm of the Red Sea serving the Israeli port of Eilat. I had never myself been a Zionist by conviction. But from my wartime experience in the Middle East I was never in any doubt about the hostile feelings innate in every Muslim and Arab about the existence of an independent Jewish state, or their intention to destroy it if they could. It was for this reason that I was originally hostile to the creation of Israel. But once the state of Israel was created and accepted as a member of the United Nations, as was the case after 1948, I was of the opinion that it would be absolutely disastrous to world peace if an alliance of Arab states were allowed to obliterate it out of existence. It was in this state of affairs that I took office in 1956, deeply apprehensive of the situation, determined if possible to defuse it. As events began to unfold themselves in the way I have described, I was never in any doubt but that if both the Suez Canal and Eilat were denied to shipping to Israel, or a threat was made by an alliance of Arab states to destroy Israel by military force, it would be in the interest of the West to intervene. The Suez Canal was already interdicted to Israeli shipping. I was also in no doubt but that, in the kind of situation which I apprehended, it would be Israel that would strike the first blow. This seemed to me to follow from the mere logistics of the case. Israel was surrounded at the time by Arab populations of not less than 35 million. At the most, Israeli mobilization would amount to about quarter of a million men, which would bring the whole economic life of the country to a standstill. It would follow that the one thing that Israeli could not afford was a long war. If they really thought their existence was threatened by a stranglehold, they would, I believed, be bound to strike the first blow and aim to win decisively at the first encounter, even risking the probable absence of air superiority. I never understood the attitude of Eisenhower or of John Foster Dulles in these matters. They could acquiesce in the destruction of a fellow-member of the United Nations if they wished. But I believed that this would be fatal to the existence of the United Nations itself, which they professed to be an essential element in world peace. Their behaviour throughout this unhappy affair seems to me to be both misguided and quite incomprehensible. I believe that both later came to hold the same opinion.

At the beginning of September when I became First Lord of the Admiralty, only the canal had been nationalized, and, though I was aware that there must have been some contingency planning, I was not told either what it was or in what circumstances it would be activated. I was a peacetime First Lord of the Admiralty, looking forward to some three years of useful and constructive work in planning the future of the Royal Navy. As with the Oxford by-election, my term of office began quite normally. By arrangement with the First Sea Lord, I was to occupy what had been designed as the First Sea Lord's flat, over the Admiralty Arch in Spring Gardens. Mary had inspected Admiralty House, then the true residence of the First Lord of the time, and decided that it was too large for her to manage and in any case unsafe for the children. As First Sea Lord, Dickie Mountbatten was not occupying the flat over the Admiralty Arch, as, being a wealthy man, he preferred to occupy his own London home in Wilton Place as well as Broadlands, his lovely seat in the country. Following my appointment, I was sworn to the Privy Council on 9 October 1956, which happened to be my forty-ninth birthday. I was, I believe, the forty-ninth Privy Councillor to be sworn in the Queen's reign. I have been a Privy Councillor ever since.

The first weeks were spent uneventfully, if not blissfully. Mary loved being the First Lord's wife, and the children were unexpectedly and excitedly happy in their new home over the Admiralty Arch. I myself was less comfortable there. I found it difficult to sleep owing to the roar of lorries accelerating under the arch and echoing back under the vault above my head; and, from early morning onwards, the amours and squabblings of that lascivious and quarrelsome bird the pigeon made it difficult to resume my slumbers. The work I found interesting, and, thanks to my experience as a staff officer in the war and my experience for that brief period in the Air Ministry as a junior minister, the paper work was relatively unexacting. The press had speculated that, with my well-known conservative views, there would be personal difficulties between the Hailshams and the Mountbattens, with their pinkish left-wing views and immensely distinguished military past and royal connections. The contrary was the case. They could not have been more gracious and understanding, and this was an immense source of strength in the exacting period which lay ahead. We remained friends through the whole of the remainder of our joint lives.

The last time I spoke to Dickie was a fortnight or so before his murder, at Peter Thorneycroft's seventieth birthday party in 10 Downing Street. Our last conversation was a moving one, since he spoke to me of his affection for his relative the Queen. 'Do you realize,' he said, 'that she is the most experienced head of state in the world?' This was not quite true owing to the continued if rather shadowy existence of the Emperor of Japan. But it is certainly true now, and my own limited experience as a minister has left me not only with a profound reverence for the person of my sovereign, but also with a deep admiration for her sagacity and judgement, for her wide knowledge and information, always accessible in her mind, and above all for her understanding and consideration for those who officially have to come into contact with her.

I was well served by a Principal Private Secretary, a Naval Secretary who was the last officer in the Royal Navy to command a battleship, Sir John Lang, who held Samuel Pepys's old job as Secretary to the Admiralty, and a much decorated Flag Lieutenant to the Board with whom my admirable daughter Mary Claire, then aged nine, immediately fell in love. When she was asked by the press what she would most miss as the result of my leaving the Admiralty, Mary Claire replied without hesitation and without a blush: 'Commander Houldsworth.' He was entirely worthy of her admiration.

Under the Ministry of Defence, the old Board of Admiralty, founded long ago when the sovereign put the office of Lord High Admiral into commission, was still in existence. Apart from the First Lord, the First Sea Lord and the Secretary, there was a bevy of other Sea Lords each more distinguished and more highly decorated than the last. The Second Sea Lord, Sir Charles Lambe, responsible for personnel, had been Dickie's best friend at Dartmouth. The Third Sea Lord, responsible, I think, for equipment, enjoyed the formidable title of Comptroller of the Fleet. There were also a Fourth Sea Lord, and a recently created office of Fifth Sea Lord, in the remarkable person of Sir Caspar John, son of Augustus, and responsible on the Board for the Fleet Air Arm. We were a happy team. I presided over a number of formal meetings at which there were always interesting discussions. Decisions were taken more informally as and when required. But I remember one discussion in particular when I was briefed on the number and proliferation of the Soviet submarine fleet – unlike our own surface ships, utterly useless in diplomacy or in time of peace, but a deadly threat to our islands if war should break out and continue beyond a catastrophic nuclear exchange. I was also warned by one of their Lordships that the real way to tell whether any of the powers had serious aggressive intentions would be to examine the extent of their preparations to defend their civilian population against air attack, another lesson which the unilateral disarmers might care to ponder.

There were also visits, always delightful, to Portsmouth ('Rule Britannia' played on the open space outside HMS *Victory*), Plymouth, Chatham (a seventeen-gun salute for the First Lord, and an inspection of the last 'rope walk' in Britain), various demonstrations of fire and damage control, which often went laughably wrong, and always, but always, lavish naval hospitality with the Queen's health always drunk sitting, as at Lincoln's Inn and the Rifle Brigade dinners, but this time with the respectable excuse that the ship's timbers in the deck above were supposed to be too low for a standing posture at attention. I was also introduced to the secret language of Navy comparable to the Wykehamist's – 'notions', 'heads' for latrines and so on. It was a delightful contrast to the strenuous life at the Bar and, if it had not been for one overshadowing dread, exciting, stimulating and challenging.

But ever present at the back of my mind was the shadowy spectre of the Suez Canal and the military preparations about it, of which I had been told nothing. From the first, my own preoccupation was what in the event actually happened, namely an Israeli reaction to Nasser's obviously aggressive intentions based on a coalition of Arab powers. By contrast, the press, the government and the public, national and international, seemed more concerned at the unilateral closing of the Suez Canal, our supposed imperial life-line. I was told nothing of the contingency plans, and when ships were actually beginning to move I was misled as to their true purpose, and given to understand that they were precautionary measures in case we might have to act in our capacity as guarantor of Jordan. In the end, I found my situation intolerable, and I told Dickie that I simply must be told the true story or else I would leave – a desperate step after only a few weeks in office. He said that the Prime Minister's express permission was required, and I said that it must be procured. It was obtained, and a young naval captain high up in the operations section of the Admiralty was duly instructed to brief me, and he did so. I forget his name, or the precise naval designation of the post he held. I heard him out, and then asked one question.

'What do you think of it?' I said.

'I think it is madness,' was his reply.

'So,' said I, 'do I,' and I took steps to see that my view was passed on to the right quarters. I still think I was right. From my war experience, I knew something about the nature of naval gunnery, since my brother officers had observed and described to me a bombardment, during the Wavell advance of 1941, by two First World War flat-bottomed monitors called, I seem to remember, *Erebus* and *Terror*. The thing about naval guns as they were used at the time was that, in contrast to land-based artillery and particularly the gun howitzers of the Second World War, they have an extremely flat trajectory and so, if they go a little over their target, they travel a long way devastating everything in their path. If there is a danger of hitting a built-up area, the effect could then be truly awful. I personally believe, though I cannot prove, that it was principally owing to the discussions that followed my conversation with the young naval captain that the plans were changed. I myself was glad that it was so, although, in my view, nothing can excuse the somersault we performed, once we were embarked on the operation, in stopping short halfway down the Canal, somewhere in the neighbourhood of the Bitter Lakes, when a simple piece of motoring would have enabled us to reach Port Suez, clear the Canal on our own, and then withdraw at our leisure, handing over the waterway either to the government of Egypt if it were still in place or, preferably, to an international organization.

I must make it clear that at no time before the plans were complete was I a party to the diplomatic negotiations which led up to the actual operations. I had formed my own appreciation of the international situation before I learned the true facts. My appreciation was that Nasser had determined to eliminate the state of Israel from the map of the world by heading a coalition of Arab states, and that his nationalization and occupation of the canal were simply preliminaries to such a move. I thought that, when this became obvious, Israel would strike and under Article 51 of the Charter of the United Nations would be entitled to do so in self-defence. I do not believe that the right of self-defence permitted by the Charter (or indeed in national law or morality) condemns the intended victim of an outrage to wait until the aggressor fires the first shot. Of course, this must be so on many and probably most occasions. But that will depend on the facts. I also thought that, if my analysis were right, Britain, France and, although I was disappointed in the result, the United States would have to intervene, in effect, on Israel's side. Of course, I know now that this is not a correct analysis of what actually happened. But it was so like it that, when I spoke on the situation to an international gathering of journalists at a luncheon a few days before the outbreak of hostilities, I thought that they would afterwards infer that I had known of everything in advance. In the result, although the matter was little short of agony to me, and although by a train of reasoning which did not involve itself in any way in the degree of secrecy or hypocrisy (if it was so) which accompanied what was actually done, I never doubted that Britain and France were right to intervene. I thoroughly disapproved of both the attitude of Eisenhower and Dulles, and our tergiversation in not completing the job before it was finished. In this, I gather, my own view coincided with that of Winston at the time and, in a death-bed repentance, of the lamentable John Foster Dulles.

Though, not being a cabinet minister, I was not there at the fateful cabinet meeting and sent in a message that we should go on, I have no doubt that the cause of our change of policy was a somersault by Harold Macmillan, then Chancellor of the Exchequer, who had been completely unnerved by the run on the pound which had been engineered by Eisenhower and Dulles, and which, had the operation succeeded, would never have lasted. This, I believe, has now emerged from being speculation into the field of established fact. The result of the disingenuousness of our original approach followed by our tergiversation when victory was assured was the fall of the Hashemite dynasty in Iraq, the murder of the boy king Faisal, whose poor little body was dragged by a hook round the streets of Baghdad, and of his civilized uncle Abdulillah (a friend of my brother Neil during the war), the present communist-orientated Iraq regime, indirectly the Iran–Iraq war, possibly even the triumph of the ayatollahs, the temporary obliteration of British influence in the Levant, and the cooling of relations with our natural ally, France, which led to our exclusion so long from the European Community. A sorry business, and for this I believe Macmillan must bear the responsibility. It would have been legitimate to be a dove throughout, or a hawk throughout. But to be a hawk in advance of the event, and a dove when success was certain was to get the worst of all possible worlds.

During the actual conflict, there was more than one tense moment of drama affecting myself as First Lord. The Navy then looked for guidance more to their First Lord than to his superior, the Minister of Defence. On one occasion I was woken up during the night to be asked what was to be done by a naval captain who was being shadowed by an Egyptian destroyer. So far as I remember, I replied that he must make his own appreciation as to whether the Egyptian's intentions were or should be assumed to be hostile and, if so, warn him off and, if the Egyptian did not take the hint and sheer off and the commanding officer thought his ship to be in danger, he should fire. I seem to remember he acted on this advice, but there were no political repercussions. The other event was potentially more embarrassing, and I would not now have recorded it had the facts and documents not since been published. During the crisis I found the flat almost untenable as, in addition to the pigeons and the lorries, the evening sounds from the constant demonstrations in Trafalgar Square were most disturbing. One weekend, having cleared with the department that my physical presence was not considered necessary, I determined to go down to Carter's Corner for Saturday and Sunday for a little peace and quiet. I had driven down as far as East Grinstead when my old A70 Austin was gonged down by a police car. I was to go back to the Admiralty at once since my presence was urgently required. When I got back I found Dickie and the Second Sea Lord in the First Sea Lord's office in a fine state of excitement. Dickie was having a brainstorm. Understandably, he had hated the whole operation from the start. He handed me a letter (since published by Philip Ziegler in his biography and by Robert Rhodes James in his life of Anthony Eden) to the effect that the honour of the Navy was at stake and he was tendering his resignation. Here my service experience and my recollection of Winston's experience during the First World War when he was faced with a similar brainstorm by Jackie Fisher came to my aid. I turned on him firmly and with the full approval of the Second Sea Lord told him that I was the political head of the department, that if the honour of the Navy was in any way impugned it was I and not its professional head who would have to resign, that he was entitled to the protection of a direct order from me, and that I would go at once to my room and write out and sign a direct order to him to stay at his post until further notice, but that I would report at once directly to the Prime Minister what I had done and ask him either to confirm or countermand it as he thought best. I did this at once, taking only Sir John Lang into my confidence. Needless to say, the Prime Minister supported my action and, until the publication of the papers, apart from a somewhat inaccurate account in Dickie's memoirs, no more was heard of it. Still, it was a somewhat embarrassing decision for a newly appointed minister to have to take in his first months of office, especially when the man who was technically his subordinate was a war hero of immense and deserved reputation, and as closely allied as Dickie to the royal family. Still I had no doubt as to where my duty lay, nor as to the constitutional propriety of the responsibility I took in doing it. As my father used to say, 'They pay for your opinions and not your doubts.' I am happy to say this odd episode did not interfere with my cordial relations either with Dickie or with Edwina. I had the right constitutional answer ready and gave effect to it. The paradox was that, though for different reasons, I hated the whole operation quite as much as Dickie. I had not joined the Government for this sort of experience. The thought of innocent civilians being put at risk as the result of actions for which, politically and constitutionally, I would certainly be treated as if I were technically responsible was an absolute agony for me, and, though I regarded the operation as a necessity, I could not approve of everything which had been done in preparation for it. Nevertheless I would have regarded it as an appalling dereliction of duty on the part of the political head of a fighting service to resign during the conduct of an actual operation of war. The time for such resignations is surely before or after, not when forces are actually engaged in combat and serving men's lives are in the balance.

Despite my disapproval of our own somersault, it was an immense relief to me when fighting came to an end. There were by-elections in progress while it was all going on, and I had to speak at all of them. At one of them – Preston, I think – I was accompanied by my Naval Secretary who, being non-political, esconced himself in the audience. The hall was vast. The noise was terrific. Nothing, said my Naval Secretary afterwards, had been heard like it since the battle of Jutland. It is worth recording that, despite all the opposition, the deafening screams of hysteria in the House of Commons, and Gaitskell's deplorable and tearful appearance on the television screen, the public supported us in what I have always thought was a difficult issue.

The end of the affair did not immediately put an end to my tenure of the Admiralty. In the first place I had to make a long-prepared official visit to the Mediterranean Fleet then engaged in clearing the canal and occupying Port Said, which I had last visited in 1941 when we were guarding the canal against the acoustic mine and used to mess in the Casino Palace Hotel. It had not been intended by my office or by my cabinet superiors that I should visit Port Said, but the Fleet was there and the Navy was evidently determined that the First Lord should visit it. As I understand it, the plan was that I should only visit the Navy and the Fleet at sea. The trip was enjoyable. I had not been to Malta since 1926 on the occasion of my memorable Mediterranean cruise in *Arcadian*. But the Grand Harbour at Valetta is an unforgettable sight. I visited the workshops at the docks and the workers in them, and I was amazed at the religious emblems at the benches and the uninhibited enthusiasm for them of the workers. I was received by the formidable Dom Mintoff, a somewhat hysterical figure, I thought, but then in one of his less disagreeable moods. I was let down on a string from a helicopter on to the catwalk of a submarine in the middle of the Mediterranean, and saw through its periscope *Ark Royal* as an enemy submarine would have wished to view her. I addressed several ships' companies on board their several frigates and, travelling east, spent a night or two in the captain's cabin of a cruiser. It was there that one morning, as I awoke, I saw the unmistakable figure of de Lesseps's statue sliding past the cabin port and knew that I was at Port Said. I was not particularly pleased by this departure from what I had been led to expect. But I was not particularly surprised, either. The Navy's judgement on what was expected of its political chiefs is very rarely at fault, and, although I was extremely apprehensive of what might be said when – as it was bound to be – news of my visit leaked out, I was secretly certain that *vis-à-vis* the Fleet itself the decision, which had not been mine, was correct. I dressed, came out on deck, boarded a launch which was to take me round the harbour, and there, straight in front of me, were the representatives of the world's press watching from the deck of a submarine depot ship, *Maidstone*, armed with binoculars, cameras with telephoto lenses and other apparatus, watching the portly figure of the middle-aged QC who was First Lord of the Admiralty climbing down the ship's side. I was taken straight away to *Maidstone* and had to give a press conference. I thought that after that I would quite certainly have to resign from the Government. In point of fact I was wrong. It was really from that time that, from being a person on the periphery of the political scene, I became a personality of national and, from some points of view, even international notoriety.

After the fiasco of our somersault, the canal had remained blocked by the ships which Nasser had placed in it. Thanks to the skill of the Admiralty staff, a large fleet had been assembled under charter, composed of salvage vessels of different nationalities and ownerships. My visit to the canal had convinced me of the urgent necessity to clear the canal and to set these vessels to work. Since there was a clear move afoot to turn Britain into a sort of international pariah as the result of what had taken place, I was determined that she should play a leading part in the vital work of salvage. The Secretary-General of the United Nations, whom I had never met, had been making a series of bold and, it seemed to me, overconfident statements as to the ability of the United Nations to carry out the work. They obviously could not do so without using the vessels under charter or contract to us, and it seemed to me to be perfectly natural that they should be allowed to do so, but of course on condition that we should also play our proper part. I saw nothing undesirable, whether for security or other legal reasons, in the whole salvage fleet operating under a single, nominally United Nations, command. One of a number of the British ships involved was an unarmed Admiralty survey-ship named the *Discovery*. She was not a warship but, being in the ownership of the Admiralty, she carried and wore the white rather than the blue or red ensign. (Incidentally all the members of the Royal Yacht Squadron at Cowes and myself as a former First Lord of the Admiralty are, I believe, entitled to do the same.) It seemed to me both natural and proper that she should participate in the work, and that it was particularly important that she should do so in the light of the tendency on the part of some misguided persons to make Britain *persona non grata* in the enterprise. I decreed that she should participate on the same terms and conditions as others. The more lunatic fringe of my own party seized on this and attempted to pillory my devoted self as the man who 'hauled down the White Ensign'. As a matter of fact I was extremely proud of the part I had played both in securing the rapid completion of the enterprise which could never have been undertaken with such speed and efficiency without British co-operation, and of my insistence that our ships should be seen to play a leading part in the clearance. Nothing could have been more lamentable than that they should be excluded either as the result of Third World hostility or from some ill-considered point of punctilio of our own.

After the shattering experiences of the past few months, I thought it right to restore morale among the Board itself, and so Mary and I gave a dinner-party in Admiralty House for the whole Board and their wives, all wearing full uniform or white tie and decorations. We brought out all the ceremonial plate, the Dolphin furniture, and used the state dining-room for the purpose. My first private secretary, Jean Crawford, stood in for Lady Lang who was unwell. Mary was on good terms with Madame Prunier, who personally put on a splendid repast fully worthy of the occasion. Dickie looked particularly resplendent opposite me with his rows of medals.

January came, and with it Douglas's birthday, his twelfth, and we gave a children's party to celebrate. It was only the second time we had used Admiralty House. There were conjurors and a sliding chute down the stairs. Suddenly, while all this was going on, there came a message from Number 10. I was to repair to the Cabinet Room at once. I rapidly thought of all my possible misdeeds, hastily collected all the controversial files I could find, and made my way to the seat of power, mentally padding my spiritual trousers as I went against the beating that I was sure was coming. When I got there, I found Nigel Birch and John Hare looking equally uneasy. From the bundles of documents each was nursing under his arm I could see that they had been doing exactly the same thing. None of us was expecting what was actually to happen. Anthony Eden had sent for us to say that his doctors had commanded him to resign.

I was absolutely appalled. Nothing, it seemed to me, was now wanting to complete our humiliation, and in a sense this was true. I had not found Anthony a particularly easy political master. He was far too fussy during the actual conduct of the operations. But, day after day, he had faced an appalling barrage of abuse and misrepresentation in the House of Commons, some of which I had heard from the Peers' Gallery. It was a sound, a colleague had said, to make angels weep. I had not realized the extent of his physical weakness following a mismanaged operation. I did not wholly share or even then know his almost extreme picture of Nasser playing the role of Mussolini in the run-up to the Second World War. Nevertheless I do not now believe that his analysis of the situation in the Middle East was as wrong as is now generally thought to be the case. So far as we were concerned, the consequences of our volte-face at Suez were bad enough, but in my view the civil effects were more due to our tergiversation and our desertion of our French allies than to our intervention to prevent what might well have been total obliteration of Israel from the face of the map as the result of a concerted aggression by her Arab neighbours.

The week after our interview with Anthony in Downing Street I was promoted to the Cabinet as Minister of Education, an unprecedented advance after only four months in office as a minister of middle rank. Neither Mary nor I, however, was happy at the change. We had given our hearts to the Navy and had been looking forward to our lives at the Admiralty. I am told that when someone asked Harold Macmillan to account for my promotion he replied gloomily: 'He wanted to rebuild the Fleet.' So I did. But now I had to start thinking all over again, this time about the schools. I still hankered after my first love, which was the law. Much was to happen before I saw the inside of my chambers again, in 1964. It was still only January 1957.

THIRTY-SIX

The Cabinet

THE FIRST THING I had to think about was the strange body of which I was now a member, the heart of our constitution, the British Cabinet with the Prime Minister in the chair. Very few people understand either the detail or the machinery of our government, all the more difficult to comprehend because it is constantly changing and depends so much more on convention than on strict legal doctrine. We sometimes say that we have no written constitution. Literally speaking, this is both true and false. It is true in the sense that there is no single document or collection of documents to which we can point, like the Americans and say: 'This (or these) make up our constitution.' But it is also false in the sense that much, probably most, of our constitution is in fact in writing. Magna Carta is in writing. So are the Bill of Rights, the Act of Settlement, the Representation of the People Acts, the Supreme Court of Judicature Act and the Local Government Acts. But it is both true and false in senses far deeper and more significant than these obvious and relatively trivial aspects. We have no separate kind of special law called 'Constitutional Law' which can only be altered by a peculiar procedure, like the American or, for that matter, the Australian constitution, or which, like the American Constitution or many others, is ultimately to be interpreted by a special court or class of courts. The Act of Settlement, which decided the descent of the Crown, and therefore the tenure of the office of head of state, can be altered by the same procedure as the Road Traffic Acts or the legislation dealing with dangerous drugs, and the pyramidal structure of our courts, culminating in the House of Lords (theoretically, but not in practice, the same body as the second chamber of our legislature and incidentally the only court whose jurisdiction extends to all three parts of the United Kingdom), makes no distinction between those courts which do and those which do not interpret and enforce constitutional law. This is just as much within the jurisdiction of a judge sitting alone in the Chancery Division, as was Mr Justice Astbury when he pronounced on the legality of the General Strike, as is the House of Lords itself, which, by the same token, is not specifically a constitutional court like the Supreme Court of the United States, but a court of appeal of general jurisdiction like the Court of Appeal itself. I myself have presided over an appeal in the House of Lords on a straightforward accident case in which we held that there was no evidence on which a motorist could be held to blame when he injured a schoolboy who rode his bicycle out of a side-road into his path.

There is an even more important sense in which one can assert that we have no written constitution. In its strict sense, law is something which can be interpreted and enforced by a court with competent jurisdiction. But this is not true of some, probably most, of the fundamental rules by which we are governed. Thus, theoretically, the Queen can veto any Bill which comes before Parliament by the use of an ancient Norman French formula when the Bill comes up for Royal Assent. But the last time this was done was in the reign of Queen Anne. In actual practice the Queen can no more veto such a Bill than any of her subjects. Once a Bill has passed through Parliament, Her Majesty automatically gives it Royal Assent.

So far as I can ascertain, the Cabinet, whose membership is perfectly well known, has no formal existence at all. It is a collection of ministers each with individual responsibilities. If it has any such existence at all, it is as an informal committee of the Privy Council. We all take the Privy Councillor's Oath, a formidable set of obligations but wholly unsuited to modern constitutional situations. Like President George Bush, William III could and did appoint and dismiss his cabinet ministers at pleasure; so in strict legal theory can Her present Majesty. But we all know that this does not correspond with the facts. The Queen's function is to select a Prime Minister whom she believes to be capable of commanding a majority in the House of Commons. Thereafter, and assuming that such a majority proves to exist, she appoints or dismisses only those whom the Prime Minister advises her to appoint or dismiss; and, whoever is to blame if a mistake turns out to have been made, it is not the Queen but the Prime Minister who must be held to account.

Until about the turn of the century the Cabinet was only a collection of ministers who happened to be members of the Privy Council, each with a separate but fairly well defined set of departmental responsibilities. It met in what, I suppose, must once have been the breakfast-room of one of the two houses since thrown together and called 10 Downing Street. Until well into the twentieth century they did not even keep minutes of cabinet meetings until the sheer inconvenience of not knowing what had been decided led to them doing so well in time for the First World War. The Prime Minister (an office formally existing only from the time of Mr Baldwin or, as some others would claim, 1905) is said to preside only because George I did not know enough English usefully to take the chair, so that the First Lord of the Treasury (the old office of Lord High Treasurer having recently been put into commission) conveniently did so in his stead. Incidentally, the old Treasury Board Room, where some cabinet committees are still held, has a royal throne, duly placed on a convenient dais, ready for Her Majesty should she care to attend and preside. It is never filled.

By the time my father, exceptionally for an Attorney-General, joined the Cabinet in 1924, government business had increased to such an extent that a system of cabinet committees based on different departments of government underpinned cabinet government, and when I first joined the Cabinet in 1957 these were still the permanent framework within which the cabinet system operated. The Cabinet itself met twice a week with a formal agenda – a practice which was of fairly recent origin, since, in my father's time, the summons to attend simply said: 'A meeting of His Majesty's Servants will be held at 11 a.m. on Tuesday, 4 November [or whatever] at Number 10 Downing Street.' I once knew a Cabinet summoned by one of the old forms. But this was exceptional, to learn of a royal occasion which was to take place.

The existence of the several standing committees has never been formally announced, and when I was first a member it was supposed to be a breach of the Privy Councillor's oath to refer to them. In January 1957 and throughout the Macmillan and Heath governments (and I have no doubt in Labour governments, too) the Cabinet normally met twice a week. This placed a considerable burden on cabinet ministers (most of whom have other things to do) as attendance in cabinets is supposed, in the absence of some special dispensation, to be compulsory, and all cabinet ministers are normally and in addition to attendance at cabinet meetings expected to be regular members of one or more of the regular cabinet committees. Since Mrs Thatcher became Prime Minister, cabinets are once again held only once a week, and the Prime Minister has acquired the habit of taking many important decisions by assuming the chair at one of a series of informal meetings of ministers affected, whose titles are miscellaneous and whose membership is fairly fluid. As Lord Chancellor, I found this a considerable convenience, as I liked to get on with the work of my office and to distance myself from as many current affairs as did not affect it. But for all its advantages the practice has undoubtedly diminished the intimate sense of collegiality which animated us when I first belonged. In fact, however, any minister who is dissatisfied with the decision of a committee, whether formal or informal, has both in theory and in practice the right of claiming a discussion in full Cabinet with or without the submission of a formal paper setting out in writing the subject-matter of such a disagreement. I was not present on the famous occasion when Michael Heseltine stormed out of Cabinet and announced his resignation on the steps of Number 10 since my duties had taken me to Delhi at the time to attend a Commonwealth meeting of Speakers or law ministers. But I had seen a fairly formidable preview of this performance early in December on the same subject. The only moral I can draw from histrionic performances of this nature is that they should not normally happen without a formal discussion based on one or more cabinet papers, and that the dignity of cabinet government is hardly enhanced by dramatic charades or displays of personal passion. My own view is that, on taking office, cabinet ministers should be given a short formal induction course in staff duties by the Sir Humphrey Applebys of the system. I learned mine in the War Office in 1940 and in GHQ Ninth Army in the Lebanon in 1941. Histrionics and puerile fits of temper are wholly unsuited to the activities of serious statesmen, and hardly enhance the dignity of public life.

Incidentally, I greatly deprecate the habit of keeping private diaries giving blow-by-blow accounts of cabinet discussions especially if these are kept with subsequent publication in mind. It is inevitable of course that some *aide-mémoires* on matters affecting public policy are occasionally in order. But when and if my papers ever reach the public eye after my death they will not be found to contain much more than a daily list of engagements, a few amusing anecdotes and a few nature notes about my garden such as 'Willow warblers on Putney Heath' or 'The martins are nesting again above the bedroom'.

The size of the Cabinet is really dictated by the size of the room and the numbers at a committee capable of engaging in collegiate discussion. This has long ago been pointed out by Professor Parkinson of Parkinson's Law, and is pretty obvious when you think of it. Over the years it has seldom exceeded twenty-five, and seldom, perhaps never, gone below eighteen. War cabinet groups of four or six should in my view be limited to military matters or informal discussions. I would personally resist to the death any attempt to introduce presidential-style government by any prime minister. Under the cabinet system, 'The Buck Stops Here' may be a suitable motto for the Cabinet Room at Number 10 with Robert Walpole appropriately gazing down at us from his portrait above the fireplace. But it is distinctly inappropriate for any minister or prime minister to apply to himself. Collegiate discussion, collegiate loyalties (which should in my view continue after relinquishment of office) and collegiate decisions are not only the marks of civilized behaviour, but also guides to wise decision-making and morally justifiable personal conduct.

This brings me back to the absent figure at the Cabinet Board, namely the head of state herself. I was brought up to take our monarchy for granted in the evolved form in which it had come down to us. I regarded it as a thoroughly wholesome influence on our national life, a focus of patriotic loyalty, a source of legal authority divorced from politics or party, a reaffirmation of the need for living worship in religion, but without undue emphasis on denominational allegiance, a guarantee and symbol of historical continuity, and a pleasing occasion for various impressive and traditional forms of pageantry. But in 1957 I had not reflected much on the nature of the institution as a working part of our political machinery. The phrase was that the sovereign reigns but does not rule, and that is still true. Without contradicting anything of the above, I have come to think rather more positively since. One of the great benefits which we enjoyed as the result of the Glorious Revolution and the Hanoverian succession was the separation of the duties and functions of the head of state in the person of the sovereign from that of leader of government in the person of a prime minister.

To begin with, I thoroughly endorse the separation of the two offices of head of government and head of state, even when their unity continues to exist in the comparatively harmless form in such democratic republics as the United States or France. Even in this form the head of state is a party politician who has won his position in the teeth of opposition from a rival, and exercises a high measure of actual and direct political power, at times in direct conflict with majority opinion in the legislature. I far prefer our own system which not only separates the two offices of head of state and prime minister, but also by convention decrees that of the two Houses of Parliament one should be elected and predominant, and the other not elected, critical and endowed with sufficient powers to be able, if need be, to be a focus of criticism and to make itself a nuisance. Once it is accepted that the two offices are separate it seems to me far better to secure an automatic succession of heads of state surrounded by a numerous circle of members of a supportive family than the appointment or election from time to time either of an active party politician or of some respected figure too far spent in years and vigour to be the source of action or even a target for hostile criticism.

It is, I believe, a great mistake to suppose that a constitutional and hereditary monarchy can never be of practical use. In my own life, the part played by George V in 1931 was not one of inertia, and the visit to Germany of Edward VIII in 1937, whether or not condoned by ministers at the time, was almost certainly an error. But there are more important matters which may be at stake. When Juan Carlos reascended the restored Spanish throne after the demise of the Franco regime, did anyone foresee that it would fall to his lot to get rid of an attempted coup by yet another set of Hispanic colonels? Could a respected but elected septuagenarian President-of-the-Republic-type have succeeded? My guess is not. Could anyone but Haakon VII of Norway have led his country, abandoned by its allies on all sides and thrown into confusion by its politicians, to such a dignified retreat in 1940? Could anyone but a royal representative have played the robust part of Sir John Kerr in effecting a dissolution of both Houses in Australia in 1975? Evidently Gough Whitlam thought not, and in consequence retired into the dreary wastes of republicanism in which, so far from being the ultimate safeguard of constitutional rule, the president would be permanently at the mercy of the transitory tenant of the office of prime minister. What is the explanation of the curious oscillation which seems to afflict the South American republics between an impotent and anarchic democracy and a repressive military or Peronist dictatorship? I cannot answer these questions wholly satisfactorily, especially in the light of the unfortunate unilateral and ethnic takeover by the miserable Rambuka in Fiji. I can only say that, the more I reflect on the matter, the happier I am that I live under the British regime with a hereditary, well-conducted, decorous monarchy at the head, supported by a numerous and hard-working family. Of all the republics I know (except the Swiss) I would far rather live under the kind of regime we possess than either a Reaganite or a Gaullist republic or one like that of Italy where the unfortunate, but innocent, president has to choose a new prime minister every few weeks or months according to the state of the parties elected by a system of voting where nobody gets what he wants since the number of parties virtually precludes the electorate from any effective choice. One is bound to ask questions, even if one is unable to supply the answers. Would the state of Europe not have been happier if the head of the House of Savoy had sent Mussolini packing earlier than he did? Was the choice of the Queen of the Netherlands to set up a government-in-exile rather than shut herself up in a castle and treat herself as a prisoner of war not a wise one in the light of subsequent events? Owing largely to the operation of the separation of powers, is it a wise provision which secures that a newly elected president of the United States is almost always inexperienced, either in parliamentary government, being all too often the ex-governor of an individual state, or in parliamentary realities unless he has previously been elected to Congress as a Senator or Representative? Is it a wise provision which secures that the choice of vice-president (who automatically succeeds in the event of assassination, or other misfortune, neither an uncommon event in the history of the presidents) has had little to do with his merits as a potential head of government or head of state, and usually only a nodding relationship with the popular choice, and is mainly influenced by the internal pressures on a candidate immediately after nomination? The Bagehot formula of the right to advise, be informed and to warn is hardly a sufficient safeguard. Should we not now add that the constant necessity of exposure to the public gaze of a hereditary king or queen has much to be said for itself in comparison with other systems of government? To me at least, no system of government is perfect. But, although ours has constantly changed and must inevitably alter in future with the development of the European structures, I can only say that, viewed simply, pragmatically and by utilitarian and aesthetic criteria, our own constitution has many advantages and should not be despised.

THIRTY-SEVEN

Minister of Education

I WAS MINISTER OF EDUCATION between January and September 1957 – not long enough, one might think, to achieve much in the history of a great department. Up to a point I must agree. But it is worth recording that this was not the view of a senior civil servant, since much promoted, when he accompanied my wife Mary down to Reading one day to attend a meeting at which I was making a speech. The next day Mary reported him as saying: 'We reckon we have got everything out of a minister that he is capable of giving within eighteen months of his appointment.' By this standard I had got about halfway when my next unexpected and, I must add, undesired promotion took place. But it would be wrong to think either that I gained nothing from the experience or that I gave nothing in return.

The problems which I had to face were almost exactly the opposite of those facing a secretary of state at the present time. I had no responsibility for universities, nor, as such, for science, and the Ministry of Labour was primarily responsible for industrial training. At that time universities were the responsibility of the Treasury, and technology did not then come within the remit of the Ministry, but of Labour. So far as the sciences were concerned, they were largely within the remit of the Research Councils under the aegis of the Lord President. We were in the throes of a popular explosion in the schools. My principal preoccupation was with quantitative questions: the need to provide enough roofs over heads, to reduce the swollen size of classes, and, more qualitatively, but quantitatively as well, the supply of teachers. The supply of pupils was, of course, wholly outside the Minister's control. A mistake by the experts in calculating the rate of human reproduction in the following five years destroys all the plans of the best-regulated education department. Now things are different. Contemporary secretaries of state are faced with a predictably shrinking school population both in the higher grades and lower ones. I was faced with the consequences of a series of underestimates in the human reproduction rate extending over a number of years and over several successive generations of school entrants. I was also faced with the partial breakdown of the tripartite system of secondary education envisaged by the Butler Act. Except in a few places, the technical secondary school had never really got off the ground, and the system actually being put into place was a binary one, consisting of grammar schools which provided roughly for the top 20 per cent of ability and secondary modern schools for the remaining 80 per cent. The change from primary to secondary education was settled by statute for logistic reasons at eleven plus, instead – as is normally the case in the independent system, and as I would have preferred – at between twelve and fourteen. It was all too easy to misrepresent this system as elitist, and to categorize those sent to secondary modern schools as having 'failed' the selection process. The idea that it might actually be more in the interest of a child of average ability to join a relatively small community with a good chance, before leaving, of reaching a responsible position at the top did not enter the doctrinaire minds of the theoreticians, nor did the possibility that the age of change might be altered to twelve or thirteen in the medium-term future enter into the realm of the practicable. My own view is and was that education is far too important an issue to be made the plaything of party politics and that doctrinaire theories based on the preferability of one sort of structure rather than another have no objective reality at all, and ought to give way to an atmosphere of objective analysis, open-mindedness, variety and parental choice. I was beset by Catholic parents, whom I was largely able to satisfy. They were faced with high financial burdens owing to the constant need to provide new schools, or schools with greatly improved accommodation, to meet the need for increased numbers. They were shackled by a resolute intention, which I had to respect as a given reality, to make sure that their children were not educated in the same institutions as their non-Catholic neighbours, even if separate facilities for religious instruction were made possible. I can see the point of this philosophy, which contends that the ethos of a truly religious school must permeate the whole school community. I am not sure that I agree with it. When I was at Eton, our biology teacher was manifestly agnostic. Others were, to a greater or lesser extent, eccentric or heterodox. I think I would have gained rather than lost by earlier contact at an earlier age with those of views other than those in which I had been brought up. But, given the system which I had to administer, it seemed to me to be reasonable to get the maximum of satisfaction I could for those for whose children I was, up to a point, responsible. Given that at this stage I had only eight months to work at the task, I do not think I did too badly, although, as it seems to me now, I only scratched at the fringe of the problems of state education. In the face of considerable criticism, I was able to lengthen the teacher training course from two to three years. Thanks to the genius of a young Jewish civil servant, I was able to give support to a more standardized and cost-effective design for the construction of schools. I did a good deal to lay the foundations for the development of polytechnics. Apart from this, owing to the limitations then of the functions of the Ministry, I was quite unable to face the problems of succeeding ministers and secretaries of state to deal with higher, further and tertiary education. Nor did I begin to grapple with the question of comprehensivization; nor with the question, then only just beginning to rear its head, of the ethical content which state education can presume to introduce into the teaching of schools catering for such a wide variety of children. Comprehensivization was only just beginning to be a subject of controversy. My civil servants, mostly of different views from my own, made me realize that the problems were not quite so easy as originally I had thought. But I flatter myself that I would never have been so foolish as to embrace the doctrine of universal and compulsory comprehensivization, so disastrously attempted with such a calamitous degree of success by my socialist successors after 1964. They never seemed to me to grapple either with the wide range of abilities catered for in secondary schools or the real degree of cruelty caused by flinging an eleven-year-old into a community composed of at least one thousand adolescents without the subdivision into houses which breaks up our residential boarding schools. I do not believe they even considered the unpleasant fact that to subject children of promise to injustice is every bit as distasteful as to do the same to children of average or below-average ability. To produce a viable sixth form (that is, a minimum of about sixty) you need a school population in a selective grammar school of not much less than 600. If you are catering for a comprehensive range of abilities, this means a school population in each school running into thousands. The whole policy once adopted was dictated by sheer doctrinaire egalitarianism and not at all by real concern for the individual children or the wishes of their parents. The result brought about problems of discipline and order which have yielded a harvest of evils in present-day youth culture going far beyond the schools. On one occasion, one of my children who qualified as a teacher at Homerton College, Cambridge, was attacked by a pupil in a comprehensive school armed with a knife. Happily her experience with her male brothers (older and younger) had taught her to bend his fingers firmly backwards so that he dropped the dagger with a yell of pain. Had it not been for this sound home background, I might be writing about the popular socialist educationalists in somewhat harsher tones.

Where I think I succeeded in my brief period of office was to restore the morale of the educational world by persuading it that a Conservative minister could be at least as much an enthusiast for education as any member of the Opposition.

One of the abiding weaknesses of the school educational scene, then as now, was the number, quarrelsomeness and sheer vulgarity in behaviour of the teaching unions. At that time, so far as I can recollect, the most respectable of them, as well as the largest, was the National Union of Teachers (NUT), which, I believe was the only one then formally recognized by the Ministry representing the teachers, apart from the smaller and elitist body representing the head teachers. But at that time there were two rather sexist little unions representing the supposedly separate interests of male and female teachers respectively. I never quite understood what useful purpose their separate existence served. They afterwards amalgamated, when I found their separate existence, though for opposite reasons, still less easy to justify. But that was after my time. In my day I was duly instructed by my civil service advisers that the real chip on the shoulders of the teaching profession was that they wished to be recognized and did not feel themselves recognized as a profession. Until that moment it had never occurred to me that teaching was anything else than one of the noblest if not the best of such callings. It was only after I was given this piece of unexpected information that I found myself wondering whether it was really the best way to achieve this avowed purpose to affiliate yourself with the TUC and stage protest demonstrations, for instance, at meetings attended by my predecessor, David Eccles, with placards so obviously vulgar as the slogan 'More Shekels, Eccles'. However, I was myself asked to address their annual conference, was courteously treated and heard, and endeavoured, like Jeeves, to give satisfaction. Since then, being myself of the professional middle class, I have given a great deal of thought to the nature of professional status, its role in society and, indeed, what seems to me to be the immense value to society of the professional class generally. In some ways we seem to be in the unenviable role of pig in the middle, between the great industrial colossi of Management and Labour. The Marxists, wholly mistakenly, but inevitably in order to promote their absurd philosophy, tend to characterize us as lackeys of the ruling class and to analyse our school and university background, our supposedly vast but actually largely imaginary wealth, and, in the case of the judiciary, the alleged, but again wholly imaginary, bias against the working class. Management tends to regard us as a kind of yuppie trade unionism, our entry qualifications, internal ethics and discipline as restrictive practices to be dealt with by legislation or even as evidence of a closed shop. Not unnaturally, I regard the professional middle class as the salt of the earth, the leaven in the lump. The name of the game, so far as regards, for instance, our entry qualification is concerned, is consumer protection – in other words, in areas like accountancy, medicine and the law, protection against quackery; and our alleged restrictive practices and internal system of ethics and discipline, so far as they can be justified (and not all can), as means of ensuring fair competition and, particularly in fields where advertising is capable of misuse like claiming to have a cure for an incurable disease, a means of insurance against misleading claims. The marks of a profession are the imposition of a high and uniform qualification for entry, a system of special ethics enforced by a just form of self-government, openness to criticism, and a determination never to deprive the public of access to our services in order to secure personal or corporate gain. Above all, the mark of a profession is the right and duty fearlessly to exercise independent judgement to the best of our skill and understanding. While I was Lord President of the Council, by means of the charter giving functions of the Crown, I was able to institute an enhanced degree of professionalism amongst the various bodies constituting what are now known as Chartered Engineers, and I must have given at least some satisfaction here as some at least of the bodies concerned admitted me to their honorary fellowship. As for our alleged closed shops, I have always steadily opposed them. Always, whilst I practised, and a subscribing member of my professional association, the Bar Council, myself, I have steadfastly opposed compulsory membership. Membership of the Inns of Court, of which there are four, is no more trade unionism than membership at the appropriate level of an Oxford College, and call to the Bar is no more trade unionism or a closed shop than the professional entry qualification required of a solicitor, an accountant, a registered medical practitioner or a state registered nurse.

The real weakness of our system of state schools is the creation during my lifetime of what seems to me to be something in the nature of a spiritual desert. The enemy is not atheism, though I believe the loss of religious faith has much to do with it, since I believe religion, particularly theistic religion, gives a rational intellectual background to morality. But religion is not the same thing as morality. The most deadly enemy of morality is not atheism, agnosticism, materialism, greed nor any other of the accepted causes. The true enemy of morality is nihilism, belief in, quite literally, nothing, the creed of the despairing Macbeth that:

> [Life] is a tale
> Told by an idiot, full of sound and fury,
> Signifying nothing.

Though I am not myself a Jeffersonian, and do not share his belief in a total separation between church and state, and that the state has no business teaching religion at all, there is much more to his creed, embodied in the American constitution, than is readily admitted over here. I am all against indoctrination in the state schools. It must be admitted that, in the American system of state education, where the teaching of religion is not permitted at all, attendance at church and religion in general seems to flourish like a green bay tree. But there the trouble is not that religion does not exist or is in decline but that it sometimes takes absurd, bizarre or even undesirable forms. For myself, I welcome an opportunity to give religious instruction within the school hours according to the wishes and beliefs of the parents. What I am certain of is that neither in education nor elsewhere can the State be indifferent to virtue according to what I call natural morality: respect for parents' authority and one's neighbours' rights, kindness, patriotism, courage, responsible sexual behaviour, respect for the environment, respect for one's own body, truth-telling, financial integrity, loyalty to friendships, tolerance of differences of opinion, openness of discussion, and forbearance to intrude into the private lives of others. I do not believe that it is at all easy to comprehend all these things within the bounds of a formal curriculum. But means must be found within the state system of making sure that the practice of and respect for virtuous behaviour is not an optional extra, but a condition of belonging to any human community and from which no man, woman or child is permitted to opt out. I find it easier to express these beliefs in the context of my own Christian faith. But I do not believe that Christian faith is specifically necessary to assert them. I find them recurring in the works of pagan historians and philosophers, in eastern mysticism, in the Tao, in Confucianism and, above all, in Judaism. In my own intellectual shorthand I think of all this as the *philosophia perennis*, the eternal philosophy, as natural morality, the truth of which can be apprehended by the use of one's own natural gifts, and, though not directly capable of being translated into law, without a belief in which no just system of law can be enacted or developed.

When I joined the Cabinet in 1957 I thought my tenure of the Ministry of Education would last as long as the government of Harold Macmillan. I did not expect this to be long. My judgement was that, after the humiliation of Suez, we should be skittled out of office by July if not earlier, and, if not earlier, very little later, and for quite a long time it very much looked as if I was right. The by-elections, the polls, the press, the media were all hostile. My belief was that, after this brief period of office I should be back at the Bar by Christmas and resume my practice with the ultimate ambition of being offered ordinary judicial office.

As usual, in my estimate of my personal prospects for the future, I was entirely wrong. All the more important turning-points in my life have been dictated to me by external events which have always taken an unexpected course. In this case, the external event was an invitation from the Prime Minister to lunch with him at the Turf Club. I now believe that this invitation was prompted by Oliver Poole, then the Chairman of the Conservative Party, an office in the gift of Harold Macmillan in his capacity as Leader of the Party and not as Prime Minister. I do not believe that it was Harold's idea to remove Oliver. I believe that it was Oliver's deliberate plan to step down himself, to act as my deputy if I would have him, which of course I did, and that I would couple the post of Chairman of the Conservative Party with a seat in the Cabinet in the position of one of the great officers of state, as it turned out that of Lord President of the Council. The offer was not particularly welcome to me. But, after consulting Mary, I accepted. The job needed to be done, and I was the one chosen to undertake it. I was quite convinced that, after accepting office in the post-Suez Cabinet, we needed to rehabilitate the fortunes of the Conservative Party. For this purpose two things were necessary: to prolong our term of office and win the following election. My life has never been quite the same since. Nor, I am persuaded, has that of the country. Without this event I do not believe we should have won the election of 1959, nor even stayed in office long enough to fight any election as late as that. Nor, I believe, would Harold Macmillan have remained in office as Prime Minister till 1963. Thus, once more, all my plans were thrown into confusion, and I was once again at the mercy of unexpected events.

THIRTY-EIGHT

Lord President of the Council and Chairman of the Party

LOOKING BACK at those events at a distance of more than thirty years, I find them as bewildering as ever. Within the course of twelve months the whole course of my life had been changed dramatically three times, each time without the smallest degree of enthusiasm on my part. Before September 1956, I was a young silk of middle rank aiming at nothing so much as working my way up the legal ladder. I accepted to become First Lord of the Admiralty with no expectation of political advantage and considerable misgivings as to the effect of my doing so on my professional prospects. At the time of that appointment I had no thought but to plan and accomplish a new role for our maritime forces at a time when the whole future of the armed services was under debate. Within weeks, I found myself at the centre of perhaps the severest international crisis since the Second World War. I had given my whole enthusiasm to the honour and integrity of the Royal Navy and to the defence of government policy at the time. Our humiliating retreat at the time when military victory was within our grasp had caused me infinite distress. The resignation of Anthony Eden led to my promotion to the Cabinet and a totally unsought-for transfer to the field of education. Again I had flung myself into the task in a spirit of dedication and service and had no thought whatever of personal advancement beyond that point. I now had this cup snatched from my lips and, again by way of promotion, found myself given the totally different and, at the time, uncongenial task of restoring the fortunes of the Conservative Party. I can remember actually bursting into tears at the last function I attended as Minister of Education, a dinner given in my honour at a teacher training college just after the new appointment had been published. At the time, I genuinely regarded the task with which I had been entrusted as by all human standards bound to end in failure. It was not for this that, just twelve months before, I had left my Headship of Chambers for what I thought was a brief spell of public life in a second-rank ministerial office. The appointment was announced with just enough time to play myself in before the Conservative conference in October. I can only genuinely express my surprise that I had so permitted myself to be flung about at the whim of circumstance. Searching my conscience now, I can honestly say that, whether or not misguidedly, I genuinely believed that I was doing my duty in accepting what at the time I regarded as a burden. Every government of any political persuasion has need of a senior cabinet minister whose function it is to act as a sort of liaison officer between the party organization in the country and the Cabinet. In a Conservative government, the only person who can perform that service is the Party Chairman. In the nature of things, a prime minister has too much to do to concern himself with party organization, discipline, morale and public relations.

Despite the fact that from the first it was clearly my duty to put as brave a face on it as possible, and to try my best, I must say that I regarded success in my new assignment as virtually impossible. It is hard to exaggerate the disarray and loss of morale in the party, and unpopularity with the press and media of the Government in the months following Suez. The party was split three ways. There were those like Edward Boyle who had resigned office because he did not agree with the operation, and Anthony Nutting who had gone so far as to resign his seat and cause a by-election because we had embarked on it. At the other end of the scale there was a disaffected section among the Conservative backbenchers on the right of the party (which included my successor as MP for Oxford, Laurence Turner). These banded themselves together as a group opposing and violently criticizing our action in ending the operation before it was complete. By-election after by-election was destined to result in new humiliations. But, having put my hand to the plough, there was no turning back. Apart from the political skills of Harold Macmillan, I had three assets. One was Oliver Poole as Deputy Chairman, to whom I was determined to stick through thick and thin. With him I enjoyed one of the most loyal and fruitful partnerships I have ever had during my public life. Whenever things were going badly, there he was beside me, never without constructive and helpful advice, never criticizing but always telling me what to do next. The only collaboration I have enjoyed in the same class, though even that was not quite so close, was with Peter Carrington in the House of Lords during our period of opposition. But that was in the future. With Oliver Poole there were a good many storms which we had to weather together. There was the fatuous mare's nest of the Bank Rate Tribunal, all the more embarrassing because, owing to press gossip, Oliver, the soul of financial integrity, felt himself to be personally involved. I have never really forgiven Harold Wilson for his part in the affair, nor quite understood how he managed to live down the scornful rejection of his innuendoes by the Tribunal report. There was the absurd row in the Bournemouth East Conservative Association over their member Nigel Nicolson, and 'Chummy' Friend, the candidate who endeavoured to supplant him, not rendered more easy to handle by Harold Macmillan's endeavours to muscle in on the scene. In the end I had to be rid both of 'Chummy' Friend, who had been found guilty of entering into clandestine correspondence with our sworn enemies the League of Empire Loyalists (now happily defunct), and of Nigel Nicolson by means of a somewhat unorthodox plebiscite of the membership which he himself had requested. I was sorry for this. The tradition in Central Office (of which I heartily approve) is to back the sitting Member in such cases. But Central Office has no power to enforce its writ. The trouble was that there is no room for compromise with a constituency association which was on the extreme right of the party, from questions as different as Suez to hanging and flogging, and a very decent Member with a good war record behind him who disagreed with them on every contentious issue. The plebiscite was only arranged after a meeting with me in the chair which I had to sustain with dignity despite the Empire Loyalists chanting their ludicrous slogans out in the street. There was naturally a good deal of contention as to the cut-off date for new members entitled to vote in the plebiscite. Actually, Nigel Nicolson did a great deal better than one would have expected and lost only by a narrow majority. I also had difficulty with the 1922 Committee, a committee of backbenchers founded in 1922 to get rid of the Lloyd George coalition, and by this time at least to be counted on for disloyalty to the leadership of the party at any moment when steadiness of nerve was both important and difficult to maintain.

Worst of all there were the Thorneycroft resignations which took place at the exact moment when, as Oliver was beginning to tell me, things were at last beginning to go our way. We were talking in January 1958. This was a particularly painful moment for me. Peter was and is an old friend and at that time was an ally. He had been a fellow-member of Theo Mathew's pupil room in Crown Office Row when I was called in to the Bar in 1932. We had been staunch allies on the Tory Reform Committee when I had returned from the Middle East at the end of 1942 until the general election of 1945. We had been junior ministers in the caretaker government and, after a brief spell on the opposition front bench after 1945, had retired in concert to the back benches. It was therefore particularly painful to me, in concert with Oliver Poole, to spike Peter's guns as effectively as possible. This, with Oliver's help, I did pretty efficiently by sending off simultaneous telegrams to the whole network of chairmen of Area, Constituency, Conservative Teacher and Conservative Trade Unionist organizations throughout the country, in fact anyone in the party network who could put 'chairman' after his name. Peter was less than pleased, and for a time our friendship cooled. My problems were accentuated rather than eased by Harold Macmillan's imminent departure on his projected Commonwealth tour. On Oliver's suggestion, we laid it on that the whole Cabinet should assemble on the tarmac to see him off. It was then that he made his famous 'playing down' gambit about 'little local difficulties', and this in turn was what led me to make one of my few genuinely original contributions to current demotic English usage by coining the word 'unflappable' and sticking it on to the Prime Minister's lapel.

I certainly coined 'unflappable', which has come into common use, as a compliment which I had applied to Macmillan in 1958 in the 'little local difficulty' of the Thorneycroft resignations. I also believe that I am responsible for 'lunatic fringe', later adopted in a revue and by the BBC in the programme 'Beyond the Fringe'. I also claim 'elective dictatorship', the title of my Dimbleby Lecture. This I did quite deliberately because, ever since the party conference in 1957 (to which I will come shortly), people had been saying of me, quite unfairly, that I had been drawing attention to myself rather than praising the leader. Still, it was a major setback to have not only the Chancellor of the Exchequer resign over the coming Budget, but also his two junior cabinet ministers, Enoch Powell and Nigel Birch, resigning as well. One can only speculate as to what led them to do it, but at the time I was prone to regard their defection as betrayal of the common cause which had been committed into my hands, namely the restoration of the fortunes of the party from the shambles left behind after our premature withdrawal from Suez and the resignation of Anthony Eden. I still think that the resignations were unreasonable to the point of being perverse. Peter had shown his usual prescience in identifying the danger of inflation as one of the greatest perils of modern democracy and the need to defeat it as one of the main tasks laid upon the Conservative Party as the party of sound currency, good housekeeping and stable society. But the discussions which had led up to the ultimate split had narrowed down the difference between the contending sides to a mere £50 million. It seemed to me that this was a margin far too small to endanger now what already appeared to be the prospect of a coming electoral victory, snatched out of the jaws of defeat. I felt this all the more strongly as the result of defeat would have been the triumph of a party whose whole theory of financial management appeared to be that every problem could be solved first by throwing money at it, and then by slapping on physical controls and imposing crippling taxation as a device which would obviously prove ineffective to hold the inflation which would inevitably follow. As so often happens in this seemingly perennial dispute, the argument in Cabinet was between the danger of inflation as expounded by the Treasury ministers and the need for adequate social services. As always, Harold Macmillan had his prewar experience in Stockton and the North-East very much in the fore-front of his mind, and a majority of the Cabinet who, uniquely in my experience, were polled one by one on the issue were firmly of the opinion that the Treasury ministers' perfectly legitimate stand was more rigid than the occasion demanded. I still think in the interest of nation and party alike they should have given way, but they refused to do so. I did ask Macmillan later to what he attributed their intransi-gence, and he obstinately adhered to what he was pleased to christen the 'Svengali' theory of the resignations, with Enoch Powell playing the name part and Peter Thorneycroft as the innocent Trilby. At the time, I was not disposed to accept Peter in this uncharacteristically alien feminine role. But, having regard to Enoch's subsequent performance, I am not quite so certain of this now as I was then, though, remembering as I did, both then and now, Nigel's uncertain trumpet sound at the time of Suez, I did not feel certain that he was not also playing a dominant role in the operation. However that may be, the Thorneycroft resignations formed the nadir of my hopes of success in my assignation as Chairman.

Because it was so traumatic, my description of this episode has led me somewhat out of strict chronological order. After my retention of Oliver as Deputy and staunch ally, my second asset in chairmanship was the solid and loyal party organization, then divided, I believe, into thirteen regions in England and Wales, but not in Scotland, where the party is organized separately under a different Chairman, nor in Northern Ireland, although at that time we could rely on the solid support of a still undivided Ulster Unionist Party which would certainly win the vast majority of the Northern Irish seats. I capital-ized this asset with all the enthusiasm at my command. Oliver organized for me a series of meetings at area level of all thirteen regions at which I harangued the faithful, and I myself introduced a practice of writing a monthly letter to the 'chairmen' of the different organizations down to constituency level describing events of the previous month from the government point of view. But, of course, my first and principal means of imposing my own personality on the party was on the occasion of the two party conferences, at Brighton and Blackpool respectively, between my appointment and the election in 1959.

Of these, immeasurably the more important was my first conference as Chairman, in Brighton in 1957. I was totally inexperienced and absolutely new in that office. As matters turned out, I had one weapon already in my hand. For some time, whether by accident or by design – and, so far as I was concerned, by accident – I had been designated to speak at what would now be called a 'fringe' meeting to be held in the Aquarium and not in the main conference-hall, under the auspices of the Conservative Political Centre, a sort of Conservative Fabian Society, but strictly under party control, which had been invented by R. A. Butler as a sounding-board for ideas. I took particular trouble with the preparation of this speech, since I knew that the whole of my future plans depended on its success, and full arrangements were made for television and the immediate publication of the text in pamphlet form under the title *Toryism and the Future*. Happily the speech was kept carefully under wraps and was not leaked. As always before a critical event in my life, I prayed hard for success as I walked with Mary along the front towards the Aquarium. The speech succeeded beyond my wildest dreams, and I duly returned thanks on my return journey.

The two other items of the conference which have dogged me for the rest of my life were unpremeditated. Being a Sussex man myself, I was aware of two facts about the south coast which are not known to the general public. The first is that in October there is generally a spell of fine sunny weather in the nature of an Indian summer. The second is that the Channel itself is generally warmer in October and right up to the beginning of November than it is even at the beginning of July and even supposing that the surrounding air in July may well have been hot. I remember one year at Eastbourne swimming out so far from the beach at the beginning of November with my cousin Quintin Hoare that the authorities actually sent out a boat to compel us to turn back. So, in October 1957, I came down to Brighton fully equipped with my latest acquisitions, a pair of flippers and a snorkel of a type now no longer on the market in the wholly fallacious belief that it is dangerous, and consisting of a mask

The endless beam of publicity at the
Brighton Conference, 1957.

I bought my Moulton bicycle after visiting the Moulton factory in 1960.
I always found cycling the best method of getting around London.

With Mary.

The pageantry and the reality of office: giving an interview at my desk, surrounded by the usual quantity of paperwork; and in the Lord Chancellor's procession from Westminster Abbey during my first term. The leading figure is Sir Denis Dobson, Permanent Secretary and Clerk of the Crown in Chancery; the mace is being carried *pro hac vice* by Anthony Blair, then my Principal Private Secretary.

London   Lotte Meitner-Graf

Lord Chancellor, 1970-74.

My last walk, in 1979. The Widderfeld, in the Engelberg group, is in the background.

In the garden at All Souls, 1985. The statue I mutilated as a young Fellow by removing its spurious fig leaf has, as can be seen, weathered remarkably well.

Spot, my Jack Russell terrier, has played a prominent role both during my visits to Buckingham University, of which I am Chancellor (here with the Duchess of Kent in March 1986), and at my wedding to my present wife *(below)* in the same year.

covering the whole face and so permitting breathing through the nose with a valve at the top in the form of a ping-pong ball, preventing water coming in at the wrong moment. (I kept this wonderful equipment, in the case of the snorkel irreplaceable, until the last year in which I was Lord Chancellor, when I lost it on a beach in Jamaica in the course of a Commonwealth Law Conference.) I happened to mention to the press who were monitoring my activities that I would be swimming from the Grand Hotel the next morning, and I do not believe that they thought I was telling the truth. At any rate they sent out a reconnoitring patrol next morning at 7.30 a.m. and to their evident surprise there I was, in my dressing-gown and bathing-pants and swinging my snorkelling equipment, and I duly obliged by swimming for fifty minutes in the water with a large number of the brethren waiting for me to emerge. The sea at Brighton is much cleaner than people think – far cleaner, for instance, than at Norman's Bay, opposite Carter's Corner. The sea is cloudy from chalk and sand, though the beach itself is pebbly. But, given a good pair of flippers and a snorkel, one can swim for miles. In fact, in 1959, in the run-up to the general election, I used to swim right across the bay at Cuckmere Haven and back – a distance, I should think, of at least four miles – with genuine enjoyment. At any rate, at the 1957 conference I had a pleasurable bathe every day before breakfast, to the delight of the press.

The other incident was even less premeditated. In those days by convention the Leader was not present at the conference itself, which then finished on the Saturday morning, but in the early afternoon gave a speech before the faithful in the conference-hall at what was technically a post-conference rally. The conference itself drivelled away to an anticlimax with a series of debates on subjects balloted for by the faithful but usually only of peripheral interest. Then as now, when these debates had ended, the Chairman of the Party had to wind up the conference with a short speech culminating in a brief, harmless, but somewhat absurd little ceremony in which the bell used by the Chairman of the Conference, duly inscribed with his or her name, is presented by the Chairman of the Party to the Conference Chairman. That year the Conference Chairman was Kay Elliot, now

Lady Elliot of Harwood, but then the wife of Walter Elliot who saved Westminster Hall from destruction in the great air raid of 1941 and in 1957 was in the last year of his life. The bell then becomes the property of the Conference Chairman, who retains it as a memento of his chairmanship. For about twenty-four hours I had been somewhat irritatingly nagged by party officials who adjured me not to forget this little ceremony, and I was somewhat puzzled by the purely technical problem of how to send the party with adequate rapture to the afternoon rally if, at the end of my speech, in place of a peroration I had to undergo this somewhat funny little piece of ceremonial. About half an hour, not more, before I was due to stand up, the light began to dawn. There was no other solution but to turn the ceremony into drama. So I made my humdrum little speech closing the conference and then swung into the ceremony. I made a few complimentary remarks about Kay Elliot and said how well she had handled the conference. I then took the little bell in my right hand, and tinkled it mildly like a hostess ringing for the next course, saying: 'We hope you will ring it from time to time just to remind yourself of us.' Then said I, suiting the action to the words, ring it more loudly, as if sounding an alarm of some kind. Finally, said I, 'Ring it more loudly still,' and swung the bell wildly over my head with a slightly modified quotation from John Donne's famous words indicating that this time it tolled for the defeat of the Labour Party at the next election. The effect on the audience and the media alike was all the more electric because the pantomime was wholly unexpected. Indeed, the effect has followed me ever since. The audience got up laughing and cheering. The cameras and the television buffs insisted on my continuing so that each could get his shot, and ever since then I have been pursued with a reputation for self-advertising publicity which I never deserved, but had to repeat the next year in the far less salubrious surroundings of Blackpool for fear of giving offence to the inhabitants of that splendid borough. Blackpool may be 'famous for fresh air and fun', but in truth, apart from the Tower and the fun-fair, it is endowed by nature with a sea which, at least in the autumn of 1958, was rough and cold and, I thought, somewhat redolent of human effluent. The only episode which gave me mild *Schaden-*

freude was that one hardy photographer, following after my retreating flippers into the surf, was knocked over by a wave and had to be lifted out by his sympathetic companions.

The only remaining episode of my chairmanship worthy of mention, apart from the 1959 election itself, was the problem of its date. By the party conference of 1958, the opinion polls indicated clearly that things were definitely going our way. The change in climate had begun between the two sets of local elections in May. The borough elections, which came second, showed a definite improvement, and at the conference I was able to sound a note of optimism at our recovery. The actual date of the election was of course for Harold Macmillan to decide, but he consulted me, and of course in turn I consulted my fidus Achates in the form of the ever faithful and almost infallible Oliver Poole. There were three dates possible: May or October 1959 and early summer 1960 when, under the statutory code, our legal time-limit would expire. I was particularly anxious to avoid the third. Opposition can usually take advantage of a government which is running up against the buffers. There were many advocates of May as the polls showed us with a slight advantage and there are always people, whom I call the 'cricketers', who urge one to 'put the others in to bat and see what a mess they will make of it'. Moreover, and rather more dangerously, prime ministers are always apt to overestimate their own popularity. Oliver advised me to wait. He said the margin showed by the polls for May was too narrow. In October, a month I have always favoured for Conservative governments, despite 1970, 1979 and 1987, Oliver more or less promised us a majority of fifty. I advised Harold accordingly. He advised Her Majesty, and we won by a majority of one hundred. Harold's motto was always 'Play it long; play it down; play it slow'. This may be good policy. But it is not always good politics or, necessarily, good election advocacy. Oliver rang me about halfway through the campaign.

'You know,' said he, 'we are losing.'

'I know,' said I and we contrived to warm things up accordingly.

Thanks to Hugh Gaitskell, the ruse worked. We had fought on the extravagance of the Labour programme, and its unfulfillability (if there is such a word) without inflation or crippling taxes, and he was so incautious as to claim that he could do it all and reduce income tax as well. The news was brought to me when I was speaking for Anthony Barber in Doncaster. I was also incautious enough to observe: 'The Lord has delivered him into our hands.' And it was so. I had won the most difficult case I had ever fought or would ever fight. I had fought the campaign on the sound principles of advocacy taught me by my father and identified the correct issue. I had paid enormous attention to the party organization and party morale. As Prime Minister, but in startling contrast to his performance after 1959, Harold Macmillan had hardly put a foot wrong. He had restored relations with the United States, reunified the Commonwealth, dominated the House of Commons, shown himself a moderate and progressive Conservative in home affairs, and disproved Peter Thorneycroft's dire predictions of immediate economic ruin. The only thing he did not understand was the party, and the principles of advocacy in party warfare. Between us, Oliver Poole and I remedied this. I did not get many thanks. Harold Macmillan wrote me a reasonably polite letter of thanks after the result, and immediately demoted me. I learned the reason later: he had misunderstood my role in an entirely private matrimonial matter in which I had been called as a witness. It was thoroughly unjust, wholly unfounded, and to have been influenced by it was very discreditable to him. What to me was intolerable was his almost Borgia-like behaviour in his use of his public position to pursue what he made into a private vendetta. But he made amends afterwards, when quite accidentally he discovered the truth.

THIRTY-NINE

Macmillan's Second Term

I DID NOT EXPECT to remain Chairman of the Conservative Party after the 1959 election and, had I been asked to do so, except for the briefest period necessary to identify a suitable successor, I doubt if I would have accepted the request. But, on discussing the matter with Oliver, whose disinterested loyalty and skill had been as indispensable a condition of our joint victory as anything I had planned or done, I learned that he was irrevocably committed to return to the City as, in my opinion, he was well entitled to do. I consulted him not because I was aware of his intentions but precisely because I was anxious to go myself back to my profession at 4 Paper Buildings. So anxious indeed was I to leave the scene completely that, as soon as the result of the vote was known and the cheering had stopped, I actually went back to the Royal Courts of Justice and crept round them by myself. It was like waking up after a nightmare to recapture even for a moment the atmosphere of the place. Oliver told me that we could not both honourably leave and that I must stay. Almost immediately after this, I received a summons from Number 10. I was received frostily, and offered the choice of my former post at Education or a new portfolio which Harold intended to create for Science and Technology. It had not yet been discovered by the pundits who affect to control these things that it was possible for a prime minister who wishes to create a new post to make as large a number of new secretaries of state as he desired without recourse to Parliament in order to create a new minister with a new ministry by Act. The reason is an odd one. Apparently, in strict legal theory the secretaries of state, though different people, are, like the blessed Trinity, of one

Substance. This was brought forcibly home to me some years later when, in the absence of the Home Secretary, but a secretary of state myself, I was asked to sign an urgent warrant for the tapping of a telephone in a case of serious crime, and discovered to my astonishment that I was actually empowered to do so.

I had consulted Oliver, not about which of the two offers I should accept but as to the feasibility of my retiring from the Government altogether. This I did partly because I was fed up with being cold-shouldered and snubbed after I had given my very best and achieved success in a seemingly impossible task at the expense, as it seemed, of my whole professional career and an almost infinite amount of ridicule and hostility from the media, but also because I genuinely misunderstood the reason for the personal distaste which I sensed in the attitude of the very man I had sought to serve. Oliver told me again that, since he was committed in any event to return to the City, it was my duty to stay on in the Government since, he said, 'it was unthinkable that we should both leave together'. It seemed to me impossible to return to my former post in Curzon Street after I had left it to become Chairman. I therefore decided to accept the new portfolio of Minister for Science and Technology, which, not being a ministry created by statute, would be unpaid, coupled with the existing office of Lord Privy Seal, which carried a salary but which, apart from responsibility for the Chevening Estate and the Crown Commissioners, was virtually a sinecure. It was also, in its way, a second demotion, as I had also to give up the Lord Presidency of the Council, which was not quite a sinecure, and entailed minimal responsibility in connection with the Privy Council itself and with the civil service which I had much enjoyed, the latter only of which would be transferred to my new portfolio.

My relations with Harold came to a crunch the following year when, as part of the appointment of Alec Home to be Foreign Secretary, he proposed to promote a junior minister over my head as Leader of the House of Lords, leaving me to remain as deputy. I told him frankly that this time I had had enough and would leave if he continued to treat me in this fashion. He looked at me oddly and capitulated at once. If he had told me of the real reason for the *refroidissement* between us, one of two things would have happened. Either I would have got up and left the room, or I would have told him the truth about the matter and he would have apologized. As it was, I was under the impression that his treatment of me was due to political considerations.

In fact the new appointment proved one of the most delightful and fruitful in my life. But it was not at all well received at the time either by the press or in the scientific world. Both had formed a peculiar impression of me as the result of my two years in chairmanship. Putting it bluntly, they had positively revelled in representing me as an ambitious and self-advertising buffoon, without taking into account the desperate nature of the task I had undertaken in September 1957. People had forgotten both my serious academic background in politics, classics, ancient history, philosophy and law, my devotion to my church and society, and the very simple fact that every common lawyer with any sort of a practice has got to know a good deal about medical and mechanical science in the course of his work.

I have always myself believed that science, the universities, the polytechnics and, above all, scientific and technological research should be separately represented in the counsels of government. I do not think they should be under the same sponsorship as the schools, and when, against my better judgement, I became myself Secretary of State for Science and Education I was careful to see that the higher reaches of education and science were separately represented in the Cabinet under me by Edward Boyle, as different a type of Conservative from myself as can be imagined, but one of the dearest and most affectionate political friends I have ever had. All parties are coalitions of disparate elements, and the Conservative Party suffered a grievous loss when, as Vice-Chancellor of Leeds, he thought it necessary to distance himself from the party in the House of Lords by retiring to the cross-benches. I think I was well qualified to be the first holder of the portfolio. I think I did it well, and I think that the fact that five years after I had parted from the responsibilities I was rewarded by the Royal Society with their Fellowship and, even earlier, by most of the Chartered Engineering institutions with theirs gives me sound ground for believing that my efforts to give satisfaction had answered reasonably well.

Before I deal with the more serious sides of the matter there is one absurd episode, my election by Cambridge to an honorary degree, which deserves some mention, since in some ways it contrasts itself with, and was in one sense a previous run of, the humiliating and shameful conduct of Oxford University in vetoing a similar award to Margaret Thatcher. In view of the various honours with which I was subsequently invested by the scientific world which I was doing my best to serve, there is something paradoxical about the whole episode. I certainly bear no malice about the whole thing, which ended in my favour, but if I allow an element of acerbity to enter into it it is perhaps in the hope that academics will realize that hypocrisy and malice, bad manners and intrigue are a form of disloyalty to the academic ideals of objectivity, sincerity, scholarship and civilized good manners which ought to characterize every community devoted to the higher learning.

If anyone has borne with me thus far, he will have realized that, if there has been one thing to which I have been devoted since my earliest days, it has been enthusiasm for learning. It may be that the discipline in which I was nurtured, that of the ancient languages, philosophy, poetry and literature, has scarcely any representatives left in contemporary society. It matters not. Before I was a lawyer, a politician, an officer in the Army, a minister of the Crown, I was a devotee of learning, of meticulous scholarship in the world of arts and sciences. It seems to me that a country which fails to nurture these in an atmosphere of freedom and security scarcely deserves to be called civilized and has failed to honour one of the undoubted sources of political freedom. Yet look how my own university of Oxford treated Newman in the nineteenth century, or read *The Masters* by C. P. Snow to savour the full atmosphere of academic hypocrisy and intrigue. All the same, I can still say honestly that there are no honours that have pleased me and flattered me more than the academic honours which have been bestowed upon me from various quarters, but particularly from my own university and from Cambridge. These are two institutions unique in the world, from the high quality of their scholarship, the beauty of their buildings, the civilized atmosphere of their Common Rooms and Fellowships, the constant contribution they make to the education of our youth, and the constant flow of new knowledge in the academic spectrum. I have always bitterly resisted the doctrine of the two cultures, the so-called literate and the so-called numerate. To my mind here is a single spectrum of knowledge, and the practitioners are all free to enjoy the company and enrich their own hearts and minds with the wisdom and insights which they can obtain from one another.

Imagine, therefore, my delight when the appropriate authorities of Cambridge honoured me with the proposal that I might accept a doctorate at their hands, and imagine, therefore, my dismay when a letter appeared in a reputable journal attacking the proposal after I had been known to accept and inviting others to reject me on personal grounds. It was a most dishonest letter carrying political bile on its face and, incidentally, attributing to me in quotation marks words which I had never used, and for which they have never had the decency to make any attempt to justify or any offer to apologize. Not uncharacteristically, one of the signatories was later appointed a bishop of the Church of England and subsequently became as such a member of the House of Lords.

Of course, this put me in an embarrassing position. No doubt those signatories imagined that I would retire at once with what semblance of grace and dignity I could muster. But this would have been an act of disloyalty to those who offered the honour and an admission on my part that this calumny inspired by atrabilious political spleen had some measure of substance in it. My enemies had miscalculated my reaction. I decided to stick it out and outface my detractors. Happily, the constitution of Cambridge University is more democratic and more responsive to public opinion than that of Oxford. Such matters are decided, not in the secluded atmosphere of the closed academic bodies on whose gowns the mantle of *odium academicum* fits as snugly as the mantle of Torquemada on the Inquisition, but on a plebiscite of residents who hold the degree of Master. I took no steps until afterwards when I wrote to the newspaper concerned to disclaim the calumnious misquotation, but until the outcome I let matters take their course. It was quite a near-run thing. By a curious but pure coincidence I was due to stay the weekend with my old Oxford friend Denys Page, the most glorious of men, and his American wife Katie. He was then Master of Jesus and was himself the victim of academic intrigue in being deprived unjustly of the Vice-Chancellorship. We went for a pleasant walk on the Backs and fell in with Harry Willink, an old colleague at the Bar and in Parliament, who was most encouraging and full of indignation on my behalf. I won by a very small margin, and at the degree ceremonies at the Fitzwilliam enjoyed the eloquent tribute of the public orator, with a little mild *Schadenfreude* thereafter at the social receptions when I had to make a speech in honour of Tom Denning. If the constitution of Cambridge had been the same as that of Oxford, I have no doubt that my own doctorate would have suffered the same fate as Margaret Thatcher's. My own doctorate at Oxford conferred in his splendid anglicized pronunciation of Latin by Harold Macmillan, Oxford's best Chancellor in my lifetime, was unopposed, probably because I was not considered sufficiently important to humiliate. It is a pity that dons cannot be made to see that meanness and bad manners actually damage the institutions of which they are members. Fortunately the institutions themselves are too great and too permanent a glory of English society to worry about the possession of such a slack standard of behaviour.

In the event, apart from my two periods on the Woolsack, my time as Minister for Science and Technology was among the most rewarding and stimulating of my public life. The scientific set-up which I had inherited in 1959 was altogether different from that which now exists. Thanks, I think, to the genius of Lord Haldane and others in the palmy days of Liberal government, science was largely administered through research councils under the general administration of the Lord President of the Council. The universities and the University Grants Committee were administered as a sort of secret spending vice by the Treasury. Polytechnics were still, like the schools, classed as a local-authority responsibility. Industrial training and apprenticeships were the responsibility of the Ministry of Labour. It was not a coherent system, and obviously did not yield all the funds which the subject required, and it was my business as Minister of Science and Technology to tidy it up, which I did, but retained the semi-detached character which the University Grants Committee, the research councils, the Atomic Energy Authority and the research associations (run in conjunction with industry) already possessed. In many ways this principle of partial independence under the separate bodies administered by scientists made for better relations with government than the more authoritarian regime in which schools, science, tertiary education and technology are grouped together under a Secretary of State for Education and Science. Its continuance more or less in the form in which I had left it was the main recommendation of the Trend Report, rejected by subsequent governments. It may have been that the vast increase, not before it was time, of university provision prompted the change towards closer government control.

The general trend of Macmillan's second administration was, however, one of slow and irresistible decay, coupled with a number of personal scandals for the extent and mismanagement of which Harold himself was at least partly responsible. His vision of the new Commonwealth structure based on a series of independent federations – for instance, in Nigeria and in East and Central Africa – never really got off the ground. His one great success was the Test Ban Treaty, for which he and Jack Kennedy can jointly claim credit, and in which, it so happened, I was privileged to take part. Since, except for a memorable encounter with the late Bob McKenzie on television, I was only marginally concerned with them I do not feel I should say much about the Blake, Vassall and Profumo affairs; nor, save for what I have already written, about the Bank Rate Tribunal, or the extraordinary business of the so-called Night of the Long Knives, when some of the most senior and trusted members of the Cabinet were removed overnight. Vassall and the Bank Rate Tribunal were mare's nests, and so, apart from one vital difference (that a false statement was made to the House) was the Profumo affair. Profumo was the victim of a really foul conspiracy between the late Dick Crossman (utterly unscrupulous) and the late George Wigg (positively evil) and some shockingly bad advice from friends and advisers who should have known better. I well remember the personal misery of Oliver Poole over the Bank Rate Tribunal, and of Tam Galbraith and Peter Carrington over the Vassall affair. All were absolutely spotless and horribly maligned. As for the two journalists who were punished for failure to disclose their sources, no one will now ever know whether they had ever possessed any sources to disclose or, if they had, whether the sources had given them information which in any way justified their behaviour. Harold's acceptance of Tam Galbraith's resignation was, I believe, an error, and his realization that it was so may be the true explanation of his subsequent mishandling of the Profumo affair. I have never, myself, been a great friend of inquiries, occasionally necessary though they may be. I am certain that the behaviour of the Select Committee over the Marconi affair rightly discredited Select Committees as a means of discovering the truth. It is a great pity that, out of a misplaced desire to borrow from institutions of the American Congress, they have been allowed once again to rear their useless heads. The Denning inquiry, a panic measure introduced in the wake of the Profumo affair, was a ghastly error and should never be repeated. When inquiries are really necessary, in my opinion they should normally be conducted under the Tribunals of Enquiry (Evidence) Act. They should never be indulged in to satisfy public prurience or salacity nor simply to enquire into allegations into the private sexual lives of public figures unless genuine questions of security are involved. A strong prima-facie case that there is something serious to enquire into and that material is likely to be available to an inquiry which will yield a worthwhile result are the minimum requirements to justify a demand.

Having, to my surprise, survived the so-called Night of the Long Knives, at the end of 1962 or the beginning of 1963 a dramatic change took place in my affairs as the result of which the year 1963 proved to be amongst the most extraordinary of my public life. A chance conversation at a cocktail-party disclosed, to my astonishment, the true reason for the estrangement between myself and the Prime Minister referred to earlier, and at the same time that it was simply due to misinformation or misunderstanding on his part. The result was that, in 1963, first one and then another special responsibility was thrust into my hands. I became Minister with special responsibility for sport, Minister with special responsibility for the North-East, and the leader of the British team which negotiated the Test Ban Treaty. In 1963 I began as a hereditary viscount leading the House of Lords and with a special responsibility for Science and Technology. I ended it as a commoner, once more in the House of Commons as Member for my father's old constituency of St Marylebone and Secretary of State for Science and Technology under a new Prime Minister. Like all the other most important events in my life, all this was altogether the consequence of happenings of which I had absolutely no prevision and which, so far as I know, I could not reasonably have been expected to plan.

In order to understand the central features of the matter, one has to go back to 1960 when the first Viscount Stansgate, a war hero of the First World War and a former Labour cabinet minister, died and was succeeded by his son Anthony Wedgwood Benn. As I myself had done when my own father had died ten years before, Anthony Wedgwood Benn attempted to disclaim his peerage. Indeed, I have some recollection that he made some sort of pre-emptive strike some five years earlier when his father was still alive. Having received a negative reply in 1950 from Mr Attlee, I had proceeded to make the best of a bad job. Indeed, as Margaret Thatcher is fond of observing, I had no alternative. As long ago as 1895, when an earlier peer had made a similar attempt on succeeding to a hereditary earldom, it was evident that primary legislation of a general character was the only solution to my problem. I had asked Mr Attlee to support primary legislation for this purpose, and had received a blunt refusal coupled with a deliberate distortion of the nature of my request. Either because he did not know what the legal position was, or because he wished to test it, Benn took the opposite course. He stood for election to his former constituency but was later told by the Committee of Privileges, as was obviously legally correct, that as a peer he was debarred from sitting in the House of Commons. But Harold Macmillan was more just than his predecessor. Negotiations followed through the appropriate channels, and early in 1962 these resulted in the setting-up of a Joint Select Committee of both Houses. It so happened that, somewhere in the summer of 1962, I got wind of the course which their deliberations had been taking. They were going to propose that in future hereditary peers by succession should have a right to disclaim, but only prospectively. If, as I had done, they had done their duty, obeyed the law, applied for their writ of summons and actually sat in the House of Lords, they were to be excluded from exercising the right of disclaimer. This seemed to me to be grossly unfair. Benn, who in my view had flouted the law, would be privileged. I, who had obeyed it because it was the law, would have been excluded. I do not think that at the time I had the smallest idea of disclaiming my viscountcy. Indeed, in the summer of 1962 I had no inkling of what was to happen twelve months later. None the less, for whatever reasons, I felt so strongly on the issue that I put in a memorandum to the Committee stating my views. I cannot now remember when my memorandum was submitted. What I do know from the record is that by the end of the session 1961–2 the Committee had not reported. The Committee was reappointed at the beginning of the session 1962–3 and reported on 5 December 1962. Its report gave effect to the view which I had expressed in my memorandum. It did not go through unopposed, especially by most of the Conservatives of the Committee. The effective division in the Committee was on 21 November 1962 and my recommendation passed by one vote only. There is a divinity which shapes our ends, rough-hew them how we will. In essence the Committee's report became a Bill. The Bill became an Act of Parliament in July 1963. Otherwise I would still be a viscount. As it was, under the Act as it passed in 1963, I had a year in which to make up my mind. As matters turned out, events took place which made it up for me.

FORTY

The Strange Year 1963

OF THE VARIOUS STRANGE EVENTS which befell me in 1963, none was more bizarre than my appointment as Minister with special responsibilities for sport, and my commission to the North-East of England, comprising the North Riding of Yorkshire (as it was then) and the two counties of Durham and Northumberland, including Berwick-on-Tweed. Yet both commissions flowed naturally from contributions I had made in cabinet discussions and from the experience I had gained from dealing with academics and scientists since 1959. I am no athlete, and no economist. I am no particular admirer of organized and commercialized sport, nor for that matter of artistic and cultural chauvinism. I would abominate anything like a Ministry of Sport, which, I seem to remember, was one of the options being seriously advocated. But my experience of the previous three years had led me to believe that there are quite a number of subjects out of which government cannot afford to opt either on a local or a national level, and to which, in one way or another, it is bound to find itself contributing, either specially from time to time or generally as part of its natural contribution to the general culture of society, but for which no single Ministry is the natural friend at Court. Such matters, I thought, were better not dealt with directly by government departments. If they were, they would be likely to lose their autonomy. Nevertheless, existing as they do on a nationally organized basis, they are too wide to be left to local authorities, especially local authorities as narrow in their geographical limits as our own. It follows that, in order to preserve their independent spiritual being, they must be funded mainly by the generosity of private donors, by industrial concerns, or by endowments, however originally obtained. I had learned to deal with such bodies through the research councils, research associations, the Royal Society, the Arts Council, the British Academy, the vice-chancellors of universities, and other bodies. In so far as they concerned government at all, their interests spanned a number of ministries, local bodies and private associations. But, in the view I had come to hold, they needed a friend at Court, preferably a senior minister fairly experienced in the ways of government and parliaments, who would be a friend, but not a master, and in the last resort could offer nothing but good offices, good advice and where necessary co-ordination of effort. Such a minister would be an honest broker rather than an administrator with actual powers.

Sport, I believe, is just such an activity. It is an essential part of education. Years later, in my judicial capacity as Lord Chancellor, I was part-author of a judgement which authenticated the legal status of a fund for Association Football as a charitable trust. Organized sport is undoubtedly part of our national culture. In mountain-climbing, cricket and most kinds of football, in hunting, fishing and game-shooting, the British were the pioneers in the field of sport as it burgeoned in the nineteenth century. In a sense, there is no such thing as sport. There is only a heterogeneous list of pastimes, with different governing bodies, different ethics, and different and constantly varying needs. There are funds to pay for the training and fares for Olympic athletes, there are demands for sports centres, problems of law and order connected with sporting contests, questions relating to the safety of sports grounds, varying views about bloodsports, boxing, horse racing and many other topics. All this and more I canvassed in Cabinet and urged the need of a small secretariat under a minister who might be more a liaison officer than a government spokesman. Whether I was right or wrong in the views I then expressed, I do not know. Things have developed on rather different lines. But I soon discovered that I had talked myself into a job, and was myself the first to attempt the task I had tried to outline. I had a small secretariat, with a retired civil servant in charge, Sir John Lang, who happened to be available and who had been Secretary to the Admiralty when I was First Lord. Evidently my idea responded to some kind of need, as in a rather different form the post has survived under different ministers and governments of different complexions.

My commission to the North-East had a somewhat similar origin. Harold Macmillan was a strange mixture of loyalties. One of these was Stockton, until it had finally rejected him, his first constituency. Early in 1963 the North-East, of which of course Stockton is part, was undergoing one of the more acute moments in its chronic malady of unemployment, and the matter duly came up for discussion in Cabinet. Although the subject-matter was utterly different, the problem itself had something in common with that of sport, science, the arts and higher education. A number of ministries were involved, and these often possessed divergent and competing interests. There was a huge number of local authorities at various levels from parish councils to county councils, and among these were two or three really large boroughs and cities. The nature of the chronic problem of the region was the obsolescence of the main traditional industries. This was easily diagnosed, but the remedy was not easy to see. The emotive content was high, since, even more than today, the Jarrow March was relatively fresh in the memory of the elderly and middle-aged. There was, moreover, a special dimension to the problem. Many of the ills of the North-East had analogues in London, Scotland, Lancashire, and were even capable of showing up in the then prosperous areas of the Midlands. It was important not to create jealousy or hostility between the competing demands of different claimants. All this I ventilated during the discussion. Macmillan showed intense interest. I pointed out that the work could not be the subject either of a separate ministry or a permanent minister. But I recommended a special project. A senior minister should be sent up to reconnoitre the scene. He should not be given power to act on his own but should report back to the Prime Minister and the Cabinet. It should be no part of his function to take money away from other areas. He should not ask to prop up foundering or decaying industries. His duty would be to take a sort of Domesday Book or bird's-eye view of the whole area without regard to local-authority boundaries, aim at growth-points, look at the quality of the infrastructure, like roads, railways, ports and airfields. He would not seek continuing subsidies but, with cabinet approval, would be able to advocate expenditure on hopeful projects. He would try to suggest plans to make the area more attractive for people to live in. Thus he would be able to consider in relation to the whole area the availability of further and higher education, the quality of schools and housing in each part, and whether tourism or other magnets of attraction could be made available. The minister would have at his disposal a temporary team of youngish civil servants, chosen from among the most promising, to co-ordinate a Regional Plan, and when the task was complete the minister would cease to operate, though I secretly hoped that a nucleus of central government would remain behind, perhaps in Newcastle, so as to prevent what was obviously one of the problems, the centrality of government in Whitehall and the parochial interests of the departments within it.

Harold was intensely interested, and again I found that I had talked myself into a job. It cannot be pretended that the press received either of my two new responsibilities with enthusiasm. All the usual clichés were brought out. Cries of 'gimmickry' were uttered, and ritual references to the bell-ringing of my past chairmanship formed much of the material of the commentators. Worst of all, after a lightning reconnaissance to the region with my team, my first public act had to be to accommodate an important public engagement in the United States. All this was adduced as evidence of the frivolity with which I approached a task to which in fact I attached the highest importance. The reconnaissance was to be followed by a prolonged visit after the civil service team, duly briefed by me before my departure, had worked out a scheme for an extended visit to churches, trade unions, employers' organizations, individual industrialists and, of course, local authorities in which, after due preparation, I would formulate a coherent plan. I was proceeding in a methodical way to prospect and to change the face of three counties viewed as a separate region.

I do not pretend that the plan succeeded to the extent that my visit to the North-East permanently solved the chronic difficulties of the region. But I do claim that it succeeded in changing for the better the face of the three county areas, transforming the infrastructure, providing two modern airfields, improving the tertiary education, attracting new industry and laying the foundation of what subsequently became regional policy under Ted Heath and ultimately the Department of the Environment. There was certainly no gimmickry either in my intentions or in the action which followed. I resolutely refused to be photographed against the ageing technology of the Newcastle bridge, chatting to the unemployed or any of the clichés to which the illustrated press is so prone. There was only one mishap: I left my bowler hat behind me in the car which took me to the sleeper at King's Cross. This led to my seeking replacement headgear in the cold winter's air of a Newcastle morning. I was offered the choice of a vile little pork-pie affair and a comfortable cloth cap which I could wear with profit out shooting and on my farm. I sensibly chose the latter. The extraordinary use which the press made of this perfectly innocent transaction only underlined the correctness of my determination to avoid anything which could be interpreted as endorsing the stereotype of the area as cloth-capped, obsolescent or down-at-heel, and to concentrate entirely on modernity, modern technology, new science like cryology, scientific research, housing, education, airfields, transport and port facilities. On one occasion only was I ill-received and that was when I had to say that there was no prospect of preventing the closure as such of the railway-wagon works at Doncaster, and on that occasion I was able to prophesy correctly that, once they were closed, a new use would be found for them within a matter of weeks.

Apart from the actual benefit to the region, I believe that permanent value was obtained in planning regional development elsewhere. A more or less exact replica of the mission itself occurred more than twenty-five years later when, partly on my initiative, Michael Heseltine descended on Merseyside and the North-West. But regional policy generally – indeed, the creation of the Department of the Environment under Ted Heath – was, I believe, a by-product of my own, and later his, experience in launching the plan for the North-East.

In two or three respects I failed, then and later, to get my way. On my visit to Tynemouth, the stench of the river, at the point at which it entered the sea, led me to recommend a cleaning-up of the pollution in the stream. It had become an open sewer. The cost, in the currency of that time, would have been £22 million, and I was told I could not have that money. More generally I had hoped that the experience of this project would by now have led a Conservative government to remedy what, then and now, I have believed to be one of the defects of the Westminster model of government, namely the small size of our local government organs, and the separate independence of their several functions on the umbilical cords tying each to a different department of Whitehall. This I regard as due to the failure of central government to create any authority at regional or provincial level to gather under a single umbrella of accountability the various quangos and regional authorities of the several regions, or potential provinces, of the United Kingdom. Parliament at Westminster has never been prepared, or perhaps able, to come to real terms with subordinate assemblies to cover regions of the sort of size of Scotland, Wales, the North-East, the North-West, the Midlands, East Anglia, the West Country, and the South-East of England, and the only example, Stormont, has never been resurrected after the failure, by a near-miss, of the Sunningdale agreement. The attempt to remedy the scandal of the rating system by a community charge is partly, of course, the result of some Labour-dominated local authorities attempting to sabotage national economic policy as approved by Parliament, but it is also partly due to the failure of English (as distinct from Scottish, Welsh and Northern Irish) public opinion to harness regional patriotism into coherent regional institutions and policies subject to the sovereignty of Parliament. I had hoped that this would be one of the spinoffs from my mission. But the idea has never really caught on in England, and in Scotland and Wales has been taken over by the fissiparous movements of a misguided nationalism.

Even more interesting than my visit to the North-East of England and my foray into the world of sport was my appointment to head the British team to negotiate the Test Ban Treaty of 1963. This, too, arose out of a discussion in Cabinet following an exchange of telegrams between Harold Macmillan and Jack Kennedy and between them and the appropriate Soviet authorities, which would have included Nikita Khrushchev, Andrei Gromyko and others. The mission was very much after my own heart; I am no unilateral nuclear disarmer, and firmly believe that the generation of electric power by nuclear means is, and is likely to remain, the safest, cheapest, least polluting and most inexhaustible method of electricity generation, apart from hydro-electric schemes and the possible use of windpower and tidal or wave energy. It does require a very precise and careful system of engineering and perfectionist discipline in design and maintenance; but, given these requirements, it is by far the best yet devised. These facts and the foreign policy and defence requirements had made me no enemy of nuclear power generation for civil purposes, nor a friend of unilateral nuclear disarmament in defence. Nevertheless my contacts with the scientists had led me to entertain real anxieties about the dangers of the emission of radioactive isotopes into the atmosphere as the result of the tests of nuclear weapons by the then three main nuclear powers, particularly the 'dirtier' tests then being carried out by the Soviet Union on Novya Zemlya, and I realized that the only way in which these could be reduced or ended was by a tripartite agreement, as I thought at the time, to abolish tests altogether but, if that were not possible, at least all tests capable of emitting isotopes into the atmosphere, that is, on the surface of ground, into the water or into the air. If this were not done, there would be, or at least so I believed, a very real danger to the health of the world, particularly as the result of the emission of the long-lived calcium-related isotope of strontium and the isotopes of caesium which were the inevitable accompaniment of 'atmospheric' tests. Again, I had talked myself into a job and found myself nominated to head the British team. I took with me Solly Zuckerman, as a knowledgeable friend who had strong views on these matters similar to my own, Sir John Penney, the nuclear physicist, for his knowledge of nuclear scientific matters, and a very knowledgeable team consisting of two very skilled and brilliant Foreign Office officials (one of whom was a lawyer), an interpreter, a private secretary and, of course, the British ambassador to Moscow,

Humphrey Trevelyan, at whose embassy opposite the Kremlin on the other side of the Moscow river I was to stay. I was carefully warned about listening devices, and the counter-measures which could be taken against them, and I also had the considerable privilege of being asked as a guest to dinner at the Soviet embassy here in Kensington Palace Gate where the Soviet ambassador, who bore the distinguished name of Romanov, entertained me royally, gave me some hints on protocol and etiquette, and, taking me into the garden, gave me some very useful and precise warnings about what was and was not likely to be negotiable with his political masters. The Americans had a much bigger team, reflecting, as so often with them, the quite openly differing views of American departments and headed by the already ageing Averell Harriman, with whom I also held preliminary talks. In the immediate prelude to the adventure, for such to me it was, Jack Kennedy himself came over and we all spent a day at Birch Grove discussing our strategy and tactics. Naturally enough, the press was immensely excited about all this, and, equally naturally, I could tell them precisely nothing. I was excited, too. It had always been something of a regret to me that my public career had never taken me near the Foreign Office, and here I was, with no previous diplomatic experience except my experience at the Bar in settling cases (much more extensive than people imagine a barrister's life to be), right in the centre of things, negotiating, at top level, what turned out to be the first real breakthrough in Soviet–Western relations since the beginning of the Cold War nearly twenty years before. Looking back on the whole affair, I believe that the presence of the small British team, few in number, handy, professional and, apart from myself, immensely talented, and the wholehearted support of Harold Macmillan were absolutely crucial to the success of the whole project. The Americans and the Soviet leaders had quite a gift for mutual misunderstanding and getting on each other's nerves. We were much more relaxed, extremely unprovocative and made it our business to be as agreeable as possible. It was here, I think, that my own professional training at the Bar came into its own. The art of settling cases depends very largely on tact and on the necessity of not getting what I call 'too close to the case or the client', that is, it involves being wholly impervious to personal insults or rudeness, and not getting emotionally involved in the merits of the issues at stake. For this very reason, although I was invited to do so, I declined to make any mention in my relations with the Soviet leaders of two or three human rights cases which had no bearing at all on the enterprise on which I was engaged. In advocacy one must always avoid any conceivable conflict of interests.

In the event, I did have to meet a good deal of aggressive behaviour, not least from Khrushchev himself. Alec Home, then Foreign Secretary, had warned me of the extraordinary character of this very remarkable human being whose coarseness of language and anecdote absolutely beggared description. His changes of mood between the aggressively ferocious and comradely genial never ceased to astonish me. I had to deal with him only twice before the actual business meetings began and after they had succeeded. I believe I dealt with him successfully, since he had me to sit next to him at the dinner celebrating our success, and told me some absolutely astonishing and intimate stories of his adventures during the Stalin era. I made use of his Russian interpreter in preference to my own, good as he was, since Victor, the Russian, had been in England during the war and was absolutely bilingual in idiomatic English, only omitting phrases in the original which he thought would shock me as a prudish English gentleman ('And then the Chairman, he used a very rude word'). When it was all over Khrushchev was good enough to ask me to accompany him on a duck-shoot in the Crimea, which I had to decline, partly because I was absolutely exhausted at the end of the fortnight. But I have no doubt we would have enjoyed ourselves together. Throughout our meetings, which included a number of receptions, meals and social occasions, he invariably greeted me as 'the Imperialist'.

'Here comes the Imperialist,' he said to me at one reception.

'Yes,' said I, 'an imperialist; but unfortunately without an empire.'

'Oh, ho, ho! Imperialist byez imperium.' (I had taken a crash course in the Russian tongue and understood the original here.)

Khrushchev was a country man to his fingertips. The only man I have met at all like him was Millington, my own farm foreman, who in some way was a sort of pale reflexion of what Khrushchev was like to meet. When I first turned up at the Kremlin, full of doubts and anxieties, I was shoved into a room with the television lights full on me to be greeted by this rhinoceros of a man who charged forward at me with the veins standing out on his forehead. He immediately explained that, on war breaking out with the United Kingdom, he would give his bomber pilots instructions to omit my residence from their attack. He also told me that he would put a convenient cell at my disposal at one of the best-conducted of his labour-camps. I said that he would find that I was a man with simple needs. 'That picture was painted with a donkey's tail,' was reportedly one of his comments on modern painting. Anyone who knows what a donkey's tail is like will see at once the bucolic aptness of his remark. I could not help liking this extraordinary person.

Gromyko, whom I also liked, was the exact opposite, taciturn, gruff, reserved, and giving nothing away whatever. I remember at one stage in the negotiations the American team (despite my love of them, they are a nation of litigants and hypochondriacs) began to insist that the Treaty, the draft of which had by that time made considerable advances, should expressly reserve the right of the parties to employ nuclear weapons in actual warfare. I am afraid I pooh-poohed this suggestion. It is called a *Test* Ban Treaty, said I, which means that it only bans tests. Gromyko took exactly the opposite line. He said that by the inherent right of sovereignty (by this time relations would have deteriorated) the parties would have implicitly denounced the Treaty.

'Funny you should say that, Mr Gromyko,' said I. 'My father always took much the same view when he argued that there was really no such thing as international law.'

'Oh, ho, ho,' said Andrei Gromyko, 'they were not always wrong, these old people.'

It was one of the most strenuous fortnights of my life. We worked for two long sessions in a pre-Revolution palace of some capitalist, named, I believe, Morozov, which was by now owned by the Soviet Foreign Office. One was a plenary at which the political leaders attended and proceeded to hammer out the text of the draft. It was followed by a session at which the officials tried to incorporate into the draft text anything we might have agreed. The Western political teams would spend the afternoons in the secure rooms of their embassies discussing progress and the next day's work. During the fortnight I became convinced that the American secure room had been penetrated whereas ours had not. I also thought that the habit of the American team of writing furious little notes to one another in the plenaries was highly insecure. Being uncertain myself in every way, I did not discuss these doubts. The Soviet team was bigger than our two teams put together. They seemed to have a number of little men during the discussion doing nothing else but staring at the ceiling. The British team also passed notes to one another. But these contained nothing more secret than jokes and limericks. A welcome break came on Saturday when I was briefed to suggest that we took a break on the Sunday, and I duly did so.

'Mr Tsarapkin,' said I, 'wishes to attend divine service.'

'Oh, yes, he is very orthodox.'

Tsarapkin was a prominent member of the Soviet side. We spent part of Sunday bathing in the Moscow river about twenty miles from Moscow. We also had a good deal of sightseeing. The 'sobors' in the Kremlin, sometimes wrongly referred to as cathedrals, but in fact desecrated orthodox churches, were undergoing a facelift at the time, and some of the icons on the iconostases were being wonderfully restored. The Armoury Museum in the Kremlin also has some wonderful art, including a miraculous collection of English silver dating from before the Civil War, presented by successive English ambassadors when they showed their credentials to the tsars. There was also, made in England, a marvellous coronation coach acquired by one of the tsars – Ivan the Terrible I think – and, housed separately, a wonderful collection of French Impressionist paintings.

It was obvious to me from almost the very start that the total ban on tests which I had been briefed to propose was a cock that would not fight, for the simple reason that neither the Soviet nor the American team wanted one. I have since been told that if atomic weapons are to be maintained at all there have to be occasional tests to prove that they are still operational. If I had known this then, I would not have wasted my breath. The rest of the negotiation was about the details of the three-environment ban – in the air, on the ground's surface, and under water, but not underground – which we hammered out line by line as the fortnight drew on. Each day I would send Harold Macmillan a summary of the day's proceedings drafted by Humphrey Trevelyan, and received encouraging messages in reply. From my beloved Mary, there came a telegram *en clair* which to the best of my recollection read as follows: 'Gutters in Putters blocked. Have put work in hand. Love, Mary.' I was told by our experts that the Soviet intelligence officers were absolutely convinced that this contained an important piece of political instruction in code. Alec Home confirms this story in his book *The Way the Wind Blows*.

At length it was all over bar one point, and I forget what that was, which Harriman said required Jack Kennedy's express approval. I relied on Macmillan's plenipotentiary *carte blanche* to agree anything in reason provided that a sensible treaty was signed. But I was privileged to hear what took place between the President and his emissary. It took place on an open line from the Morozov Palace where we had been negotiating. There was no difficulty in getting through to New York. The American official then asked for the White House.

'The White House?' said the American voice. 'Where's that?'

'In Washington, DC, you know. It is where the President lives.'

At length Jack Kennedy was found and rapidly gave his consent.

The Treaty put an end to testing by the signatories in the atmosphere, on the surface, or underwater, but not, if no leaks occurred, underground. So ended my one lesson in top-level diplomacy. The Treaty was well received at home, and the British team, having given me a wonderful dinner the night before at their hotel, including a disgusting drink made of fermented mare's milk, returned in triumph to Heathrow, bearing the text and a lot of generous gifts of caviare, Crimean wine, Stolychnaya vodka and Armenian brandy pressed on us by our Soviet hosts. We were met by

Alec Home, and a clapping crowd watching our arrival from the airport terminal's roof.

One thing surprised me enormously about Moscow. In spite of a totally authoritarian regime, the Moscow pedestrian is an almost suicidal jaywalker, not at all successfully controlled by uniformed police blowing whistles and crying 'Grazdanka' and 'Grazdany' at frequent intervals. I did not venture into the stores, GUM or what not. Not only are there no goods to be had and, if there are any, none at reasonable prices, but also the actual procedure of purchase is so complicated and distrustful of all and sundry that it is almost impossible to achieve anything. First you have to queue to inspect the goods, then you have to queue at another counter to pay for them and in return receive the voucher, and then you have to go back to the counter to collect the goods in return for the voucher. So much for mutual trust in the workers' paradise. Let us hope that *glasnost* and *perestroika* have changed all that.

But the weirdest of all the things which had happened to me in that strange year of 1963 was still in front of me.

FORTY-ONE

Blackpool 1963

IN 1963 THE CONSERVATIVE CONFERENCE was due to be held in Blackpool. Entitlement to become a delegate at the annual conference of the Conservative Party (confined to England and Wales; the Scottish Tories have a separate conference in Perth, and there is still virtually no Conservative Party in Ulster) had for years been so numerous that Blackpool and Brighton were virtually the only seaside resorts which could house us. This was not always so. My first party conference, which I attended in 1929, was in Yarmouth, and at different times I have been to conferences in Scarborough and Llandudno. Immediately after the war there were even conferences in London. But by 1963 it was virtually alternate visits to Brighton and Blackpool. The 1963 conference was remarkable in that it coincided with the end of the reign as leader of Harold Macmillan.

It had been obvious since 1959 that Macmillan's last government marked a slow decline from the peak of the 1959 election, and was punctuated by a series of what have since become known as banana skins. Some time in the summer – I think in June, but before I went to Moscow – I had received a visit in my office in Richmond Terrace from my old friend Oliver Poole. The purpose of his visit was to tell me that I should prepare myself to become the next leader of the Conservative Party. I had not, at that stage, decided to disclaim the two peerages successively conferred on my father, but I was at least sufficiently aware of the possibility to have refused an earldom for myself, which, under the legislation then passing through Parliament, would have precluded my doing so. I had no idea that I would, or could, be in the line of succession for the leadership, or that, apart from his obviously fading sense of direction, Macmillan was on the verge of leaving the scene. At that particular moment my mind was completely preoccupied with the traumatic crisis caused by the fact that Mary had virtually ordered me to get rid of Carter's Corner to which, as my home, and out of regard to my father's express wish that it should remain in the family, I was deeply attached. By way of preparing me for my future role, Oliver pressed me to read the American bestseller *The Making of the President*. I did not think much of this piece of advice since the methods of selection seemed to me to be wholly different. I had already discussed the possibility of disclaimer with Alec Home, I am almost certain at his suggestion. He was Foreign Secretary, and I was leading the Lords. The one thing we were both agreed on was the absolute impossibility of our both disclaiming while this continued, and we then went on to agree that each would consult the other should the possibility become real. I did not in fact take Oliver's *démarche* particularly seriously. At that time I regarded Butler, who had been passed over in 1957, as at least heir presumptive, with Iain MacLeod as a possible outsider. I had not seriously considered my own chances, nor, as a matter of ethics, would I have thought it right to do so. In point of fact, I would have said that the image that had become attached to me as the self-advertising bell-ringer was hardly calculated to endear myself to the party if the office of prime minister were in question. I have since learned that, at least since February, Macmillan had been speaking to his intimates of myself as possible successor; and, had I thought about the matter, I would have realized that, as the result of the series of important missions with which I had been entrusted since January, something might have been in the wind. My recollection is that Oliver's meeting with me took place before I took off for Moscow, but after I had been entrusted with the mission to go.

However this may be, things turned out very differently after the summer holidays. At that time, the Conservative conference in October, then, as now, the last of the series of party conferences, did not take place until the Wednesday of the week in which it was held. It was preceded on the Monday or the Tuesday by a local-government conference with the same representation on the floor but no general attendance of cabinet ministers. On the Monday I was summoned to Downing Street by the Prime Minister. I had not the smallest inkling of what was to take place. He told me, formally, that he wished me to succeed him, and gave me to understand that he expected to retire about Christmas. He certainly then had no more suspicion than I that, before the end of the week, events were going to overtake him. Though my recollection of the exact sequence of events is distinctly hazy, I do remember being almost struck dumb with surprise at the content of our conversation and do not remember a thing that I said. I was not due to visit Blackpool until the Tuesday evening. But, for the first time since that memorable experience in the Brighton Aquarium in 1957, I was due to address the annual Conservative Political Centre meeting on the Wednesday evening. There was, so far as I recollect, a cabinet meeting on the Tuesday morning less than twenty-four hours after my meeting on Monday at which Harold, manifestly ill, and deeply moved, but apparently unaware that an emergency operation was going to take place the following day, told us that the state of his health was now so precarious that he was going to have to submit to a medical examination followed by an operation. In fact he had an enlarged prostate. On Tuesday morning I fulfilled a long-standing engagement to speak at a trade-union gathering in London and moved on to Blackpool by train and car. The next day (Wednesday) was my birthday. I was just fifty-six years old. I had a public speech at Morecambe that evening. It might well have been, as I was told at the time, that they would have been willing to select me as their candidate to succeed their sitting Member had I been prepared to announce my decision to disclaim. I thought that this would be jumping the gun. Harold had not declared his intention to resign, and all I could say was that I hoped he would get better soon.

I cannot now remember whether it was the Wednesday or the Thursday that I had a conversation with Alec Home about the situation as we walked back together from the conference. I think it must have been the Thursday since *The Times* that morning had carried a report that 'a fourth hypothetical candidate [for the leadership], Lord Home, would probably be the choice of perfection of the party's organization men.' The other three, of course, were Rab, Reginald Maudling and myself. At that time, and despite Harold's direct intimation of his preference for me, I did not personally doubt that Rab would easily emerge as the winner. I never took Maudling very seriously as a candidate. In Cabinet he was a good counsellor, though on the soft left of the team, what would now be called a wet. He had a first-class brain, and in counsel had a good line in detecting and deflating nonsense. But he had no great charisma and a certain lack of decisiveness, and his performances in public, including those at the critical conference itself, were distinctly lack-lustre. As we walked, Alec told me that he was under strong pressure to disclaim and throw his hat into the ring. I was not surprised at this intimation. But by this time I regarded the two most promising candidates as Rab and myself and possibly Iain MacLeod as a compromise.

Together with Edward Boyle, Iain MacLeod was one of the two left-wingers in the party I most admired and differed from most often. Iain had the best mastery of the House of Commons on our side. To hear him wind up a debate on the side of the Government was an education in the parliamentary art. He scarcely had a note in front of him, spoke admirably to the point with hardly a word out of place, and held the House in the hollow of his hand with the sheer enchantment of his debating skill. He was the one Conservative who had the measure of Aneurin Bevan. But for his tragic death at the very beginning of the Heath government when he had achieved the post of Chancellor of the Exchequer he might, for aught I know, have prevented its premature end in March 1974 and, if not, possibly have provided a different successor to Edward Heath. In 1963, however, Iain was, of course, still alive and active and may have had ambitions for the ultimate succession. I never quite knew why Reginald Maudling and not Iain was, with Rab Butler and myself, the third contender for the succession to Harold Macmillan. Perhaps this was because Salisbury's cruel and unjustified gibe of 'too clever by half' had left an unmerited stain.

Meanwhile I reminded Alec of our previous agreement about disclaimer, and gave him to understand that I did not think it was at all a good idea for him to stand. He asked me why, and I replied that I did not think his knowledge and understanding of home affairs was adequate. This was, and is, in my opinion; but, not unnaturally, he was not best pleased. He reminded me that he had been Minister of State in the Scottish Office. 'That,' I replied, 'is not enough. They would skittle you out in six months.' We remained, and remain, on the best of terms. He is, and I believe he has always been, a sincere Christian and by any standards a super person. We left it at that, but the conversation remained in my mind. The Conservative Party has always been reluctant to take a calculated risk, and I knew myself to be regarded in that light especially by many on the left of the party. Rab would have been their preferred candidate, but the same factors which stopped him being chosen in 1957 were still operative, and I have since come to believe that Harold Macmillan was distinctly persuaded that he would not do as leader. I believe that he might have done quite well. So Alec and I parted amicably, and I hope have been friends after, as before, our talk. He is a good and wise man.

The pot suddenly came to the boil that afternoon. Maurice Macmillan and Julian Amery (Harold's son-in-law) came suddenly down from the sickroom in London. Harold had taken a turn for the worse and was going to resign at once before the conference had ended. Their joint message was clear and was conveyed straight from Harold himself. 'You must act at once,' said Julian. The question was how. I had about a couple of hours in which to make up my mind, and then I had to go and make my speech at the CPC conference, at the Empress Hall, on the same occasion as my Aquarium speech in Brighton seven years before, almost to the day. The speech was in print and would be on sale after the meeting. It could not be altered. Two things, in all decency, I had to do. The first, in all loyalty to him, was to tell Rab. I did so, in his suite, at the Imperial Hotel. He was not pleased, and tried to dissuade me. But by this time my mind was made up. One way or the other I must act at once, and there was only one decisive moment at which I could do it: the end of the CPC meeting when I replied to the vote of thanks to myself as the principal speaker. This was the one moment when I could say whatever I would then have to say. It would be one of two things. I would have to say that I did or did not intend to disclaim my peerage. Anything else would be to dither. If I said that I would not disclaim, I would be out of the race, to make way, as I then believed, for Rab. If I said that I would disclaim, I was making it plain that I was available, if wanted, as Leader. So I made it clear to Rab that, in reply to the vote of thanks, I was going to announce that I was going to disclaim my two titles. And that is what I did. The prepared speech which I delivered for a totally different situation did not go down either particularly well or particularly badly. But when I came to reply to the vote of thanks, totally impromptu, and at the very end made my decision known, the effect was one of the most dramatic in my lifetime. The whole audience, and the platform, went mad, standing, cheering and waving in the full light of the national television; and, of course, the whole press was full of it the next morning. *The Times* reported my end remarks verbatim. The *Daily Express* carried a banner headline 'Enter Mr Hogg'. I tried to keep out of the public eye for the rest of the conference and in the main hall I absolutely succeeded, seated behind the pillars except that when the main speakers went in, including MacLeod, Maudling and Alec Home to make their own speeches, I applauded each with enthusiasm, as I did also when Rab came to make the final speech which in the ordinary case would have been made by Harold Macmillan. It was otherwise outside. Randolph appeared, bearing with him badges for delegates to wear marked 'QH'. I did not approve of all this. It was too like the Republican and Democratic conventions in the United States. How I lived through the rest of the day I simply do not remember. But one thing I do remember. Mary had stayed behind in London to look after our youngest child, Kate, who had been born the previous year on St Luke's Day in the middle of a lecture by Sir Harold Himsworth, the charming and brilliant secretary of the Medical Research Council. The message announcing Kate's arrival was brought to me while the lecture, in what is now Canada House, was still going on. The reason why Mary had stayed behind was because our domestic arrangements were such that we had no one else to look after Kate. But after my meeting with Rab there was one more thing I had to do – which was to ring up Mary in Putney Heath and ask her, in view of the developments, to come down, and she duly came, as there was no alternative, with Kate in her arms. Some odious people subsequently tried to make out that I did this only to advertise my candidature, and I am sorry to say that this abominable calumny was fed by my detractors to Harold in the nursing home, duly appeared in his diary, and was subsequently swallowed hook, line and sinker by Alastair Horne. The case was quite the contrary. There are times when a man needs his wife by his side, and this was emphatically one of them.

We went back on the Saturday, and what used to be called 'the usual consultations' then took place. To these I was not, of course, a party. At that time the present written and formal mechanism for selecting a leader was not in place. The sovereign body of the Conservative Party was, and still is, the same body as decided to pull Conservative ministers out of the Lloyd George coalition. It was then called the Carlton Club meeting, from the fact that, when the old Carlton Club was standing in Pall Mall before the bombing, it came together on the first floor of the building exactly where the high-explosive bomb later fell. The gathering consists of all Conservative MPs and prospective candidates, Conservative peers and certain other dignitaries. It meets now only as a sort of formal body to crown the leader already selected by a new written procedure in which the decisive vote takes place after successive ballots by Conservative MPs. In 1963 I believe it did not meet at all. Instead there took place the 'usual consultations', whatever these may have been, largely conducted through Lord Dilhorne, helped, it would appear, by Martin Redmayne, and perhaps others. I have never discovered quite what these 'usual consultations' were except that in this instance they could not have been 'usual', since never before in the history of the office of Prime Minister had advice as to his possible successor been tendered to his sovereign from a bed of sickness, based on hearsay evidence prepared for him by others which he apparently had no possible means of verifying and which, from Alistair Horne's somewhat garbled account of the matter, he appears to have swallowed hook, line and sinker. Iain MacLeod, who may well have harboured ambitions of his own, was always of the opinion that the whole thing had been fixed by a tight inner circle composed of old Etonians and their friends. I was never convinced by this, and Alistair Horne's version of the matter, which appears to be based largely on Macmillan's own recollections, which I do not believe to have been accurate, makes it clear that, whatever else may have taken place, it was neither usual, rational nor well thought-out and was largely based on erroneous and, in one respect at least, deliberately malicious hearsay evidence.*

So far as I am concerned, therefore, the matter remains wrapped in mystery. No doubt the subject of the Leadership had been a topic of conversation for some months between knowledgeable people and there would have been nothing improper in this, and if the 'organisation men' of the party, whoever these may have been, had decided that Alec Home was the ideally safe compromise candidate instead of the supposedly weak Rab and the supposedly flamboyant Hailsham, either of whom might have been expected to be a cause of division amongst the faithful, I should have had nothing whatever of which to complain. The constituency organisations would undoubtedly have favoured myself. But then Britain is governed by Parliament and not by constituency organisations. In the outcome, however, I was bruised and angry when I read for the first time of the malicious nonsense which was being fed into the sick-room from what should have been reputable sources. Fortunately, perhaps, I shall never know the whole truth and I lost no friends, even among the rival contenders. Although the time was a painful one for me, I do not think that any of us was guilty of disreputable conduct. By Monday, 14 October, after the conference, *The Times*' centre page relating Dilhorne's activities was headed: 'Cabinet Move to Make Home Leader.' On Tuesday, 15 October, referring to Monday, we read: 'Butler Sees Lord Dilhorne and Lord Home' (but not Lord Hailsham). On Wednesday, 16 October, *The Times* read: 'Macmillan Sees the Possibles.' In addition to the others these interviews did include

*What I have learned since I first published my own account of the matter (which so far as concerned my own part, was purely factual) is that my previous speculation based on a visit by Edward Heath to John Morrison at his island home in Scotland somewhat earlier in the summer is not at all correct, as I have Edward Heath's own word to this effect which, of course, I wholeheartedly accept, and I am now sorry I included it in my narrative.

me. I visited Harold in the King Edward VII Hospital, where the operation had taken place. He said nothing to me of the slightest importance. Least of all did he refer to our previous week's meeting in Downing Street, nor the urgent message he had sent me via Julian and Maurice on the eve of the operation. I had the distinct impression that he had done another of his famous somersaults. So he had. It was another retreat from the Roman Catholic Church. It was another Suez, another Night of the Long Knives. By Saturday, after advice from her retiring Prime Minister, the Queen had sent for Alec and invited him to form an administration.

But this is to anticipate events. After my return with Mary to London and my hospital interview with Harold, I had tried my best to secure a meeting with Rab and Maudling to point out to the two of them that no one could form a government if we all three acted together, and to disclose to them that I was tolerably certain that the choice would not fall on myself. In other words, I would offer it to Rab on a plate. I was unable to set up such a meeting until it was known to all three that Alec was already on his way to the Palace. I placed my cards on the table. I said that, if we all declined to serve in it, Alec would not be able to form a government and that I no longer regarded myself as a candidate. But Rab then said that he had already given his word to Alec. I cannot remember what Maudling said. But it did not matter anyway. Ferdinand the bull had preferred to sniff the flowers rather than take what would have been his if he had wished it. Harold had done another of his somersaults under the influence of Reggie Dilhorne, who before the matter was settled had distinctly urged me to 'throw my hat into the ring', and presumably of Ted Heath. Later that day I agreed to serve Alec in my existing capacity as Minister for Science and Lord President of the Council, with the reservation that honour demanded that I should adhere to my proclaimed intention to disclaim my peerage. This I did despite coming under very heavy pressure from persons I deeply respect to go back on what I subsequently said at the meeting and stay on as Viscount and Leader of the House of Lords. I did not then, or later, think that was an honourable course. I am neither a card-player nor any other sort of gambler. But when one has put one's stake on the table and lost the coup I do not think it open to a man of honour to pick up his counters, put them back in his pocket and walk away whistling a merry tune.

I was sad to renounce the peerage because, in addition to having had to sell Carter's Corner in opposition to my father's wishes, I felt there would now be many who would regard my disclaimer as some sort of implied slur on my father's noble life and achievements.

I had once said to Christopher Chataway in the course of a television interview that the man who actually wanted to be Prime Minister was a fool. I stand by that, and I sincerely say that, although I would have been proud to accept the leadership if the cards had fallen that way. I was not sorry that they did not. But the whole experience had been miserable. I would not have allowed my name to go forward at all had Harold not pressed me to do so at that Monday interview and by the message sent to me on the Wednesday by his son and his son-in-law. I do not think I was greatly influenced by Reggie Dilhorne's urgings, and I persuaded Randolph, to whom I divulged my side of the story when he was researching his book, to take out a slighting reference to Reggie which he had originally inserted. But during the course of the crisis a number of wounding things had been said about me in private and in public which I did not think I deserved, and I do not pretend that at the end of it I was not bruised and battered to an extent which I had not endured since my unhappy return to England at the end of 1942.

In the mean time I had a constituency to find and a by-election to fight. I had an offer of more than one safe seat. But, of course, as soon as it was made open to me, I selected my father's old constituency of St Marylebone, in which three generations of my family had lived and in which my grandfather's life's work in the Regent Street Polytechnic had been consummated. The by-election itself was squalid and painful and accompanied by a totally false charge of assault against me by the Liberal candidate, who withdrew it after an agreement between counsel on both sides. I was, of course, elected, but on a low poll and with a reduced majority, and I consummated my unhappy standing in the country by making thereafter in the House of Commons one of the worst speeches I have ever made, during the course of which I inadvertently addressed the House, out of sheer force of habit, as 'My Lords', an error which so far as I know has been made by no one else in the world in the history of British politics. Not for the only time in my life was I spiritually, and physically, at a very low ebb indeed.

I have often been asked what I think would have been if the result had been different. That is a question which it is impossible to answer. But I hope I would have reacted to the challenge honourably and courageously. What I feel quite sure of is that either Rab or I would have won the 1964 election, and I believe that that would have been an important event in constitutional history. After four consecutive defeats, for reasons I will indicate in the next chapter, I believe that it would have destroyed the Labour Party. In its place I believe would have arisen in time a radical party composed of moderate Labour, Liberal and a few left-wing and dissident Tories. If so, the Wilson era would never have come about and, I believe, British politics would have reverted to its two-party norm. At the time I thought that Rab Butler would have made an above-average Conservative prime minister, under whom I would have been happy to work in any capacity. His performance at the time of the events of 1963 has since led me to doubt this, since his failure to take what was his for the asking has led me to wonder to what extent he would have had the temperament to lead. But I feel sure that, under Rab, we would not have lost the 1964 election. As it was, we were only defeated by a whisker. Two hundred and fifty thousand votes would have done the trick, and we lost more than that as a result of the decision, before that election, to abolish resale price maintenance. Being no economist, I say nothing about the merits of that, though as a politician I am convinced that, after proper preparation and consultation, resale price maintenance might very well by now have gone the way of all flesh. No Labour government would have restored it, and it is possible that a Rab government would have got rid of it in a fairly short time. As it was, Alec allowed it to be forced through by tiny majorities in advance of the election, without mandate and without adequate consultation, in the false belief, engendered by one cabinet minister, but against the advice of more experienced colleagues, that it was an election vote-winner instead of a certain loser. When colleagues selected by himself agree, the office of prime minister is one of the easiest to fill. When they differ, the art consists in the possession of knowledge and instincts capable of backing the right horses at the right time. In matters of foreign policy, Alec had all the makings of a more than adequate prime minister. But in home affairs his lack of perceptiveness led him astray. When, after the 1964 election, he decided to throw his hand in, I begged him to stay. As it was, my prophecy in Blackpool was only a few months out. He is one of the most deservedly popular and beloved public figures in the country. But in the House of Commons and the country he was no match for the Labour Opposition generally or Harold Wilson in particular, and proved unable to sustain the mounting unpopularity which inevitably attached to a party continually in office for more than thirteen years. In the next Parliament, I was to become the opposition spokesman in the Commons on Home Affairs, and it seemed possible that, should we be returned to power, I might even have become Home Secretary. It was not to be. Since that office is more often the grave than the foundation of reputations, perhaps it was as well.

FORTY-TWO

Member for St Marylebone

THE DYING YEARS of a Parliament are not good ones for either side. That which ended in 1964 was an extreme example of this. Owing to the course which things had taken, Alec was virtually compelled to let the old Parliament, elected in 1959 and its mandate exhausted, virtually run out of its statutory five years on time. This gave Harold Wilson the chance of squeaking home, and he thus saved the Labour Party from what I believe would have been annihilation had they lost. I bitterly regret this since, though by this time I was a dyed-in-the-wool Conservative, I had come to believe, as I still do, that the traditional Labour Party, with its undemocratic card vote, its organic link with the unions, and its shackling devotion to Clause 4 of its constitution, committing it unconditionally to the common ownership of all (yes, all) the means of production, distribution and exchange, had outlived its usefulness, having obtained all the legitimate objectives for which it was formed. It had become a danger to political navigation and should have been sunk without trace. I desperately longed for a return to the two-party system to which, I believe, our constitution as a norm is best adapted. This would indeed have meant what has since been referred to as the breaking of the political mould. It would have involved not only the shattering of the Labour Party, and a sprinkling of left-wing Conservatives with experience of government, probably including Edward Boyle, possibly Iain MacLeod, conceivably Enoch Powell (who had not, at that time, acquired his fixation about 'the Tiber flowing with blood') and possibly Nigel Nicolson and Humphry Berkeley. The Unionists of Northern Ireland, still responsibly served by their leaders, at that time reasonably liberal and notably unbigoted in their attitude to the minority community, were still affiliated, as they should always have remained, to the Conservative Party in England, Wales and Scotland. The civilized but somewhat harem-bred Hugh Gaitskell was already dead, and had been followed by the far more politically astute, though perhaps less politically idealistic, Harold Wilson. Neither the SDP, the SLD, nor the Green Party had even been thought of. That, at least, was the idea I had as I toured the country in support of my own party, to which, of course, as a middle-of-the-road Conservative and former Party Chairman I would always have continued to belong.

In the few remaining months of the 1959 Parliament a certain amount of harm had already been done. Except that I believed it to be an election-loser, I have very few strong views about the abolition of resale price maintenance. There are, I believe, arguments on both sides, but for the reasons I have already given my conviction is that long before now it might very well have been abolished – if not before, at least after, we entered the European Community. But, although loyalty to my successful opponent led me to accept the office of Secretary of State for Education and Science, I was myself an adherent of the Trend Report. With the Labour government and the calamitous appointment of Frank Cousins as a separate Minister of Technology, a disastrous brainwave of Harold Wilson's, the possibility of a useful separation of political control of science, technology and the universities from that of schools became irreversibly damaged and has since proved unattainable. Technology cannot be separated from science for the simple reason that science and technology form a single spectrum of knowledge characteristic of modern culture and both, separately and together, are themselves a necessary component of education, where teaching, research and even development go hand in hand. Happily the separate Ministry of Technology no longer exists. I still think, however, that the present portfolio contains too many disparate elements to rest easily in one department.

All this, of course, is largely speculation. Harold Wilson, perhaps a better Leader of the Opposition than Prime Minister, squeaked home in 1964 and improved his majority in 1966 until it gradually disappeared after his mismanagement of the election of 1970. During the whole of this time, I was in opposition in the House of Commons, on the front bench, at first as opposition spokesman on Science and Education, but latterly, under Ted Heath, as spokesman on Home Affairs.

One of the traditions of the Bar is that one should try to keep on good personal terms with one's opponent, and I made it my business to remain on friendly personal terms with Roy Jenkins and, later, with James Callaghan. In litigation this policy is not always popular with one's lay client. In politics, it is also a doubtful source of popularity with one's own supporters. Nothing annoys some lay clients more than seeing their counsel lunching or walking off after court hours apparently on intimate terms with the very opponent with whom he has been waging fierce and apparently bitter battles during court hours. Equally, nothing annoys one's political supporters more than seeing one failing to take advantage of inadvertent slips of a political adversary on the opposition bench.

However, I have a definite policy in such matters. At the Bar, like my father, I never failed to take full and ruthless advantage of what I regarded as deliberate errors of tactics by opposing counsel. In libel cases, if he alleged the truth of a libel when he should have contented himself with a plea of privilege or fair comment, or in an action in contract if he pleaded fraud instead of alleging negligence, innocent misrepresentation or breach of warranty, I was never slow to exploit any advantage that I might gain from such tactical mistakes to the full extent and to the bitter end. But, in the case of inadvertent mistakes, such as inaccurate recollection of the evidence, or failure to spot a relevant authority, the error should be remedied with the greatest delicacy, and above all one should never seek to humiliate an honourable opponent. This I believe to be part of one's moral duty both to the opponent himself and to the tradition of general decency in which controversy should be conducted whether in litigation or across the floor of the House of Commons.

There is one occasion during my period of opposition which remains much in my mind as it illustrates the point I am trying to make. On the very first day when he became Home Secretary, after what must have been a painful resignation from an even higher post, James Callaghan made a most appalling gaffe. Answering a question asked by Jeremy Thorpe, then Leader of the Liberal Party, about a rather terrible crime, James said with evident satisfaction that the House would be glad to know that the criminal had been arrested. Quite reasonably Jeremy pointed out that the man had not even been tried and was therefore presumed innocent. The House was naturally outraged. But James had been through a difficult time, it was his first day in office, and he had not erred intentionally or maliciously. I therefore came to his aid. 'What the Right Honourable Gentleman meant to say, Mr Speaker, as I understand it, was that the *alleged* criminal has been arrested.' The tension subsided, but when I left the chamber shortly afterwards I was sternly rebuked by Iain MacLeod. 'You were too generous,' he said as I passed him, and he added that he would not have been. I had missed a point deliberately. But I believe I made a friend and added to the decency of public life.

When Roy Jenkins was still Home Secretary I was able to work quite amicably with him on some at least of his proposals in the field of criminal justice. One of these was his proposal for majority jury verdicts. There are, on every jury, almost always one or two oddballs conscious that they have a right to veto a verdict and sometimes with quite preposterous ideas of the kind of consideration which is appropriate to the case. Sometimes the minority of eccentrics manage to sit the majority out and secure a verdict to their liking. More frequently, before the Jenkins reform, a jury faced with this kind of problem simply disagreed, with the result that the trial had to begin all over again, after a delay of weeks or months, and the accused, committed for trial for the second time, would remain in gaol for an offence of which he might ultimately be acquitted. There was a terrible row about this. *The Times* wrote leading articles prophesying the end of our most cherished liberties, regardless of the fact that the Scots, with their juries of fifteen and despite their horrible verdict of 'Not proven', have been doing perfectly well for centuries on majority verdicts of as little as eight to seven. The Criminal Bar Association, not perhaps the most erudite of bodies, emitted fumes of sulphurous vapour like Vesuvius on the verge of eruption. Jenkins had consulted me before the event, and I had promised to back him through thick and thin, but not before I had consulted the eight or nine senior legal Members (some of them more distinguished at the Bar than myself) and got their promises of support. In the end, overcome by the superstitious public outcry, all these ratted and voted the other way. I kept my word to Jenkins and backed his proposals for all I was worth as a welcome, if minor, rationalization of the creaking old eighteenth-century ox-wagon of our criminal law. Ten to two seemed to be a perfectly adequate majority with the proper safeguards which Jenkins offered, and I prophesied, rightly as it turned out, but with some experience of juries, that most probably the first majority verdict would be one of acquittal. It duly was. Later, the Peter Hain trial, a nine-day wonder, ended, rightly in my opinion, in an acquittal equally by a majority. So far from being a fetter on liberty the Jenkins proposal turned out to be an aid to criminal justice, the purpose of which is the conviction of the guilty and the acquittal of the innocent. Of course, both the burden and the standard of proof have remained unaltered, and, once introduced, majority verdicts have come to stay. No one, least of all my profession, realizes how absurdly antiquated, rigid and irrational some of our rules of evidence and procedure have become. Many, if not most of them, date from the time when it was not open to an accused person to give evidence on his own behalf or, if accused of felony, even to have legal representation; when there were no disciplined police, no judge's rules, and no proper guarantee that a prisoner on remand was not bludgeoned or even racked into confession; and, perhaps above all, when there was no right of appeal, and no transcript of what had taken place at the trial. My profession has always had a love–hate relationship with juries, pretending on the one hand that they are the great bastion of our liberties and then refusing to let them have the relevant and logically probative facts for fear that they might let their emotions run away with them or prove incapable of judging the relevant reliability of witnesses or the inferences which can permissibly be drawn from given evidence. Readers of *Pickwick Papers* may well wonder how it was that neither

Mrs Bardell nor Pickwick was able to give evidence when the sole question at issue was whether or not Mr Pickwick had given or Mrs Bardell had accepted a proposal of marriage which Pickwick had admittedly been unwilling to perform. The whole trial in the Court of Common Pleas, like many of Dickens's assaults on our customary law, was perfectly good legal history. The course of the proceeding, though of course a caricature, was none the less based on the perfectly sound premiss that, being parties to the case, neither Pickwick nor Mrs Bardell was a competent witness. Right up to my own time, the civil law contained, and to a very large extent the criminal law persists in retaining, the hearsay rule in its full rigidity. Lawyers and civil rights enthusiasts still defend what Bentham rightly called the thieves' charter (the so-called right of silence), the trial within a trial, the absurd pretence you can get a random jury by subjecting twelve unwilling subjects to day-to-day attendance at a trial expected to last six to nine months, and many other minor anomalies too numerous to mention. Most have now been abolished from the civil law, many during my lifetime, but even then not without much misgiving and tooth-sucking. The criminal law has not progressed so fast, and every time a move towards rationality is proposed solemn leading articles and senior legislators with long faces proclaim with dire forebodings the end of civil liberties as we know them, oblivious of the fact that our own irrational procedures exist in only a handful of civilized countries throughout the world. However, in the matter of majority verdicts, Jenkins won the day; and, deserted by my eight colleagues, I kept my bond to support him in the letter and in the spirit.

When, in 1956, I had left the Bar for high office in Eden's government I had not expected my absence to last more than three years, when I expected to resume my practice as a silk. My unexpected success with Oliver Poole in assisting the party to victory in the 1959 election for Harold Macmillan had caught me like a mouse in a trap in cabinet office, and Olive Poole's determination to resume his City career had left me high and dry in the administration, at first despite my forfeiture, for irrelevant reasons, of Harold's good opinions. I did not escape until 1964 when Wilson's government came into power. To everybody's surprise I went back to the Bar and resumed my place in chambers, and equally to everyone's surprise except that of my clerk, Sydney Aylett, and myself I succeeded. To say this is not mere immodesty on my part. I had done it before. In 1945 I was pushing Douglas in his pram in the Flower Walk in Kensington Gardens when I met Hubert Hull, a leading member of Theo Mathew's chambers. I told him of my intention to return to the Bar after the election if it went against us, and he told me that the thing was impossible. It never succeeds, said he. But it did then, and in 1964 I pulled it off again. The fact is that, despite two absences of about seven years each, my love and knowledge of law and my capacity to win cases and settle the unwinnable ones were such that, although obviously never in the top earning class, I was able to win back a respectable practice and keep my family. To do so when something of a figure in public life and to finish up as Lord Chancellor is something of which, perhaps understandably, I remain rather proud.

In the present case, however, my return was the occasion of a rather unpleasant incident which I recount only to show how beastly people can be when they are motivated by political hostility. Naturally enough, the press was full of enquiries after the election as to what I was going to do now after more than six years in office, and I told them that I would be returning to my chambers in the Temple. They asked me about my practice, and as I had absolutely no idea what would be coming my way I gave inconclusive answers. Later the same year I attended a dinner in New York to celebrate Winston's ninetieth birthday. There was an American speech to mark Winston's half-American parentage and – for reasons, I suppose, similar if not identical – I was asked to make the British response. Present was a very select and distinguished gathering including Averell Harriman, my former colleague at the Test Ban negotiation but by this time very old indeed, with whom I exchanged affectionate recollections on our joint endeavours in Moscow. Later that night or the following night, I was asked to a drink by the charming daughter of the late Lord Beaverbrook, and we enjoyed a very nice glass or two of Glenlivet together. In the course of conversation she asked me about the Bar and enquired what sort of case I preferred doing best, to which I replied 'a nice clean case about money', explaining that I did not like having my withers wrung by pain, injury and suffering and that the violence or the squalor of sex and marital unhappiness made me, too, unhappy. All this, though I did not then think of it, and in perfect innocence and good faith, she duly reported.

A few weeks later a letter came on my desk out of the blue from the disciplinary committee of the Bar Council. They had received no less than three complaints, odiously expressed from obviously politically motivated (that this was so was apparent from the language used) persons wholly unknown to me to the effect that I was engaged in touting for work. If the charge had been substantiated, I was liable to be disbarred. I was not so much outraged as totally devastated and went round to John Hobson, our previous Attorney-General who was most considerate, sympathetic and supportive, and he promised to represent me in any disciplinary proceedings which might ensue. Happily this was not necessary. I replied to the Bar Council with some heat and considerable distress, setting out the above facts and expressing a degree of indignation that they should have taken seriously poison-pen letters so obviously inspired by political malice. Even now, the thing has left a scar.

The most notable event, however, of the period of opposition was Enoch Powell's extraordinary speech about immigration in 1968 on the occasion of the imminent Second Reading of the Labour government's Race Relations Bill of that year. Under Ted Heath's Leadership of the Opposition, I was at that time the opposition spokesman on Home Affairs: in the pompous jargon of the trade, the Shadow Home Secretary in the Shadow Cabinet. Except possibly in the fields of tenancy and employment when American experience and evidence led me to believe that the civil law had a role to play, I have never favoured legislation in this field. Race prejudice is a detestable thing, but its existence is a fact of life, and my belief is that to legislate about it normally makes things worse, especially if the legislation involves the creation of enforcement agencies especially constituted to hunt out and persecute those alleged to be guilty of it. Like blasphemy and other public-order offences, I believe that criminal offences like the use of racially abusive language should be defined in such a way as would proscribe as criminal only such conduct, whether class, racial or religious, as is likely to lead to ill feeling between classes of Her Majesty's subjects and not simply refer to some particular source of social friction (like the old law of sedition, now largely obsolete). Religious and class prejudice can be every bit as hurtful as racial prejudice. But everything depends upon the circumstances in which the prejudice is displayed.

In cases of discrimination in the grant of tenancies or employment rather different considerations apply. It is a protection to landlords and employers to be able to reply to concerted attempts by others to lead them to indulge in discriminatory practices, to be able to resist by explaining that such discrimination is against the law and that there exists legislation capable of enforcement which would make concession to discrimination ineffective. But in this case it is a mistake to single out ethnic prejudice, or sex discrimination, and to exclude, for instance, religious, class or political discrimination, since one form of prejudice against minority groups is as disreputable as any other, and one can easily be masked by conduct prima facie attributable to any other. So many ethnic or political prejudices may be masked by legislation based on superficially religious or other differences. This was the real difficulty underlying the House of Lords judicial decision about the Sikhs, who are basically a religious denomination rather than an ethnic group. It is also part of the difficulty in tracing and outfacing anti-Semitic prejudice.

When, in the early part of 1968, the Shadow Cabinet chaired by Ted Heath met to discuss the Second Reading of the new Race Relations Bill then proposed by the Government, it was my duty as opposition spokesman on Home Affairs to advise my colleagues as to the attitude we should take. It was the last meeting we should hold before one of the short recesses, and the debate was to be held on the day after our return which, unless I am wrong, was a Tuesday. Mine was neither an easy nor an agreeable task. I began by saying that I did not intend to play the numbers game, much in vogue at that time, of guessing either the number of immigrants at present within the country or prophesying their rate of increase.

I said that it was unthinkable that we should countenance differential treatment aimed at those lawfully present in the United
Kingdom, still less their offspring, or that we should encourage
in any way discrimination against persons on account of the colour
of their skin. Apart from the obvious political and moral objections
to doing so, we would quite certainly incur great odium abroad and
encourage retaliatory action against our own expatriate nationals,
always more numerous than those of most other nations. I had to
report that in the House our party was split three ways. The Bill
had enthusiastic supporters, including Edward Boyle, whose zeal for
what seemed to me a largely misconceived measure was such that
he had told me he would support it through thick and thin whatever
advice came from the Shadow Cabinet. On the other hand, I said,
there was a numerically larger section of the party determined, at
least unless restrained, to vote against the Government on any
possible occasion. The great mass of the party, like myself, was
unconvinced either of its necessity or its timeliness but preferred to
give it qualified support in the field of landlord-and-tenant and
employment. I thought we could improve it a good deal in Committee, though in the event my attempt to include religious discrimination within its orbit was ruled as outside the scope of the Bill by the
Standing Committee Chairman. In the circumstances I could only
recommend colleagues to present as united a front as possible by
abstaining on Second Reading and taking an active part on Committee and Report. I warned colleagues that this stance would be
denounced as pusillanimous by the opponents of the Bill in our own
ranks and by populist opinion outside. The only alternative was a
'reasoned amendment' on Second Reading which would inevitably
be interpreted as unqualified opposition and would emphasize rather
than diminish the dissension in our ranks. After discussion, however,
which was prolonged, a reasoned amendment was agreed. Enoch,
with a face like a sphinx, remained silent throughout the debate, and I
was under the impression that he acquiesced in what had been
agreed. To make certain, I said to him as we left the room: 'I hope I
explained it fairly.' His reply reassured me. 'You could not have put it
more fairly,' he said. At no stage did he indicate that he differed, still

less that he contemplated a speech of his own. I departed for the recess with a sense of relief. I was to spend the weekend in the Lake District with Willie Vane, a former colleague in the House as Member for Westmorland, by this time Lord Inglewood. My younger son James would accompany me. Willie and I would walk the fells near Ullswater. James and the young Vanes, accompanied by a schoolmaster, would indulge, more ambitiously, in rock-climbing. Willie and I duly performed our fell-walking. The younger Vane had not gone climbing, but stayed indoors. I met him shortly before six o'clock. 'Have you heard about Enoch Powell's speech?' he said, and when I said 'No' he went on to suggest that I should watch the six o'clock news shortly coming on BBC television. I duly took the intelligent boy's advice, and to my horror heard and saw as the main item Enoch's warning about the Tiber 'foaming with blood'. To say that I was outraged would be a considerable understatement. Even in Shadow Cabinets, I had always regarded it as my duty to circulate all my public speeches through Conservative Central Office and, in case I spoke on a subject within the responsibilities of another colleague, to make sure that what I said was known in advance. No one had ever told me about this, but I had always regarded it as an obvious corollary of the essential collegiality of cabinet and shadow cabinet decisions. Enoch had circulated his speech on plain paper, to all editors, bypassing Central Office and concealing from Ted Heath and all other colleagues his intention of making any speech at all on the subject, still less one plainly inconsistent with the decision arrived at the meeting on the previous Thursday at which he had remained silent. However, I bottled up my fury, and rang up Willie Whitelaw who lived only about fifteen miles away and was at that time not merely a local MP but our Chief Whip in the Commons. There was an ITV news bulletin at that time at about 6.30 p.m., and there were just a few minutes in which to act. After asking whether he had heard of it, all I said was: 'Enoch has been making a rather odd speech, and I would ask you to listen to the news on ITV when it comes on in a few minutes' time.' I made no other comment on the nature of the speech. But I fully intended to have a blood row when the House met again after the recess. I clearly understood that if Enoch's speech was not publicly condemned by colleagues I would have to resign as Home Affairs spokesman and, barring accidents, my public life would be effectively at an end. It did not come to that. Willie Whitelaw watched the speech on ITV, rang Ted Heath, and without further ado, and without consulting me, Ted Heath sacked Enoch from the Shadow Cabinet. I have always been grateful to him for this.

I cannot conclude this episode without one further reflection. Race relations have now developed almost into an industry without, it seems to me, in the least improving the actual relationships between ethnic groups. After the general election of 1974 another and further Act of Parliament found its way on to the statute book during the four years of Labour government without, so far as I can see, simplifying or clarifying the complexity and prolixity of the law. On the contrary it seems either to have made things worse or, at least, left things much as they were before. I am fully persuaded that in some fields such as education, employment, tenancy and house-ownership some sort of legislation of a simple kind is necessary in order to prevent injustice and to protect those who might otherwise be placed under pressure to be guilty of discrimination against their will. A quite eminent lawyer of my acquaintance believes that a very short Bill prohibiting discrimination in certain fields and giving a remedy in damages would be enough. This would leave the courts to apply the principle. I am not sure that I agree with this. It must be possible for the owner of a French or Italian restaurant to give preference to cooks and waiters of the appropriate breed without incurring the penalties attaching to a hotel-keeper refusing admittance to a respectable customer because he has a black face or a factory-owner employing only white workers or workers of a particular religious denomination. But in the end more ought to be left to public taste and opinion than to precise regulation. Some laws are better left in general normative terms without erecting too many precise regulations or creating elaborate institutional structures dedicated to their enforcement. The United States Supreme Court has, however, improved race relations in the United States when confronted with blatantly unjust acts of segregation by state legislatures and executives, and it may be that a normative Act of

Parliament in general terms might usefully impose on the courts here a similar role. In the mean time, but not, I believe, solely or even principally owing to his dismissal by Ted Heath, Enoch went on to advise voters in one or it may be two general elections thereafter to vote Labour, and then, abandoning his Conservative allegiance altogether, to accept membership of the Unionist Party in Northern Ireland. Big-game shooting has never attracted me as a sport but, were I to be tempted to bag the occasional tiger, I rather doubt whether I would choose Enoch as a companion. This is a pity because I greatly admire his intellect and his scholarship, even when his conclusions are of the most bizarre, and I greatly regret that, despite our remaining on mutually courteous and friendly terms, what happened in 1968 still remains an obstacle to renewed intimacy.

One further incident belonging to this period remains in my memory. This is Ted Heath's mission to me to visit Northern Ireland in the wake of the civil rights marches and the dreadful riots in Belfast which followed. I have no doubt that he entrusted this mission to me as opposition spokesman on Home Affairs, which at that time included the affairs of what is left of the province of Ulster in the United Kingdom. I doubt if, at the time, he realized what an emotional experience this would be for me. The Hoggs come from Northern Ireland, and until 1914 we should undoubtedly have described ourselves as an Irish family. We regarded ourselves as Unionist and Irish rather than Conservatives until the unity of the Irish people was irreparably destroyed in 1921. In 1922 it fell to my father as Attorney-General in the Bonar Law government and Member for St Marylebone to make his maiden speech in the House of Commons from the dispatch-box to propose the enactment by statute of the terms of the Irish Treaty which he abominated but which he regarded as binding on us in conscience as we had pledged our word to it. Since that time we have regarded ourselves as British. But we have never forgotten our origin. In 1928 I had once visited the province as the guest of my friend Richard Best; and now, as Ted Heath's representative, I was to be hospitably put up by my friend in the House of Commons, Robin Chichester-Clark.

Naturally, apart from the scene of the riots, I visited the old home town of the family in Lisburn, now enriched by a statue of John Nicholson, the hero of Delhi, whose mother, Clara Hogg, was the sister of my great-grandfather. I also found time to visit Cardinal Conway and the Church of Ireland Archbishop of Armagh, the Moderator of the Presbyterian Church, and the chief of the Methodist Church. But my most poignant visits were to the Bogside in Londonderry, at that time a no-go area designated by its inhabitants as Free Derry (or Doire) and the scene of the riots in Belfast, whose pitiful inhabitants, Protestant and Catholics, showed me the burned-out ruins of their homes. At that time by far the worst damage had been caused to Catholic homes by Protestant mobs. But they were not the only sufferers. One Protestant shopkeeper told me miserably how a Catholic customer had lobbed a bomb at him. 'And I thought he was a friend,' he added bitterly. In Derry I was handed over by my guards to the representatives of the no-go area in the Bogside. I was utterly alone and unprotected, but they all treated me hospitably, feeding me lavishly with chicken sandwiches and beer as they aired their grievances, imaginary and real. For me, the whole experience was a searing one and, spiritually, tore me apart. I had immediately afterwards to report what I had seen to the Tory conference, and I almost broke down in describing what I had seen and heard. My own family connection with the place no doubt explains the depth of my feeling, but what had chiefly shocked me was the sheer evidence of mutual hatred exposed by the burned-out living-rooms and shattered windows and, in the Protestant areas of Londonderry, the places pointed out to me by their families where people had actually been done to death. Even my pleas, spoken from the bottom of my heart, for faith, hope and charity, above all charity, angered my Unionist hosts, at that time welcome affiliates of the Conservative Party conference, and Robin Chichester-Clark and some of the others actually walked out. Only two good things happened as the result of my visit both of which assisted me later in my work as Lord Chancellor. The first was my friendship, which I date back to that time, with the late Cardinal Conway who averted what might have been a terrible misfortune when I wrote to him to seek his assistance. The second was a warm friendship I struck up with James Callaghan, at that time Home Secretary, whom I visited after my return. I remain heartbroken at what has happened to the land of my fathers, and I remain, as was my father before me, firm in my belief that, though there is no going back on the treaty which we signed in good faith, the future of these islands, from Jersey in the south through Scotland and Man to the Orkneys and Shetland Isles and equally to Cork and Donegal, must be together or not at all. Independence is no answer. If Benelux can be effectively a unity within Europe, so can these islands. Men and women can surely be persuaded to seek friendship and co-operation rationally, without recrimination, and within the bonds of charity as demanded by all branches of the Christian faith.

In the mean time, and wholly unsuspected by me, a new chapter in my life was about to open out. After all the work I had done in Marylebone and as Shadow Home Secretary I was not to be Home Secretary after all. Yet another unforeseen turn in my fortunes and activities was about to occur.

FORTY-THREE

Lord Chancellor and Life Peer

ONLY ONE, and that also a wholly unexpected, episode should have given me some warning of what was in store for me. Fairly late in the life of the 1966 Parliament, I received a totally unexpected invitation to a meal from Gerald Gardiner, at that time Lord Chancellor. I could not imagine what it was about. It is not uncommon for senior barristers to receive a summons to meet the Lord Chancellor, but only in his office, and then usually only as a prelude to being offered some judicial preferment. I knew of course that this was not going to be one of these. The invitation was to his flat, and to a meal. Despite politically opposed loyalties, Gerald was of course well known to me. We had always been friends at the Bar. Indeed, he had led me once in a tragic civil case in which we had both appeared for Sybil Lygon, a former acquaintance and friend of my late brother Edward Marjoribanks. At the time of our meal together Gerald was living a solitary and lonely existence in the austere discomfort of the Lord Chancellor's flat above his office, cared for by an elderly Spanish maid, Maria. His first wife had recently died after a long and melancholy illness, and he had been left a widower. Gerald had formidable gifts as an advocate and a passion for law reform, usually of a politically controversial nature. But he had no leanings to join the judiciary, and, as Lord Chancellor, seldom sat as a member of the Appellate Committee. We ate our meal amicably together; then, to my astonishment, he disclosed to me that he did not think that the Labour government had a long period of office in front of it and asked if, should an election take place and a Conservative majority be returned to office, I would be prepared to accept the Woolsack.

Obviously I had to take the suggestion seriously, but I was absolutely at a loss to know who could possibly have put him up to ask such a question. I still do not know. He was a socialist of left-wing views, held with a highly respectable sense of constitutional propriety. I had friends among the higher judiciary, including both Hubert Parker and John Widgery. But the Woolsack is in the gift of the Prime Minister, and Ted Heath, then Leader of the Opposition, who would be Prime Minister if the election went our way, as at the time did not seem particularly likely, had not so much as given me the whisper of a hint that this was likely to be my lot. I naturally made deprecatory and noncommittal noises, and we parted on the best of terms. I still do not know the inner history of this remarkable episode in my life and I soon put it from my mind. I do not think that I even told Mary about it. At the same time there could have been no doubt in my mind that I should accept. I was approaching sixty-five and, although I believe he liked and trusted me as a colleague, not particularly close to Ted Heath. Even if, which was by no means certain, I was offered the Home Office, my tenure of it could not conceivably be long. I had no pension, and my variegated career had never permitted me to make much money. I knew that as Lord Chancellor I would throw myself wholeheartedly into the role.

When it came, the outcome of the 1970 election did not look propitious for my party. The polls were against us. Harold Wilson strutted around like a member of the royal family going walkabout. The only thing that could be said for electioneering was the weather, and I campaigned by road in glorious sunshine, driven about highways flanked in the country gloriously with Queen Anne's lace. In my own constituency, I wandered the streets of Marylebone with a loudspeaker into which I declaimed, 'Turn out to vote, and vote to turn them out,' a slogan of my own invention. This is in fact what happened. Our majority was not large but it was enough. I was summoned to Downing Street and offered the Woolsack by Ted Heath. I consulted Mary, and our decision was 'Yes'. I had to give up St Marylebone and take a life peerage. We looked forward to our joint future with hope and enthusiasm. I was measured for new knee-breeches, and Mary modernized the Lord Chancellor's flat. It was as well that I had sold Carter's Corner as we decided to cling to our family house in Roehampton where the family could get together. Never since the Admiralty had Mary been happier. We hardly used the flat at night except for official entertainments.

We both realized that my acceptance of the Chancellorship was a watershed in our joint lives. For me it meant a final end to any leading part in the life of the Conservative Party. Whilst he was Chancellor, David Kilmuir continued to address party political gatherings at every level. I never did. I treated my appointment as a signal that that side of my life, so prominent since 1956, had come to a full stop and that, except at election times, and speeches for special friends or, later, members of my family, I must henceforth confine myself to being as good a Lord Chancellor as I knew how and to avoid any activities which conflicted with this. I was not sorry. My double life at the Bar and in the House of Commons had not improved family life. Henceforward, free from the harassment of being an MP's wife, I believe Mary became a good deal happier than she had been for years. To my considerable surprise she expressed a desire to become a magistrate. At first this was an embarrassment to me as, technically, all magistrates are appointed by the Lord Chancellor. But she was obviously eminently suitable. I told her what hoops she would have to jump through, but that if she managed to jump them without my active support I would not, and could not, refuse to endorse her simply because she was married to me. This duly happened. One does not ask magistrates whether they actually enjoy the work. But it is a satisfying piece of public service, and it enabled Mary to blossom out as she had never done since the earlier days of our marriage. I cannot remember now when she actually qualified, but she became an experienced and seasoned member of the Inner London Bench with a group of friends of her own and with a great deal of self-confidence. This gave her a really satisfying life after living so long under the shadow of her husband's career.

In my second term of office I had a similar difficulty. In a particularly busy week I was asked to approve a batch of more than a hundred (I believe) nominations for the Bench from the Hampshire Advisory Committee. I do not think my office ever really believed that it was my invariable practice to look through every nomination form. But in giving my approval I wrote at the head of the submission: 'I think you might have told me that one of these candidates is my own daughter, and that she has put down her politics as Liberal.'

I thought I knew the nature of the office better than most. My father had been Lord Chancellor twice and, particularly in his earlier term of office, whilst I was still living at home, he had discussed the duties fairly freely with me. Of course, in the intervening years much had changed. When my father was Lord Chancellor he had presided in Appeals as a judge almost every day. The political sittings of the House of Lords did not begin till 4.15 in the evening. Then, as now, Appeals to the Privy Council were held in Downing Street. But Appeals to the House of Lords were held in the chamber. The Lord Chancellor clad in wig, gown and bands, but in long trousers, would come down from the Woolsack (then stuffed with horsehair) and counsel (silks wearing full-bottomed wigs) would address him and his four colleagues from an uncomfortable little box at the Bar of the House. The hearing would stop at 4 p.m. My father would then adjourn the House, don his knee-breeches and silk stockings, drink his cup of tea and resume his seat on the Woolsack at 4.15. Sittings seldom lasted later than 6.30 p.m., and usually fewer than fifty peers attended. By the time of my meal with Gerald Gardiner all that had changed. As I have already written, the bombings of London put an end to evening debates. The Commons Chamber had been destroyed, and the Commons took over the Lords Chamber as their own. The Lords betook themselves to the royal robing-room. To hear appeals, the Law Lords, usually in two divisions of five, sat upstairs in the Committee Room in plain clothes, and were duly addressed by counsel in robes but short wigs. Their judgements continued to be given in the House, but in the form of a report from what was henceforth known as the Appellate Committee. After the war, the new system continued, and, since both Houses now sat in their political capacity at 2.30 p.m., the Lord Chancellor could not be in two places at once. He either had to abandon the Woolsack to the Lord Chairman of Committees as Deputy Speaker and hear appeals as President of the Appellate Committee or, vice versa, he had to leave the Chair in the Committee Corridor to the senior Law Lord available and sit in the House on the Woolsack at 2.30 p.m. to attend debates. In practice he usually chose the latter course. He was not altogether sorry to do so because, quite apart from appearances, the administrative duties of the office, though far less than at present, had increased enormously since my father had finally left office. The only function which had diminished was the ecclesiastical patronage. When my father was Lord Chancellor, he was besieged by a plethora of parsons seeking livings. By the time Gerald was Lord Chancellor, the livings vacant vastly exceeded in numbers the suitable potential incumbents. Moreover the Patronage Office itself had been amalgamated with that of the Prime Minister. By the time Gerald demitted office the judicial functions of the Lord Chancellor, which for constitutional reasons I was to revive, had almost begun to atrophy. This would have been a disaster, as their regular discharge is the only factor ensuring that a politically motivated prime minister does not give the office to a no-good lawyer.

Though the constitutional functions of the Lord Chancellor have varied greatly throughout the ages, the office has always been exacting. In addition to their duties as judges of equity, Wolsey and More were virtually Prime Minister. They served under a tempestuous, savage, conceited, treacherous, authoritarian sovereign who has always had a better press than he deserved. As one born out of due time, Clarendon was, I suppose, the last of this series. During the eighteenth century, the Lord Chancellors of the day were virtually the monarch's private spies on their colleagues and constantly intrigued against them. Once appointed, they lasted a long time. Eldon, over separate terms, was Chancellor for twenty-seven years, Hardwicke for twenty years, and Thurlow for sixteen. Their main judicial work was at first instance sitting in the Court of Chancery, which, if the Chancellor, like Eldon, was slow to make up his mind, got frequently into the kind of muddle pilloried by Dickens in *Bleak House*. Almost alone, More and Brougham, very different characters, but both from Lincoln's Inn, acquired a reputation for the rapid disposal of business. From the nineteenth century onwards until the

Appellate Jurisdiction Act 1976, when the Law Lords appeared to take over the judicial work of the House of Lords, that work was largely performed by the Lord Chancellor of the day with any of his former colleagues who might be available and any retired judges who might be in the House of Lords also assisting. In the eighteenth century, Lord Chancellors virtually performed the Appellate work alone, sitting, but solely to make up a quorum, with a couple of bishops and perhaps a lay peer. By the time I was appointed in 1970, administrative duties had practically taken over. Until the end of the slightly ascetic Gerald Gardiner's tenure of the office the hours spent on the Woolsack had increased until they had become unbearably long. This was owing to the increased number of peers and the consequent lengthening of the duration of debates. I determined to reduce this drastically and, with the approval of the House, designated something like twenty-six deputy speakers, under the Command of the Lord Chairman of Committees. This was not out of laziness, but because it seemed to me a waste of time and money to employ a highly paid and heavily worked official in a task where he had no disciplinary functions and, unless he was actively engaged in a debate, no function at all except to put the correct question at the appropriate time and read out the result of any divisions.

Apart from the office work which has vastly increased since the reorganization of the Circuits and the vast increase in the number of judges, part-time and permanent, the Lord Chancellor does play an important part in the work of the Cabinet. In addition to cabinet meetings themselves he is almost always a member of more than one of the Standing Committees of the Cabinet. Until halfway through my second term, when the duty was, in my view rightly, placed on the shoulders of the Leader of the House of Commons, the Lord Chancellor was Chairman of the Legislation Committee (which eliminates the bugs from draft legislation after the policy issues have been approved). He remains a member of this Committee, and of its sister the Future Legislation Committee which discusses the size and shape of the sessional programme of legislation, and is virtually always a member, in the absence of the usual chairman sometimes presiding, of the Home Affairs Committee. I myself served on the

Defence and Overseas Committee and was so serving (though not a member of the so-called War Cabinet) at the time of the Falklands operation, and of course was summoned from time to time to Downing Street to take part alone or with other colleagues in *ad hoc* discussions with the Prime Minister. The sheer weight of public business led Margaret Thatcher, in my view wisely, to reduce normal meetings of the Cabinet to one on a Thursday, and to confine its business, so far as possible, to parliamentary affairs, foreign affairs, and any pressing topic requiring attention and which could not be otherwise handled. This has the disadvantage of still further reducing the collegiality, and so the feeling of joint responsibility, in the Cabinet. But it has the advantage of flexibility and the more efficient disposal of business. In addition to his responsibilities for law and legal or quasi-legal responsibilities, the Lord Chancellor is also responsible for the Public Trustee's office (an office which might well be a candidate for removal from direct ministerial responsibility; I could give an example of undue Treasury interference in invest-ment policy) and for the Public Record Office, which, during my second term, I made the subject of a special Committee report chaired by a former diplomatist of distinction. Every year, such is the abundance of Government paper, a mile and a quarter of shelf space is added to the public archives, that is approaching thirty-seven miles of public records since 1958 when responsibility was transferred from the Master of the Rolls to the more accountable Lord Chancel-lor. By the year 2000 another twelve miles or so will have been added to this deluge of paper. Yet even this mass of material represents only 1 per cent of the total paper generated. The remaining 99 per cent is pulped. All that remains is supposed to be in aid of the 'historian of the future'. Every January, under the thirty-year rule, the greater part of whatever material is thirty years old, save that certified by the reigning Lord Chancellor to satisfy one or more of certain published criteria, is exposed to the public gaze, together with any more recent material which he certifies to merit immediate exposure. The rest (probably the most interesting to the 'historian of the future') is held for fifty, seventy-five or a hundred years. The mind boggles at the number of 'historians of the future' there would have to be to digest even a hundredth part of the material which must have been added to the store during my own career as a Minister in the Cabinet or on the front opposition bench. Sometimes the most absurd things spring to the eye as having been withheld. On one occasion I discreetly enquired what advantage there was in withholding (or for that matter disclosing) some papers relating to Morris Motors in 1929. I was told with great firmness that their disclosure would possibly damage British exports. If I had had my way, the whole file would have been consigned to the dustbin. But that would have been a crime which it would be unthinkable for a Lord Chancellor to commit. So there they are still, presumably still awaiting the researches of the 'historian of the future'. The thirty-year rule can also be embarrassing. Fortunately, in 1986, I reflected that the archives of 1956, when, during Suez, I was First Lord of the Admiralty, should be examined by someone else and extracted a promise that nothing should be withheld on the ground that it might be embarrassing to myself, but that otherwise the ordinary criteria would be followed. Of course, nothing embarrassing to me emerged since, so far as I know, there was nothing there except what was already known. This did not prevent Lord Hatch of Lusby from asking a question on 14 January 1987 as to whether in the light of what had emerged the Lord Chancellor would resign. It emerged from the exchange that he had nothing whatever against me, but relied on the general doctrine of cabinet responsibility, being apparently unaware that at the relevant time the First Lord of the Admiralty was not a member of the Cabinet. For this constitutional ineptitude he was very properly squashed by Baroness Seear.

I also came to an arrangement with Ted Heath that the custom which had grown up of asking the Lord Chancellor to investigate internal government scandals which were not thought important enough for public inquiry should be given its final quietus, and the Lord Chancellor should not be asked to act in such matters for the future. This was both for reasons of principle and to allow him to concentrate on his legitimate duties. It is quite improper that the Lord Chancellor should assume the mantle of Grand Inquisitor. I also took the view, which is more controversial, that either the

Leader of the House of Lords or of the House of Commons should normally take the chair at the Legislation Committee of the Cabinet, which scrutinizes the details of legislation before it comes before Parliament, a post which, until then, had normally been allotted to the Lord Chancellor of the day. Reggie Dilhorne had rather revelled in the detail of this task, but personally I regard it as a waste of time for a senior minister, who is neither in charge of the policy nor responsible for the work of parliamentary draftsmen, to trouble himself more than with the ordinary functions of a chairman, and that this role is better discharged by those responsible for the carriage of business in the House.

Gerald Gardiner had left me with two valuable legacies both of which gave him the right to claim an important place amongst twentieth-century Chancellors. Like the Forth Bridge, the law is constantly in need of maintenance and repair, and, until the twentieth century, no proper mechanism for law reform had existed apart from the creation of committees or Royal Commissions, set up to investigate particular questions. Lord Sankey had appreciated the need for something more permanent and had created the Law Reform Committee, a standing body which from time to time still deals with items specially referred to it by appropriate ministers. His example had been followed by a succeeding Home Secretary who, as the minister responsible for criminal law, had set up a parallel body called the Criminal Law Revision Committee to advocate changes in that area. But it remained for Lord Gardiner to establish the two Law Commissions, English and Scottish, with a permanent and general obligation to investigate particular questions referred to it or, of its own motion, to pursue a regular programme of inquiry into the general state of the law or any particular respect they choose to select. Originally, I believe, the idea was to achieve total codification, but on the whole this has proved an *ignis fatuus*. However this may be, the two Law Commissions, particularly the English Commission, equipped with a permanent library, office and staff, and under the chairmanship of a High Court judge, have proved an invaluable mechanism of reform, with an established methodology and the services of at least one permanent draftsman. In both my terms of office I made full use of their services and, during my second term of office at least, including Consolidation and Statute Law Revision, between myself, the English Commission and other departments, we passed eighty-one Acts through both Houses. In any one year these would include at least one and preferably two or three main programme bills, and usually one or more minor and technical bills which could safely be entrusted to Private Members. That such a large number of measures should have been passed is largely due to the procedure evolved, involving preliminary discussion followed by a consultation paper, followed by a final report, preferably with a draft Bill attached, and finally incorporation into the government programme. Admittedly those areas of law in which the Lord Chancellor's office holds the labouring oar have been most consistently successful. Neither the Department of Trade and Industry (responsible for commercial law) nor the Home Office (responsible for criminal law) has been anything like so keen or positive. But, by any standards, Lord Gardiner's initiative deserves to place him as one of the more considerable holders of the Lord Chancellor's office during my professional lifetime.

The other great legacy which Gardiner left me during my first term of office was the reorganization of the criminal courts by the amalgamation of the Courts of Quarter Sessions and Assizes following the report of the Beeching Commission. This was by far the heaviest task in law reform I undertook during the Heath government, and added a great deal of work permanently to the work of the Lord Chancellor's Department. Still, it is not too much to say that, with indictable crime increasing since the war at something like 10 per cent a year at compound interest, the work of the courts would have come to a grinding halt in the early 1970s without the Courts Act 1971 and the ancillary work, largely my own achievement, that went with it. This involved the reorganization of the Circuit System, the crash programme of court-building, the new method of appointing judges by giving them a trial run as deputy judges, assistant recorders and recorders before according them permanent status by pensionable appointments, and the Judicial Studies Board which provides for induction training, refresher courses and seminars. All this was very largely my own work. In co-operation with County Court judges I also introduced the small-claims procedure in the County Courts and, by a system of revised forms, systematized and simplified them. The method of appointing silks, and the declaration required of silks before appointment, was also reformed. In neither of my two terms of office was I able to achieve in the field of civil law my ultimate aims of doing for the civil courts what I had achieved for the criminal courts by amalgamating the jurisdictions of the County Courts and the High Court, without of course eliminating the distinction in grade and status of High Court and Circuit judges, by reducing to a single complex with a unified pyramid of appeals the complicated and unjustifiable confusion of jurisdictions in family matters between magistrates, County Court and High Court. These pieces of unfinished business remained for my successors in office after my second term as Lord Chancellor, together with the other items on the agenda of the Civil Justice Review.

The most important constitutional function of the Lord Chancellor in the twentieth century remains to preserve the integrity and impartiality of the judiciary against all comers. This is not as easy as it sounds. Nor, until recently, was it observed as consistently even in the twentieth century as it has been by Chancellors of very different political outlooks since 1945. In theory, of course, everyone is in favour of judicial independence in the same way as they are in favour of virtue and against vice. But in practice this is far from the case. The Glorious Revolution had brought about the separation of powers between the Executive (first the King, later the Cabinet), the Legislature and the Judiciary, thenceforth secure in salary and appointment pending good behaviour. Since then the Legislature and the Executive have become inextricably intertwined, while the Judiciary has been left out on a limb as the weakest power in the Trinity. Only the Lord Chancellor is a member of all three branches of government: of the Judiciary as presiding officer of the Appellate Committee of the Lords; of the Legislature as Speaker of the Lords (and its member during legislative debates); of the Executive as member of Cabinet and head of a spending department. All this was, of course, unforeseen by the orchestrators of change in 1688.

The independence of the judiciary, wrung by Parliament from the Crown with much difficulty by the Glorious Revolution, is open to a continuous process of erosion by backbenchers and pressure groups, always ready, without hearing the evidence or listening to argument, to demand the removal of judges with whose particular judgements as published in the tabloid press they happen to disagree. More seriously, judicial independence is constantly open to intrusion from the government or opposition front benches, often eager to create new offences or rules of law which would deprive the judiciary of the ability to act according to the justice of the case. Then members of the Cabinet, the popular press, and academic lawyers take part in this activity. These approaches, in cases amounting almost to mob rule, cannot be protected by constitutional law, since we have no separate body of constitutional law which can only be amended by special procedures. On the contrary, judicial independence, like freedom itself, needs eternal vigilance and sometimes considerable courage on the part of the temporary, often extremely temporary, holder of the Great Seal. Hitherto the line has been held, even more successfully in recent years than before the war. When I was first called to the Bar more than half the Common Law judges had, at one time or another, been Members of Parliament, and therefore active party politicians, and it was a commonly held convention that a Member of Parliament who was also a member of the Bar had only to ask for a silk gown to be accorded it almost as of right. It was also commonly assumed that to have held a law officership gave an automatic right, almost on demand, to a seat in the Court of Appeal on resignation from office. Fortunately, all that has now gone by the board. But there are disadvantages as well as advantages in this. There is nothing like experience of politics to knock the angularities off a man, whether it be due to religious, social or political prejudice. I certainly left the House of Commons a man far less prejudiced than I had entered it. Some of the judges holding strong political views that I have known have been those promoted without experience to the House of Commons. Among Lord Chancellors, both Maugham and Simonds held stronger right-wing opinions than most Conservative politicians, and Gardiner was rather left of the centre of his party in his political orientation. On the other hand there has been considerable loss in mutual understanding between the Bench and politics. This has been caused by the growing loss since the war of the close relations which had existed for centuries between the legal profession and the House of Commons, which no doubt originated in the close proximity between St Stephen's Chapel, where the Commons used to sit, and the Courts of Justice formerly located in Westminster Hall. There is also a certain and regrettable absence of understanding on the part of the judges of the actual working mechanisms of the constitution, and this is certainly not an advantage. On the whole, however, I have to say the quality of judges, despite their vastly greater numbers, is higher now than when I was called to the Bar in 1932. Some of the County Court judges were holy terrors, and, though this was sometimes an advantage to a young man who knew his law and had the courage to stand firm in the face of judicial onslaught in that it deterred solicitors from briefing the timid, the ignorant or the inexpert, the picture presented to the average litigant or witness of the quality of the Bench was not always as happy as it is now.

I suppose I must shoulder my own share of the blame for the dissolution of Parliament and subsequent electoral defeat of the Heath government in the face of the miners' strike in February 1974. There had been those who were for going to the country from the first. I was not. I was originally for sticking it out as Mrs Thatcher subsequently did in the 1980s. But this was conditional on our rather slender majority in the Commons standing firm in the face of national stoppage, and I changed my mind when the whips advised us that they could not guarantee that this condition could be met. At all events, the blame cannot be attributed, as it often has been, to Ted Heath alone. As he was entitled but not bound to do, he consulted his colleagues before making his request at the Palace, and his request when it came was the result of a collective decision. It must be said that we had no reason to expect the infinite harm which was done in the Midlands by Enoch Powell's advice to vote Labour, nor the general damage done by some singularly inept, foolish and misleading speeches by Mr Campbell Adamson of the CBI and by a member of the Relativities Board which gave the impression of an ineptitude in two relevant fields of policy of which the Heath administration had certainly not been guilty.

At all events, by the beginning of March I was out of office. When I had accepted the Woolsack in 1970 I had said to my family that the next chapter would be 'Eventide' or 'Last Days', and it now looked like this prophecy coming true, at the somewhat early age of sixty-seven. I did not at all realize then that the most serious crisis of my life and the longest period in one office still lay ahead. I fully expected the Labour government to last for two full Parliaments, and that was long enough, I thought, to see me permanently retire from public life. In the mean time I betook myself to the front opposition bench in the House of Lords under the able leadership of Peter Carrington, and to authorship.

FORTY-FOUR

'The Door Wherein I Went' and 'The Dilemma of Democracy'

EVER SINCE THE FAIRLY EARLY 1930s I had intended to write some account of my beliefs and fundamental philosophies, both of which were based on intellectual rather than purely emotional grounds. Indeed, at one time before the war I had even signed a contract to write such a book, but had to escape from it somewhat ignominiously owing to the rapid increase in my practice during my early years at the Bar. Thereafter I put the project aside until the Greek Kalends.

Even during the period of my first Chancellorship I had begun to receive approaches from publishers suggesting that I write my autobiography. With one exception I turned them down flat. At that time I had set my face against writing anything of the kind. My reasons were complex. One was very simple. I had read the introduction to Anthony Trollope's own autobiography in which he candidly faces the fact that it is not possible for an autobiographer to tell the whole truth about himself. The second was that, although I had kept a whole cartload of papers and could have had access to all the cabinet papers, memoranda and letters I had written when in office, I had kept no diaries, except the rather intimate one which I wrote during 1941 and 1942. Apart from this I shrank from the labour and doubted the interest of readers in the kind of three-decker record of facts and opinions which would emerge from a painstaking study of official papers. The third and most conclusive reason was my Privy Counsellor's oath. The Cabinet and its organs have no legal existence as such. But all the members of the Cabinet are automatically members of the

Council, and, although the actual terms of the oath which, I think, could only have been invented by Henry VIII in one of his less agreeable moods, or someone like him, are infelicitous, archaic, and in parts absurd, I have always regarded it as imposing an honourable and religious obligation not to disclose what has taken place between colleagues, or between oneself and members of the government service. I was appalled by the Crossman diaries and by the Widgery judgement which licensed their publication. The calculated and politically motivated leaks by individual civil servants and ministers continue to fill me with disgust. When they prattle about 'public interest' and 'public good' it seems to me that, in a parliamentary democracy, the one overriding public interest in this field is that those in government should be able implicitly to trust colleagues and public servants so that government may take place as the result of free discussion uninhibited by the possibility of premature or unauthorized disclosure. In a democratic context I regard as the purest hypocrisy pleas of public interest or public duty. Obviously conspiracies must be disclosed to proper authority. Indeed, the Privy Counsellor's oath says as much. But these I regard as a theoretical possibility, and I become particularly disgusted when the Scribes and Pharisees refer to totally inapplicable outrages that might have happened under some authoritarian regime like that of Hitler or Stalin.

The one exception to my doubts was the result of a luncheon-party with Collins, at which, in the course of voicing these sentiments, I disclosed my ambition of telling the story of how in my youth I came gradually to return from a position of virtual agnosticism to one of total commitment to mainstream Christianity. To my surprise, this suggestion received a favourable reception. The consequence was that I spent much of the year after our defeat in 1974 in writing *The Door Wherein I Went* whose title was a quotation, of course, from the final edition of *Omar Khayyám*. The book, which I intended to be, and honestly believed would be, my last word to the world was unexpectedly successful and was commended for a literary prize promoted by the *Yorkshire Post*. It went through a hardback and a paperback edition, and, wholly to my surprise, triggered off my temporary registration for VAT. This caused me nightmares, since my faithful bankers, who had done my income tax ever since I was seventeen, resolutely refused to have anything to do with Value Added Tax and, for the first time in my life, I had to keep some sort of accounts. Much of the book was written in the idyllic surroundings of the garden of my brother's hotel on the outskirts of Lucerne, looking across the lake to the magnificent silhouette of Mount Pilatus, named, following a medieval legend, after no less a personage than Pontius Pilate, whose body is supposed to lie in a little lake on the side of the mountain, now silted up to form a delightful glade in the forest overlooking the Eigental.

In the immediate aftermath of the election I took Mary, and our youngest daughter, Kate, on a Hellenic cruise in a superannuated American liner, the first time I had seen the classical sites since my ill-fated voyage in *Arcadian* in 1926. It was lucky that I went then. The sightseeing involved a good deal of walking, and in June 1974 both my injured ankles packed up in the course of a single week and thenceforth I was able to walk only for the shortest distances and with the aid of two sticks. Poor things, both ankles had been broken before the war in the Alps. I had treated the fractures only as sprains. With the exception of one unhappy incident on a company commander's course near Heliopolis they had bravely seen me through the war, in the desert, and on night patrols, canvassing in the streets of Oxford, and in numerous mountain walks and climbs, in Skye, Snowdon and the Lake District at home, and in the Alps. But from June 1974 onwards they struck work, and ever since I have been heavily handicapped.

Another book emerged from my pen in 1978. It was entitled *The Dilemma of Democracy* and was based on my pessimism about the future of our democracy during the period of the Wilson and Callaghan governments of 1974 and 1979. The theme underlying *The Dilemma of Democracy* was that there were two basic models on which countries claiming to be democratic could base the structure and philosophy of their systems of government and that there really was no halfway house between them. I labelled them the theory of elective dictatorship, which was wrong wherever it was claimed and wherever it was applied, and the theory of limited government, limited even in a democracy. I believe that there are inherent limitations on the exercise of authority whether by aristocracies or by oligarchies, or by popular assemblies whether or not based on universal franchise and whether or not accompanied by a powerful executive. This was the theory first formulated by Bracton, the earliest serious writer on English law, who composed his work shortly after the signature of Magna Carta in 1215 and therefore at a time when England was anything but democratic. The king, wrote he, should be under an obligation to obey God and the law, because it is the law which makes him king. As I read this in modern language I translate it to mean that there are moral and practical limitations on governments, however constituted and however popularly based. All governments are in the business of sticks and carrots; this means that, from their very nature, they are operating codes of conduct less far ranging and less exacting morally than the dictate of conscience which is based on the free will of individuals. A majority of 51 per cent of any given group of human beings has just as much to justify the use of compulsion or bribery on the remaining 49 per cent as any monarch or dictator exercising power over a majority under an authoritarian constitution. The divine right of majorities is just as fallacious in conception as the doctrine of the divine right of kings, and although there is a qualified duty of responsible obedience imposed on the governed by either type of constitution there comes a theoretical limit beyond which duty can no longer be demanded, and a practical limit beyond which it cannot be enforced.

When Mrs Thatcher's government was formed in 1979 a meeting of ministers was held to discuss constitutional questions and I was invited to attend. *The Dilemma*, written in the failing years of the Wilson and Callaghan regimes, was fairly fresh from the press. The book averred that our traditional constitution was breaking down under pressure of the immense volume of work which the central government was undertaking. This could be exemplified by comparison between the sheer quantity of legislation being passed through Parliament – say, 450 pages in 1911 under a reforming government with only a small proportion of subordinate legislation emanating from it, compared with some 3,000 pages in any typical year of a fairly typical government, Labour or Conservative, with 10,000 pages of subordinate legislation in the 1970s and 1980s. A similar comparison could be made in the relative sizes of the annual budgets, £150 million gold sovereigns in Lloyd George's controversial budget of 1909, compared, say, in 1988 with more than £170,000 million paper pounds of the present day. The thesis was that the constitution was being subjected to strains greater than those it was designed to bear.

At the same time, I called in aid the fact that almost alone amongst civilized nations our own legislature had no constitutional limits to its legislative powers. The dilemma consisted in the fact that any similar government subject to the pressures of the postwar era must choose between two alternative ideals. Either it must recognize that any government, whether democratic or authoritarian, must accept that there are limitations inherent in the practice of government which it must respect, or alternatively it will be driven by the sheer pressure on its working parts, if a democracy, to attempt methods which are so inimical to human freedom that it would merit the description, which I had coined a few years before in my Dimbleby Lecture, of elective dictatorship.

I made it quite clear to the readers of *The Dilemma of Democracy* that I favoured a limitation of the powers of government by structural changes. These would have included a much smaller House of Commons, a system of elective regional assemblies with limited powers and elected by methods different and in constituencies separate in extent from the reduced number of parliamentary constituencies, balanced by a second parliamentary chamber based on the regions and elected by a proportional system of one of the fourteen available kinds and to some extent the adoption into our municipal law of the European Convention on Human Rights, which I rather envisaged – though I do not think I said so – would take the place of the existing system of judicial review founded on the old prerogative writs of *certiorari*, prohibition and *mandamus*. Although this was a fairly radical programme, at no time did I envisage encroaching on the position of the present hereditary monarchy, the sovereignty of Parliament or the primacy of the House of Commons based on the existing system of first-past-the-post voting, or on the existing cabinet system embodying a strong central executive commanding a majority in the House of Commons (but not necessarily in the second chamber). At no time, except to the extent I have indicated in relation to the European convention, did I suggest a written constitution, although, in the nature of things, the powers of the regional assemblies would have been subject to some scrutiny by the ordinary courts. I pointed out that such a structure, with our existing monarchy at the head, would have various advantages. To some extent it would placate nationalist feeling in Scotland and Wales and provide a degree of devolution for Northern Ireland. It would put the various regional quangos which now exist under the control of the regional assemblies in place of Whitehall, together with control of the health boards, water, electricity generation and distribution, higher education, airports, port authorities and most roads. It would render possible a system of regional taxation less unfair and less irrational than the local rates (the Community Charge was not then under discussion), and it would greatly reduce the pressure on the central administration while not undermining the monarchy, the cabinet system or the sovereignty of Parliament. Although it was written under a Labour administration with strong centralizing authoritarian and regulatory tendencies, *The Dilemma of Democracy* was not an essay on policy or on party politics. It was an attempt to cope with the problem of over-centralization which had been growing on us since the end of the First World War. Above all, it did not suggest any particular solution to economic problems. As it turned out, ideas such as these foundered on national repulsion evidenced by the results of the Labour plebiscites under the Callaghan administration, and I aborted my crusade.

As a publication the book was a success. But it was obvious from the first that, whatever advantages it might have in Scotland, Wales or Northern Ireland, in the regions of England at least there was insufficient support for regional autonomy to justify immediate legislation. To some extent my ideas have since been hijacked, at first by the SDP and the Alliance, and since then by Roy Hattersley. I treat this as a compliment to their rationality, but I repeat that the scheme was designed as an essay on structure and not as a critique of policies or ideologies and all three have turned it into both.

Some people have asked me why I have not continued since 1979 to write and speak in the sense of *The Door Wherein I Went* and *The Dilemma of Democracy*. In the first place the answer is that I had said what I had wanted to say. But in the second place, soon after *The Dilemma* had been published, I had returned to public office and was constrained by the ordinary limitations imposed on ministers by the conventions of the constitution. I was always a little disappointed that my suggestions for regional government and the incorporation of the European Convention have not been taken up. But I have come to realize that one reason at least was the absence of popular demand, particularly in England as distinct from the other parts of the United Kingdom. Another was the fact that the necessary legislation would have taken up the legislative time of Parliament at the expense of the radical reforms which have been enacted during the leadership of Margaret Thatcher. As will appear, I am sure that, in this at least, her sense of priority was right.

By 1979, it was quite clear that the growing effect of inflation and countering the 'ratchet effect' of socialism had to have priority over my suggested constitutional changes, especially since it had become evident that some of these did not, at least as yet, command a sufficient degree of support. This was the result of the discussion which was called in 1979. I was fully concurrent with the outcome then, and am entirely satisfied with it now. The policy of financial controls, despite which public expenditure has steadily risen, of denationalization, of lowering the proportion of income extracted by the Exchequer, the increase in house- and share-ownership and the wider distribution of property and income, together with the general rolling back of the frontiers of the intrusive state, the remodelling of our legal system, and the increase in the numbers and powers of the police in order to counteract the growth in crimes of violence and dishonesty were rightly given priority over structural changes in our constitution for which there was insufficient demand and which would have had to be introduced as a package and not piecemeal and would have involved the postponement of anything else. I believe the changes since 1979 have paid a dividend. Apart from other considerations it is insufficiently appreciated that under the first two years of any government, and maybe for the best part of five, the administration of the day has to live with the economic consequences of the policies of its predecessors. However, I believe my basic analysis still stands. While I realize the time was not ripe in 1979, my manifesto of 1978 still remains on the agenda and should the need arise, and if support for it were increased, would at least form part of the agenda for constitutional reform. In the mean time any government has to operate under the existing system whatever the defects of that system may be. This is true of a Conservative or any other administration. The most important improvement in our constitution which I could advocate at present would be the dissolution of the present Labour Party with its organic relationship to the trade unions and its undemocratic card vote, and the emergence of a new progressive party which could form a credible alternative to a Conservative government when the time came, as in the end it will, for it to go. Since I remain, as I have throughout all my life, a Conservative in politics with a big 'C', this is a process in which I can play no useful part and offer no advice as to the means of a solution. Perhaps events will take charge.

FORTY-FIVE

Third Bereavement

I HAVE VISITED AUSTRALIA twice in my life, and I love Australians. My first visit was to celebrate an anniversary in the history of the country. Sir John Kerr was still Chief Justice of New South Wales and Gough Whitlam was still Prime Minister of the Australian Commonwealth. The great constitutional crisis of 1975 about which so much has been written was still in the future.

My second visit was to have been, indeed was, to speak to a body largely confined to a political party. Bob Menzies was still alive, though too sick to be present. The main event was to be in premises belonging to the University of Sydney, and I was to be the principal speaker. I was to be accompanied by Mary, my wife. In the events which happened, I returned alone.

Whilst I was still in England, my hosts had telephoned me from Sydney asking me what Mary most enjoyed doing. I replied that she enjoyed horse-riding most of all, and in this artless answer I signed her death warrant. Mary was an experienced, though not particularly accomplished, rider, and every week she used to take her part in a little company which used to exercise Billy Walsh's stable polo ponies in Richmond Park. The ponies themselves were lively creatures and needed experienced horsemanship to keep them in order. But they were well trained and amenable to the ordinary skills. Since 1974 I had ceased to accompany Mary on these jaunts even during the parliamentary recesses, since the pain in my ankle joints was sufficiently tiresome to make riding rather less than a pleasure. But we jointly determined that, if it could be arranged, Mary would be mounted by the local police, and that I would accompany her. When

397

packing I received a warning like the warning to lock the gun-cupboard before Edward's death in 1932. I was warned to tell Mary to pack her reinforced riding-cap. I omitted to do so.

After a rather exhausting journey, in which the plane was diverted to Melbourne, we arrived in Sydney and were comfortably housed in a very pleasant social club with rooms enjoying a fine view of the harbour. Our hosts were attentive and hospitable, and we were together almost the whole time. With neither having much responsibility, the week was one of the most gloriously happy in our entire married life. Mary was even more attentive and loving than usual, steering her somewhat disabled husband across the street with affectionate care. There was an enchanting public garden almost opposite the club where we sat and talked and watched the graceful flight of the Australian 'Welcome Swallow' to all appearance exactly like an English swallow, though I am told that it does not migrate. The month was May; in the southern hemisphere the glorious weather reminded me of an English October. Sometimes I bathed in the sea and Mary sat on the beach with towels. It was like a second honeymoon. It will always be a joy to me to remember that our last week together was one of unadulterated happiness. But when the blow fell it was like a thunderbolt from a clear sky, and for that reason all the more difficult to bear.

For some reason, our ride had been postponed until the after-noon of 10 May. I had just made a speech at a luncheon. We went back to the club and changed, Mary into her breeches, I into jodhpurs. We were motored to the Centennial Park where there was a riding-track rather like Rotten Row, only bigger. We entered the park by a gate beside which were some bollards joined by chains. There were four horses waiting, two ridden by police officers in uniform, the other two for Mary and me. The only anxiety I had was lest with my painful ankles I would be unable to get my heels down hard enough to grip with my knees. We had the park track nearly to ourselves, though I do remember the odd party riding to meet us anticlockwise. We walked for a bit to get the feel of our mounts, and then trotted for a time, and I began to feel the pain in my joints. All the time we were chattering away as happily as birds on the bough.

There was in fact one bird that seemed to be going along with us on our right outside the park. It was a peewee, also known as the Murray magie. I have since heard that it is sometimes regarded as a bird of ill omen. Mary was mounted on a mare, reputedly the quietest in the police stables, but when we stopped trotting she did say one odd thing to me. She said: 'I don't think I have ridden as strong a horse as this for a long time.' Almost immediately one of the police officers said to me: 'Do you think you would be more comfortable if we cantered?' Immediately I kicked my horse into a hand canter, holding it in rather firmly with my left hand. The other police officer was on the inside, beyond Mary on my right. Almost immediately Mary drew in front of us. I was glad, as I thought she had found it irksome to ride at such a slow canter as the pace I was setting. The track veered round to the right as we were riding clockwise round the park. Mary seemed to be following the track, after a few seconds the officer on my left said: 'Shall we go on, or shall we go straight ahead?' Straight ahead was the asphalt road round the park and the gate by which we had entered the park, and I thought I saw a stationary car by the bollards. Thinking Mary had gone round to the right, I said: 'Let us go round; that is the way she has gone.' Almost immediately the officer said: 'I think we had better go straight ahead.' At that moment I saw that what I had taken to be a stationary car by the bollards about two hundred and fifty yards away was in fact a stationary horse and that it was riderless. So we went towards it. By the side of the horse was Mary, lying on her back, and behind her head was a pool of dark blood. Why, oh, why had we not packed her riding-cap with its reinforced crown? Just as when Edward died I had had then a momentary impulse to lock the door of the gun-cupboard, so on this trip I had had a momentary impulse to tell her to pack that cap. I got off and knelt beside her. I called her name three times. She did not answer. I felt her pulse. It was still beating strongly. I knew from the blood that she must have cracked her skull, and I began to have pictures of a crippled wife, propelled by me in a wheelchair for the rest of our joint lives. Oddly enough, it did not occur to me that she was dying. We sent for an ambulance, and it seemed, in my anguished state, an unconscionable time a-coming. I got up and said to the officer: 'Remember that, whatever happens, no one is to blame.' The ambulance came, and our car came, too, and I sat alone in the back where so short a time ago we had sat together looking forward to our ride. The hospital was a Roman Catholic hospital. Nurses came and went by the little waiting-room where I sat. 'How is she?' I asked. They only said: 'Sister will be here shortly.' Sister came. Urgently I said to her: 'Sister, I must know the truth. Is my wife alive?' Something about the way the nurses had looked at me had given me a grisly warning that things were worse than I had thought. Sister replied: 'Your wife is dead.' The words struck me like a bullet, and I cried in great sobs, and then apologized. 'We have been married thirty-four years.' It was about four o'clock in the afternoon, and I felt I must ring through to England and tell my children and my old widowed father-in-law before the thing got out on the morning news at eight in their morning. I got through to my eldest daughter. Later, she told me she had had a presentiment. I laid on her the obligation to tell the others. They gave me a cup of tea, and I cried into it. Then a priest arrived, Father Vincent. 'Father,' said I, 'I must pray.' 'Bring me to her.' There she was, looking peaceful and calm, lying on a slab. I burst into prayer. 'The souls of the righteous are in the hand of God,' I prayed, 'and there shall no torment touch them. Though they be punished in the sight of men, yet is their hope full of immortality.' I can remember every word I spoke in that dreadful agony. 'Oh Lamb of God that takest away the sins of the World, have mercy upon us. Receive our prayer. Have mercy upon us. For Thou only art holy. Thou only art Lord, Thou only, O Christ, with the Holy Ghost art most high in the Glory of God the Father. Grant her eternal rest, O Lord, and light perpetual shine upon her.' Father Vincent was visibly shaken at this agonized utterance by a Protestant husband of the torrent of familiar words and said a prayer of his own. So I went back to the club to the little room where her nightdress lay just under the pillow and her slippers by the side of the bed. Two good Samaritans, Lloyd and Edwina Waddy, moved into the club in rooms next to mine and comforted me. The Archbishop of Sydney took care of Mary's body in his private chapel and held a special service of prayer for her when I was permitted once more to look on that beloved face, calm and composed in death, lying in her coffin. There is something unbelievably horrible in looking at the form beside which one has lain so often, and which one has held lovingly in one's arms, absolutely cold and without life. But I kissed it gently, and the Archbishop read from the eighth chapter of Romans:

> . . . I am persuaded, that neither death, nor life, nor angels, nor principalities, nor powers, nor things present, nor things to come, nor height, nor depth, nor any other creature, shall be able to separate us from the love of God, which is in Christ Jesus our Lord.

It was small help to me at the time. But one decision I made that very same day. I had come over to make that speech at the express invitation of those who had paid for my journey. I had forty-eight hours of misery before it was due to be delivered. Whatever happened, that speech I would make. There were those who thought of this as a considerable act of courage. Though no one actually ventured to say it to me, I have no doubt that there were those who thought that it showed disrespect to the memory of my wife. In fact it was neither. You do not live with a woman for thirty-four years without knowing what her wishes would be in given circumstances. Mary had all the constancy and integrity of the Southern Irish Protestant. I knew what her wishes would be as clearly as if she had been standing at my side and telling me from her own dear lips. She would have told me at whatever cost to make that speech, come what may, and I obeyed. Happily the speech was already in draft. I added a paragraph at which my voice wavered a bit. I have the soundtrack and I know. But for the most part I delivered it as calmly as if she had been sitting behind me. My life was in ruins, but I could not shame her. When it was over kind Edwina earned my eternal gratitude by packing Mary's beloved things which I could not bear to see, still less to touch. For years they remained packed up at the top of my house in Roehampton. By chance her little dog came into the room in which they were, much more than a year after the event. She had neither pined nor complained when I came back without her mistress. But when she smelt those suitcases with the familiar scents, little Mini, the Jack Russell bitch, went nearly mad with joy and had almost forcibly to be removed from the room.

In the mean time I had to go home and face the future. The Qantas aircrew had been briefed. I was almost out of my mind. Throughout the long journey home there was always a steward with me. I talked incessantly always of Mary, my love for her, our children, her constancy and love, our last days together. Mary returned in the hold of the aircraft, in her coffin. Her death was by far the most horrible thing that has happened to me. We had been married thirty-four years. She rescued me from the blight which settled on my life after Natalie's desertion in 1942. We had had five children, and there were four grandchildren. A fifth grandchild was on the way, and in the event was born a few days after my return. I learned a great deal about human kindness in those days. Messages came flowing in, from the Queen and Prince Philip, from friends and political opponents, from total strangers. I was quite beside myself. My family came in a body to greet me on my return. We all embraced. I went to see Margaret Thatcher, by this time the Party Leader, on my return. I told her: 'I have decided to stick it out.' I said the same to Elwyn Jones, the reigning Lord Chancellor. I said: 'There is one thing you can do for me. Give me some judicial work.' He arranged for me to sit in the Privy Council and the House of Lords and I have been eternally grateful for his kindness. I do not believe I let him down. Work is therapeutic, perhaps the best therapy.

But grief is an illness. It is not easily overcome. Beware of the stiff upper lip. Coming back to the empty house in the evening. Worse still, lying alone in the empty bed at night. Tears are nature's safety-valve, and they came every time I went upstairs to bed. In the dark hours I called her name. C. S. Lewis has described the sensation to perfection. His marriage was totally different from mine. But he lost his wife and described his experience in his book *A Grief Observed*. My own experience was the same, and I can only repeat what he wrote:

> After the death of a friend I had for some time a most vivid feeling of certainty about his continued life, even his

enhanced life. I have begged to be given even one hundredth part of the same assurance about 'H' [the name by which he refers in the book to his wife]. There is no answer. Only the locked door, the iron curtain, the vacuum, absolute zero. 'Them that asks don't get.' I was a fool to ask. For now, even if that assurance came, I should distrust it. I should think it a self-hypnosis, induced by my own prayers.

Even more poignantly, in a later passage, he wrote:

Talk to me about the truth of religion and I'll listen gladly. Talk to me about the duty of religion and I'll listen submissively. But don't come talking to me about the consolation of religion or I shall suspect that you don't understand.

The worst thing about grief is the length of time during which the experience lasts. For the first weeks one is in a state of shock. But the agony lasts long after the state of shock comes to an end. After a year, or about two, the agony gives way to a dull ache, a sort of void. During the night in one's dreams, and in the morning when one wakes, one is vaguely aware that something is wrong and, when waking is complete, one knows exactly what it is. On many occasions I was asked in private by friends and, since I was a public man, in interviews by the media whether my religion was not a great help to me during my trial, and, being truthful, like C. S. Lewis, I had to answer: 'Not at all.' This caused surprise and, sometimes, shock. People thought that I had lost my faith. But I dispute the basic premiss underlying their question. The Christian religion is not a painkiller, no analgesic, no patent medicine. It is not there to make tolerable the intolerable suffering that, at one time or another, we all undergo in this world. It is not to be abandoned because we are in pain. The Cross was suffered without an anaesthetic, and so have our several and lesser Calvaries. Christianity does not cure the toothache or alleviate sea-sickness. It did not prevent the cry of dereliction from the Cross. Why, then, should it reduce the pain of bereavement? There was, however, one definite and sensible consolation. There were among my friends those who feared I was losing my faith. But there were more – not less than twenty or thirty – total strangers who, having heard my frank admission on the radio, instead of being shocked or angry, wrote that my own feeling of helplessness in misfortune had strengthened them in their own suffering, even restored their faith, by the knowledge that their own experience was not unusual, and not, as they had feared, a fault to be ashamed of, a sin requiring forgiveness. They learned from me that, in this vale of tears, pain at parting is the price we pay for love. All that summer the sun no longer shone by day. The stars did not shine at night. The flowers did not bloom in the garden. The birds were silent in the tree-tops. As the good book says, I was a pelican, that, is a water-bird, in the wilderness; an owl, that is, a woodland bird, in the desert; a sparrow, a most gregarious bird, alone upon the house-top. But at least I knew what I had to avoid. I knew that, whatever happened, I must not despair. I knew that the arguments which had appealed to me as true when I had written my book were not less valid because of my new experience of desolation than they had been when I was happy. I continued to pray, to go to church, to attend communion. I did not suffer less thereby, but I was very conscious that, had I not followed these disciplines, I would have suffered even more, because I would have despaired of the nature of things and not merely suffered from the course of events.

Also, I avoided the pitfall of spookery, the road to Endor. So, like the Abbé Sieyès in the French Revolution, I survived, I hope without loss of integrity, and without causing too much embarrassment to my friends and those with whom I came in contact.

Mary's grave bears an inscription of my own composition paying tribute to her qualities as wife, mother and grandmother, and ending with the words 'radiant and joyous companion'. The flowers that adorn her grave are planted or sown by myself and come mainly from the home we shared together in Roehampton. I go there regularly to tend the plot and hope that, when my turn comes, I will lie there with her once again.

FORTY-SIX

Margaret Thatcher and My Second Term

SOME TIME IN 1978 my friend Patrick Reilly asked me, on behalf of the English-Speaking Union, to undertake a tour of lectures on the eastern seaboard of the United States. I agreed, but on one condition: that as part of the tour I should be allowed to visit my mother's home-town of Nashville, Tennessee. Ultimately, apart from Boston and New York, and Louisville, Kentucky, my visit took me as far south as Jackson, Mississippi. After the loneliness of London, it was a wonderful therapy for my desperate condition. My family in Nashville were wonderfully supportive, and hauled me off from the Holiday Inn (opposite the full-sized replica of the Parthenon built in 1949 by one of my two American great-grandfathers, Josiah Nichol) to the comfort and hospitality of their homes. But it was in Louisville, Kentucky, in the home of my friend Kay Bullitt, that the news came through that the Callaghan government had been narrowly defeated in the Commons and that a general election was in prospect. I was able to complete my obligations to the English-Speaking Union and return to take an active part in the election campaign.

In the interval between the defeat of the Heath government and the general election of 1979, Margaret Thatcher had become the Leader of the Conservative Party. Under the new regulations, the constituency with a vote for the leadership is effectively the Members of the House of Commons in receipt of the Conservative Whip. Senior members of the party are of course consulted, and as a leading member of the party in the Lords I was naturally asked for my opinion. Having been a loyal colleague of Ted Heath's and a recipient of an honour in his Dissolution Honours, I had not played an active part, but indicated that I must remain loyal to my former chief. The candidates were all friends and former colleagues of my own. But I must record my surprise when, after the withdrawal of Keith Joseph, Margaret Thatcher emerged decisively victorious. She had, of course held the Education portfolio with distinction. When her appointment was first announced in 1970 in the rather sour world of the educational establishment she was at first treated with almost universal derision. By the time the Government fell at the beginning of 1974 that derision had changed to one of almost universal respect from those who were in a position to judge. Still, one swallow does not make a summer, and to be elected leader of a party without having held any of the senior offices in the Cabinet must be regarded as astonishing. In the remainder of our period of opposition I had served as a representative of the Lords in her Shadow Cabinet. I had one serious disagreement with her on the subject of devolution, but she proved to have popular opinion on her side.

We fought, and won, the 1979 election on virtually the same platform as that which had carried Ted Heath to victory in 1970. Those who talk about Thatcherism and suggest that Margaret Thatcher revolutionized the thinking or ideology (if there is one) of the Conservative Party should, I believe, ponder this fact. When I discovered that we had won, I was pretty sure that the electorate was less determined to support what they already knew to be the general outlook and ideals of the Conservatives than to turn their backs on the miserable experiences of the so-called Winter of Discontent in 1978 and 1979, the shoddy behind-the-scenes bargain of the so-called Social Contract and the miserable expedient by which David Steel and the Labour leadership had prolonged the life of the Labour government long after the general mass of the voters had decided that they wished to be rid of it. Some of the hospitals had been closed. Some of the schools had been unable to open. Some of the dead had been unburied. The principal culprits had been the two local-authority unions COHSE and NUPE and the fecklessness of the Labour government in failing to cope with them firmly. From my point of view this disaffection was increased by my dismay at their capitulation to the sort of general strike organized by the so-called loyalists of Ulster. The Labour government had shown the yellow underbelly of surrender to blackmail. It was our business to restore national self-respect.

What I was totally unprepared for was the extent and duration of Margaret Thatcher's hegemony of British politics in the ten years which followed. Whilst I was still lecturing in the United States I had been impressed by the scale on which her personality had made an impact upon American opinion generally and particularly upon my cousins in Nashville. But what in 1979 I was totally unprepared for was her continued dominance of national politics, and the vast influence and admiration she has aroused in Western and even Eastern leaders outside the United Kingdom. When I resigned from the Chancellorship in 1987 I wrote to her in admiration that she had succeeded in changing the face of British politics. She has in fact done more than that. She has halted and perhaps reversed the decline in British prestige throughout the world which had followed the retreat from Empire, the volte-face over Suez, our long exclusion from the European Community and our repeated and seemingly endemic economic crises, largely caused, at least in my eyes, by our inability to cope with trade-union selfishness and their repeated attempts at domination. Others, including former colleagues, have written disparagingly of her personal characteristics. Her opponents and critics assail her personal reputation with almost paranoid execration. But I wish to pay her tribute. She has succeeded where others failed. It has not been an easy victory. The Falklands War, the miners' strike, the hideous rise in inflation in the first years, and the continued high number of the unemployed have not been easy crises to surmount. They required perspicacity and above all nerve to an extent which no prime minister since the war, including the failing Winston between 1951 and 1955, has managed to display. She has not hesitated, sometimes to their intense displeasure, to dispense with the services of colleagues whom she thought unprepared to face the consequences of her decisions. She knows very well that personally I have not hesitated from time to time to voice my considerable disagreements when I have differed with her views and opinions. Sometimes I have come off best, and sometimes she has prevailed. In my professional experience a strong judge requires a fearless advocate to keep him (or her) on the rails. But it has also been my experience as an advocate that a good judge respects fearlessness and despises subservience in those who have to present their cases to their court.

Very different was the Falklands episode in 1982. After hearing the military advice, I never had any doubt about the righteousness of that cause. Even if I had had any doubt about the root of our title to the Falklands, which was not the case, it seemed to me that the matter spoke for itself. For 150 years a humble community had lived there asking for nothing but peace from their neighbours and only to be left alone, speaking English, and preserving intact their contact with their mother country which was Britain, only to be made the subject of a treacherous attack by a military dictator to whom they presented no threat whatever, but who, for some reason, believed that the comparative proximity to the coast of South America would give him some military superiority which would boost his own prestige. Not that it did not require some courage in the Cabinet to support what was being done. The one thing I had always been taught in the Army was that an opposed landing from the sea was a peculiarly hazardous undertaking, required air superiority, and should be undertaken only with a secure and fairly short line of communications. The success that followed deserves the highest possible praise for the sheer professionalism of the fighting men, the magnificent planning of the staff and the realism of the professional advice they gave the Cabinet, neither craven nor underestimating the risk. But it is right, now that I am no longer her colleague, that I should pay my own tribute to the courage of Margaret Thatcher. Unlike the few of us who had survived the last war, she had never been under fire. But she never wavered for an instant even when *Sheffield* went down or the Exocets caused lamentable casualties among the Welsh Guards and others in Bluff Cove. She was quite right not to make political capital out of it in the election of 1983. This would have been dishonourable, though the Opposition like the Church in Laodicea had blown both hot and cold in their support. After the invasion, Peter Carrington felt it necessary to resign. Though I admire his courage and sense of honour in so doing, I never understood why he did so and I tried to dissuade him from that course. It seems to me that we had acted absolutely correctly throughout. In Peter I lost one of the two colleagues I have most admired in public life.

A crucial factor in the diplomatic scene was the support which came from the United Nations even from those who are usually our critics on the basis of our imperial past. A decisive consideration in establishing this support was that we had made no gesture of any kind which by the wildest stretch of the most jaundiced imagination could be described as provocative, even to the extent of sending a survey ship and even though a serious naval force was being assembled on the other side under cover of 'annual exercises'. If we had done anything it would have made no difference to the resulting invasion except to sacrifice, or at least risk, the loss of innocent British lives.

I never can understand why the Spanish American countries seem to oscillate aimlessly between feckless multiparty democracies and thuggish military dictatorship. I fancy it is because they have not learned to separate the office of head of state from the head of government. To my mind military dictators who break their oaths to the constitution and assume the role of head of state and head of government by force of arms are fit only for the firing squad. But it must be very provoking to be subject to the impotence of a multiparty government without the strong executive provided by our present method of voting.

Above all Margaret has succeeded because she made and adhered to a correct analysis of the political situation, which I will admit frankly I either had not made at the time or, in so far as I did make it, to which I attached insufficient importance. I do not know that she was the inventor of the phrase 'the ratchet effect of socialism'. I rather think that she was not, but even if that is so she was the first leader of the Conservative Party to draw the correct lessons from it. From the end of the war onwards I had stated my political convictions under the rubric 'privately owned industry and publicly organized social services', and my ultimate political philosophy as 'freedom under the law' to which, if challenged, I added the essential corollary, 'the freedom of virtuous individuals responsibly exercised under a just law'. But, as I pointed out in *The Dilemma of Democracy*, and have said earlier in this book, so long as the Labour Party – throughout the period our only serious political competitor – adhered even nominally to Clause 4 of its constitution which pledged the party to the public ownership of all the means of production, distribution and exchange, Britain was certain in the end to become an Eastern-type 'people's democracy', that is, an elective dictatorship with an all-powerful parliament, elected on the first-past-the-post system of voting. It might well be true that periods of Conservative rule, like the thirteen years between 1951 and 1964, might temporarily arrest the advance of the socialist juggernaut. But the end was certain, given the working of the two-party system of government and the swing of the pendulum. Ever so often the periods of intermission would give way to Labour governments armed with a mandate for a new 'shopping-list' (which was the current phrase) of private-sector industry destined for the chop. The only way out of this dilemma was to roll back the frontiers of the socialist state during the periods of Conservative government by reversing the ratchet effect, and this meant turning the Conservative Party from its traditional conservatism into a party of change committed to a reversal of its natural role and to turning back the whole bias of society to something nearer the ideal of the liberals of the previous century. I was for a long time myself a determined supporter of Macmillan's 'Middle Way'. It was not an ignoble ideal. It was based on the belief that, irrespective of the damnable Clause 4, a *modus vivendi* would ultimately be arrived at between the two rival philosophies, that is, the public ownership of a few natural monopolies supported by a privately owned industry which would achieve efficiency through the operation of market forces and competition. It is not true that Margaret Thatcher was the first to perceive the fallaciousness of this analysis. The Heath government's manifesto of 1970 was largely a recognition of it, but the change was not complete until the advent to power in 1979 of Mrs Thatcher's administration. There were, of course, some other conversions to be made. I have never turned my back on my immediate acceptance of the Beveridge proposals in 1942. But they are now hopelessly outdated, and if anyone wished to go back to them they would soon find they were hopelessly inadequate in aim, scope and scale. No doubt, as a matter of history, the modern Welfare State dates back to Beveridge and even before, to the reforms of 1911 and 1925. None the less, we are now far more comprehensive in our objectives and in our recognition of the needs of education, of the elderly, of the handicapped and the sick. Beveridge was a cautious innovator in the field of social security to which his Report was limited. By 1979 the Welfare State was inadequate both in scope and in sources of finance. Quite apart from this was the need to accept that the philosophy of equality is quite incompatible with liberty, and that the gospel of uniformity quite inconsistent with progress and a sure producer of shortage. It is no more self-evident that the natural human instinct to acquire material wealth is productive of social evil (even though avarice may be one of the deadly sins) than that the normal sexual drives of adult human beings should be restricted by law, despite the fact that lechery is another. None of these perceptions is peculiar to Margaret Thatcher. There is in fact no such philosophy as 'Thatcherism'. Nevertheless the advent of Mrs Thatcher as Prime Minister in 1979 did mark a turning-point in political action in the country, and the remarkable combination of personal courage and tenacity in the face of economic blackmail and external aggression which she displayed during the miners' strike, the Falklands operation and the long years of continued inflationary pressure between 1979 and 1985 did change the whole ethos of the British people and stemmed the tide of national decline which had set in in 1945 and which led to the pessimistic mood in which I published *The Dilemma of Democracy* in 1978.

I must confess I was thoroughly surprised, but completely delighted, when she invited me to resume the Woolsack after our victory in 1979, and I look back on the eight years which followed, apart from the loneliness of widowhood, as one of the happiest and most constructive of my long life.

FORTY-SEVEN

Lord Chancellor Again

WITHIN A WEEK OF MY APPOINTMENT for my second term of office as Lord Chancellor one thing became abundantly apparent. The reforms in the law of divorce brought about by Private Member's Bill in 1969 and consolidated in 1973 were producing almost incredible misery. The shoe was pinching not in one but in half a dozen places, and it was obviously necessary to introduce widespread reforms.

Those who have not come into contact with divorce concern themselves primarily with a large number of non-questions. This was so before 1937 when, after about quarter of a century's wrangling, some at least of the proposals of the Royal Commission appointed before the First World War were passed into law by a Private Member's Bill carried through as the result of the literary and parliamentary skills, legal knowledge and prescience of the late A. P. Herbert. It was so again after 1969 when, as the result of a further Private Member's Bill, less skilfully thought out, and which I had strongly criticized from the opposition front bench, the present basic law was introduced. The real crux of any divorce law is about money and property, or about children, or both. It was true when I first practised at the Bar from 1932 onwards. It was true in 1979 at the commencement of my second term. It is true today. The use of the civil law to hold together parties who wish to live separately is almost always misguided. What ought to be explained to parties who contemplate divorce is that, although a marriage may or may not be brought to an end, the consequences of divorce are long-lived and may be permanent.

When I reached office in 1979 the unfortunate spouses who had brought their marriage to an end under the new law had formed themselves into two irreconcilable and quasi-Marxist classes, each represented by strong pressure groups with incompatible aims, with which the courts, partly as the result of the inherent facts of the case, were quite unable to cope. The two classes were the ex-husbands with their second or subsequent wives and children, and the ex-wives (whether first or subsequent) with the children of the first marriage or of subsequent marriages prior to the latest one.

I am not talking in terms of religion or morality. When my marriage to Natalie had come to an end, though I had not realized it at the time, I had been extremely lucky. Owing to the fact that she could not bear children, there were no children. Her one desire had been to marry her latest paramour, and she immediately did so. There were thus no problems about custody or control of children. There was a clean break and it took place almost immediately so that there were no disputes about money. It is simply not practical politics for a man to allow his wife to set up an establishment with another man and allow the two to live together in a state of permanent bitterness with him because it is not within the power of the cohabiting couple to regularize their relationship. But this is only one situation amongst many. A friend of mine was told by his newly married wife on their honeymoon that she had only married him as a blind to cover an immoral relationship with a French aristocrat. The Roman Catholic Church would have no difficulty in allowing a nullity in such a case. The English law allowed him to proceed by way of divorce. But the majority of cases are different. Leaving for a moment the question of fault on either side, a wife who has been married for some time almost invariably loses or impairs her earning capacity, and is surely entitled to maintenance at any rate for a period of time, and of course in the normal case where there are children of school age the difficulty is compounded. In the mean time the ex-husband marries again, and normally has more children. The economic facts of life are such that one man's earnings or property are normally insufficient to meet the needs of two separate households even when they do not include two families of children, and that in such cases, although the matrimonial tie may be broken, the consequences may remain for life. I myself have frequently endeavoured to persuade friends or, where it was appropriate, clients of the desirability of effecting reconciliation. But I do not think I have had a single success. I did my best to save my marriage with Natalie, but failed. Those who have not had to face the consequences of broken marriages of their own or between others often talk in unrealistic terms of 'making divorce easier or more difficult'. By the time things have reached a certain stage, divorce in one form or another is, I believe, inevitable. The Roman Catholic Church recognizes this in practice by having a fairly elaborate jurisprudence of nullity even where there have been children and has to bow to the inevitable in cases of fault where cohabitation is no longer a practical possibility, by recognizing 'divorce from bed and board', that is, in effect, judicial separation without licence to remarry. But, without a nullity on technical grounds, and given a marriage valid by canon law, the Roman Catholic Church refuses a licence to marry on the ground that a true marriage is indissoluble, at least in secular law. I do not myself think this is a valid option. Since it was clear that my own marriage to Natalie could not be saved I do not like to think what my own life would have been if I had followed my original plan of judicial separation from her instead of following my father's and brother's advice in pursuing the clean-break principle. Whether or not I was right to take the course I did, I would not like to impose it on others by law, but I should like them to have the opportunity to follow the same course. Professionally, I have known husbands who wanted to be rid of their wives proceed to knock them about until they were forced for their safety to leave home. Moreover, and more frequently, they committed adultery. Even the charade described by A. P. Herbert in *Holy Deadlock* of the feigned adultery to deceive the court is better than an inescapable tie. Like Lord Simon of Glaisdale, however, whom I once heard say in the House of Lords that under the old law he had never in the whole of his long experience come across an adultery petition in which the act had been deliberately set up to deceive without commission of the act, I would endorse this hard saying out of my own experience. In the whole of my professional career at the Bar I have never known anything quite so degrading to all, to the parties, their friends, their servants, their counsel and sometimes their children and of course the judge, as the former 'defended cruelty' case in which, whoever won, the parties left the court permanently scarred and embittered, and incapable of forming any rational and civilized arrangements about custody, control or access to children, or about maintenance or the division of property. The real trouble about the proliferation of divorces is partly that parties who enter into a marriage only too often do so without a real intention to make it permanent, and too often allow a temporary quarrel or a casual and perhaps almost venial act of infidelity to be made the occasion of a permanent separation.

The change from fault to irretrievable breakdown as the sole ground of divorce had already taken place before I assumed office in 1979, though the ghost of the old system still remained in place, as it still does, to some extent by virtue of the first three of the five sets of facts by which irretrievable breakdown must be proved. In 1979, however, the evil was compounded by three absurdities which made matters much worse, all of which made rational and relatively amicable arrangements more difficult and, in some cases, virtually impossible. The first was a provision of the 1969 legislation, which provided that, in arriving at a financial settlement, the court was required to try as nearly as possible to bring about a solution similar to that which would have obtained had the marriage not broken down. This was about as sensible as telling the court to treat a triangle as if it were really a circle. The second was a survival from the Herbert Act, which he had been persuaded to insert in a vain attempt to placate the churches, which of course it failed to do. This was to the effect that, after the celebration of a marriage, no petition of divorce could be filed until three years after the date of celebration unless it could be proved either that the respondent had been guilty of 'exceptional depravity' or that the petitioner would otherwise suffer 'exceptional hardship'. This nonsensical formula had survived the 1969 legislation, probably for the same reason, and obviously with the same lack of success. It had led to quite deplorable results. Since neither phrase was capable of definition, it had led parties eager to be rid of an unwanted and detested partner to make allegations against him or her of a preposterous kind, thus reproducing many of the horrors of a 'defended cruelty', or alternatively to give reasons more or less plausible for saying that the remedy would save the petitioner from a hardship which was not merely ordinary hardship but exceptional hardship. The litigation to which these disputes gave rise was not only preposterous, and from the public point of view time-wasting, but also, from the point of view of the parties, calculated to make rational conciliation impossible, if only because the court had to insist that the statutory conditions were met. All the time there was an example, north of the Tweed, where the grounds of divorce were broadly identical to the English, but where no comparable statutory time-bar of any kind existed, and where, after seven years, it could be shown that the incidence of breakdown in marriage was statistically identical with that in England and that complications did not exist at all. The genesis of the problem lay in the fact that the 'churches' (whatever is meant by that) in England (but not in this context in either Scotland or Northern Ireland) wished to make divorce 'more difficult' or 'less easy' whereas the real problem was to make the unavoidable consequences of a broken marriage more tolerable to the parties and their children without unnecessarily undermining the public interest which lies in the permanence of the marriage bond.

The third problem lay in the emphasis laid or not laid by the courts on the question of conduct between the estranged spouses. In the euphoric aftermath of the 1969 legislation, a case had arisen in which, to use a popular oversimplification, conduct was never, or at least hardly ever, relevant in deciding the ancillary questions of maintenance and the division of property following the substitution of 'irretrievable breakdown' as the sole ground for divorce for the 'fault criterion' previously obtainable. The churches had been much too ready to say that in every case both parties were to blame. Since no one is perfect, this is quite possibly true. But I have heard it said – I think it was by Lord Simon of Glaisdale – and it is certainly my own experience, that although obviously in the course of matrimonial estrangement both parties had from time to time committed faults it was seldom difficult to identify the party really responsible for the final breakdown. The relevance of this fact to the various questions to be argued after dissolution varies from the trivial to the decisive. I found that, as the result of one rather slap-happy decision of the courts, the solution of these questions became more difficult and less and less relevant to the continuing situation.

The difficulties of ignoring the previous conduct of the parties during marriage were accentuated by the total impossibility of ignoring the behaviour of the parties, good or bad, after divorce. This was all the more unjust because the types of such conduct differed from the exemplarily good to the appallingly bad. In the euphoria following the passage of the 1969 legislation abolishing fault as the ground of divorce the Court of Appeal had delivered a judgement which appeared to say that conduct, good or bad, was no longer relevant to the proceedings ancillary to divorce. This was so deeply offensive to the conscience that the registrars and judges who had to administer the law had in practice begun to ignore the decision and to do what seemed to correspond to the justice of each case, where strict adherence to the decision would have led to a result too absurd to be tolerated. But this, too, was unsatisfactory, and statutory effect had to be given to the dictates of conscience. There were cases when wives were left stranded and broken by their husband's cruelty and desertion. There were cases when ex-wives deliberately lived with their paramours without marriage in order to maintain themselves in comparative affluence out of the former husband's maintenance while leaving his second household in penury. There were the non-paying ex-husbands, the refusers of access to the children (both sexes), the concealers or deliberate dissipators of assets or income (also both sexes). Once bitterness and antagonism have set in there is practically no length to which ex-partners will not go to assuage their own unhappiness or advance their interests, real or supposed, at the expense of the other party. The children can be made mere pawns in an ugly game of post-divorce battledore and shuttlecock. Baseless accusations proliferate, and each class of evil compounds the effects of the others.

The difficulty about all law reform is that most is contentious, and this is doubly the case when the litigants divided, as here, into two easily defined classes whose mutually incompatible interests are each strongly supported by plausible and powerful single-purpose pressure groups, each in turn backed by an influential and sometimes emotive lobby of MPs. These considerations, though at that time in fields totally distinct from family law, had led Lord Campbell, when he was composing his *Lives of the Lord Chancellors*, to remark that 'law reform is either by consent or not at all', and Lord Haldane, another predecessor of mine, to observe in his autobiography that it normally took three successive Lord Chancellors to effect anything really worthwhile in the field of legal change. He was thinking of the reform in property legislation which he set in motion before the Great War but which did not come into fruition until the successive terms of Lord Birkenhead at the time of Lloyd George and of Lord Cave in 1925.

But the necessity of the reforms with which in 1979 I was faced could not wait, and most of them, however long they waited and however little connected they might be with party politics, would never be uncontroversial. Moreover their very nature involved long drafts upon the time of Parliament and enabled well-meaning enthusiasts to attempt to overload any Bill with well-intentioned and sometimes intrinsically desirable remedies which, as my colleagues with rival Bills for the government programme were only too ready to point out, would crowd out their own proposals for legislation from the sessional programme.

Happily I was armed with an institution which neither Campbell nor Haldane had enjoyed during their Chancellorship. This was the Law Commission. During most of my second term as Chancellor the Law Commission included amongst its members a highly knowledgeable expert on family law and a succession of highly co-operative chairmen of High Court judge standing or above. I referred a number of questions to the Commission on the subject, and the result was a flow of Bills coming from them for which, in successive sessions, I was able to secure a place in the government programme; and, although one of them received some ill-informed and obstructive opposition from the bishops' benches, all became law, some with improvements and some without alteration.

One thing in the field of family law I was unable to achieve was the so-called Family Court. The present situation is highly unsatisfactory. The jurisdiction in matters of Family Law is divided between three separate groups of court: the magistrates' courts, the County Courts, and the Family Division of the High Court, which I instituted. All these systems have overlapping jurisdictions relating to family law, varying from adoption to matrimonial disputes, and this leads to undesirable forum shopping and confusion. There is no reason in principle why restructuring should cost an additional penny. But it was pointed out to me that an almost inevitable consequence of restructuring would be a transfer of some business, the extent of which was not measurable, from the magistrates' courts to County Courts where the fees chargeable on legal aid would be higher. I believe that all the difficulties could have been resolved and that the annual cost in legal aid would, in 1986, have been about £30 million. My own view is that there should be a single point of entry in family cases at the local County Court, which would then transfer the simpler cases to the local magistrates, take the run-of-the-mill cases itself and transfer to the High Court cases really deserving the attention of a High Court judge in London or on Circuit. But I know this would be controversial.

I have dwelt at length on the single topic of family law reform for a variety of reasons. The first was because it was the topic which impressed itself most forcibly upon me during my first days in office during my second term as Lord Chancellor, and because it remained so during the remaining years. But, in truth, it was only one of a vast number of subjects with which I found myself concerned as needful of reform during the same period of years. I have always regarded myself as a conservative with a small as well as a large 'C'. I have instinctively more sympathy with those who stress the need for continuity, durability and precision in a legal system than with the enthusiasts for legislation as the automatic response to the identification of any perceived human need or social anomaly. There are times and seasons for reform, but there are also times and seasons for staying put, or waiting until the moment is ripe. Marriage is, in fact, an excellent case in point. You cannot be for ever tinkering with a fundamental change in a social institution of the importance of the family if it is to continue to command respect or even to retain credibility. But once the dissolubility of marriage had been recognized, as it was in 1857, the shockwaves engendered by the initial change in outlook have continued to have their repercussions throughout the century and a half which followed. At the other end of the scale, there are very few legal institutions which do not stand in need of regular maintenance work, sometimes of a fairly radical kind, more than once in any century. This was the explanation of the Insolvency Act in 1986. Bankruptcy law had hardly been effectively reformed since 1914, and maintenance work was clearly overdue. The same consideration applied to the overhaul and subsequent consolidation applied to the law relating to companies in 1981, 1985 and 1986. What is needed for these cases is a wide selection of instruments of reform, but the general acceptance of a single methodology. Before Sankey's Chancellorship in the 1930s almost the sole effective instrument was the Royal Commission or the *ad hoc* Committee. These are still valuable but they take a long time and still longer for their proposals to be accepted. It took from 1912 to 1937 for the Royal Commission on Marriage and Divorce to put even part of its recommendations on to the statute-book. The Pearson Commission on personal injuries, for whose institution I was primarily responsible in my first term of office, has not produced to date more than a handful of alterations in the law, largely because its main recommendation foundered on objections of principle. So did the Faulks Committee on Defamation. The foundation of modern law-reform methodology began with Sankey, reached the criminal law with R. A. Butler as Home Secretary, was improved by Simonds, and was finally perfected under Gardiner with the institution of the two Law Commissions. It is now fairly clearly laid down that you begin with preliminary identification of a problem. You then start work with questionnaires directed to interested persons or bodies. Based on the result of the answers to these questionnaires you then issue a consultation paper for discussion and lastly publish a final report by a professionally drafted Bill. You then have to struggle for a place in an overcrowded legislative programme. You have to overcome the resistance of the obscurantists and the forces of inertia. You have to control the enthusiasts, and finally, if you are lucky, and after immense discussion in both Houses of Parliaments, you may have achieved a worthwhile change. On the way, you have to face a number of unnecessary obstacles, the division of responsibility between departments, each, like the DTI and the Home Office, sovereign in its own field and each embued with an orthodox tradition deeply embedded in the thinking of its own departmental officials. In Parliament you have to reckon with the loquacity and insensate zeal of enthusiasts, the hostility of single-purpose pressure groups, nearly always well motivated but sometimes wholly misguided. I once saw a pure Consolidation Bill – a Bill which simply consolidates the existing law in a simple enactment, without amending it in any way – destroyed by a foolish use of their immense power and the public sympathy they engendered by a group representing the disabled. The task of the reformer is thus strewn with pitfalls. My own view is that the Lord Chancellor's office should carry the initiative even outside his departmental interests – the Law Commission's sensible proposal for simple interest in delayed-contract debts has always been blocked by the DTI, who inherited their present viewpoint from the old Board of Trade – and that almost all proposals, except those required by an emergency, should be processed by the methodology I have described, that the length of parliamentary procedures by oral discussion should be curtailed by the use of written documents, and that it should be recognized, apart from Private Member's Bills, that at least one law reform measure should be included in every session of Parliament, as part of the government programme.

However, enough of law reform. The late Mr Justice Astbury is credited with the saying 'Reform? Reform? Are not things bad enough already?' Fortunately, though his remark was witty, it was not generally followed.

Important as it may be that the Lord Chancellor of the day should keep up the momentum of necessary law reform, whether on radical or evolutionary lines, I am sure that if all my postwar predecessors were lined up in a row and asked what is the most important function of their office all would reply that it is to maintain the independence, integrity and impartiality of the judiciary and of the judicial process. To enable them to achieve this it is essential for the Lord Chancellor and his officials to retain the confidence of the profession and the judiciary on the one hand, and that of his political colleagues and of Parliament on the other.

This is not always as easy as it may appear at first sight. Over the years, the executive and the legislature in this country have become almost inextricably intertwined as the result of the development of cabinet government and of the party system, and of the sensitivity of both to passing waves of popular emotion. This tempts both ministers and Parliament constantly to encroach of what belongs properly to the judicial process and the judgement of the courts. This means that of the three branches of government recognized at the time of the Glorious Revolution the courts and the judges are far the weakest and the most vulnerable to attack, both from the executive and from individual members of both Houses. It is the function of the Lord Chancellor to hold the balance between the three, and for this purpose to retain the confidence of all three elements in the equation: his colleagues in the Cabinet, both Houses of Parliament, and the judiciary whose independence and impartiality it is his duty to protect.

The judges themselves are not always their own best friends. I speak not of their occasional lapses from good taste or common sense – failings to which all of us are subject from time to time when under stress – but of the sad disease to which I sometimes give the name Hewartitis, from a celebrated incident in December 1934 when the Lord Chief Justice of that name solemnly denounced the Lord Chancellor (Lord Sankey) and, worse still, his permanent officials then led by Lord Schuster as a sort of Quisling army determined to abase themselves before popular pressure or the financial demands of colleagues, or even, in acute cases of the complaint, avid of power themselves at the expense of those they are employed to protect. It is essential for the proper discharge of his office that the judges should retain their confidence in the Lord Chancellor of the day as their appropriate and dedicated friend at Court.

When asked from time to time to lecture to schools and colleges on the nature of my office I was often asked questions on two equal but incompatible lines of reasoning. The first was to ask whether I found my membership of three separate branches of government incompatible with one another. To this I had no difficulty in answering that, given an ordinary degree of personal integrity, they were not merely compatible but complementary. It is essential that the Lord Chancellor of the day should be a judge, and a judge capable of sitting and presiding over the highest Court of Appeal. There is no other way in which he can command the respect and confidence of the profession. More important still, there is no other way in which prime ministers could be prevented from appointing a political Lord Chancellor interfering with the very independence he is supposed to protect, possibly directly, though that would be difficult, or indirectly by accepting political advice in making judicial appointments – a practice not altogether unknown until a little before my father first held the office in 1928.

The other, and incompatible, line of questioning was to suggest that everything would be much better if the Lord Chancellor's office be converted into a Ministry of Justice in the Continental sense. This would be to make the office political in the most overt sense. Although a Lord Chancellor is a useful working member of the Cabinet and even in party political matters is free to take part in controversial debates in the Lords, and capable of giving useful advice in Cabinet in foreign and legal matters and of representing the view of the judiciary to his colleagues as strongly as might be, his position on the Woolsack and in the House of Lords prevents his sitting as a member of the House of Commons. If this were to happen, the substituted Minister of Justice could be directly interrogated in the House of Commons as to the discharge of his office (and by one device or another, whether by the Speaker's permission or not, this would certainly happen), as to the qualities of particular judges, and as to their possible removal, their observations, obiter or otherwise, and as to sentencing or other judicial policy in criminal or civil cases or classes of case. In short, judicial independence would be at an end.

Equally important, a Continental-type Minister of Justice would certainly be made responsible, as they all are, for the conduct of prosecutions and the penal treatment of offenders including the operation of prisons. In my view, these responsibilities, at present divided respectively between the Attorney-General and the Home Secretary, are mutually incompatible with one another and with the administration of the courts and the preservation of judicial independence which are the function of the Lord Chancellor. The fact is that those who criticize the existence of the Lord Chancellor's office from these mutually inconsistent points of view have utterly failed to analyse the delicate balance of the different working parts of the British constitution.

Another line of criticism, which is equally short-sighted, is to attack the method by which judges are appointed, and in which the Lord Chancellor of the day inevitably plays a key role. In all the Common Law countries, judges are appointed from successful practising lawyers. The problem is to secure that the criteria for appointment should be unaffected by political considerations or personal prejudice. It is the function of the Lord Chancellor to secure that this objective is achieved; and, in my opinion at least, the conventional machinery which has evolved is the best so far designed to achieve this purpose.

In theory, of course, all judicial appointments are by the Queen herself in virtue of her position as the Fountain of Justice. But, to protect the sovereign, the Queen must always be acting on appropriate advice from a minister accountable to Parliament. All are made on the advice of the Lord Chancellor, except the highest of all where the accountable minister is the Prime Minister. In practice, however, the actual appointments are arrived at by a delicate mechanism, composed in part of the judiciary themselves, the Lord Chancellor and the Prime Minister (who must never act out of political considerations), with the officials of the Lord Chancellor's office acting as secretariat and liaison between the working parts.

Under the American constitution, at state level some at least of the appointments are often directly made by election at the polling-booth (to my mind the abomination of desolation and a direct contradiction of judicial independence). At the higher levels in the United States the appointment is by the executive, in the Supreme Court by the President himself 'by and with' the consent and advice of the Senate. No one who, like myself, has seen the examination of Judge Bork on television by a Congressional Committee, and his subsequent rejection, could regard the process as other than degrading and highly political even in the most partisan sense. Sometimes it is suggested that, in place of the Lord Chancellor, there should be some committee of the great and the good. But how this could be constituted or appointed no one agrees. This, too, is a constitutional solecism and based on ignorance of what actually happens. The Lord Chancellor's position guarantees accountability to Parliament in the last resort of judicial patronage and is at the same time the guarantee of the independence of the system from political pressure. What actually happens depends upon the particular appointment to be filled, and for this a single body of advisers would be wholly inappropriate. It would be useless to seek advice from the same sources to appoint a judge to sit in Brighton and Lewes, or in Manchester or Wales or Leeds or Northumberland, or to appoint a judge to sit in the Family Division, or in the Commercial Court. What actually happens at Circuit judge level and below is that it is considered correct for barristers and solicitors to apply for appointment by giving particulars of where they would like to sit in relation to their homes and the availability of transport. From time to time officials make a trawl in the various Circuits of likely candidates, enquiring unofficially what their private plans may be. Before appointments are made, advice is always sought from the presiding judges of the relevant Circuit, and, where appropriate, the Court of Appeal, through the Master of the Rolls, the Vice-Chancellor, the President of the Family Division and the Lord Chief Justice, according to the needs of the Circuit and the nature of the vacancy. Sometimes, though more seldom in Wales or the North, the potential runners are actually known personally to the Lord Chancellor. Actually my own views were only valuable where I had known candidates at the Bar, and in latter days this was the exception, and with the passage of time of diminishing importance. Where I was able to have a favourable influence was that I was able to make allowance for the several enthusiasms and prejudices of the candidates' supporters and opponents, and I simply cannot think of a better way of getting at the truth of things. Occasionally I interviewed the successful candidates themselves where some contentious matter had arisen. But I can honestly say that, having appointed, particularly in my second term, more assistant recorders and Circuit judges than any other Lord Chancellor in history, I never came to grief at all on a pensionable appointment. Only once did I incur public criticism when I refused to renew the appointment of a recorder who held the misguided view that I had it in for him because he was Irish and claimed to be a Roman Catholic. He then went public into the bargain, and his grievance was published in the press. In that case my conscience was entirely clear. At the time the decision was made the man was unknown to me from Adam. I acted solely on the consensus of others who knew his peculiarities and actual performances, and I have rarely read a submission with a more unanimous series of observations. However, the case did establish one point, of which I was glad. It established the vital constitutional necessity for the existence of a minister with ultimate responsibility accountable to Parliament, and therefore capable of being there instead of simply being made the subject of ex-parte statements to the press.

In the case of High Court appointments, the method was similar in principle, but different in detail. Persons who wish to serve as High Court judges or above are not supposed to apply for appointment as such. The trawl is therefore more careful, and the consultation with the higher judiciary more comprehensive. Also, High Court appointments depend more directly on the nature of the vacancy and the job specification required for the particular replacement. One would be unlikely to appoint a criminal-law specialist to the Chancery Division, and one would be unlikely, even within the Chancery Division, to replace a specialist in patents with an expert on revenue law or vice-versa. In the Common Law and Family Divisions, there is a greater demand for all-rounders, but one must always keep up the supply of Family and Criminal specialists and Commercial judges,

and, at a lower level, of Official Referees (to my mind a somewhat underestimated and possibly undervalued class of judicial
officer).

When it came to prime ministerial appointments, I always
respected the right of the Prime Minister to make the actual decision
by submitting a short-list of two or three names. But I always put
these in an order of merit, giving reasons, and also mentioned why
other likely names had, for the particular occasion, been omitted
from the list. Obviously the particular nature of the vacancy to be
filled was uppermost in my mind. I only once had a disagreement,
when my second choice was chosen, and on that occasion the Prime
Minister's selection was an outstanding success. If an unsuitable
name had been appointed on any occasion, I would have tendered my
resignation.

Only one of my High Court appointments ever came in for public
criticism, and that was from the egregious Paul Foot in the *Daily
Mirror*. It was the first appointment of all that I made in my second
term. We had been in office not much more than a week. The
vacancy was for a High Court judge to sit in the Family Division.
There had been a long and somewhat divided discussion with the
Heads of Division. Many candidates were discussed, but no name was
agreed, and my own preferred candidate was unanimously rejected
by the other participants. Eventually I said: 'Gentlemen, as we do not
seem to have reached agreement, have you any further suggestions to
make?' The then President, Sir George Baker, spoke up. 'Why do
you not appoint a registrar?' he asked. It had never been done
before.

'A good idea,' said I. 'Have you any particular registrar in
mind?'

'Yes,' said he. 'Mrs Butler Sloss.' There was a chorus of approval
from my colleagues.

'Well, then,' said I, 'so be it. Mrs Butler Sloss will be appointed.'

A timid voice from the end of the table then intervened. 'I think
you ought to know, Lord Chancellor,' said the civil servant present,
'that she is the sister of the new Attorney-General.'

I had known Elizabeth Havers as well as her brother and her father quite well. But until that moment I had no idea of her married name.

'If she is otherwise suitable,' said I, 'is that a bar to appointment?'

The question only had to be asked to be answered. The day after the appointment Paul Foot attacked me in the *Daily Mirror*, accusing me of political bias and suggesting as alternatives a number of quite unsuitable names which had rightly never been under discussion. I think it was probably one of the best appointments I ever made. But neither Paul Foot nor Captain Bob Maxwell ever apologized to me for their slur on my integrity. That sort never do. There was not a squeak out of the profession except sounds of approval, nor, so far as I remember, in Parliament. But again the moral is: how excellent is a constitution which makes the Lord Chancellor in the last resort accountable to Parliament as a whole, and how wise a practice by which he consults the senior judges. Left to myself it would never have occurred to me to make that appointment since I knew the lady only by a different name, had never appeared before her as a registrar, and it had not occurred to me at that particular time that an appointment of a registrar would be desirable.

In the case of removing judges the position is far less satisfactory. As a result of the Glorious Revolution, High Court judges and above hold their office during good behaviour and, it is generally believed, can only be removed by resolution of both Houses of Parliament. But no one has ever defined exactly what 'good behaviour' means or exactly what happens administratively if such resolutions were passed. As the situation has never arisen in England (although I believe there may have been precedents in Ireland in the remote past) it remains a doubtful area of law.

But in the case of Circuit judges the case is different. Following earlier Acts of Parliament, section 17 of the Courts Act 1971 places the onus on the Lord Chancellor to remove Circuit judges for 'misbehaviour or incapacity'. When, during my first term of office, the Courts Act was going through Parliament, I expressed the view that this was unlikely to happen. In this I was mistaken. Unfortunately, during my second term the issue arose twice, and I believe that, under previous legislation to the same effect, it had done so once before in the twentieth century under Lord Chancellor Kilmuir. Actually the provision is not quite so draconian as it seems, since it is quite certain that an improper use of his power by the Lord Chancellor would be subject to debate not only in Parliament, but, by way of what is now called judicial review, also in the courts. Nevertheless I regard the system as wholly wrong in principle. To name only three examples, Scotland, Canada, and Australia have a different and more satisfactory provision by which the indispensable executive act of removal is preceded by a quasi-judicial hearing of a disciplinary panel of a judge's peers. This is far better and, behind the scenes, I have campaigned for years for the introduction of a similar practice, suitably adapted, for England. Astonishingly, I have only been prevented from achieving this purpose by opposition from within the judiciary itself, on what possible ground I am quite unable to understand. However, during my second term of office I was faced with the question twice. On the first occasion, my decision, although an unhappy one, was not attended by controversy or by personal risk to myself. Although not guilty of any misbehaviour on the bench itself, a Circuit judge had been convicted on his own confession of offences against the Customs and Excise. He obviously could not remain in office. But I was advised that if he were simply allowed to resign as I would have preferred I would have no power to award him any part of the pension he had already earned. I enquired of the precedents, and, though there was none affecting a judge, a very senior civil servant who had been guilty of a much more serious offence had been awarded at least a proportion of his pension and I thought that this was also a suitably humane action in this instance. The trouble was that under the regulations a pension was available only if the judge were removed and not if he voluntarily resigned. This seemed to me both anomalous and unjust. But I had to take the law as I found it. The only criticism I received was from individual members of the public who thought, understandably, but as I thought unduly harshly, that he should have been deprived of all pension whatsoever. I took a different view. The pension had been contributory in part, and the judge's work had been properly performed. In Parliament there was no criticism of what I had done. In this world there is a place for mercy as well as for justice.

The other case was when I was strongly advised by two of the most respected members of the senior judiciary and by my own office that a particular judge had also been guilty of misbehaviour within the meaning of the Act and should be removed. I myself was inclined to agree and, had the Scottish system been in place, would have referred the matter for advice to the advisory board of the judge's peers. But it was not in place, and it had come to my knowledge that the judge in question had, amongst other misdemeanours, made a number of what, rightly or wrongly, I thought to have been quite unjustified and scurrilous criticisms of myself. This put me in an awkward position. In spite of advice to the contrary, both from the higher judiciary and from the office, I thought that, in this particular instance, and even supposing the case for the prosecution was unanswerable (which was never tested and as to which therefore I kept an open mind), the principle that justice should be seen to be done meant that I could not act as victim, prosecutor, jury and judge in the same proceeding. What astonished me was not so much the misdemeanours themselves (if they were such) of a somewhat obscure and absurd judge whose only real claim to fame was the number of times when his behaviour had been criticized and his judgements reversed by the Court of Appeal as the purblindness of my senior colleagues on the Bench in failing to see the desirability (which I had been urging for years) of superimposing on the statutory duties of the Lord Chancellor the Scottish, Canadian or Australian methods of securing a fair trial compatible with judicial independence.

Another difficult conundrum arose from the so-called Kilmuir Rules. Rightly, in my opinion, David Kilmuir had laid down in a letter the undesirability of judges discussing controversial matters in the media. But they were, and are, under constant pressure to do so. The protocol formulated by David involved the proposition that, before doing so, they should seek the advice of the Lord Chancellor's office and ultimately of the Lord Chancellor himself. The enormous majority of judges needed no such guidance. They simply rejected all such approaches, which might take a number of very different forms and might be made to retired as well as to serving judges. But there were exceptions and I personally had some reason to think that there were instances in which a handsome fee had been paid – a course I considered highly undesirable. One judge who had been particularly vociferous actually promised the Lord Chief Justice that he would desist from the practice and later, as he put it, 'withdrew his undertaking' and went on as before. In other words, he deliberately broke his word. There were also more approaches than one to me from the media themselves that the 'Kilmuir Rules', as they had come to be called should be modified or revoked. The issue arose, according to my recollection, on four or five occasions, during both my terms of office. In each instance I referred the matter to the judiciary themselves, both the higher judiciary (excluding the Law Lords, who are peers of Parliament and so not subject to the rules) and the Circuit judges. Although I held strong views on the subject myself, what seemed to me important above all else was that judges should observe a common practice in the matter. It was not simply that I did not wish to dictate to the judges. It was that, whatever practice ultimately emerged, it should be a practice common to all and consistently observed. Being themselves an independent branch of authority, it seemed to me obvious that judges owe a common duty of loyalty, not merely to the Crown, but to one another as a common brotherhood, subject to the same dangers and always liable to be criticized in public. On each occasion I received the same, unequivocal answer. By an overwhelming majority, the judges of every grade did not wish the Kilmuir Rules to be altered. I had given no prior indication of my own views, but I was always convinced that, had I been one of their number, I would have given the same reply. Public indulgence in publicity off the Bench is in my view quite incompatible with proper performance of the judicial office. Apart from anything else, I have to record my experience, which is that the judges most eager to air their opinions are precisely those whose opinions are least representative and least worth listening to. On occasions when judges, or former judges, appeared on the screen I made a point of viewing or listening to their performances, and I saw nothing in these to alter my mind. Quite apart from this, once I had received an emphatic and unequivocal opinion from the horses' mouths, there was no possibility that I should impose an alteration to the Kilmuir Rules upon an unwilling judiciary, although in my earlier terms as Lord Chancellor I had wondered whether some accommodation could be found. After all, a judge's office is an important one, and the public are rightly interested in what they do and how they operate.

Quite different from this issue was an occasion when two quite similar judges expressed from the Bench, and in open court, controversial opinions about the merits of a particular proposal coming before Parliament. This seemed to me a clear breach of the constitutional rules and convention about the separation of powers, and I sought, and obtained, apologies from them both. If anxiety is to be expressed about particular proposals, there are ample means at the disposal either of the judiciary or of individual judges to make their views known in the proper quarter. This could be done quite easily by approaching the Lord Chancellor privately, or in public on the floor of the House of Lords through the mouth of one or more of the Law Lords (usually nine in number) or retired Law Lords.

As I have said, I am sometimes asked whether I did not find my political and judicial functions incompatible or personally embarrassing. The answer is not at all. I would never have allowed myself to sit on a case with party political implications, and I can only remember three occasions when, as often happens to ordinary judges, I was approached by members of the public or by Members of Parliament with reference to a case where I had given judgement. One was the case of the proposed sterilization by occlusion of the fallopian tubes of a mentally retarded young lady of seventeen referred to, as is customary, in the reports by a letter of the alphabet. In that case a Member of Parliament foolishly yielded to the importunities of a religiously motivated constituent and wrote to me to justify my decision. To him I simply wrote a polite letter explaining the constitutional position and sending him, without comment, a print of all five judgements (which were unanimous). The second was a pathetic case of a young boy injured in a road accident whilst riding his bicycle out of a side-road, who was unfortunately not able to produce any evidence of negligence on the part of the motorist who had collided with him. The third was a letter from a mother thanking me for allowing the appeal of her son who had been convicted of murder. None caused me the smallest embarrassment at all, and none had the smallest political implication. All judges receive such letters from time to time. Most go straight into the wastepaper-basket, but in each of the last two cases compassion led me to explain that I fully understood their feelings but could not expand in any way on the judgement delivered. The part of the Lord Chancellor's function I most enjoyed was sitting as a judge myself, presiding either in the Appellate Committee of the House of Lords or in the diminishing but still important minority of cases coming before the Judicial Committee of the Privy Council. I only wish that the pressure of administrative and legislative business that has grown up round the office of Lord Chancellor had allowed me to do more judicial work.

FORTY-EIGHT

The Legal Profession

IN SOME DEGREE the professional classes are the Cinderellas of the modern economic scene, Cinderellas without a Prince Charming to protect them. They are not part of the workforce and do not belong as affiliates to the TUC. They are not part of management. Whether they are dentists, accountants, solicitors, surgeons or barristers, their activities are hedged about by somewhat arcane ethical rules, which can easily be misrepresented as restrictive practices, but which, for the most part, are really imposed in the interest of professional integrity and consumer protection. The housewife can readily discern the relative value of the services of a butcher, a baker or a candlestick-maker, and her husband and she can readily exercise consumer choice between different makes of motor-car or television set. But what standards should be set before a doctor, a dentist, a chartered engineer, a solicitor, a barrister or an accountant in order to qualify as such? The same difficulty pertains to the respective ethical codes to be observed towards one another by the individual members of what are essentially competitive and, in the case of lawyers, reciprocally adversarial professions.

Long before my father entered politics, I was aware of him as a practising and of myself as a potential member of the Bar, and after precise scholarship in academic studies, which I learned from a series of gifted teachers during my formal education, the Bar was always my first love. I well remember Esmond Rothermere's surprise and, I thought, disapproval, when at a dinner-party at which he was the host I professed my preference for the law over politics. For the last thirty years, I have had perforce to be active in both fields and thus, perhaps falling between two stools, never achieved my full potential in either. But, despite sometimes hostile comment in the press, I have never ceased my sense of loyalty to the profession to which I belong, and in spite of a critical attitude to some recent developments, and in some ways to its intense natural conservatism and dislike of change, I have never ceased, to the best of my ability, to maintain its traditions and promote its interests. A particular interest in recent years has been the consideration that, in all common-law countries, professional judges of all grades are recruited from successful practitioners, and in all countries, whether common-law or Code Napoléon (where judges are a separate profession recruited directly from the law schools), remain a sturdy and independent bastion of freedom. Quite apart from this there are two factors peculiar to the law in all countries. The first is that in all contested litigation, criminal or civil, there is an inherent danger of corruption and dishonesty, both in the advocate and in the judiciary, and I believe sincerely that we are insufficiently aware of the extent that our own professionals, whether judges or advocates, show a shining example to the rest of the world, and of the extent to which that shining example is the direct product of the particular internal arrangements which excite most criticism from members of the public and the media.

Since the war the numbers of the profession have vastly increased and, in spite of the difficulty in foretelling the future, I believe that growth will continue, though at a decreasing rate. Of two branches of the profession, there are at least nine practising solicitors to one practising barrister, and there are about nine practising juniors to one practising silk. In the mean time, while at the time I left the Woolsack in 1974 the numbers of the Bar had increased to approximately 2,500, when I returned about five years later in 1979 they had about doubled to above 5,000, and the solicitors' profession had increased about proportionately. The increase has continued. The practising Bar now numbers over 6,000. In addition to these, industry, finance and commerce have offered salaried posts to a very large number of qualified lawyers of both branches, and with the proliferation of public work the legal civil service and lawyers in the employment of central and local government have also increased in number.

Whether this has been altogether good for the profession and its standards I will not discuss. Various opinions are expressed. But legal education has certainly improved, and I am perfectly certain that despite huge increases in numbers the training and quality of the judicial Bench has also improved greatly.

The causes of this huge increase are manifold. There has been an enormous expansion of the volume of the work available, whether non-contentious matters, or in divorce, personal injuries, criminal, constitutional or international cases. But one of the main causes has been the provision of legal aid, initiated by the Rushcliffe Committee report after the war, at first only in civil, and from 1962 also in criminal cases. In 1972, during my own first Chancellorship, legal advice and assistance, which come directly within the province of the Lord Chancellor, was also instituted. Socially, of course, legal aid and advice has been an immense improvement, satisfying an overwhelming need. The change has been at the expense of a certain amount of idealism and a growing trade unionism among the professional organizations, the members of which were accustomed to giving many of their services for nothing or next to nothing. On the other hand, the provision of legal aid has virtually eliminated the legal underworld of ambulance-chasers who, in cases of personal injury, were a feature of the profession before the war and who, in the United States, in the absence of legal aid, and with contingency fees the rule rather than the exception for plaintiffs in personal injury cases, have been such a disagreeable feature of the litigating scene there, where the evil is compounded by the continued use of the civil jury and awards of damages more than discounting the contingency-fee element in every case.

A more serious difficulty has been the separation of the profession into two classes: those who depend mainly for their income on state funds derived either from legal aid, or, since the adoption by the present government of a centralized prosecution service on prosecution briefs; and those who operate partly or mainly in the free market, and who, if they succeed in making a living at all, earn very much higher sums than did even proportionately the great advocates of Victorian, Edwardian and prewar Georgian days. The effect on the profession has been largely to trade-unionize the two professional organizations of barristers and solicitors, some of whom have yet to learn the lesson that to overstate even a good case is not necessarily the best way to win it. I have also noticed a considerable increase in the number of what seem to be avoidable demarcation disputes, between solicitors and other professions in the conveyancing field, and between solicitors and barristers in the area of rights of audience and appointment to the judicial bench. Both tendencies, I believe, were largely avoidable, and should have been avoided with wiser and more statesmanlike leadership from the top. The first dispute led to the institution of the licensed conveyancer as an alternative to the solicitor in house purchase. The second has not yet run its course. In 1971 I was happy to accept the appointment of solicitors as recorders and, if successful in their recorderships, as Circuit judges. The remainder of these arguments still continue. The few solicitor recorders appointed have undoubtedly been a success, as have the fairly numerous permanent appointments to which some of them have subsequently led. But, for reasons which I predicted at the time, the numerical addition to the Bench has proved disappointingly small. The reason lies deep in the nature of the economics of the two branches of the profession, the solicitors being a profession with high overhead expenses, paying high rates, high rents, and high salaries to a large number of salaried partners, executives and clerks, and being therefore unable to acquire many of the skills peculiar to the Bar. On the other hand, the barrister in his nature belongs to a set of chambers which necessarily has to maintain a low overhead expenditure employing few clerks, junior clerks and typists. Much of his time is spent waiting for the case to come on for hearing, and much spent in the library in reading and research. He neither employs partners, writes letters, keeps other people's money, nor interviews clients directly coming to visit him. What the public sometimes fails to realize is that, in course of time, the functions of the two professions have become largely complementary and, therefore, mutually exclusive. Of the two professions I suspect the solicitors' is the more permanently lucrative, and leads at the end to the acquisition of the goodwill in a practice which may be sold for cash. On the other hand, the barrister, when he retires, no longer even enjoys the modest cash concessions in relation to fees paid late after retirement, which were taken away by Roy Jenkins when he was Chancellor of the Exchequer. But, in terms both of taxes and of clients, he can afford with relative ease to extricate himself from his practice and accept a place on the Bench which, though far less lucrative, is probably less exhausting and is rewarded by a substantial though not overgenerous pension for himself when he reaches retiring age or is afflicted by ill-health, and for his widow when he dies. These differences have become more rather than less marked over the years as the result of the exponential increase in legislation passing through Parliament or contained in subordinate legislation. No practising lawyer can do (if that) much better than keep pace with legislation in his own particular field. No firm of solicitors, except perhaps for a handful of very big City firms with literally more than a hundred partners, could conceivably provide personal expertise in more than a handful of areas, or employ more than a handful of expert partners or clerks. No individual solicitor or barrister can be himself expert in all the various specialities: income tax, patents, family law and divorce, planning, local government, personal injuries, road, rail and air traffic, commercial law, trusts, charities, judicial review and crime. The solicitor makes his business the interviewing of clients, the identification of issues, the reparation of documents and accounts, and above all the selection of an army of counsel from various specialist chambers of varying degrees of experience and distinction to whom he can turn for expert advice or professional advocacy. Even a solicitor with a medium-sized provincial practice must have very many specialist or general-purpose counsel on his books. In their turn, counsel are in a complementary position. They will naturally tend to specialize in a relatively few fields, sometimes exclusively in one or two, and in the mean time have perhaps thirty or forty firms of solicitors in that field regularly sending them instructions, for some of which they may think leading counsel indispensable for a favourable outcome. Though I would be the first to agree that the system, like Topsy, has largely growed, I cannot myself see that any positive advantage to the public is likely to occur by attempting to blur the separation of functions between them which has gradually developed. Facility of transfer is quite another matter. One of my ablest pupils became the senior partner in a well-known firm of solicitors and ultimately a registrar in the Family Division, and two at least of my colleagues on the Bench as Heads of Division and members of the Court of Appeal began their professional lives as qualified solicitors.

The profession had two legitimate grievances, for the remedy of which I fought hard, and in the end successfully, with my colleagues. Both were questions of principle, and, though increases in the remuneration of the profession are never popular with the public, I found it hard to restrain my impatience at the resistance I received. The first, and to my mind the less important, was the reduction by 10 per cent, which was made by statute, of the remuneration payable for work actually done and adjudged to be fair and reasonable. I suppose that it had its origin in the fact that most of us of a certain age – and, at the time of the introduction of legal aid, almost all of us – gave much service to impecunious clients for nothing or for next to nothing, both in court and in 'poor man's lawyer' centres for non-contentious business cases. In criminal cases, the old 'dock brief' system whereby anyone accused on indictment could secure the services of a junior barrister not otherwise engaged for, at the time of my call, the rather meagre sum of £1 3s 6d (£1.18) – of which half a crown went to the clerk – and the hardly more generous poor prisoner's defence (awarded by the court at its discretion) both meant in practice that one's services were given for less than nothing apart from the gain in experience which work of any kind afforded the briefless barrister. In civil cases, one was entitled to look to the client solicitor for the fee agreed and marked on the brief, but in practice, in suitable cases, one did work marked 'No fee', and I never remember insisting on my rights against a respectable solicitor who said that if I did it would come out of his own pocket. The danger of this, of course, was that, if not done scrupulously, it could easily degenerate into a system of contingency fees. In my case, it never did, and in addition I gave my services by way of representation to two charities who took up meritorious cases for the impecunious and would nowadays be entitled to legal aid. They were, respectively, a Roman

Catholic society called Our Lady of Good Counsel and a non-Roman Catholic society called the Bentham Committee largely supported by the near-communist D. N. Pritt. There was an element of sheer idealism, at least in my case, in all these activities, and I suppose this element spilled over when legal aid was introduced after the war and justified the statutory 10 per cent deduction from the proper fee. By 1979, however, it was an unjustifiable anomaly. It took me all of seven years of hard bargaining to get the Treasury to agree to its abolition and even then it did not become law until it was enacted by my successor, Lord MacKay, in the Legal Aid Act 1988.

Far less justifiable even than the 10 per cent deduction was the system of the deliberate late payment of fees, for work actually done by lawyers who voluntarily, and as a matter of professional duty, undertook legally aided work. I suppose this had its origin in a bad old practice whereby even respectable solicitors put counsel's fees actually received from the lay client on deposit for a year and pocketed the interest. When my father was first called to the Bar one eminent firm had £30,000 of unpaid counsel's fees permanently on deposit in this way, and this sum, accountable in gold sovereigns, earned 5 per cent interest. I believe that this wretched practice no longer persists in private practice among respectable solicitors. But in the hands of the Treasury it had become downright dishonest. It meant in effect that in an inflationary situation, and at relatively high interest rates, the Treasury was paying counsel and solicitors anything up to two and a half years in arrear in depreciated currency whilst enjoying the benefit of the equivalent of interest on the sum due and owing over two years before. This meant that counsel was paid anything up to one-third less than he was entitled to, when inflation was at a high ebb. Inside government, I used to refer to this practice as the Lord Chancellor's bucket shop, much to the displeasure of David Kilmuir, then incumbent at the Woolsack.

This was straightforward dishonesty, but verily I believe that I would not have succeeded in getting it abolished without the stalwart support of the Prime Minister. The fact was that I had no knowledge of the vastness of the sums involved, since, in addition to keeping current payments up to date, the Treasury had to fork out huge amounts to restore to the profession the sums being dishonestly kept from them in the form of arrears. It was characteristic of the bad judgement of the profession in arranging their priorities that they did not put this unanswerable claim at the head of their list. I put it at the head of mine, and secured my purpose after a bloody battle and even then only in three tranches. I believe, though I am not quite certain, that the operation is now complete but, to show the immensity of the sums involved, I know of one instance where in the case of one junior family practitioner in moderate practice, where the work is more generally dependent on legal aid than in any other field except criminal defence, his reimbursement came to no less than £12,000. During the continuing battle for the remaining tranche I mentioned this figure to some ministerial colleagues who used it against me in order to prevent the operation proceeding at all. To indicate how unpopular lawyers are, I can remember one occasion when a colleague who had been opposing me stormed out of a meeting as red as a turkey cock saying that he was not going to be a party to paying lawyers so much money. Incidentally, he was in fact one of the 'caring' fraternity commonly known as 'wet'. The legal profession should not underestimate the extent to which it is rather less than popular with press, public and politicians. To my mind this unpopularity is wholly undeserved and is due to a false stereotype. Caricaturists always depict judges as sentencing defendants in full-bottomed wigs and capes (neither of which they wear in court whilst trying cases or delivering judgement). Editors and sub-editors describe recorders and assistant recorders (part-time judges, and in effect probationary) as 'top judges' whenever they say something rather less than sensible, and editors habitually place criticisms of the Bench alleging an unduly severe sentencing policy as responsible for the overcrowding of prisons and on the next page howls of execration against sentences alleged to be too lenient, without pointing out the inconsistency between the two stereotypes. For some reasons utterly unknown to me they always represent counsel as addressing the court as 'M'Lud' instead of 'My Lord', even when the judge in question is a Circuit judge (and thus entitled only to 'Your Honour') or even a stipendiary magistrate (entitled only to 'sir'). They also habitually misunderstand the perfectly reasonable convention of pretended judicial ignorance, when the judge quite rightly demands a more precise definition of a popular phrase with which, of course, he is perfectly familiar. For instance, when a witness refers to 'snogging', 'petting', 'heavy petting', 'bonking' or whatever, a judge is entitled to insist on an explanation in ordinary language of exactly what a couple is alleged to be doing. Jurors are not always as well up on popular language as the court. The fact is that, in this age of supposedly explicit language, such perfectly familiar phrases are used to cover a wide range of quite different activities.

Rather less successful, and rather more unfortunate for my reputation, was the course of my negotiations with the Treasury in connection with the Bar's annual claim for enhanced remuneration for legal aid. In fixing, as he was bound to do by regulation, the various levels of remuneration for different types of work, the Lord Chancellor of the day, by the terms of the statute then in force, had to 'have regard to' the principle of 'fair remuneration for work' actually and reasonably performed. Had I been trying to advise myself, and thereby had a fool for a client, on the meaning of both phrases in this curious formula, I might have had some difficulty in finding accurate definitions. Happily I was not in this position, as I felt I was under an obligation to take, and follow, the advice of the Treasury devil, which I will not disclose. The Bar took the view that I could in effect only 'have regard to' the principle by actually paying the 'fair' remuneration. If that were the true meaning of the words, I can only say that I could have wished that Parliament had said so. My Treasury colleagues seemed to think that I could 'have regard' to the principle by first genuflecting in front of it and then doing what they told me was appropriate having regard also to other claims on the public purse, the general state of the economy and (in the jargon of the time, though I never used the phrase) 'the principle of affordability'. I did think it was relevant to point out that, on the general principles of constitutional law, and explicitly elsewhere in the Act, any money spent on legal aid was to be paid out of moneys voted by Parliament, and that any regulations made by the Lord Chancellor were subject to the negative veto of either House (in practice the House of Commons) and that my own view of what was fair remuneration must bear some relation in practice both to what was being currently paid to the newly formed Crown Prosecution Service (not a reform of which I had actively approved) and to the vagaries of the market in private practice. In the present Legal Aid Act, in broad terms being actively canvassed as a piece of proposed legislation whilst I was still Lord Chancellor, and now enacted under the guidance of my present successor, the problem will never arise in quite the same form as an attempt has now been made to identify and define the relevant factors. I hope that at least to this extent Lord MacKay will be spared my own disagreeable experience.

Both extreme views, however, left wide open the question what remuneration in each separate item of work in each separate field was in truth fair. Unfortunately it was here that the Bar had slipped up badly. They had obtained a broadly favourable report from a most eminent and honourable firm of accountants. But, like computers, even the most eminent and most honourable accountants are not to be relied on unless fed with wholly accurate information, and in feeding information to them each separate error can have the effect of compounding the others. Unfortunately, though it never crossed my mind at the time and does not cross it now that the errors were deliberate, it was pointed out to me that the Bar Council's figures were very badly flawed indeed. In some respects I was able to check these errors for myself. For instance, it is by no means true that the average plea of guilty in the Crown Court takes, as the Bar had suggested, two hours to dispose of. Based on my own experience, I set the figure at thirty minutes. This obviously needed checking by an actual scan. But this was undertaken and the answer was forty-five minutes, less than half the figure the Bar had put forward. Nor could I accept that pleas of guilty took on the average five hours for a barrister to prepare. This of course could not be checked. Some barristers take longer than others. I would certainly have taken less than half the suggested time. Quite apart from this, there was a calculation of the gross amount an average barrister of particular call might hope to earn in the course of a month. It was easy to check this by accounts for sample months, and the error was significantly large. Quite obviously there was room here for continued discussion, and I made it clear to the Bar that such discussions would be welcome to me and would have to take place. In the mean time the Treasury had dug their toes in and Christmas was approaching. So I summoned a meeting of my own officials and the main representatives of the Bar. As usual they were courteous, respectful and reasonable. It was here that I made an error, or rather two. I decided to take them into my confidence. I am sure they acted in good faith and that what followed must have been due to some misunderstanding. I explained to them that I had reached a complete impasse with the Treasury and that further progress could not be made until steps had been taken. The first was that I must be in a position to present my colleagues at the Treasury with a set of figures in which I myself could have implicit confidence and that, for this purpose, further discussions would be necessary between them and my officials. These discussions could proceed but, owing to the fact that Christmas was at hand, it would be unlikely that they would be finished until the Houses resumed in January. The second, and more important condition – and this I told them in strict confidence – was that no further progress could be made in the bilateral conversations between my own officials and those of the Treasury until I could set up a meeting with the Prime Minister in the chair at which not only the Treasury but also ministers from the other principal spending departments, and the Attorney-General, who was directly affected because he was involved in discussions over the remuneration for his Crown Prosecution Service, were all present. I explained that this would be difficult to achieve since I myself had to attend a Commonwealth Conference in Delhi, whether of Commonwealth Speakers or Commonwealth law ministers or both, during the vacation, and doubtless the other ministers, probably including the Prime Minister, would be performing analogous and unavoidable duties. In the event I was rather angered when subsequently the Lord Chief Justice calmly said in public that I had chosen to go off 'on my holidays' rather than continue the negotiations with the profession. I can only suppose that the Bar representatives had taken my stern injunctions of confidence rather more literally than I had intended. I did, however, tell them that, after the two conditions had been met, I expected to continue negotiations with them and would expect to come back with a proposal which, although not meeting their claim, would be an improvement on what I was in a position to offer them at the time. At no time did I suspect that they were contemplating taking me to court. Indeed, had anyone suggested to me that such was likely to be the case, I would have said that I would have regarded it as most improbable, since the only effect of their doing so would be to suspend all negotiations while litigation was in progress, and the only effect of their winning (if they did) would be to set aside my refusal to make any formal offer before Christmas. It was here that I made my second mistake, which led to a public rebuff at the hands of the Divisional Court which caused me deep distress. I explained to them that the only answer I could give them as of that day was contained in a letter which had been drafted for me by the Treasury rejecting their claim in its existing form. *The Times* subsequently described the letter as 'insensitive' and, in spite of the fact that I had toned it down significantly, that was exactly what it was. Of course, even in its modified form, I should never have signed it and, if I had signed it, I should never have actually delivered it but adjourned the meeting until my two conditions had been met. By signing the letter and then delivering it while negotiations were still pending I had, from the point of view of the litigation which I had not anticipated, simply played into their hands. But they, equally foolishly, by taking me to court, simply delayed by three months the concessions I had confidently expected to obtain for them once the facts had been ascertained correctly and the meeting of ministers, ultimately achieved in January, had taken place. So the case was settled, as often happens, with both sides the losers, a bad loss of face for me, and an unnecessarily delayed increase in remuneration for them. I should never have taken them into my confidence to the extent I did, and I should have found the means of adjourning the meetings without delivering the letter prepared for me by the Treasury.

FORTY-NINE

The End of the Flight

MARGARET CONTINUED ME IN OFFICE after the 1983 election. This was something of a surprise to me as I was past seventy and had had various points of difference with some of my colleagues. Before embarking on my election tour in support of the Government, I had arranged for a champagne farewell-party to take place immediately after polling day for my official staff in the Lord Chancellor's room with toasts and all to celebrate the end of my second four years in office. The party was interrupted by a summons from Downing Street continuing my second term as Lord Chancellor which, as it turned out, lasted until after the 1987 election, by which time I was very nearly eighty. I had been Lord Chancellor longer than any others in this century, unless you include Lord Halsbury, whose period of office dated well back into the nineteenth. Despite the innate caution and conservatism of my disposition, more changes, I believe, had been effected in the judiciary, the office itself, the profession and the substantive and procedural law of the land during my two terms as Chancellor than under any other occupant of the Woolsack. To my successors after 1987 I left a menu of change in the shape of the options on family courts and the civil law review which should occupy them until they have time to arrange further changes of their own. Law is a family mansion whose upkeep requires constant maintenance and repair, as well as demolition and extension. As Lord Haldane observed, in his time it usually took three Lord Chancellors to effect really serious reforms. With the modern apparatus in position, I would myself reduce the necessary period of gestation to about five years, since the whole secret of the thing is to identify the right questions and then assemble support for the appropriate changes. I was sorry to leave. But I trust I went with a good grace and, until the issue of the unfortunate Green Papers, did support both my successors on the Woolsack and my former colleagues in government. For a man who thought when his father died in 1950 that his public life was at an end and that henceforth he must devote himself to the practice of his profession, I have had a pretty good innings and a full and satisfying career, and although I miss the fun and strain and responsibility of office it would be churlish in me not to express a profound sense of thankfulness at the opportunities I have enjoyed. When I entered politics in 1938 as the newly elected Member for Oxford, my father gracefully retired as Lord Chancellor. My son Douglas is now a minister of state. Since 1922 there has not been a moment of time when one or more of us has not been a member of at least one of the two Houses of Parliament. I have no complaints. No doubt I have made many mistakes but, in public life at least, I have, I believe, acted in good faith. I have now reached the end of the road. I must now bring my narrative to its appointed end. But I should like to conclude with one more word about the development of my religious and fundamental beliefs since 1975, when I published *The Door Wherein I Went*.

My course is run. Except for repentance, it is too late to make amends for anything I have done amiss. It is too early to make any assessment of anything positive I may have achieved. There is nothing morbid in recognizing that in front of me there is nothing but increasing dependence on the love and support of others, and there is nothing but love and gratitude that I can hope to offer in return.

After my tour in support of the Conservative cause in the general election in 1987, I received the expected summons from Downing Street. I was a few months short of eighty years of age, and this time there could only be one subject under discussion. As usual, Margaret was kindness itself. She evidently found our meeting difficult. I made it easy for her. I had always determined that I would stay on as long as others believed that my continued presence served a useful purpose, and go without question and with a good grace the moment it was conveyed to me that the time had come to make my exit. We parted affectionately, and at her request there was the usual exchange of letters, my own founded on the poem written by my beloved brother Edward at the beginning of his life of Edward Marshall Hall:

> Fold the worn silk, and let the wig be laid
> Into its battered box. Their use is done
> For ever; now the final cause is won;
> The long term closes; the last speech is made.
>   No prisoner at the Bar may seek his aid;
> No judge will hear him now; beneath his flail,
> No witness now shall writhe – no felon quail,
> No jury by his eloquence be swayed.
>
> The Roman head on Saxon shoulders set,
> The silver hair, the tall heroic frame
> Are seen no more. But some will not forget,
> And, till they die, must reverence the name
>   Of him, who, as they struggled in the net
>   Rose in his strength & to their rescue came.

I have enjoyed my supposed retirement even less than I expected. Every post brings me in innumerable and flattering letters based on the belief that, since I am presumed to have nothing to do, I can do no better than attend some social or political function which my increasing infirmities make it impossible for me to reach. Every post also still brings me letters both from home and abroad based on the assumption that I am still Lord Chancellor. In the mean time there is nothing morbid in the reflection that I am faced with gradually declining powers, physical and mental. It has required some moral effort to adjust to the implications of this.

My one decision of policy has been to write this book. Apart from any literary imperfections, I have deliberately avoided quotations from speeches, letters, diaries or the cabinet papers to which I have access, but to quote from which would have required official permission. Relying on memory, as I have, there are no doubt errors of fact which others will gleefully correct. I have made as little effort as I can at self-justification. In a fairly continuous and chronological narrative I have tried to set down my life as I recall it. It has been long, varied and satisfying. If there has been little self-justification, I have not felt it necessary to load it with apologies for past errors or past faults. I do not believe I have breached any confidences, personal, professional or political, and I hope that, even where I have expressed criticisms, I have done so fairly and without offence.

There is one plain omission which I shall now attempt to justify and, to some extent, perhaps remedy. This is the omission of the various vicissitudes of my inner moral and spiritual development.

As I explained at the beginning, when I wrote *The Door Wherein I Went* in 1974 I had intended it to be the last public utterance I would make about my religious beliefs, and had not the slightest idea that in front of me lay the greatest spiritual crisis I should ever encounter in the aftermath of my wife Mary's death, and by far the longest and most constructive period of political office I should ever enjoy. So far as possible I have tried to keep my religion out of my public narrative. *The Door Wherein I Went* was designed to explain my progression from the virtual agnosticism of my youth to the mainstream Christianity which became and has continued to be the abiding religious background to my personal, family and public life. In the main I would prefer it to remain like that. But it is inevitable that my views on life in general and my outlook on life should have evolved in detail if not in principle in the fifteen years since that peaceful summer of 1974 when, secure in a happy marriage, and with five young but maturing children, I wrote those chapters of my book under the pollarded trees of my brother's hotel on the Lake of Lucerne, looking towards the lights and shades on the magnificent silhouette of Mount Pilatus facing me on the opposite side of the Lake of Lucerne. I thought then that I was in calm water, expecting a smooth passage into port. Instead of that, storms and a long voyage lay ahead, and it is not quite finished yet.

The first thing I had learned by that experience was that religion is no automatic comfort in adversity. But faith is not the same thing as belief in an objective state of affairs like the existence or non-existence of the Loch Ness Monster, the validity or invalidity of astrology, the existence of ghosts or the effectiveness or ineffective-ness of alternative medicine, homoeopathy or chiropractic. Certainly faith must be rational, that is, comfortable to reason, or it is pure superstition, and in *The Door Wherein I Went* I tried to show that my faith in the Christian religion had intellectual rather than purely emotional foundations. But in the twelve years following Mary's death I have come to realize more and more that faith, *fides*, *pistis*, *foi*, *Glaube*, is a continuing act of the will and not a simple statement of intellectual conviction. Without some element of conviction faith cannot exist. But basically faith is trust. It is founded on a conscious reliance on the ultimate rationality and goodness of things, and it involves continuous action, commitment, prayer, communication and, above all, love. Without it, life is a tale told by an idiot, full of sound and fury, signifying nothing. I do not believe that life signifies nothing any more than the continuing fall of the apple on Newton's head caused him increasing surprise as (perhaps) without belief in the rationality of things logically it should have done. Locke incurs much ridicule amongst modern philosophers by his theory of 'innate ideas', and Bacon much criticism by his theory of induction *per simplicem enumerationem*. But both were ahead of their time. Both were trying to say that, without a fundamental belief in the rationality of things, human reason could not operate at all. There could be no science or scientific knowledge without an innate belief in the rationality of the material world. 'Don't chatter, make trial,' said Charles II (who never said a foolish thing even if he never did a wise one). There can be no religion without prayer, private and public, and sacrament. There can be no public religion without priest or pastor and congregation, without private meditation, without a constant struggle for the light, without a constant searching-out of the dark places of one's heart and soul. Since faith is not knowledge, doubt is no sin. God has His doubters, as well as His devotees. There can be no faith without continuous questioning. Without questioning faith becomes super-stition. There can be no faith without a straight confrontation with the forces of unbelief. When hundreds of thousands are killed in an earthquake, when an innocent and vulnerable and helpless child is tortured to death or dies of leukaemia, when at thirty-one thousand feet more than two hundred passengers are blown up in an aircraft and come cascading out of the sky, and the aircraft itself falls in flames on sleeping villagers, we are bound to question faith and the grounds of faith. In the face of famine, pestilence and sudden death we have to question. But the fact that we question is also part of the answer. If our soul revolts at the bitterness, the strife, the malevolence we see about us, what are we asking questions about if we think that there is no sense in anything? If there is no one to listen to the questioning of our outraged conscience at the prevalence of evil, why do we indulge in the vacuous process of asking questions of nobody about nothing? If someone tells me that he does not believe in God, I ask him to describe the god he does not believe in, and I nearly always have to tell him that I do not believe in such a God, either. Despite all the destruction and malevolence of the world, I do not believe in a malevolent deity. I do not believe in an uncaring deity. I do not believe in an irrational universe. I believe in goodness, truthfulness, loving kindness, beauty, generosity, loyalty. They all exist, and they are all qualities which demand just as much explanation as malevolence, mendaciousness, cruelty, ugliness, meanness and treachery. God is the beginning of our understanding. It is futile to believe that we can search out the reason for suffering. We must not forget that enjoyment is as difficult a thing to account for as misery. The more committed I feel to the Christian faith, the more I feel drawn to others who seek the answers to the same questions as I am asking, and the less sympathetic I feel towards those who assert dogmatically that there is and can be no answer to any questions, or those who assert that theirs is the only possible answer. Less sympathy still do I feel for those who wittingly or unwittingly seem to be on the other side, who consciously pursue injustice, who deliberately deride the things of good repute, who cultivate hatred, who practise cruelty and pursue triviality, foolishness or prurience. I am acutely aware of the inadequacy of mere words, of prosaic language, of literalistic expressions to formulate my belief in words. As I approach the throne of the ineffable, the more mere words fail to express my inmost feelings, and I take refuge in metaphor, in poetry, in music, in admiration for beauty in a landscape, in a sunset, in the plumage of a bird or a butterfly, in the works of man, in stone, in colour, in sound. But my doubts finally dissolve in wonder, in longing, in adoration. And, lo, a paradox appears. I seek God, and behold a bedraggled human figure impaled for public ridicule upon a gibbet. I despair of man, and behold the same figure, enthroned in majesty above the clouds. If I go up to heaven, He is there. If I descend into the depths of misery and grief, He is there also. He is Alpha and Omega, the source of my being and the end of my pilgrimage. He is love, at once the beloved and the eternal lover. He is Father, Son and Holy Spirit, at once the creator, the redeemer, the inspirer of suffering humanity, the companion on my way and strengthener of my steps. But He is Himself the Way, the Truth and the Life. He is unknown and unknowable, yet constantly revealed, revealed in nature, in beauty, in goodness, in knowledge, but always absent in the negative, the hated and the hateful. He is always present and yet constantly eludes my grasp. Being infinite, he cannot be comprised in my understanding. Nevertheless as constantly he reappears in my need. Remaining Christian, I am constantly reassured in my wandering, in my doubting, and as constantly led back by my trusting. I do not know. I do not pretend to know. But I trust, and therefore I believe. Now I see through a glass, darkly. The time is not far distant when, infinitely contrite, I must seek the mercy of an infinitely compassionate judge, and then, face to face, I shall know, even as I am known.

The Sparrow's Prayer

Father, before this sparrow's earthly flight
Ends in the darkness of a winter's night;
Father, without whose word no sparrow falls,
Hear this, Thy weary sparrow, when he calls.
Mercy, not justice, is his contrite prayer,
Cancel his guilt, and drive away despair;
Speak but the word, and make his spirit whole,
Cleanse the dark places of his heart and soul,
Speak but the word, and set his spirit free;
Mercy, not justice, still his constant plea.
So shall Thy sparrow, crumpled wings restored,
Soar like the lark, and glorify his Lord.

Index

Index